A SPITFIRE PILOT'S STORY

This book is dedicated to Pat Hughes and all the others like him – men and women – who bore the brunt of the first impact of war. May they never be forgotten.

A SPITFIRE PILOT'S STORY

PAT HUGHES
BATTLE OF BRITAIN TOP GUN

Dennis Newton

AMBERLEY

ABOUT THE AUTHOR

DENNIS NEWTON is an aviation journalist and author of six books, including *A Few of the Few, Clash of Eagles, Australian Air Aces* and *First Impact.* He edited the Battle of Britain memoir of Gordon Olive, *Spitfire Ace*, also published by Amberley. He lives in New South Wales, Australia.

First published in 2016
This edition published 2018

Amberley Publishing
The Hill, Stroud,
Gloucestershire, GL5 4EP

www.amberley-books.com

Copyright © Dennis Newton 2016, 2018

The right of Dennis Newton to be identified as the Author of this work has been asserted in accordance with the Copyrights, Designs and Patents Act 1988.

ISBN 978 1 4456 7149 9 (print)
ISBN 978 1 4456 5415 7 (ebook)

British Library Cataloguing in Publication Data.
A catalogue record for this book is available from the British Library.

Typesetting and Origination by
Amberley Publishing.
Printed in the UK.

CONTENTS

INTRODUCTION

Flight Lieutenant Paterson Clarence Hughes DFC was ranked sixth among the Royal Air Force's highest-scoring aces of the Battle of Britain, and he was the most successful Australian pilot. He joined the Royal Australian Air Force in 1936 and was then accepted by the Royal Air Force in 1937.

As a flight commander in 234 Squadron, he scored the squadron's first victories during July 1940. The burden of command fell on his shoulders before the squadron transferred to Middle Wallop, a forward airfield, in August and from there he led it into some of the heaviest fighting of the Battle of Britain. Revered by his fellow pilots, Pat began a shooting spree on 15 August that only ended when he was killed during the first huge daylight attack on London on 7 September 1940.

He advocated bold 'close-in' tactics and inspired his pilots, in his last three days alone contributing at least six victories to the squadron's tally of sixty-three. What exactly happened to him on 7 September 1940 remains uncertain but Kathleen, his bride of just six weeks, was suddenly a widow.

This is Pat's story ...

PATERSON

Paterson (Pat) Clarence Hughes was born on 19 September 1917 in the Cooma district of New South Wales, Australia. He was the son of Paterson (Percy) Clarence Hughes and Caroline Christina (*née* Vennel) and the eleventh child in a family of twelve. They were descendants of John Nichols, a convict transported to New South Wales in the First Fleet of 1787–88 (see Appendix 1: The Ancestry of Pat Hughes). Aviation entered young Pat's life dramatically before he reached his teens.

Cooma today is the largest town in the Snowy Mountains, generally known as the Monaro country, and is regarded as the gateway to the alpine area of New South Wales. Set within a region of rolling plains, rivers and snow-covered peaks in winter, it is located at a junction south of the national capital, Canberra, via the Monaro Highway and on the Snowy Mountains Highway connecting Bega with the Riverina. Cooma is several miles south of the banks of the Murrumbidgee River, a main tributary of the Murray–Darling River basin from which it sources its water.

Indigenous tradition and the evidence of archaeology shows that before European settlement the aboriginals had lived in the vicinity for more than 20,000 years. By the 1800s these were mainly the Ngarigo people who camped and trekked in and out of the area in accordance with the seasons. Cooma's name may have been derived from an indigenous word 'Coombah', meaning 'big lake' or 'open country'.

The region was explored in 1823 by Commander Mark John Currie RN in the colony's never-ending quest for new pastoral land. Passing through part of what is today's Australian Capital Territory (ACT), he traversed 'fine forest country intersected by stony ranges'. In 1827 cattle were brought south from Sydney and the area quickly became popular with settlers. The first surveys of the area occurred in 1840 and the village of Cooma itself was surveyed in 1849.

Discoveries of gold in the 1860s at Kiandra, forty miles to the north-west, brought about a permanent increase in Cooma's population, and the railway opened in 1889. Cooma prospered and boomed, and by 1900 the town boasted of having the status of a 'Regional Capital' with numerous grand official buildings. Back in 1851, the estimated population of Cooma was forty-seven people. It grew to 2,330 in 1911, but by the early 1930s this had dropped back to just under 2,000.

In the 1920s and 1930s, the entire world became air-minded for the first time in recorded history. The exploits of record-setting pilots who were adventurers, showmen and barnstormers abounded.

The four years of the First World War (1914–18) had brought about a revolution in early aviation. In Britain, businesses tied to the war effort, like Avro, Bristol, de Havilland and the Sopwith Aviation Company, mushroomed and flourished. Towards the end of the war Sopwith alone had four factories employing a total of 3,500 people. More than 1,000 were women. After the Armistice, the situation changed almost overnight. Military contracts stopped. Instead of needing more aircraft, the new Royal Air Force (RAF) had far too many – an overwhelming surplus. Work for the aeroplane companies dried up. For Sopwith's older employees and the majority of the women, who had stayed on or joined the company to 'do their bit for king and country', it was time to depart.

One of those who left Sopwith was Harry Kauper. He returned home to Australia after the war, and in 1919 he and another Harry, Harry Butler, formed Harry J. Butler & Kauper Aviation Co. Ltd in Adelaide, South Australia. One who stayed with Sopwith was Harry Hawker, who had come to England with Kauper before the war. Hawker by war's end was Sopwith's chief test pilot and a proven designer and innovator for the company to boot, but now the company needed contracts to avoid liquidation. It had to diversify, but how?

A new organisation was devised by Tommy Sopwith and H. G. Hawker Engineering Co. Ltd was registered as a private company on 15 November 1920. As well as aircraft, it had to manufacture a wide variety of products: motorcycles, internal combustion engines, steam engines and motor cars. Sadly, Harry Hawker never saw the company that bore his name develop into one of the outstanding success stories of Britain's aircraft industry.

For the Aerial Derby of 1921, Hawker elected to fly a one-off, single-seat biplane racer, the Nieuport Goshawk. At Hendon on 12 July, four days before the big race, he took the Goshawk up on a test flight. What happened next is not known exactly. The aircraft was seen to lurch in the air and it appeared as if it was trying to land, but instead it crashed and burst into flames. Harry Hawker did not survive.

During the immediate post-war years the sight of an aeroplane was an exciting rarity in Britain, but country-wide aerial joyriding and barnstorming shows gradually led to thousands becoming familiar with the sight. In Cornwall, for example, Captain Percival Phillips, known locally as 'P. P.', established the Cornwall Aviation Company from his motor garage just outside Trewoon, ready for the 1924 summer season of joyrides and stunt-flying. His first aircraft was a bright red reconditioned Avro 504K biplane, G-EBIZ, that he bought for £250. It was his pride and joy and he gave it the pet name 'Geebies'. Each summer during the late twenties and early thirties Phillips and his pilots thrilled crowds across Britain.[1]

It was in America that the flying phenomenon took off. The tactical importance of aircraft was obvious by the time the US entered the war in 1917, and the hard-pressed French and British sought more planes and pilots from their new ally. America's already vast production capacity was put to work. Thousands of flying machines began to be churned out in which thousands of young Americans were taught to fly, but Armistice Day arrived before most of these men could reach the battlefront. The energetic new aircraft industry found itself producing machines which suddenly had no useful purpose. Fliers, and aviation itself, seemed out of place. These men had been denied the excitement of flight and were dismayed at the prospect of going back to ordinary, humdrum lives. Many didn't.

The 1920s and 1930s in the United States became an era of freewheeling flying circuses, barnstorming shows and air races by the hundreds. America was flooded with cheap aircraft and dashing young fliers to use them. Air races and air shows captured headlines and made the names of fliers like Frank Hawks and Jimmy Doolittle familiar to the American public. Barnstorming pilots were adventurous, romantic figures clad in leather helmets and goggles, shiny riding boots and white silk scarves as they climbed out of their open cockpits. They captured the imagination with their dangerous wing walking and aerobatics.

Hollywood came to the party in the 1920s as it began to recreate the Great War, especially the air war, on film. Barnstormers-turned-stunt pilots flew mock dogfights over Southern California, creating an image of air fighting that seemed even more dramatic, and certainly more romantic, than the real thing. The legend of the ace scout pilot was born. He was a chivalrous knight of the air, a scarf-wearing hero who lived for today because tomorrow he could die. Many still consider the air war epics they created the best movies of their day. In 1927, *Wings*, starring Richard Arlen and Buddy Rogers, won the first Academy Award for Best Picture. A year later, Howard Hughes risked a fortune on *Hell's Angels*. When Howard Hawks' talking picture *Dawn Patrol* threatened to surpass it, Hughes reshot *Hell's Angels* in sound and won the Oscar in 1930.

Australia, since 1901 no longer merely a collection of separate British colonies, was caught up in the phenomenon too, and had its own pioneering aviation heroes. In 1919, the Australian Government put up a £10,000 prize for the first Australians to fly from England to Australia. Many applied. Ross Macpherson Smith and his brother Keith, both experienced former RFC and AFC pilots, approached the Vickers company to supply a Vickers Vimy, G-EAOU, a large twin-engine biplane originally designed as a bomber. In it with two sergeant mechanics, Jim Bennett and Wally Shiers, they survived severe storms over Europe and monsoons over India to land at Darwin on 10 December. The flight had taken around four weeks, but actual flying time was 135 hours 50 minutes. They won the prize and both Ross and Keith Smith were knighted. Later, Ross Smith and Jim Bennett were killed in a crash on 13 April 1922 while testing a Vickers Viking amphibian in which they were planning to make a flight around the world.

The first woman to fly from England to Australia was Jessie 'Chubbie' Miller who, aged eighteen, had married a journalist named Keith Miller. The marriage did not last and a few years later Chubbie found herself alone in England. She met Bill Lancaster, an Englishman who had previously worked in Australia and was trying to finance a plan to make the first flight by a light aircraft from England to Australia. Chubbie persuaded him to take her as a passenger if she could raise half of the money required. She did, so he did!

They bought an Avro Avian biplane (G-EBTU), named it *Red Rose* and on 14 October 1927 departed from Croydon in England on their epic flight. Along the way they made numerous stops, usually normal stopovers, but sometimes there had to be necessary running repairs. Some trouble was not of their making, such as a week spent quarantined in Basra due to a cholera outbreak, and on 2 January 1928, just after leaving Rangoon, a brown snake appeared from under Chubbie's seat; Lancaster tried to kill it by stamping on it and failed, but after a hurried forced landing Chubbie finished it off. However, within a day's flight of Darwin, the Avian's engine failed. In the ensuing forced landing at Muntok Island, the aircraft was severely damaged. They were grounded for three months while the plane was repaired, and during that time Bert Hinkler passed them. It was he who accomplished the first flight to Australia in a light aircraft. They had missed their chance.

Nevertheless, on arriving in Darwin at 2.30 p.m. on 19 March, they received a message of congratulations from Prime Minister Stanley Melbourne Bruce, and Chubbie gained renown as the first female passenger to fly to Australia. They arrived at Mascot in Sydney at 5.20 p.m. on 31 March at the conclusion of an aerial pageant and derby, where they were welcomed by a large crowd. They and *Red Rose* were celebrities, and over the following months there were tours and visits throughout New South Wales, Victoria and Tasmania.

Another major record was set on 9 June when a Fokker F.VII/3m tri-motor aircraft by the name of the 'Southern Cross' landed at Brisbane airport, Queensland. It had just made the remarkable epic first crossing of the Pacific Ocean by air from Oakland, California, to Australia. Its crew consisted of Charles Kingsford Smith (pilot), Charles Ulm (co-pilot), Harry Lyon (navigator) and James Warner (radio operator). After enjoying the excitement and kudos of their achievement, Kingsford Smith and Ulm would form Australian National Airways (ANA) the following December. The two Americans, Harry Lyon and Jim Warner, spent a couple of weeks in Sydney after landing in Brisbane before boarding a ship to return to the USA.

Meanwhile, Bill Lancaster and Chubbie Miller were back in Sydney again and on 13 June, four days after the 'Southern Cross' reached Australia, they departed from Mascot for a three-hour flight to Cooma in alpine New South Wales as part of their promotional tour. When they took off there was an ominous cracking sound, but they continued on their way. As the plane was landing on Cooma Racecourse, a wing spar collapsed but they touched down safely. Neither Chubbie nor Bill suffered any injuries but the *Red Rose* would need a major repair.[2] They might have had to go back to Sydney by train to continue with their other plans, but before that they were entertained at the Blue Bird Tea Rooms, which was run by the local Country Women's Association to raise funds for a local maternity hospital.

The enthusiastic people of Cooma came from miles around to gaze at the plane and welcome the two fliers. Among them were members of the Hughes family from Peak Hill. It was an exciting occasion for everyone, including young Pat Hughes, who was by then a boisterous and impressionable youngster almost eleven years old.

When the aviators left, Chubbie left behind a souvenir, her old flying helmet which, in all likelihood, she would not need again – not for a while anyway. It was retrieved by Pat's older brother, Charles, and to this day it remains a treasured possession of the Hughes family.[3]

The Avro Avian was sold to a Mr R. A. Charlton. On the following 23 June, Chubbie Miller and Bill Lancaster left Sydney aboard the SS *Sonoma* bound for San Francisco. With them were Kingsford Smith's former radio operator Jim Warner and navigator, and Harry Lyon. Lancaster and Miller had been engaged by Lyon to assist him in obtaining a prospective motion picture contract. In the arrangement, they were to fly Lyon's aircraft but the deal apparently fell through.

Although Chubbie had been a passenger for the journey to Australia, Bill had taught her the rudiments of flying. In the USA, she graduated as a pilot at the Red Bank School, New Jersey, and later became a record-setting flier in her own right.

*

Jock Goodwin grew up in the Cooma district and was a schoolboy in the late 1920s at Cooma Public School. He remembered the Hughes family from Peak Hill when interviewed in 2011.[4]

Pat was younger than me. He was one or two classes behind. One of his sisters was in the same class as me, Connie. The next girl was a year ahead and the next boy a year ahead of that again. There were twelve of them. I only knew the younger ones.

Those younger ones left Cooma long before they were married.

I understand, I could be wrong, I understand he was named after Banjo Paterson.

My family was one of the earliest settlers on the Monaro. My mother's family was there in the 1830s, I think. My father's family – I think they got to Australia in 1842 and they settled up around there.

My mother was the youngest in a family of eleven. They were all big families in those days. What else could they do? No television in those days. Excuse my quaint way of putting it.

Q: 'Were you living in town?'

No, we were living on a property twenty odd miles out of town. That had quite a history, but that's not what you're after. My mother's father come out I think as an orphan boy with some wealthy graziers. He took up a bit of country himself and gradually built it up until we had quite a big area.

Q: 'How did you get to school?'

In those early days we had a governess and, I just can't remember what age, in about fifth class – what age would you be then, about nine or ten or something? I lived with an uncle and auntie about five miles out of town and rode a horse to school. That's when I came into contact with the Hughes family.

Q: 'Where were they at this stage?'

The old chap worked on a property just out of town about three or four miles, I think.

'P. C. Hughes,
With the pinchin' shoes.'

He was quite a poet. Have you seen his poems?' [I nodded yes.]

Q: 'Were you in his class? Was he your teacher?'

Oh, no! He'd retired from teaching many years before that. He was only a country teacher in those early days when they had those part-time schools. You'd teach three days at one school and two days at another one, and then reverse the procedure the following week. I don't know their history there. He was probably retired from teaching and working on properties and that's how I knew the family.

Q: 'You said Pat was a little younger than you. Were they combined classes?'

Oh, no! When I went to school, there were about 200 to 250 kids there. It was up to Intermediate standard, no higher. I only went to sixth class there and then I was pushed off to Sydney to a boarding school. The Hugheses moved from Cooma when I was at boarding school and I knew them at Ashfield as well. I used to visit their place on days off. I didn't know of them at Haberfield until much later.[5]

Q: 'So you knew Pat at Cooma *and* Ashfield. What were your impressions of him as a young bloke?'

Oh yes. Oh, a very smart young boy, top of the class. So were his sisters. He went to Fort Street later on. Connie went to Fort Street as well but that was down at The Rocks. They had segregated boys and girls, didn't they!'

Q: 'How big of a place was Cooma then?'

At a bit of a guess, I'd estimate about 2,000 to 2,500 people. I think there were between about 200 to 250 at the school that went up to Intermediate standard.'

Q: 'Do you have any memories of Pat at school, at sport or anything like that?'

Well, they didn't have sport that much in those days, a big rough old playground at the school; they weren't fields like they are today. We had a couple of tennis courts there. I was a bit of a keen player, but not much good.

Q: 'What about Pat?'

I can't remember him playing. His sisters played. Of course, him being a couple of years younger, you didn't come into contact with the younger ones quite as much.

Q: 'You were more friendly with the sisters?'

They were more in our class. Yes.

Q: 'You came to Sydney. What was the boarding school you were at?'

I went to Holy Cross College at Ryde.

Q: 'You used to visit the family during your days off?'
I probably only visited a couple of times a year … That would be about the late 20s, or around 1930/31, I think. Pat used to build model aeroplanes in those days out of balsa wood like little match sticks.
Q: 'He must have always been keen on aviation then?'
Must have been.
Q: 'What about his older brother, Bill? He must have been there.'
I didn't know much about Bill. He was the youngest one that still lived at Cooma that I knew. The rest of the whole family had gone away. I didn't know any of them. I don't know what he even did for a living.
Pat started an apprenticeship with a watchmaker, so Connie told me once. I don't know if that's true or not. I can't verify that.'
Q: 'Around about this stage, Pat was friendly with a bloke called Pettigrew. Do you have any memory of someone of that name?'
No. Once I went back to Cooma on the property, I never saw any of them again. I only heard about them. Then Pat joined the air force so I only know there what I've heard.'
Q: 'You said he did model making of aeroplanes, does anything else come to mind?'
Not really. We were only school kids then.
Q: 'How old would you have been then?'
About sixteen.
Q: 'So Pat would have been about fourteen?'
That would be right.
Q: 'How did you get to their family home at Ashfield? Did you go by tram with your parents?'
Oh, no. My parents were in Cooma. They never moved from Cooma.
Q: 'When you arrived there [Ashfield], who would be there to greet you?'
Oh, the whole family, the old people, Mr and Mrs and I'd say from Bill down – Bill, Marge, Connie and Pat. His father was Percy.

Pat's father was the first Paterson Clarence Hughes, although everyone did call him Percy. This probably evolved from him using his initials, 'P. C.', when signing or writing poetry.

Having left home at the age of sixteen, he was a jack of all trades. As well as on occasion being 'a country teacher', he ran the post office at Peak Hill, at various times worked on and managed two properties in the Monaro district and gained renown as a 'bush poet'.

Pat's sister 'Connie' mentioned by Jock Goodwin, was Constance Olive Hughes, the tenth of the twelve children. Constance's daughter Dimity relates:

At that stage, Paterson, or Percy as he was known, divided his working life teaching school at Peak View and the nearby settlement of Jerangle. He was artistic with a gift for calligraphy and highly literate, as was his mother, which was of course unusual for people in the bush in those days, and (using a pseudonym) he contributed bush poetry to the *Bulletin*. One of his best poems was a eulogy to Henry Lawson who was apparently a friend.[6]

From Peak View the family moved to a large property called *Tarsus* on the Murrumbidgee on the other side of Cooma which Percy managed for a German pastoral company. My mother recalled that the day they arrived what passed for a ballroom was full of pumpkins at one end while a rabbiter and his dogs were camped in the other half. It sounded like a pretty idyllic place for kids to grow up with miles of country to go roaming in and orchards, one full of almond trees.

Caroline did all the cooking, housework, dressmaking and gardening – her produce often won prizes at the Cooma show – while Percy, as often as not, sat reading in a large chair by the fire. He might have been an intellectual sort of fellow but he was also tough. If he was out droving and developed a bad tooth, he would operate on himself with a penknife.[7]

Percy wrote his last poem, *The Tablelands*, while recuperating after losing his right leg when he was aged ninety or ninety-one. He was successfully fitted with an artificial leg and insisted that it was 'better than the original' up to his death in 1970. Jerangle Public School named its library the 'Percy Hughes Library' in honour of the man who was a teacher there in the late nineteenth and early twentieth century.

THE TABLELANDS

I'd like to go back to the tableland,
That world designed neath the Master's hand,
With its verdant hills and mountains grand,
And crystal streams a'purling;
To the rolling plains where the lakelets lie,
To mirror an arch of peerless sky,
With lazy cloud ships drifting by,
Their snow white sails unfurling.

When spring returns with fairy tread,
To wake the earth from winter's dead,
Her gems in all their beauty spread,
In tints and fragrance tender.
Mid every shade of nature's green,
Where shafts of sunlight romp between,
The wattle reigns - the bushland queen,
In all its golden splendour.

To me in memory still it speaks,
Of old bush tracks and shady creeks,
Of mists along the distant peaks,

And wild birds westward homing.
And when the evening shadows steal,
And daylight fades - yet I may feel,
The magic of its gloaming.

Time's ruthless hand brooks no delay,
And swiftly speeds the years away,
Far from that spacious yesterday,
When I was a carefree rover.
When the heart was young and the world was wide,
In the scented breath of the morning tide,
And magpies carolling over.

To those who wrought with me of old,
Those grand bush mates with hearts of gold.
Whose friendship I was glad to hold.
Through fair and stormy weather,
I dedicate this verse of mine,
With kindly thoughts in every line,
For good or ill through Auld Lang Syne,
T'was ours to share together.

P. C. Hughes (1874–1970)[8]

In the early 1930s the Great Depression hit Australia as it did in the rest of the world. Percy's move to Sydney seems to have been because of the need to find work, but there was also a rift in the family.

Pat Hughes' nephew was Laurence Hughes Lucas. His first memories of the Hughes family date from when half of them were living in Knocklayde Street, Ashfield, an inner western suburb of Sydney. In 2013 he recalled these details.[9]

I was born in 1929 and my 'flesh to flesh' period with Pat covered merely 1933 to 1938, but young as I was, across those years, there are vivid memories and impressions still recallable about an unusual young person. Pat was impulsive (but not without purpose) and very conscientious about his obligations to the family, e.g., his homework, house duties and relationships with his brother and sisters.

The only timeline to build upon comes from Marjorie who claimed to have gained her driving license in Cooma at the age of seventeen (?). Born in 1913, it makes the move to Ashfield at about 1930 because she said that they moved soon after that event [the license].

My earliest memories of Knocklayde Street would be from 1933 onwards. The Federation home they rented had a pond full of terrapins, so my sister and I were always eager visitors from Concord.

The family disposition at that time was something like this:
Old Perce was a gardener at Coogee;
Helena my mother, married, Concord;

Dorothy, Coogee, married;

Jack, Charlie and Fred in established jobs and married except for Charlie who married in 1938 or 1939;

Muriel, married, Kiama.

Living with Caroline and Pat were Constance waiting for her eighteenth birthday to later start nursing at Camperdown Children's Hospital; Marjorie who worked in retail and became an assistant buyer for sports and leisure wear in a city department store; and Bill, single with the PMG Wireless Regulating Authority. And finally Valerie, single, studying accountancy and working in the office of a garage on Parramatta Road.

So I guess that Caroline, Pat and Con were supported by the incomes of Marjorie, Valerie and Bill.

An undercurrent of hostility would surface towards old Perc especially when the older siblings came to visit. Some had mixed feelings but certainly no family member found fault with Grandma.

She was Pat's darling and vice versa. She was a Pollyanna holding a glass half full and standing beside a sundial (which only reads the sunny hours!).

And the two older singles, Bill and Valerie, were Grandma's rock.

All the family members (except Grandma and Pat) exhibited a measure of cynicism which came directly from old Perc. I could go so far as to say that Pat missed out because he was never really exposed to his father for a long period so wasn't he lucky to have been infected by Grandma's roseate world plus the get up and go attitudes of Val and Bill?

But, by and large, I was proud to be a member of the Hughes putsch. They were opinionated, garrulous, and quarrelsome and my sister and I loved them for their warmth and generosity towards their young cousins.

The death of our father in 1933 sparked off frequent visits to Knocklayde Street. I suppose our mother drew a little closer to the family for moral support and my sister and I naturally gravitated towards young Pat for entertainment. We were not disappointed. He would organise 'dress ups' for the three of us on the basis of popular adventure stories he would be currently reading. I remember one 'scene' was my sister Patsy (aged only seven) kneeling in an upturned cane lounge with motorbike helmet and goggles (from Bill?) as Amy Johnson battling the elements in her Moth *Jason*.[10]

It got to the stage where we would stay over weekends. I would sleep with Pat in a big double brass-knobbed bed. One night I awoke shivering and when Pat asked what was wrong I told him about my cold feet. He got up, heated Grandma's iron, wrapped it in a towel and placed it in the bed on its side so that my feet were on the sole plate. I slept like a top.

After dark the house was ablaze with lights, gas and electric, but there was no lighting in the gloomy pantry. When Grandma asked me to fetch an ingredient, I baulked at the sight of a harmless 'daddy long legs' spider on the wall. Pat was doing his homework at the kitchen table while monitoring my 'sooky' antics. He jumped up and asked me to show him the spider's locality, following close behind. I can still feel the kalsomine powder as his hand closed over mine, sweeping the spider away and filling my fingernails. His only explanation was to say to me that I should always make things happen – not just let things happen to me!

When our father died in 1933, Pat used to visit us at Concord and in 1934 he stayed for some months, commuting daily to Fort Street and keeping his favourite sister company. Pat berated our mother for not taking us out. He would say that she had to get outside herself. Magically, his fifteen-year-old entreaties worked on his thirty-five-year-old sister and it wasn't long before we enjoyed Saturdays and Sundays around Sydney: the Zoo; Hyde Park; Observatory Hill, etc. He became an advocate for our dearest wishes. My sister got a supply of Collins story books and I got a Hornby train set. He never asked our mother for anything for himself though.

He was at that early age an Anglophile *par excellence*, so he must have known that Collins was British. The same for Hornby, so I suspect he steered our mother towards politically acceptable articles!

Both he and Bill were modellers and before he returned to the family he had scratch-built me a model of Amy Johnson's *Jason*. It was either blue and silver or green and silver. It even had a spare propeller attached to the fuselage. Of course, he was an Amy Johnson fan so it was a twist of fate that Pat would ultimately be buried in Amy's home town of Hull, an end denied her because of her loss in the Thames Estuary.

I don't know why or when Old Perc left Caroline but the family were guarded about any extended discussions on the subject. It was just that all we cousins couldn't understand the situation so we were always asking questions – to no avail!

Did he feel that his own twelve kids were the turkeys preventing him from soaring like an eagle? He didn't see too much of them. He was a provisional teacher and I think it meant that for a couple of days he would saddle up and ride to one provisional school and for the remainder of the week go in another direction to another school. So Caroline managed the Peak View Post Office, grew and stored her own fruit and vegetables and generally cared for the family. There must have been compatibility though, because our own mother would tell us that both parents would 'doll up', saddle up the sulky and spend Saturday night at the local dance, returning in the early hours of Sunday morning.

It meant that the three eldest, Helena, Muriel and Jack were tasked with caring for the rest of the brood, plus themselves. Perc claimed that he and Billie Hughes were first cousins, based on his 'claim' that they had common grandparents.[11] It has never been explored to my knowledge. But I do know that Perc had visited Billie at Loyalty Square in Balmain. He said that Billie had told him to stop writing poetry and get interested in politics! Perc had those Janus qualities which would have helped.[12] In a second he could go from a Bo Jangles style singing western folk songs to a man of letters (admittedly Australian literature only).

In 1936 our mother married a navy man who was transferred to Flinders Naval Depot in 1939. We followed to reside within commuting distance at Frankston on Port Phillip Bay.[13]

Young Pat was a good sportsman, excelling at swimming and football, and as well as his keen interest in making model aeroplanes he experimented with electricity by making crystal radios and the like. His brother Bill (who Pat usually called 'Will' in his letters) recalled that on one occasion Pat fused out the whole house and consequently was 'black-balled' by the rest of the family.

When the family moved from Cooma to Ashfield and later to Haberfield, Pat at first attended Petersham Boys High School where he became close friends with John 'Peter' Pettigrew. Bill Hughes remembered them together:

Re the life of Peter Pettigrew, I can only offer a short summary of his association with our family. He was a year younger than Pat and lived in Haberfield with his mother and a sister. He had a brother and a sister married. His father was a builder in the district but had died some years before. He attended Petersham Boys High School with Pat and after having gained their Intermediate Certificates, Pat went to Fort Street Boys High but Peter was enrolled at Sydney Grammar School. At the age of 18 he left school and obtained a position with the MLC Insurance Coy and, remained there until selected for Point Cook. I only saw him several times after that as a cadet. When and how he sailed for England I do not know, but I recall that Pat wrote in one letter that Peter had arrived in England and they had met up, that is where I lost contact as I shortly joined the army myself. Somewhere I have a notice of his death, announcing that Mrs Pettigrew of Glenbrook and sister Phyllis had received news of her son and brother's death.[14] I understand the sister was living at Glenbrook for health reasons ... As for Peter himself I can only speak in the highest terms and it's hard to imagine any conduct of disrepute. He was a well mannered lad – no vices – and treated as one of the family in our home and an ideal companion for Pat.

Fort Street High School is the oldest government high school in Australia. It was on 8 January 1848, the then Governor of New South Wales, Charles FitzRoy, established a Board of National Education to implement a national system of education throughout the colony. The board decided to create two model schools, one for boys and one for girls. The site chosen for Fort Street Model School was the old Military Hospital at Fort Phillip on Sydney's Observatory Hill. This school was not only intended to educate boys and girls, but also to serve as a model for other schools in the colony. The name 'Fort Street' is derived from the name of a street which ran into the grounds of the hospital and became part of the playground during its reconstruction. The school was officially established on 1 September 1849, when the conversion of the building was approved by the government. This original school building is visible today beside the southern approaches to the Sydney Harbour Bridge. The establishment of Fort Street School marked the establishment of a non-denominational system where the government undertook education, separate from religion. Today it remains a selective public school operated by the New South Wales Department of Education and Training drawing its students from across the Sydney metropolitan area.

The school's motto, *'Faber est suae quisque fortunae'*, was adopted from a speech by Roman dictator, censor and consul Appius Claudius Caecus, translated from the Latin as 'Every man is the maker of his own fortune'.

In 1911, the school was split into one primary and two secondary schools: Fort Street Public School, Fort Street Boys High School and Fort Street Girls High School. Due to limited space at Observatory Hill, the boys' school was moved in 1916 to the school's present site, on Taverners Hill at Petersham, one of Sydney's inner western suburbs. The girls' school remained at Observatory Hill until 1975, when the two schools were amalgamated to form the current co-educational school at Petersham. During that time, its grounds continued to be consumed by the growing city such as when the Sydney Harbour Bridge opened in 1932 and took most of the playground. Fort Street Public School remained at Observatory Hill. Students past and present are referred to as 'Fortians'.

The school magazine is titled *The Fortian*. The issue for June 1934 contained an essay by Pat which revealed a sensitive character growing within an otherwise outgoing and at times boisterous adolescent:

AN AUTUMN EVENING

On a jutting crag of a mountain, a man sat, immobile, an image in living bronze, and looked into the blue distance.

It is a land, of far-arched and unstained skies, where the wind sweeps free and untainted, and the air is that which remains as God made it.

The face of the watcher shone with a look of wandering awe, and an Involuntary exclamation came from him as the wide view unrolled before him was changed by the slanting rays of the setting sun.

Under that sky, so unmatched in its clearness and depth of colour, the land 'lay in all its variety of valley' and forest and mountain—a scene unrivalled in the magnificence and grandeur of its beauty. Mile upon mile in the distance across those primeval reaches, the faint blue peaks and domes and ridges of the mountains ranked—an uncounted sentinel host. The masses of the timbered hillsides, with the varying shades of pine and cedar, the lighter tints of the oaken brush, the dun tones of the open grass lands, and the brighter note of the valley meadows' green were defined, blended and harmonised by the overlying haze with a delicacy exquisite beyond all human power to picture. And in the nearer distances, chief of that army of mountain peaks, and master of the many miles that He within their circle. Peace Mountain reared: its mighty bulk of cliff and crag as if in supreme defiance of the changing of the years or the hand: of humankind.

The gracious hand of autumn had caressed the countryside and decorated it in the purest gold and brown, which mingled with the wood and grass land flowers in a galaxy of colours.

The watcher on the peak made a frame of his fingers and looked at the scene below him. On the walls of the next Academy Exhibition will hang nothing half so beautiful.

The long shadows of Peace Mountain crept out from the base of the mountains farther and farther over the country below. The blue of the distant hills changed to mauve with deeper masses of shadows where the chasms yawned and the gullies ran into hiding in the heart of the mountain chain.

The sun hid itself behind the line of mountains, and the blue of the sky in the west changed slowly to gold, against which the peaks and domes and points were silhouetted as if cut by the tool of a master graver; and the bold facades and battlements of old Peace Mountain grew coldly grey in the approaching dusk.

The very air was motionless, as though the never-tired wind itself drowsed indolently.

And alone in the hushed bigness of that land, the man sat with his thoughts— brooding, perhaps over whatever it was that had so strangely placed him there— dreaming, it may be, over that which might have been, or that which yet might be—viewing with questioning, wondering, half-fearful eyes the mighty untamed scene before him.

The far-away cities were already in the blaze of their own artificial light—lights valued not for their power to make men see, but for their power to dazzle, to attract and intoxicate—lights that permitted no kindly dusk at eventide wherein a man might rest from the day's endeavour—a quiet hour; lights that hid the stars.

The man on the peak lifted his face to those twinkling myriads who were gathering to keep sentinel watch over the world below.

The cool evening wind came whispering over the lonely land, whilst all the furred and winged creatures of the night stole from; their dark hiding places into the gloom which is the beginning of their day. An owl flapped by, and from the mountainside below came the weird, ghostly call of its mate. Night-birds chirped in the scrub. A fox barked his staccato challenge, whilst away in the distance the clear cry of a curlew pierced the awakening sounds.

The watcher rose slowly to his feet, and with the beauty of that autumn evening impressed on his soul, he started again on his journey, For a moment he was lost to view behind an outcrop, but then for a short time he stood, vaguely outlined against the lighter gloom of the wide-arched sky—and then he passed from sight—over the skyline.

P. HUGHES, 4A[15]

Pat left school at seventeen before completing the year and in 1935 began working at Saunders Jewellers in Sydney. Was this to help support the family, or was he aiming for an apprenticeship in jewellery making or watchmaking, both highly skilled trades? The meticulous patience and expertise of an accomplished model maker would have provided a very useful lead-in to either profession. Both held the promise of a secure and successful future.

Perhaps they were too sedate for Pat. While he was working at Saunders he sent off applications to join the air force and navy and settled down to wait for replies. Shortly afterwards, acceptances came from both services. After seeking advice from his closest brother, Will, he chose the air force. He would train as an officer cadet for the Royal Australian Air Force in the course commencing at RAAF Point Cook in January 1936.

In a small 1936 *Walker's Diary* that Pat kept, for Friday 17 January he entered: 'XXX – FATEFUL DAY. LEFT HOME.'

Inside, on the page for that date, he wrote:

This is one day that I guess the outward calm of years truly deserted me.

I am leaving something that really must be classed as one hundred per cent.

It's rather hard to define it but I know the first thing I shall do when on leave will be to come straight back to see if our promises are still intact; and I make no secret of the fact that it will make the world of difference if they should have changed. Let's hope things will be the same & I am really am sure they will.

Over the page (on the page for Saturday, 18 January), he continued,

With the aid of the best family in the world, I find myself aboard the 8.20 p.m. Limited for Melbourne.

Trains usually leave later than schedule, but Fate was unkind and I was not allowed to spend with the friends on the station the few minutes that would have meant so much.

The train wheels rattled in furious rhythm to my own thoughts, and what jumbled ones they were![16]

2

POINT COOK

It was a glorious sunny morning when the train stopped at the town of Albury on the border of New South Wales and Victoria. This was for the passengers to have breakfast and change over to the day car. After arranging for breakfast on the day car, Pat contented himself with a fifteen-minute stroll until it was time to depart again. The countryside was 'definite different, quite brown and flat', cool for the moment before the build-up of the day's summer heat.

Back on board and travelling alone, he settled down after breakfast to read the epic *Seven Pillars of Wisdom* by T. E. Lawrence, the fabled Lawrence of Arabia, during the last leg of his journey to Melbourne. By reading Lawrence's book, Pat was also extending his knowledge of the role the Australian Flying Corps (AFC) had played in the First World War. Incidents involving No. 1 Squadron AFC, and in particular the remarkable Ross Smith, were related in parts. In 1918 under the leadership of Smith, two deadly Bristol F2B Fighters and a DH-9 had been detached from the squadron to Lawrence's Arab Corps' 'X' Flight. They successfully defended the Arab encampment at Um es Surab from attacks by enemy aircraft from Deraa. Afterwards, he brought the big Handley Page 0/400 bomber (C.9681), the only one of its type in Palestine, to the Arab encampment. Compared with the Bristols its sheer size made a deep impression on the Arabs: 'Indeed, and at last, they have sent us THE aeroplane of which these things were foals.'

Smith, who was nicknamed 'Hadji' and was the only pilot 'trusted' to fly the big machine, used it to bomb the airfield at Deraa, destroying any remaining aircraft and hangars and obliterating the railway station, and to open General Allenby's decisive 'Battle of Armageddon' on 19 September. As well as flights for the artillery or for photography, hazardous long reconnaissance flights were undertaken deep inside Turkish territory. Many of these were on behalf of 'our Lawrence', who needed to know exactly what was in front of him, his Arabs being prone to be inaccurate, exaggerative and vague with their military descriptions. While returning, the messages were dropped to Lawrence's camps. Sometimes, Hadji Smith ferried Lawrence himself to and from British HQ.

Pat's train arrived in Melbourne twenty minutes after midday, the book unfinished. After overnight accommodation in Melbourne, on Monday Pat went by taxi to Victoria Barracks where the cadets ('a very motley crowd') were assembling. The Royal Australian Air Force had its largest intake of new cadets so far in January 1936. After some necessary formalities and a 'cursory' examination by medical officers the cadets were transferred 'rather tardily' by air force tenders to Point Cook, their new home.

Point Cook is located on the western coastline of Port Phillip Bay, south-west of Melbourne in Victoria, It is an ideal site for an air training school as there is no sign of a hill or a rise in the surrounding land for twenty miles. It was selected for flying in Australia well before the First World War and indeed before the first aeroplane made its appearance in the country. Although Australia had been the only Commonwealth country to have its own operational flying corps during the war, the AFC was disbanded in 1919. A new 'Australian Air Force' was officially born on 31 March 1921 and the prefix, 'Royal', was granted soon afterwards, promulgated with effect from 31 August 1921.

As far as was practical, it was deemed desirable to develop the air forces of the British Empire along common lines. This would be achieved by having uniform systems of organisation, arms, equipment, stores and training. The RAAF was just two years old at the time of the Imperial Conference of 1923 in London when RAF representatives proposed having RAAF officers attend training courses in England. Short service commissions in the RAF could be offered to a proportion of the pilots being trained annually at the RAAF College at Point Cook.

Australia's fledgling, cash-short air force stood to benefit enormously from the proposed scheme. The Air Ministry would pay for the cost of initial training at £1,500 per head. This amount would be credited to a special fund in London from which Australia could pay for other goods and services provided by the Air Ministry to the RAAF. By this method, it was reasoned, a reserve of trained aircrew would be built up which could be used to reinforce RAF squadrons in an emergency, and Australia would benefit when the men returned home after four years' training and experience at British expense. With the Australian Defence Minister's approval of the scheme, the first cadets were selected from those who completed training at No. 1 FTS Point Cook at the end of October 1926.

Although the original agreement involved each RAAF transferee receiving a five-year short service commission in the RAF, with Point Cook training counting as the first year of service, the RAF soon showed interest in retaining some men for a longer period, perhaps even permanently. The Commonwealth was agreeable subject to a satisfactory financial adjustment. Then, in October 1930, the Commonwealth was asked if it wished to limit the number of officers to be accepted for permanent transfer. With the effects of the Depression resulting in retrenchments in the services at that time, Australia did not place any restriction on numbers and so the size of the courses at Point Cook increased each year.

In 1935 the British Air Ministry suggested extending the period of short service commissions from five to six years. Again, the Australian Air Board raised no objection. Several people went on to attain senior ranks in the British service. These included such men as Air Marshal Sir Ronald Beresford Lees KCB CB CBE DFC (Point Cook graduate of 1930), and Air Commodore Sir Hughie Edwards VC CB DSO OBE DFC, a 1936 graduate who was in the senior class six months ahead of Pat. Edwards, as well as being awarded the coveted Victoria Cross, went on to become Governor of Western Australia.

With the backdrop of a potential emerging nemesis in the form of a resurgent Germany, Japan's activities in China and Mussolini's Italian ambitions to expand, Britain announced measures to build up her air strength in 1935 – the RAF was eager to have as many Point Cook-trained pilots as possible. Britain's Chief of Air Staff, Air Chief Marshal Sir Edward Ellington, said the RAF would like to increase its intake of Australian pilots to twenty or twenty-five a year, and that it was looking for as many as fifty pilots in 1936. In fact, the courses of 1936–37 did result in the largest numbers going to the UK but this was in the face of growing criticism from some RAAF officers. They argued it resulted in Australia's best pilots being drained away to the RAF. Within the next three years the RAAF's own expansion program would create a pressing need to retain all the pilots it could train and the arrangement with Britain was suspended. By July 1938, when the last eight Point Cook-trained pilots sailed for England, a total of 149 officers had joined the RAF under the scheme.

*

Forty-five young men came from all over the country for Flying Course No. 20, mostly by train, some by boat. For the majority it was their first time away from home more than just a few days, and it meant a major change in their style of life. It was an extremely hot mid-January day when they were assembled. All were issued with heavy black boots, socks, overalls and a black beret followed by an army rifle, a belt and a bayonet. Then they were subjected to a pep-talk by an unsmiling, immaculately dressed flying officer in what looked like an army uniform. It was actually the RAAF's summer dress but to the untrained eye it did look like an army uniform.

At first they were grouped alphabetically into two flights but their positions in the mess were fixed so that they dined with different people. They were divided up yet again in the afternoons on the sporting fields, so it did not take long for everyone to get to know each other. For the next month the newcomers were subjected to endless military drills, physical training and gymnastic exercises, long hikes or marches – usually carrying packs as well as the rifles – and cross-country runs. This took up half the working day. The other half was occupied with lectures.

Pat's first roommate was Bob Cosgrove from a well-known Tasmanian family. He was described as 'a nuggetty, pleasant lad with reddish curly hair and a somewhat white skin which was unusual', in direct contrast to Pat. When Bob told his father, who was an eminent figure in the state's Labor government, that he was going to join the RAAF, the news was not well received. Bob went ahead with his decision anyway. Pat and Bob became close friends.

Peter McDonough in the room next door had moved from Ulverstone in Tasmania to Victoria. He had a dry but quick sense of humour matched to a lazy drawl. He walked with a slouching gait which looked like it should belong to a much taller man. As it was, Peter was short, very slim, and had all the mannerisms of a tall, gangling, uncoordinated adolescent. This was deceptive because he was actually sharp-witted and physically as quick as a cat, which showed up on the sporting field in almost any game. He was an outstanding wicketkeeper at cricket.

Peter's roommate was Gordon Olive, an equally short but talkative young man from Queensland. Everyone simply called him 'Olive'. He had a light, almost frail build and straight dark hair, and in his early years had suffered from asthma, which was diagnosed as chronic bronchitis at the time. As an adolescent, his family had moved from one side of Brisbane to the other to be closer the beach, a move which cured his 'asthma' completely. From that point onwards he hurled himself into all forms of sport with great interest and enthusiasm. He was much tougher than he looked.

Writing years later, Gordon remembered Pat and the others vividly:

Pat Hughes … was a big, well-built fellow with more boisterous life in him than anyone I have ever met. Pat just loved life and lived it at high pressure. Part of his tremendous 'joie de vivre' expressed itself as a compulsion to sing, and Pat sang at all possible opportunities. He had one volume – flat out at the top of his lungs. He was at his best in the shower, which he took three times a day in summer and on each occasion he really shook the 'Wind Tunnel' with the vigour of his delivery.

Unfortunately for the rest of the occupants of the tunnel, Pat was tone deaf and most of his strenuous efforts were supported by a rich obbligato of catcalls, groans and complaints which rose to a crescendo as the ablutions progressed. But Pat seemed oblivious to these protests – no doubt he drowned most of them out for most of the time, and when he drew breath, thought he had really got the whole camp singing. The fact that the chorus of groans and abuse was not in harmony with his own efforts would have had no significance to Pat.

Eventually we gave up trying to shut him up; we just accepted it as part of life, but it was my first introduction to someone who was virtually tone deaf and quite oblivious and uninhibited about it.[1]

Desmond Sheen had been born in Sydney but his family moved to Canberra where he was educated at Telopea Park School before joining the Prime Minister's department as a junior. Noticing newspaper advertisements inviting young men to apply for cadetships in the RAAF, he decided to apply.

Bill Edwards was from Leichhardt in Sydney's west, not far from Pat's home in Haberfield. The other Edwards on base, Hughie Edwards, was from Fremantle on the opposite side of the continent. He was in the senior course which had started in July 1935.

A Victoria native, Geoff Hartnell did not have far to travel to reach Point Cook. He was from East Malvern in Melbourne and had been educated at Wesley College. It did not take long for him to become a capable pilot, showing particular skill in navigation as he was something of a perfectionist. Pat would count him among his closest of friends.

Tall, dark-haired and handsome, Carl Kelaher attracted girls 'like iron filings drawn to a magnet', much to the envy of the other cadets. He was originally of German extraction but his family changed its surname during the First World War to avoid any problems associated with being German.

Cec Mace was called 'Grappler' because of his powerful build which was reminiscent of a medium-sized gorilla, but this was offset by his pleasant and humorous face. Grappler told jokes and had a seemingly endless supply of funny, spicy, stories. His voice was high-pitched and he normally laughed furiously at his own yarns as he habitually reduced his listeners to helpless fits of laughter.

The intense twelve-month officer cadet course was packed with some twenty-two subjects. Many of these applied to the problems of flying such as navigation, the theory of engines, the theory of flight, and airmanship – the art of 'conducting oneself around an aerodrome and an aeroplane in an intelligent and safe fashion'. There were subjects relating purely to the service such as General Administration, Air Force Organisation and Air Force Law. A comparable knowledge was required of the army and navy, and of civil aviation. All had to be clearly understood.

Tactics and strategy had to be studied very carefully and seemed to be the content of numerous lengthy dull books. Meteorology was another obscure and inexact science, as was the case with photography and photographic interpretation. In a more practical vein, Morse Code had to be learnt by using the buzzer and lights, plus each cadet had be able to read semaphore, the procedure of sending messages by flags.

Knowledge of armaments was essential. Guns of various calibres and bombs of numerous types had to be understood, their construction explained and remembered, and the theory of ballistics studied. The application of these to the aeroplane and the theory and practice of their use were important. Other requirements were that the anatomy of machine guns, bombs and cameras had to be known to the extent that cadets could dismantle and reassemble them 'without enough parts left over to go into the second-hand business'. There were also the practical sides of engineering and rigging which had to be mastered. This involved dismantling and reassembling aero engines and repairing damaged aeroplane parts. It was a formidable array of subjects, as was the six-day routine each week.

The cadets' day began with the 0600 hours bugle. From then on, the pace was hectic – bed made, room tidied, shower, shave and breakfast. Out on the parade ground at 0700 in immaculate order with boots, buttons and all leather polished followed by forty-five minutes of 'tramping up and down the parade ground learning the finer points of ceremonial drill'. Then it was back to the barracks to divest himself of his rifle, belts and paraphernalia, and grab books, pencils and notepaper ready for the mile and a half march around the perimeter of the aerodrome to 'The Flights' area. 'The Flights' were old sheds, hangars and lecture rooms where everyone worked for the rest of the morning. At 1200 hours, the cadets were marched the mile and a half back to the Mess for lunch. Forty minutes later they were on their way back to 'The Flights' on foot for the afternoon sessions.

For the most part, the days were divided into theory and practice. If the morning was all theory, the afternoon was practice, which was learning to send and understand Morse code, practical work on engines or air frames or on guns or bombs and the like, and, hopefully soon, flying. On alternate weeks the daily routine was reversed, with practical work in the morning followed by theory in the afternoon.

At 1600 hours, the cadets were marched back to the barracks for a ten-minute tea break before sport from 1630 to 1800. The choices were cricket, tennis, football or hockey and everybody had to mix in. There was no let-up here either. If the instructors found anybody shirking, the defaulter was sent for a run around the perimeter of the aerodrome, or out to a line of trees roughly a mile and a half away. The victim had to be back within a given time, or he had to do it again each evening until he could.

From 1800 to 1830 hours, cadets were supposed to maintain their personal kit, clean boots and so on, and then prepare for a formal dinner or supper at 1900. After this, by 2000 hours, everyone had to be back in their rooms studying. At 2145 hours a whistle was blown, allowing fifteen minutes to tidy up and get to bed. Lights-out was at 2200 hours sharp and by 2201 nearly everyone was asleep from pure exhaustion, particularly at the start.

The severe system of training and discipline left many new cadets in constant fear of being dropped from the course, an attitude which tended to make some fail. To overcome this fear, the attitude had to be one of 'do your best and to hell with the consequences'. For all this, the rate of pay was the princely sum of £3 10s per week, with uniforms supplied. Most, including Pat, adjusted to the long hours of work fairly quickly.

Meanwhile, there was still very much of the mischievous schoolboy in Pat. 'Everyone was trying manfully to be in good spirits,' he wrote on a Sunday, 'but we are all damn tired from yesterday's rifle drill, so I was mainly accused of being stupid by annoying and playing tricks on everybody. The weather was OK, the meals were lousy and all in all a very rotten day.'

One Sunday each month there was time off for leave to go into Melbourne to see the sights or visit local friends and relations, if any. These days were anticipated with great relish. About the worst disciplinary restraint for misconduct was to be confined to barracks for that one day of freedom.

During the practical half day the cadets were taught to fly at an average rate of half an hour per day. Again the subject was dealt with in great detail. Not only did they all have to learn to take off, turn, glide and land, they had to learn spins, aerobatics (loops, half rolls, rolls, stall turns and so on) instrument flying for flying through clouds, map-reading and practical navigation, forced landing procedure and practice, formation flying and the principles of aerial combat, bombing and gunnery.

Initial flying training was carried out in de Havilland Gypsy Moths for the first fifty hours and that was to be followed by Westland Wapitis for the last fifty hours for cadets who were still in the course.[2] A few cadets already had some flying experience. Gordon Olive had obtained his private license in Queensland but the majority, like Pat, were new at the game. To start with they had to learn to take off, climb, glide and finally land. This involved considerable coordination of the eyes and hands and feet. This was especially true of the landing when the cadet had to keep the machine straight by using the rudder pedals and at the same time hold the machine a few inches above the ground by means of juggling the control column ('joystick') backwards and forwards. To make things more complicated, the same control column moved sideways to roll or bank the Moth right or left. The skill was to keep it level both fore and aft and laterally simultaneously and place the wheels gently on the ground, keeping it straight using the rudder pedals. This was one of the most difficult parts of flying.

There were more mistakes made at the instant of landing than at any other time of flying. It always aroused the critical interest of those on the ground when not actually flying to just watch other pilots landing. As for those coming back to earth, the knowledge that critical eyes were watching for errors of judgement resulting in bounces ('kangarooing'), swings off line and other types of rough landings, could be unnerving in itself. Although the average cadet could land an aeroplane after about three or four hours of instruction, he would probably spend years perfecting his technique.

At the beginning landings were the bane of Pat's life. His regular trainer was Moth A7-69. On Tuesday 25 February, he wrote:

On the Defaulters Parade again today for no apparent reason.

Flying was worse than terrible and I don't know what's the matter. I can't even fly straight much less land a plane safely.

But I'll get over it, and I tried to forget it and went to the pictures, but alas some weepy lovesick stuff made me feel worse.

Cursed day.

His diary entry for 10 March noted:

Flying in full swing again today and in old 69 again to the general imperilment of all other planes. Mucked about and did some damned horrible landings. Went to the pictures and saw once more 'The Nitwits' and laughed almost fit to kill myself. Reminds me of Pete and myself.[3]

The next day was completely different. In capital letters at the top centre of his diary page he printed in capitals: 'SOLO'.

Today was the day. Flew splendidly in a wooden test machine, so Squadron Leader Bladin tested me and I did four corker landings in succession, then to my delirium he got out.

I flew off and around for twenty minutes, and it is quite unnecessary and impossible to tell how I felt.

I went mad, whistled, sang and almost jumped for joy.

Thursday, 19 March:

Solo period today and turned the plane upside down as usual to wear off my sleepiness.

F/O H…. was given a farewell dinner tonight as he has been promoted and posted to Richmond. We made whoopee in a big way with a bang. Ruined a dinner shirt completely, but won an obstacle race over the piled up furniture with no little applause. Needed a shower before going to bed – Hells Bells!

Formation flying had a fascination of its own. To fly close alongside another aircraft was always an exciting business. The manipulation of controls, throttle, rudder and control column required the finest judgement and in the early stages at least, the impression of nearness could be almost terrifying. To fly in formation the leading aeroplane flew at a reduced throttle setting and had to give plenty of warning of his intentions to turn, climb or dive either by hand signals or by radio telephone. The pilot of the following aeroplane concentrated on keeping in the same relative altitude regardless of what happened to the horizon. This required considerable faith in the leader and mutual confidence in the ability to act as a team.

Monday 6 April:

Started formation flying. Bloody queer – old planes bob up and down like lunatics. Damned hard at first. Got 2 good chaps with me, Jackson and Gilbert. Good pilots – not afraid to come in nice and close – but it would be funny for their propeller to chew the behind off my tail, I know.

Tons of mucking about after break up. Flat turns and dives at one another – be a smash one day.

Aerial attacks and air-to-ground gunnery were similarly exacting. The pilot had to concentrate on maintaining a steady aim through his sights whilst closing rapidly on his target. He had to judge the exact instant to break away or he would be in real danger of flying into his target. If this was a ground target, that was the end of it. Many a pilot was killed in just this way. The secret of success lay in a steady hand, holding fire until close and then flying down as near to the target as possible without actually crashing into it – all requiring split-second timing.

Low-flying practice was exhilarating and dangerous. This came into the category of the greatest killer of pilots. Normal flight above 500 feet gave almost no impression of speed on the senses. The ground appeared to move past very slowly and the higher one flew, the less the apparent movement. On the other hand, coming down low, the impression of speed suddenly increased until, when a few feet above the ground, objects loomed up and flashed past at an alarming rate. Any mistake at such a height could be spectacular and very likely fatal.

Wednesday 15 April, after the Easter break:

Hell of a day – Flew like a barn door but did some unauthorised low flying – hot stuff – should let us do it anytime we like especially after holidays. Met Gilbert at 2,000 and engaged in a restricted encounter – would have been shot to pieces if he had a gun on his plane. Escaped several times by rudder in steep turns but resulting in a sickening side slip. Gilbert – Good – Egg.

Next day there was a tragedy. Thursday 16 April:

A fearful day – Blowy and gusty.

Chaplin tore his wings off and tried to jump but his parachute tangled and he rode her in from 2,000 feet. Bloody awful – First death – boys are taking it pretty badly.

The officers put on a show in the mess tonight but even though it has taken the sting out of things – the thought of Chaplin's death still hangs around.

Vale – Cadet.

It was Pat's turn to have a mishap on Tuesday 21 April:

Positively an unlucky day. Chased Gilbert out to sea where I left him doing aerobatics. His engine cut out and he squeezed home to land by about 20 yards. Meanwhile I careered down to the deck and turned up on my nose in A7-40. I have requested permission to obtain damaged propeller.

Gilbert and I seem to be Siamese twins – either we are in or out of trouble at the same time – good effort of Gilbert's.

Monday, 27 April:

We have a cove called Eaton here, a really blinking mad snake – turned up for flying with a distorted bundle of blue wool that proved to be a helmet his lady love had knitted for him – Good God – he looks like Frankenstein. He has been reading how the German ace Boelcke wore a knitted helmet I suppose – but perhaps he doesn't know Boelcke was shot down while wearing it.[4]

The cadets were well aware of the exploits of Australian fliers in the First World War and some were instructors at Point Cook. After a guest night dinner, several legendry figures like 'Kanga' de la Rue and Adrian 'King' Cole would visit the cadets' ante room where, with a little prompting, they could be 'persuaded' to tell some first-hand accounts of combat over the enemy lines. 'Stories would flow of Spads and Sopwith Camels, Fokkers, and Albatros scouts hurtling about in monumental dogfights with their Vickers, Spandaus and Lewis guns blazing, spitting out sudden death. They could all see the bullet holes punching their way across the black crosses and into the sides of some doomed Fokker.'[5] There was much to be learned by listening.

When there was weekend leave, Geoff Hartnell ('stout fellah') often took Pat to his home at East Malvern in Melbourne. 'Makes me feel like I really know some decent people after all. P.S., Hartnell's family is all kindness.'

Despite all the pressure, the first half of the year passed very quickly and then for the young men in Flying Course No. 20 there was two wonderful weeks of leave. However, something else happened at this time which was of particular interest to them. Cadets from the senior course finishing at the end of June had the opportunity to apply for short service commissions in the Royal Air Force in England. Five of them did so, one of them being Hughie Edwards from Fremantle. They departed for England in July. Here for Pat and the others, there was a tangible chance of overseas travel and adventure, and the opportunity to fly the latest and best aircraft in the world.

After his middle-of-the-year leave, Pat began his diary again on 13 July. Flying in the second term was a matter of the senior cadets applying their knowledge of flying and the theory of flight to the actions required in war. They began by flying Westland Wapitis, biplanes with a similar performance to the Bristol Fighters of the First World War.

Each instructor was allocated four pupils. To start with, there was a great deal of cloud flying and close formation flying practice. To oblige the pupil to trust his instruments, there was flying 'under the hood'. A canvas hood was pulled over the pupil's cockpit so that he could not see out. High-altitude flying exercises usually involved two hours of extreme cold and misery. Struggling up to 20,000 feet in a winter sky over Victoria in an open cockpit with no heat and a 100 mph draught whistling around subjected the occupants to sub-arctic conditions. The temperature in the atmosphere dropped by three degrees Fahrenheit for every thousand feet of altitude. The aircraft had to climb fully loaded as if for wartime operations and clawing up the last few thousand feet was extremely slow and painful – a character-building experience! Much more to their liking was the air-to-ground gunnery and dive-bombing practice. The Wapitis gathered speed very rapidly in the dive and cadets found it 'quite impressive', with the wires in the rigging howling and vibrating as they hurtled down. The more nervous cadets tended to pull out too high and the reckless ones to go down too low.

A squadron of Bristol Bulldogs was located at Laverton, five miles to the north. Bulldogs were nimble little biplane fighters of the early 1930s and it was good sport for the Wapitis to engage them in mock dogfights. Mostly a pair of 'Dogs' would launch surprise attacks from above out of the clear blue sky, if possible from out of the sun. The idea was to evade and counter-attack. The pupil hung on, watching and learning as the instructor would weave, dive, roll and pull around in violent climbing turns, striving to keep one or another of the 'Dogs' in his gunsight. Good sport indeed! The time would eventually arrive for the pupil to take over.

The antics of another flying instructor in particular made him really stand out. He was regarded by most of the people at Point Cook as easily being the best pilot in the RAAF. This was a flying officer by the name of Sam Balmer. He was a relatively uncommunicative man with a permanently sour expression on his face and he tended to instruct in monosyllables, but when he did talk you listened. His flying ability was unsurpassed and it was he who absolutely relished baiting the Laverton Bulldogs and engaging them in pitched battles. They never succeeded in catching him by surprise. Sam was reputed to own a large, sporty Vauxhall car in which he made record-breaking runs such as Darwin to Adelaide, Perth to Adelaide and possibly Perth to Melbourne at a time when the highways were dirt tracks. Of him, Gordon Olive wrote:

Kanga had everybody bluffed except Sam who seemed to have some compulsion not only to show Kanga he was not worried by him but also to keep on showing him. As a result, Sam was more or less permanent Duty Pilot or Orderly Officer, two unpopular jobs which were normally done by turn but which were handed out as punishment to officers who were being intractable or just plain bloody minded as was Sam's case.[6]

For all the cadets these were full and heady days and time passed swiftly – but learning to fly could be dangerous too. There were the hazards of bumpy landings through lack of experience or judgement that resulted in damaged propellers and/or undercarriages the problems of becoming separated or lost sometimes resulting in occasional forced landings short of fuel and there were, fortunately infrequently, rough-running engines or similar mishaps. Pat was among those who did manage to 'bend' another plane.

On 19 October:

Had to write out a crash report today, sideslipping turn, stalled near the ground and banged A5-33 in from a great height. Major repair. Scotty must have been as mad as hell! He said the main thing in crash reports is not to incriminate oneself. Always blame the plane. Good scout.

It could even happen to experienced fliers. One day two instructors, one of them a sergeant pilot, had a mid-air collision. Their planes were observed circling the aerodrome in opposite directions, one following the circuit of the day, the other not. Both pilots were injured in the crash, badly in the case of the sergeant pilot who was not at fault. He died the following day as a result of his injuries. The accident left a dark cloud of gloom over the base for some time.

Then, all too soon, the rest of the year slipped away and summer approached. Towards the end of the course, Pat wrote to his sister Constance:

Con,

Sorry old cheese, for remembering to forget to reply to your last scrawl, but the fact I was, and still am very tired and lazy.

It's a pity that girl friend from Coonamble couldn't stay over till Christmas, as then perhaps we could possibly go surfing, as was our intention that day so long ago … She will be horribly cross if … I have to go to England won't she. Or do I kid myself?

Went to Luna Park the other night and plunged bravely into 'The River Caves' in a small canoe. But the chappie in charge didn't like it a bit when we rammed the blinking wall and caused a traffic block in the dark tunnel. The fleet was in and up some place a sailor had the misfortune to break my pipe.

Hartnell's father died last week so I'm by myself now for a while.

Another dance will come off next Friday, and by all accounts seeing as it will be our last one, it will be what is termed a 'wizzer'.

Too dammed hot to do anything today except swim and sunbake and lady am I sunburnt. I'm completely red: and by hell it is sore.

Some foul swine rigged my bed yesterday, so that when I sprang to my resting place last night the whole thing collapsed to the complete ruin of all the supporting joints.

From your letter, it appears that you are having a hell of a busy time. Me too, although mine isn't of my own making.

Nothing more to tell you, so give my regards to Rob and his exam papers.
Love and Love.
Pat
P.S., I'm flying to Albury–Deniliquin solo on Tuesday – cross/country.[7]

Almost all too suddenly the course came to an end. Despite the approaching end-of-course examinations, extroverted cadets like Pat and his friends still found time for some in-house 'fun' in the evenings. 'Gilbert and I and Mace offered to fight the Mess but we had to give it up when Kanga came in to take the dinner ceremonial.' And then it was over; practical and theoretical exams were passed or failed, newly acquired flying skills were assessed and there were important decisions to be made for the future.

On 27 August:

Paget nearly talked me into going to England again tonight.[8] Painted a fascinating picture of easy life, beer and women. And what beer and what women? They say 25 cadets are going so it looks as though I might even be going against my will. But speaking of wills, I think it is willed that I would (go to England I mean).

On 18 October:

They tell us that 25 out of the 31 left are going to Blighty. I would like to go very much, travel and all that but the being away from home for so long appears to be the worst part.

From the class of 1936, twenty-five did decide to go to England for experience in the RAF – the largest contingent to leave for the UK so far. Some RAAF officers were beginning to doubt and question the wisdom of sending their brightest and best away from the service for five years. Indeed, experience was showing that when their short service commissions were up, some earlier cadets were not returning to Australia at all. Some, like Ron Lees from the January 1930 Point Cook class, opted to accept permanent commissions in the RAF. Others like Donald Bennett from the July 1930 Point Cook class resigned from the RAF and went into civil aviation or other careers in England, although they were required to remain in the RAF (not RAAF) Reserve. The RAAF was losing too many good men.

The fortunate twenty-five were:

Allsop, J. W.	Boehm, D. C.	Brough, J. F. T.	Campbell, D.	Cosgrove, R. J.
Fowler, H. N.	Gilbert, C. L.	Good, D. C. F.	Grey-Smith, G. E.	Hughes, P. C.
Hullock, C. L.	Johnston, L. L.	Kaufman, K. W.	Kelaher, C. R.	Kinane, W.
Mace, C. R.	Marshall, D.	Olive, C. G. C.	Paine, J.	Power, R.
Robinson, A. E.	Rogers, K. R.	Sheen, D. F. B.	Wight, W. B.	Yate, E. W.

'*Faber est suae quisque fortunae*'. 'Every man is the maker of his own fortune'. It was a motto Pat knew well. He and the others had chosen the path they would follow. They had all worked for it and made it happen.

All but one left for England in January 1937, sailing from Australia on P&O's elderly liner, the 16,600-ton SS *Narkunda*, a regular ship on the Australia–England route. The exception was Marshall, who had departed almost immediately after he had finished in December. His intention was to meet up with the others again over there.

Before he left, Pat 'did the rounds' to say goodbye to his friends and members of the family. Excited by Pat's success, and the marvellous adventures that undoubtedly lay ahead of him, Pete Pettigrew was prompted into lodging his own application to join the RAAF – he would try to get to England too!

Laurence Lucas remembered his uncle calling in to see his mother before he went:

It was in the Christmas/New Year holidays early in 1937 that Pat came one weekend to our Manly flat to say goodbye. Bill had shouted him a new 'civvie' outfit: a genuine Harris Tweed jacket; slacks; and a felt hat worn 'porkpie' style. In the three years since my sister and I had been in Pat's company, he had changed. He was polite, reserved, uncharacteristically diffident. Perhaps it was too much for a twenty-year-old to take in: that he was leaving us all behind.

I personally don't know if he said goodbye to his father. I hope he did.[9]

The *Narkunda* left from Sydney Harbour's No. 21 Wharf at Pyrmont on 9 January at 11 a.m. Among those seeing Pat off were his mother, Midge, Will and Pete Pettigrew. Those who boarded in Sydney were mainly from New South Wales, Queensland and the Australian Capital Territory and included besides Pat were Gordon Olive and Desmond Sheen. Former cadets with their homes in other states joined the ship along the way.

As *Narkunda* sailed south towards Melbourne, many passengers took the opportunity to dash off final letters to the relatives and friends they were leaving behind. To Constance, Pat wrote:

Dearest sister,

This gondola is supposed to berth at Melbourne tonight sometime so if I get this finished you should get it pretty quickly.

I have not yet been very sea sick, only slight uneasiness around the centre, but it is quite OK at present.

It's pretty late now as there has been a struggle around the room, listed on the notice board as a dance. Talk about a game of Rugby. The women would never pass in a beauty show as far as our part of the ship goes but down in the tourist class, well! That's different.

Going to see Hartnell tomorrow and tomorrow night, the fat thing and suppose I shall run into the rest of the chaps staying in Australia at Point Cook.

The meals are good, but very very widely spaced, as yet, but we have made one successful midnight sortie upon the pantry steward, much to his amazement.

The deck games are good, but the swimming pool is pretty small, although the water is rather clean.

Have written the Mater a letter.

Get hold of one of those photos from Paramount and see which one is the best and give it to Judith, don't slip up on it will you, on I'll get my throat cut.

Love and Love to both Robert.

Keep smiling. See you soon.

Pat[10]

Bob Cosgrove, Pat's former roommate, was the very last to board the ship in Melbourne on the 12th. He was apparently delayed in Tasmania by his father who had not taken the news of him going very well at all, but it was Bob's decision. Whatever happened to him from now on would be on his own head.

The *Narkunda* sailed on and all too soon they lost sight of land. What was ahead of them all now?

3

ENGLAND

The voyage to England by ship early in 1937 was a colourful and varied experience, particularly for twenty- and twenty-one-year-olds who had the world at their feet. In the hot summer the boys put the ship's smallish swimming pool to good use, Pat usually grouping with Des Sheen and Bob Cosgrove. The route was by way of Colombo, Bombay, Aden, Suez, Marseilles and Gibraltar. It was their first time outside of Australia and their transitory glimpses of the East were just enough to whet their appetites for more. The strange places and foreign languages made quite an impression on them all.

One of the personalities on the ship was a much-travelled youngish Englishman of about thirty years of age who was an army officer by profession and had spent many years in the Dominions. He was an excellent companion and took a lively interest in the 'education' of the young pilot officers. Although he gave the impression that the young Australians were the first live pilots he'd actually met, he'd had a brother in the air force for years.

He went out of his way to show the Australians around Colombo and promised something special in Bombay. This turned out to be an offer of taking them on an after-midnight conducted tour of the native vice dens of the city. An Indian Army Colonel of more mature years on the ship heard of the plan and severely warned against the idea. He told them not to be such idiots as they could almost certainly end up with their throats cut at the very least. He viewed their interest in the dare with the gravest misgivings. They assured him that they were merely curious and not attracted to the enterprise in a biological sense. The colonel still insisted on cautioning them not to go.

In the long run most of the boys heeded the colonel's advice but six, being young and foolish, ignored it. With their English guide they left the ship for the native quarter at about 11 p.m. When they returned the stories they told were chilling.

It was not long before they became uneasy about the sights and sounds of their surroundings. They were the only non-natives among teeming thousands of men and women. Some wore European clothes but mostly the men had on a toga-like native sheet or were just wearing a loincloth or shorts. A great many of them were drunk. Fights were breaking out frequently and their foreign curses were mingled with feminine screams.

In Grant Road, the location of the houses of ill fame, women of all ages from what appeared to be their late sixties to teenage adolescents were caged up behind huge steel grills, gates or trellises. Entry to the houses was only possible after paying a door attendant. Inside, the interiors were poorly lit and the occupants so obviously disease ridden that the young Australians only entered a few establishments for fear of being 'done in' for the few shillings they could be carrying. There appeared to be hundreds of these establishments and they seemed to stretch for miles. In reality, they only stretched for a few hundred yards but it seemed unbelievable that there could be so much squalor and filth. The stench of degradation was indescribable and by merely seeing it they felt in some way contaminated.

As the night turned into the small hours of the morning the streets grew quieter. Drunks and exhausted natives slept together on the foul pavements with rats crawling among them and over them fossicking for something to eat. All the time as they walked past the women behind the bars continued to scream and put their arms through the cages-like bars to try to grab them. They looked and were treated like monkeys in cages – it was hard to believe that these poor creatures were humans too.

Eventually the 'tour' was declared over. They eagerly left the slums and headed back to the ship. By the time they arrived back they'd seen enough of the East to last them for quite some time. After a bath at 5 a.m. to strive to somehow wash away the squalor and contamination somehow they turned in to try and sleep. Each only had a fitful and troubled rest at best.

At 10 a.m. the Australian pilots were scheduled to visit Bombay in daylight. The half-dozen who had ventured out during the night saw a very different city. They were all conducted to first-class hotels where clean Indian servants served them long glasses of cold beer. It was difficult right there and then to realise that the other side of the Indian penny actually existed. It seemed more the stuff of nightmares than harsh reality.

The friendly colonel was obviously relieved to see them back again in one piece and cautioned once more never to do such a foolish thing again. It was obvious now what he had meant. He went on to explain that there were parts of Indian life which the British were unable to do anything about. British influence only touched the higher administrative levels of the nation. Efforts by tens of thousands of Britons to alter the ways of the people were simply swamped and lost amid the teeming, overwhelming hundreds of millions on the Subcontinent.[1]

*

Aden was incredibly barren. There was no green of plant life to be seen anywhere, only bare, infertile rocks and heat. At first sight the scenes were fascinating in a way and impressive, absolutely nothing like the deserts of Australia. Everything looked so uninviting and alien.

Once through the Suez Canal the weather turned very cool, even cold. It was winter in the northern hemisphere and in January the supposedly sunny, warm Mediterranean was neither warm nor sunny.

The Australian boys found it too cold to stay out on deck for long and had to abandon outdoor activities for an indoor existence for the remainder of the trip. This they found very tedious and by the time they reached London even best friends were becoming a trifle cranky and argumentative. Except when working, the majority of Australians spent by far the greatest part of their waking life out of doors usually at some form of sport or pastime, summer or winter. Any lengthy period of enforced confinement in a house due to bad weather brought frustration in its wake causing squabbles and petty irritations.

The *Narkunda* called in at the great naval base at Gibraltar. Many of the ships of the Royal Navy were in harbour, no doubt reminding the Spaniards, currently waging a civil war, that there was no need to become too ambitious about the Rock. The great, massive battleships and their many smaller destroyers made an impressive sight. It seemed obvious that Gibraltar had a water supply problem as great areas of the Rock were covered with corrugated iron. This was presumably to catch water for drinking and domestic use. Coming from a dry continent, the Australians knew something about that.

A few miles away across the Straits of Gibraltar was Tangier. *Narkunda* stopped there for a short time and found another fleet. It flew the Italian flag. The ships had a modern and streamlined look which made them appear to be much more impressive than the British fleet over at Gibraltar. They looked fast and efficient – more than a match for the obsolescent Royal Navy vessels. When this was pointed out to the friendly young Englishman, he said, 'Oh no! They're not so hot really. Saw over them once, wasn't impressed, all covered with rust, verdigris, olive oil and spaghetti.' He dismissed them contemptuously. Nevertheless, the Australians could not help recalling that the Italians had recently defied the League of Nations by invading and conquering Abyssinia despite general condemnation. The members of the League had just looked on and said, 'Tut! Tut!' They wondered, were the British really as decadent as Mussolini claimed?

Narkunda passed through the Bay of Biscay in full fury – there was an angry gale whipping up enormous seas. For two days the ship pitched and tossed, then the gale subsided but a steady light rain fell from the low grey skies. The seas, rain, sky, all were grey and leaden. It was impossible to tell one from the other. It stayed wet and windy in the English Channel and it was still wet as the ship tied up in the docks at Tilbury the next morning.

The spirits of the Australians were heavy as they struggled with their baggage and passed through customs. They emerged into the same biting wind and soaking rain to board a dirty, sooty train. It might have been Melbourne in winter as they were transported at an unimpressive speed through some rain-sodden marshland on to the endless dreary wilderness of London in February. It was hard to imagine anything much more dispiriting than entering

London on such a day from such a direction, yet nothing could have been more typical of an English introduction.

The arrival in London was wet and cold, and the newcomers were miserable. At other ports of call there had been something impressive, something unique. The teeming hordes of Ceylon and India; the incredible barrenness of Aden; the excitement of visiting Port Said, Marseilles and Gibraltar – but not London. It seemed drab, dirty, mouldy, wet and cold. The buildings were not tall and impressive – there were better in Melbourne and Sydney. Nowhere else had they seen as many chimney pots, which gave an impression of bleakness. It all looked so alien, and wet! Back home it would have been summer and hot. February was always hot, but not here.[2]

They were met in London by some Australia House officials who informed them they would be transported straight away to the RAF centre at Uxbridge, about sixteen miles west of the capital. On arrival, they would be 'sworn in'. There was no time to look around. The weather was against it anyway. And what was there to see around here as they departed in any case? Sombre, Doric-styled Australia House had been built in the Strand on an island site at the east end of Aldwych. Stretching from Australia House past St Clement Danes towards the great dome of St Paul's Cathedral was Fleet Street, the hub of Britain's newspaper publishing empire with its hectic traffic made up of double-decker buses, cars and cabs. On the footpaths busy people with umbrellas and overcoats still brushed by each other despite the soaking drizzle.

Lanes and little side streets branched off at right angles to left and right – Shoe Lane, Birde Lane and there to the left off Ludgate Hill was Old Bailey Street. Further along this street and higher up, just visible outlined against the cold grey sky, stood a tall bronze female figure. In her right hand was a sword held high and she balanced scales in her left – Blind Justice herself. She was on top of the courthouse. This was the Central Criminal Court, the famous 'Old Bailey'. Next, they passed around the imposing St Paul's Cathedral and up to Newgate Street to turn left and go westward, eventually leaving Central London along Oxford Street, passing Marble Arch and continuing along the Bayswater Road.

For Pat Hughes and his family, England and the Old Bailey was where their story had begun. (See Appendix 1: The Ancestry of Pat Hughes.)

The Australians were unimpressed. By the end of the first week they'd all had enough. Accustomed to fine sunny weather, they had great difficulty in accepting the confined existence of a wet English winter. The locals seemed to be completely attuned to it, but before long the disenchanted Aussies became irritable and moody.

On 19 February 1937, after being sworn in at RAF Uxbridge as 'pilot officers in the General Duties Branch of the Royal Air Force' for five years, they were instructed to go to London to buy RAF uniforms. These differed in colour from those of the RAAF, being a light-greyish blue, whereas the Australian uniform at that time was a dark royal blue similar to the navy uniform. The cost was about two years' of their salary and the instruction was to pay this off by a banker's order to deduct a set amount from their monthly salary. By this method the debt would be cleared in four years but their already very modest income was reduced to even smaller proportions. In the interim, permission was given to wear the Australian uniform. It was with mounting regret and some bitterness that they remembered the RAAF uniform had been supplied free.

For the next month the rain showed no sign of letting up. Day after day of freezing wet weather. There was nowhere to go and nothing to do – even the London tailor came to the camp for fitting the new uniforms. By the end of the month everyone was ready to go *en masse* back to Australia. Then, almost unexpectedly, they were ordered to transfer to Lincolnshire and split up, half going to Digby and some going to Grantham. The remainder were to go on to Thornaby in Yorkshire. Pat's destination was No. 2 Flying Training School at Digby. Desmond Sheen was with the group going to No. 9 Flying Training School at Thornaby.

Digby airfield was located some twenty miles south of the city of Lincoln but to travel there by train the countryside all looked the same – grey and wet. To reach there by truck or coach there seemed to be tall fence-like hedges and piled stone walls bordering endless miles of twisting narrow roads. The furthest distance they could see in any given direction was about half a mile. Digby airfield dated back to the First World War when open fields near the village of Scopwick were used as a relief landing ground by the RNAS at Cranwell. Between the wars it was used extensively for training and was extensively modernised and upgraded as part of the RAF's expansion programme in 1935 and 1936. Its commanding officer for a few months in 1920 had been Squadron Leader Arthur Harris, later to become commander-in-chief of RAF Bomber Command; other commanders included Wing Commander Arthur Tedder and Group Captain Trafford Leigh-Mallory. Following the completion of the expansion it passed into the control of No. 12 Group, RAF Fighter Command, and was to remain a fighter aerodrome for much of the war.

The Australians found Digby dreary and dismal. It was made up of small, supposedly temporary igloo-type structures that had been erected during the First World War. If they thought their 'wind tunnel' accommodation at Point Cook had been rough, compared to these igloos they had been luxurious. As one of the others, Lew Johnston, commented, 'There were two types of igloos, small and bloody small.' The smaller igloos had four 'cells' for the inmates, the larger had eight. There was an additional cell for the batman. Each just had room for a bed, a chair, a cupboard for clothes and a small fireplace in the only corner that was not occupied.

Gordon Olive, who was also at Digby, recalled:

The fireplace was there for the simple reason that the igloos were so cold. Unless they had some heating each night, the occupant was likely to freeze to death during his sleep.

Between each pair of igloos was a toilet-come-ablutions igloo. This worked on the principle that good fresh air was very healthful and that young officers should not luxuriate in hot baths under any circumstances. These were truly efficient wind tunnels and only the most determined of the Australians maintained their two baths a day routine. One thing the wind tunnel did achieve was to stop Pat Hughes' daily bath song. Pat claimed that it was just not possible to sing and shiver to death at the same time...

The Air Council of the RAF seemed to have the philosophy that all young officers were virtually inseparable from trouble, and one way to combat this was to reduce them to abject poverty. In this they were most efficient, but the theory was only partially effective.

Thus on one notable night the citizens of Lincoln (the local city) were amazed to see three young men busily erecting a toilet pedestal, seat, cistern, chain and all on the footpath outside a pub called *The Saracen's Head*. Pat Hughes was the ring leader, and proved very efficient with a Stillson wrench which he had acquired from somewhere. Pat claimed the pub was run by a pack of bums and that the toilet seat combination was a more appropriate sign outside the establishment than that depicting the decapitated Saracen of ancient vintage.

The local constabulary arrived and took the matter up with Pat, and those of us who were sober enough, took the matter of Pat up with the local constabulary. As a result, the toilet set-up was eventually replaced in its original location and we avoided the embarrassment of having to bail Pat out of the local gaol. Pat, for his part, stoutly demanded to go to gaol because he said it would just have to be warmer than the igloos at Digby.

The only break after the month of rain was a week of snow. For a while it changed the colour from grey to white but then the sun shone for a few hours turning the snow to slush. And then it rained for another month![3]

The Australians filled in some of their seemingly endless waiting time by studying maps of the area for a radius of a hundred miles or so from the aerodrome. A number of neighbourhoods were prohibited and had to be avoided. One was Cranwell, the main RAF training school. Some civil aerodromes also had to be shunned, as were gunnery ranges on the coast. There were other service aerodromes dotted about where pilots could land if they became lost, or if for some reason a landing back at Digby became difficult or impossible.

Overall, the terrain was flat with seemingly endless fields for crops but lacking in such prominent landmarks as mountains and distinctive hills. Nevertheless, there were several very valuable landmarks. The forests in the vicinity were very important, they were told. These were isolated and not particularly large but they had very distinctive shapes and were easy to pick out from the surrounding cultivated countryside. Back in Australia roads and railway lines had always been good landmarks because they were very few and far between. This was not the case in England. There were literally dozens of roads and railways weaving their way over the countryside and identifying one from another from the air was a major difficulty.

Old Roman roads were the exceptions. These ran for miles, sometimes forty or fifty miles in a straight line. This was most unusual in England because the multitude of country roads meandered drunkenly all over the place as if they could not decide which way to go. There were old Roman roads in Lincolnshire. The Australians were told that some ran along by some of the RAF airfields. These were the most useful of all the landmarks in that part of the world. Many a pilot had saved his life in bad weather by finding a straight Roman road and flying along it until an aerodrome appeared where he could make an emergency landing.

On the rare occasions when the rain did ease, several games of rugby were played with the local lads. The playing fields were as soft as sponges, and apart from churning up the mud and receiving a liberal coating of muck over everything, it was a much less violent sport than that played on the harder grounds back home. It was not as rough on the knees and other exposed parts as playing the same game back in Australia.

Even after eight long and boring weeks, the Australian boys were still trying to acclimatise to English hibernation. Some were cursing their foolishness for electing to join the RAF. The eagerly awaited mail from home added to their torture. It was full of cheerful descriptions of friends and relations swimming and baking in glorious summer sunshine. Lew Johnston summed it up: 'Even the birds walk in this bloody climate.' 'It was true,' Gordon Olive agreed. 'The waterlogged aerodrome was dotted with groups of crows and seagulls pulling up earth worms which had come to the surface to avoid being drowned.'[4] Pat remembered Cooma in New South Wales could be cold and wet, but it was nothing like this.

Eventually, as April approached, the weather did improve. At first there was one clear day followed by two or three days of rain, then two clear days followed – and then it was almost fine! The wind was still very cold, but there was more and more sunshine. The Englishmen claimed it was spring arriving.

As the weather cleared, flying started at long last. With every new day there was more activity and soon they were fully occupied. This was what they wanted! First, there were the essential familiarisation flights. Yes, the local countryside *was* as flat as the maps showed; patterned fields of crops *did* spread in every direction; and so too there *were* the irregular patches of woods and forests, but these had displays of thick greenness that complemented the yellows and browns in the fields and gave a serene beauty that was at the same time restful and surprising.

The aircraft at Digby were Hawker Harts, Furies and Audaxes, all by the Hawker Company, and Avro Tutors. The elegant Hart two-seater light bomber which had first flown in June 1928 had introduced an unrivalled dynasty of Hawker military machines to the RAF. It was an early product of designer Sydney Camm, a promising draughtsman who, with engineer Fred Sigrist, had devised a system of bolted duralumin tubes that became the characteristic fuselage construction of all new Hawker machines. Their Hart boasted a matchless performance for its time that included a top speed in level flight of 184 mph. It was chosen as the RAF's new light day-bomber and nearly 1,000 were built, with large export orders. It had proved to be one of the most adaptable aeroplanes in RAF history.

Early experience with the Hart in squadron service left little doubt that it could be adapted to fulfil a variety of roles. One of the first involved fairly minor changes to satisfy an army cooperation requirement, with the air force needing a replacement for lower-performance types such as the Westland Wapiti. A message pick-up hook and other minor equipment changes transformed the Hart into the Audax.

The Demon was an interim fighter based on the Hart bomber but the next Hawker machine, the Fury, was designed as a fighter from the outset. This graceful single-seat biplane was the RAF's first to exceed 200 mph in level flight. Ordered in 1930 and entering service in May 1931, the Fury's superb supercharged Rolls-Royce Kestrel engine gave it an impressive rate of climb, superior to the contemporary Bristol Bulldog, while its light controls made it ideal for aerobatics. They initiated the development of additional multiple types such as the Hardy, Hind, Hector and Hart Trainer, on which many future Second World War pilots would cut their teeth.

Aside from a few other stray machines, the Tutor was the other main type at Digby, and it was not from the Hawker stable. It was the A. V. Roe (Avro) and Co. Ltd's Type 621 Trainer of 1929 which had been designed as a replacement for the Avro 504N of First World War vintage. The Tutor featured a welded steel-tube structure and a 155 horsepower Armstrong Siddeley Mongoose IIIA radial engine. Eventually Avro mass-produced more than 390 of them for the RAF, including fourteen Sea Tutor floatplanes with long single-step Alclad floats.

Despite becoming busier, Pat still found time to keep up with his correspondence. To his sister, Constance, he wrote:

Con,

The address as you see proclaims my existence in the land of Eskimos and seals and other things that make up this dear England in winter time.

I won't write you a long story of the trip, as I managed to keep a sort of diary on the boat, and I, as it has just come back into my possession, am about to post it home, so you can gather it off the Mater and peruse it some afternoon when you have naught else to do.

Well, to be honest, this England, even though it has been miserable weather, is a pretty decent place.

Our quarters here are only temporary until we move on to a squadron and so we can't expect a palace, so after all life has been pretty good.

I have completely regained my land and flying legs, seen most of London, spent a fair bit of money and seen a good deal of countryside by flying over it.

The trouble is the smoke hangs around so much that I can't see very much from about 4,000 feet.

I'm flying rather nice and fast aeroplanes, single seater, 700 horse power fighter planes called Hawker 'Furies'. They are supposed to kick out about 250 miles an hour, but mine must be old as it only does about 200 and then feels as if the engine will jump out.

I hope to go to a squadron equipped with planes called 'Gauntlets' or 'Gladiators', nice and fast, much faster than these old Furies, but I'm terribly satisfied as I am.

There's only one other chap from our lot up here with me, Johnston, a Queenslander, and he is flying heavy bombers the poor sod, so it looks as if I will be going to a squadron by myself, as none of the other chaps except for Des Sheen will be flying single-seater fighters, and he's going to a squadron near London I think.

I haven't done anything this Easter as I didn't have anywhere in particular to go, and I didn't have much money so I just mooned around and played squash.

We have had snow and rain practically four days out of five during our working week, and on Wednesdays, Saturdays and Sundays, when we have holidays, it was so foggy or dull we couldn't do a thing …

… Saw Merle Oberon in a play called 'Beloved Enemy' and saw the play called 'This Will Make You Whistle' with Jack Buchanan. He's a dumb cluck if ever there was one but old Merle is a tasty dish. Yum! Yum! What would mother say?

Tell your lanky hero not to get fat and lazy just because he's married, but to look after himself. Keep on with the swimming lessons.

After 6 weeks on that boat where I spent about 4 hours a day in the pool reckon I could take on the great Weissmuller himself.[5]

Haven't bought a car yet although I hear that Hartnell, in a fit of rashness, placed all his money on a Ford, which he proudly motors to and fro in. Tough luck about the air force packing those two Demons up in Tasmania and tougher luck still on Eagerty when he fell in the water. Those three chaps were in the senior cadets when I was there. Tough luck.

We've got an old lady called the Dutchess of Bedford, she's 73 but she flies her own aeroplane.

She got lost the other day and we've spent about three days looking for her, but they found some wreckage of her kite in the sea, so it looks as though the old duck has gone and done it sort of thing. Poor old thing! Although a woman of her age should have more sense.

So sister mine, behave yourself and see that the family doesn't have too many arguments and tell everybody you see to write me or send me a telegram or some damned thing. If I don't get some letters soon I'll have to start reading books to remember what Australia looks like.

Love to all and give my love to young Judith when you see her.

Love and Love

Pat[6]

After their familiarisation flights, the flying concentrated on camera gun exercises against ground targets and then against air targets – enjoyable fun and better was to come.

For the next stage, they went to Catfoss Aerodrome in Yorkshire where they carried out the same exercises and practice sessions all over again. The airfield was located on the east coast, north-east of Hull. While they were still there, they progressed to firing live ammunition at ground targets, and then at large flags being towed by other aircraft out over the North Sea. The results were being assessed to judge their suitability for placement into either fighter squadrons or bomber squadrons.

This was the era of the bomber, it was the 'glamour' aircraft. The latest bomber types, such as the new Bristol Blenheim, Vickers Wellington and Handley Page Hampden, were more 'modern' and faster than the RAF's existing biplane fighters. Many regarded fighters as a machine of the past. Even if new fighters could make up the gap in performance, there were rumours of new hydraulic four-gun turrets (that would be fitted to the Armstrong Whitworth Whitley) which would be able to shoot them down long before they came into range. Most of the Australians wanted to be categorised for bombers or seaplanes with the object of taking up careers in civil aviation in the future, but not Pat Hughes. He knew all about the great fighting aces of the First World War like the great Irishman Mick Mannock, the Canadian Billy Bishop, James McCudden, Harry Cobby, the Australian Flying Corp's top ace; and even the legendary Germans: the Red Baron Manfred von Richthofen, Boelcke, Immellmann and Voss. Fighters were what Pat wanted!

Con,

Having just received another letter from you, I am horrified to find I actually owe you two, but you'll pardon my not having written before …

… Have been here for several months just flitting around the countryside and popping off bullets at various targets. Been doing bags and bags of flying and so far have fired off about 4,000 bullets in air gunnery. You'd be surprised to find intact the targets still are. First of all we do gunnery on targets on the ground. We fly over about a thousand feet and dive at the targets and the idea seems to be to try and fire your guns at them. Alas! Alas! but damned good fun, you know.

When at last we passed out tests on these stationary ground targets, they took up a target on a great long piece of wire, towing it behind another aircraft.

We have to go up and dive at this towed target from different angles. The hitting of the ground targets when they were still was hard enough, but when this other is tootling along about 140 miles an hour, it's almost impossible even to get near it, less alone hit the damn thing with little bullets, if they gave us a big cannon or a spear, maybe we'd mangle the target, but as it is, its damned heartbreaking.

However, compared with the RAF junior officers, Olive (Queenslander) and myself have been getting apparently decent scores. So even though I would like to be getting a hundred bullets on, I am quite content with my thirties and forties, as is Olive, so life is not so bad after all …

… I have been doing a regular amount of night flying and am just considering whether my finances would stand the hire of a tub to fly over London on coronation night, just to see things from an original viewpoint.[7] I'd like that, and if, as is at present expected, Olive and I club together we'll certainly take a trip.

People have gone coronation crazy you touch or say borders on red, white and blue. Actually, it will be a damned good job when it's over.

Hartnell has been doing nothing in the way of letter writing, nor has Peter, but I have had all the exciting of Melbourne from Peg Colville.

Old Peg is a hell of a good scout, Con, and she writes a decent letter, filled with news and such. If ever she comes to Sydney, may she call and say good-day for you? She'd like it, I know, and you'd like her.

Have been sitting around all day doing nothing, waiting for the fog to clear up and get the sun shining and at last I see they have wheeled a few single seaters out, so I'm off.

Regards to everyone around the borough and give my love to all the scattered members of our family including ye olde Robert.

Will write again soon.

Love and Love

Pat[8]

Two days after returning to Digby the pilots found out their categories and their squadrons. Because of his outstanding air gunnery, Gordon Olive was selected for fighters. His posting was to 65 Squadron at Hornchurch near London. The rest of the Australians at No. 2 Flying Training School were rostered to go to bombers, and seemed satisfied – all but Pat. When he discovered he had been categorised for bombers, Pat was disappointed and hostile. What could he do? Make it happen! Pat decided to lodge an immediate protest, appealing to be reclassified for fighters. This was what he had been seeking from the very beginning.

Gordon Olive was not happy either. He was among those who had wanted bombers. He wrote later:

I felt very unhappy. Up till this turning point I had taken very little interest in the fighter-versus-bomber debate. To be assigned to fighters was by no means accepted as a status category, and most of the boys so assigned were far from happy.

When I learned that the squadron to which I was posted was based on the Thames Estuary at a place called Hornchurch, my cup of disillusionment was full. Hornchurch was notorious for the worst weather in England, as it was always fogged in winter by the industrial murk from London. This was carried on the prevailing westerly drift of the air masses in those latitudes. If ever there was a reluctant fighter pilot, I was it. Besides, all my friends had been posted to Bombers at aerodromes with famous names like Andover and Worthy Down and Abingdon, all in the beautiful west counties. I had to get Hornchurch!

There was one redeeming thought, Pat Hughes, who had been selected for bombers appealed and was recategorised to fighters. He was the only one who was keen on them.[9]

Olive appealed to the chief instructor for a posting to bombers but because of his outstanding gunnery results the instructor scoffed at the idea. His application was refused.

At the same time, Pat's more forthright request was upheld. His posting was to No. 64 (Fighter) Squadron at Martlesham Heath, somewhere in Suffolk.

Again, he had made it happen.

4

THE GATHERING STORM

In summer the countryside of England can be strikingly beautiful. Trees that were so gaunt and black in winter become laden with masses of leaves stretching to the ground. Colours bloom everywhere. Such variation and greenery is unreal to Australian eyes that have come from where the colours are predominantly a drab olive or brown for most of the year. English temperatures can also climb to unexpected levels, but usually only for brief periods of time. This invariably follows a prolonged wet spell which can make the humidity soar to a stifling, near-jungle heat.

It was almost tropical summer heat when Pat made his way to Martlesham Heath. The aerodrome was situated seven miles from Ipswich on open heath land. Around him clumps of bright yellow gorse grew in abundance, dotting the dark heath which later in summer and autumn would float in a sea of wine-coloured heather. The countryside further south along the River Stour had a familiarity about it thanks to the famous landscapes of John Constable.

Set down as it was on acres of relatively level sandy soil overlaying gravel that provided good drainage, Martlesham Heath was a natural site for an aerodrome. Moreover, for Pat it was an exciting destination, for this was where the newest RAF aircraft were tested. The latest and the best were there.

The station was officially opened on 16 February 1917 as a centre for the official testing of aircraft prototypes. The following October, the title of Aeroplane Experimental Station was conferred. Pilots stationed there were required to fly every type of aircraft from fighters to bombers and even evaluate captured enemy machines.

Throughout 1918, extensive testing and redesign work took place place on the Vickers FB27, later named the Vimy. Although it was too late to serve in the First World War, the Vimy achieved fame as the aircraft which carried Alcock and Brown on their record-breaking flight between Newfoundland and Ireland in June 1919. But the work could be hazardous. On 11 September 1918, the third prototype, B9954, carrying a full load of bombs, stalled on take-off. It crashed and exploded, killing the pilot.

After the war, Britain's newly formed Air Ministry decided that the aerodrome site should be leased on a secure basis, and on 14 November 1921 a five-year lease was taken out with the owner, Mr Ernest George Pretyman MP. This was extended to a lease for 199 years in 1923.

On 8 July 1936, Britain's newest monarch, King Edward VIII, and his brother the Duke of York (later to be King George VI) had visited Martlesham Heath for an inspection as part of a tour of the Royal Air Force. Among the many new types they saw on display were the Hawker Hurricane, Supermarine Spitfire, Fairey Battle, Bristol Blenheim, Vickers Wellington, Handley Page Hampden and Westland Lysander – names destined to become household words in the not too distant future.

Pat's posting to 64 Squadron at Martlesham Heath seemed to be a step in the right direction – at first. The squadron's planes were bright silver, two-seater Hawker Demon biplane fighters powered by a Rolls-Royce Kestrel engine. The fuselage of each machine proudly displayed the squadron's distinctive red-and-blue trellis insignia on either side of the roundel. His new CO was Squadron Leader P. King.

In the First World War, 64 Squadron had distinguished itself as a ground-attack unit in France, equipped at first with the de Havilland DH5 and later with the SE5a. It was no slouch in air combat either, claiming 128 enemy aircraft destroyed in the period March to August 1918. After being disbanded in December 1919, it reformed at Heliopolis in Egypt on 1 March 1936 from two Hawker Demon flights detached from Nos 6 and 208 Squadrons. Italy had invaded Ethiopia in October 1935, and there was fear that the conflict could escalate into a war between Britain and Italy. In order to not give the impression that RAF strength in Egypt was being built up, it was officially announced that the squadron was based at Henlow in Bedfordshire.

The squadron moved to Ismailia in north-east Egypt eight days later. In the event of hostilities, it had orders to move west to Mersa Matruh to be able to attack Italian airfields and provide fighter cover for bombers refuelling at advance landing grounds. Such operations would have been difficult, hampered by sand which was found to be damaging to the Kestrel engines. By the beginning of June 1936 Ethiopia had been conquered, so the threat of war between Britain and Italy passed. The squadron left Egypt for the United Kingdom the following August to become part of the UK's air defence build-up.

At Martlesham Heath, although every precaution was taken before and during the test flying of any aircraft, the nature of the work being done there carried with it the impression that it could be hazardous. There existed an almost fatalistic belief that from time to time it was inevitable that there would be accidents, some of them probably serious. In fact, the number of serious accidents was relatively low but one did happen on 28 May 1937, just after Pat arrived. A Demon from 64 Squadron was carrying out spin-and-recovery exercises over the aerodrome when the pilot failed to recover in time from a spin. The aircraft crashed into the middle of the aerodrome, resulting in the deaths of both occupants.

Pat may have been disappointed to see the Demons when there were faster and newer fighters about. The Demon was just a glorified Hawker Hart bomber and not much different to the types being flown back home at Point Cook. Each was equipped with two synchronised forward-firing Vickers machine guns and the rear cockpit modified to provide a maximum field of fire for a Lewis gun operated by the observer/air gunner. They had even been known as Hart Fighters in the beginning.

In December the squadron received a new commanding officer, an Irishman from County Cork by the name of Francis Victor Beamish, one of four brothers to serve with the RAF. Victor Beamish was a larger-than-life character and an inspirational leader. He was born in Dunmanway on 27 September 1903. After completing his education at Coleraine School, he joined the RAF and entered Cranwell, graduating in August 1923. Service in the UK followed and then in India. Next, he attended the Central Flying School before becoming a fighting instructor at RAF Sealand and afterwards at RAF Cranwell. In 1929 he travelled to Canada to assist in forming the basis of fighter squadrons within the Royal Canadian Air Force (RCAF). Two years later he returned to the UK to the post of flight commander with 25 Squadron at Hawkinge, but his tenure was cut short because he contracted tuberculosis and had to be invalided out of the service. His flying career seemed over. Beamish, who was not one to just sit there and let things happen, decided to return to Canada and adopt a healthy, active outdoor lifestyle. He worked as a lumberjack and it was this that eventually brought about a spectacular cure. After three years he was able not only to rejoin the air force but to take up flying again as well. He had made it happen by sheer determination, a characteristic that would make him an outstanding leader and fighter pilot.

On returning to the RAF, he spent a year building up the Meteorological Flight. A Met Flight pilot often had to go up in spite of weather conditions that kept others remaining safely on the ground. On most days he was required to take off at dawn, midday and dusk and while climbing take wet and dry bulb thermometer readings at intervals of a thousand feet. These figures were transmitted to the ground at two-minute intervals. In this way, the wind velocities and temperature at the various altitudes were relayed for the weather men to analyse suitability to fly. It was very exacting work and conditions could frequently be extremely difficult. Beamish was awarded the Air Force Cross for this significant effort.

The influence that Victor Beamish had on Pat Hughes has not been quantified but it is likely to have been considerable. His mere physical presence could inspire those around him and he tempered discipline with disarming Irish charm. 'He was an exceptional pilot, admired, well liked and revered by all who knew him, regardless of rank.' He was also exceptionally fit. In addition to his outdoor life as a lumberjack, he had excelled at sport in his early days, representing the RAF at rugby and being reserve for the Irish team on occasion. It was his practice to often jog around the airfield after the working day rather than having an evening meal.[1] He and Pat did have something very basic in common: the innate determination to make things happen, not just to wait for them to happen.

Around the same time as Victor Beamish took over the squadron, orders came through to apply camouflage to the all of the RAF's home-based, front-line fighters (camouflage had been applied to bombers since 1923). The first fresh-from-the-factory camouflaged fighter was a brand-new Hurricane monoplane fighter delivered to the RAF from Hawker's assembly line in December 1937. It was taken on charge by 111 Squadron at Northolt in Middlesex. Now the biplane fighters had to be camouflaged too. Over the following months the natural aluminium dope/silver finishes and the bright colours and distinctive patterns of the squadron markings disappeared from all fighter units, painted over in standard configurations of matte dark brown (called 'dark earth') and dark green. The fuselage roundel on each side was retained.

These measures were taken because of disturbing trends in international affairs. Back in 1932 nearly all the major nations had been reducing their armed forces but Japan was an exception. Her economy was rapidly expanding. Coming increasingly under the control of a military junta, in September 1931 she began to occupy Manchuria. In March 1933, ruffled by the disapproval of the League of Nations of her attack on China, she withdrew as a member. In October the same year, Germany, which since January was under the leadership of Adolf Hitler, who was preaching defiance of the peace treaties of the First World War, also withdrew from the League of Nations. By 1935, the chief powers in the league were losing faith in the ability of the organisation to preserve peace, and they too began to rearm. It was becoming more and more apparent that if world peace was disturbed by a major power, it would be by one, or more, of the three most ambitious nations – Germany, Japan and Italy.

After the First World War, national pride in Germany had been left smarting over the harshness of the conditions imposed by the 1919 Treaty of Versailles. Amongst its terms, military aviation was banned. Air-minded German youths could only gain flying experience by joining local gliding clubs. Civil aircraft construction was also prohibited until 1922 when it was permitted under certain conditions – but something was stirring in secret.

In reality, the German civil aviation industry was highly centralised and largely controlled by the military. By the mid-1920s there were highly efficient aircraft businesses that included such companies as Messerschmitt at Augsburg, Focke Wulf at Bremen, Dornier at Friedrichshafen, Heinkel at Warnemunde, and Junkers at Dessau. German designers were developing advanced all-metal monoplanes with cantilevered wings, variable-pitch propellers and retractable undercarriages while the victorious Allies were still flying obsolete wood-and-fabric biplanes.

In contravention of the Versailles Treaty, Erhard Milch, who in the early 1920s was manager of Lufthansa, Germany's civilian air transportation company, created a small air force within his organization's framework. The restructured Lufthansa established routes throughout western Europe and became the most technically advanced airline in the world. Also contravening the Versailles Treaty, military crews trained at four Lufthansa flying schools to become proficient in night and all-weather flying.

Following the death of President von Hindenberg, Adolf Hitler declared himself the Führer of the German state. The armed forces were required to swear a personal oath of loyalty to him. With his rise to absolute power, the German Air Arm was created under *Reichskommissar* for Aviation Herman Göring, Hitler's Nazi Party deputy who had been an ace in the First World War commanding Manfred von Richthofen's *JGI* after the Red Baron's death. To build up the new service, trainees were sent secretly to Italy and the Soviet Union. In March 1935, 'the disguise was dropped and the Luftwaffe emerged before the eyes of an astonished world like a monument at the moment of unveiling ... The reaction abroad was just as violent as it had been when Germany left the League of Nations.'[2]

The Spanish Civil War broke out in July 1936 and there was soon international involvement. Joseph Stalin's Soviet Russia reinforced the loyalists while Germany and Italy aided fascist general Francisco Franco 'to prevent Bolshevism from getting a foothold in Western Europe'. Less than a month after the outbreak of fighting, a contingent of twenty Junker Ju52/3m transport aircraft and six Heinkel He 51 fighters with eighty-five volunteer air and ground crews from Germany arrived clandestinely in Spain. Italian aircraft, infantry and light tanks followed. For the other side, Soviet air force contingents, military advisers, artillery and tanks soon reached Spain's east coast ports.

Out of the initial small German contingent grew the Cóndor Legion. It evolved into a balanced force of forty to fifty fighters, forty to fifty multi-engined bombers and around 100 miscellaneous aircraft for ground attack, reconnaissance and liaison. The Cóndor Legion's contribution to Franco's eventual victory was considerable, but more important from a German perspective were the conclusions drawn by Luftwaffe Staff planners. Germany evaluated much of its air arm's new equipment under combat conditions in Spain. These included the Me 109B fighter, Heinkel He 111 bomber, Dornier Do 17 reconnaissance bomber, and Henschel Hs 123 and Junkers Ju 87 Stuka dive-bombers. Lessons learnt included the value of ground-attacking dive-bombers in hampering enemy communications, and the effectiveness of strafing by fighters to exploit an army breakthrough. As for fighter tactics and combat experience, the Spanish Civil War put Germany a year ahead of her international rivals. Towards the end of April 1937 in Spain, Cóndor Legion aircraft bombed the town of Guernica into oblivion, an action that prompted international outrage (an outraged horror that was expressed in Pablo Picasso's famous painting of the same name).

Meanwhile, growing more obvious was the Third Reich's ambition to expand and dominate Europe. In September 1937, Hitler unilaterally declared the end of the Treaty of Versailles, which he had ignored from the outset anyway. The following December, Italy too withdrew from the League of Nations. With the arrival of 1938 events moved faster. The world was shocked when on 12 March Austria's *Anschluss* with Germany was achieved by German troops crossing the border in a bloodless *coup d'état*. There was no political opposition to the move. The following month, because of agitation by German minorities in Czechoslovakia's Sudetenland who wanted to 'return' to the Fatherland, the Czech government ordered partial mobilisation.

From early in the year, Britain's Prime Minister, Neville Chamberlain, sought a general appeasement throughout Europe which would ensure peace. To do this he and his partners in the League of Nations found it necessary to make concession after concession to the wishes of the expanding Third Reich. In return, Chancellor Hitler assured that his re-emerging Germany had no further territorial claims. His words were hollow. By September his army was threatening Czechoslovakia. The world was tottering on the edge of a terrible abyss.

On 15 September, Chamberlain flew to Berchtesgaden for peace negotiations with Adolf Hitler. On 22 September, he flew to Bad Godesberg for more. During a speech in Berlin on 26 September, Hitler stated that the Sudetenland was Germany's last territorial claim in Europe. On 29 September Chamberlain flew to Munich for more peace negotiations. Also in attendance at this meeting were Italy's Benito Mussolini and France's Premier Edouard Daladier. Next day, the negotiated agreement weakly ceded Czechoslovakia's Sudetenland to the expanding Third Reich for more hollow assurances that Germany had no further territorial claims.

Returning by air to Britain, Prime Minister Chamberlain held up his scrap of Munich Agreement paper in front of the media, asserted 'peace for our time' and the world breathed a collective sigh of relief. The immediate crisis was over, but as the piece of paper signed by the German Government was being held up, what had been going on in Spain since 1936 was totally ignored. The war in Spain was a dress rehearsal for what was to come …

While Mr Chamberlain was going back and forth that September, Pat celebrated his twenty-first birthday. There were of course congratulations from home and Pat made mention of them in a lengthy letter to his sister Constance in November.[3]

Dearest Con,

Don't pass out with shock at getting a letter from your long lost young brother, as besides having several duties to perform by me, you are now laden with those of being a mother.

I suppose by now the infant is more or less grown up, and the day is not far off when she will be eating the same menu as the family.

Honestly Con, your letter was the most welcome thing in years so thanks again for it and the best wishes. More about birthday celebrations later.[4]

I'm quite happy, but shant be sorry to see a few familiar faces and some sunshine, so don't despair, as I'll be home in another couple of years.

Congratulations on the infant's names, and from your letter I'm glad to see you regard her as more or less an ordinary kid and not one of the prodigy with which the other married members of our family were blessed.

Midge's letter and Val's telegram arrived on my birthday and also a cake which appeared from some other person, and from Midge's letter I know all the gossip possible and what has happened in Kiama for all the last few months.

I don't seem to be a very good correspondent as far as home mail goes but Con, unless something startling happens I can't sit down and write a lot of letters on nothing but bombing and aerobatics and parties and all such nonsense as goes on every day; so there it is.

Peter has arrived and is now fairly settled, he's down in Oxfordshire at a flying training school and he's more or less accustomed to things now. I've introduced him to half a dozen people at the air force club and had him nominated for entrance, so after Christmas he'll get to know a lot of people. He and I have had several decent parties in London but now he can't get any more leave for a while, so he's got to get down to work for a while. He's going onto a fighter squadron also, and although it's too much to expect him to come to the Fighting 64th, he'll at least be in either one of the groups close by.[5]

His coming to England seems a good thing, although I fear he won't get much flying as they seem to be overcrowded at present. I'm actually luckier that most of the chaps from home because for the last 12 months our squadron has done more flying per pilot day and night than any other fighter squadron, so I'm mighty pleased.

I have just returned from a five week's leave, down the south of France. It was absolutely marvellous, miles of sun, sea and sleep, with a few decent parties flung in for good measure. My French is now colossal, and my appetite for French wine is superb. Had a hell of a good time tho' and returned through Paris. Our original intention was to stay the night and drive on immediately, but a hasty telegram to the adjutant of our squadron brought forth an extra six days leave and the necessary money to enjoy it with, and so we saw Paris in no uncertain manner.

Came back to this God forsaken place and almost had to get some more leave to recover. I should think our dear mother would have been completely flabbergasted.

Flew up to Edinburgh to see the Glasgow 'exhibits' and all that and thought it was absolute tripe and onions so to speak, and from Glasgow we flew to Northern Ireland, and the fog came up and we had to stay there for three days. Needless to say neither of us have much recollection of what happened, but the first thing which woke me up properly was finding myself about 10 feet off the water passing over the Isle of Man. You'll probably think that is nothing, but the Isle of Man was only 40 miles south of where we should have been, and what's 40 miles between friends. The funny thing was the chap with me fell asleep and when we drove up in our aeroplane to Church Fenton I woke him up and he said 'By Hell, I thought I was still in bed.' Decent chap he is. A South African Air Force chap. We have joined the same rugby club in London now. You might tell Bob that I have developed in a rugby fanatic, and except for cracking a couple of ribs last November I would have been playing for the Air Force Fighter Squadrons. The cracking of ribs isn't looked upon as a good thing I guess, and I don't think they knew at home, because you know what Mum is. She'd have a fit.

King George has come to the conclusion that Paterson C isn't such a bad type after all and although my promotion is three months late, I'm a flying officer at last.[6]

Promotion in the RAF isn't nearly as quick as at home, because Hartnell has been a flying officer for more than a year. Still, such is life, and five years flying in these weather conditions is worth 25 at home. At least I think so.

Incidentally, whist on leave I learnt to water-ski, but by hell! Con, did I come some awful busters at first. The reason why the ink is so funny is because it really belongs to King G VI's map department and is indelible. Hence the pyramids.

The world isn't such a large place after all. [I] was given a job a couple of months ago to fly an old type single seater fighter called a 'Bulldog' from here to Farnborough to hand it over for experimental purposes.

It was a bit too old however, and just as I was admiring the scenery and sunshine of the Midlands near Nottingham when the engine gave a sort of despairing cough and gave up the ghost completely. Old dame luck flung her arms round my neck and I hit in a great park next a hell of a great house without even bending the aeroplane! After being invited in to the house to telephone and have a glass of sherry I got to talking to the wife and daughter of the house. And believe it or not when they saw my uniform they got curious and when I told them I was Australian, it transpired they knew everybody for miles around Cooma, like the Hains and the Harnets and such. They asked me to go and see them again anytime so some day I'll trot along. The Bulldog was repaired and I eventually got to Farnborough.

Three other chaps and myself flew to Hendon on Monday the 19th and leaving our aeroplanes we proceeded en masse to London to celebrate the birthday.

Today is Wednesday and we've just got back; and even if we do say so, it was a good party while it lasted and although we put up various black shows round the London circle, everything is OK. I'm afraid details of the whole show are somewhat obscure, but vague recollections of four rather befuddled officers commandeering a Hansom cab in Hyde Park on Tuesday morning still come back to us.

Your letter seems absolutely chock block with news and things. I'm glad to hear (without telling Pete) that Dot Lee is more or less tangled up; and your news of the Paterson family is hellish pleasing. From all accounts my name is taboo sort of in the Appian Way and although the whole thing is tremendously funny, I am damned sorry that Judith thought you were sort of shaking her up on account of me. If old Hitler doesn't start a war I shall probably write to Judith, although I think I sent her a Christmas card which she either didn't get or sort of forgot about.

Geoff Hartnell seems to be thriving on the RAAF; and is almost married, and Peg Colville is well on the way I gather; although I don't know whether you've met them yet.

I'm still more or less unmarried and innocent, and don't smoke as yet, although some fair female presented me with a couple of pipes many moons ago on the assurance that I should be a more serious and sober man if I indulged in the solace of Barney's Punchbowle or some other such foul promise.

John MacGuire, a test pilot from Martlesham, who was in the Point of old Cook several years before me, has told the RAF what to do with his commission and returns home next Christmas. He's promised to look everybody up and take a meal off the Hughes clan. He's a hell of a good chap; and an absolute wizard pilot.[7]

Nobody knows what is happening in Czechoslovakia at present, Con, and although the only people who aren't worried are the chaps in the air force and 64 Squadron particularly, because if there's going to be a war, let's have it now. Our new aeroplanes have started to arrive, and they are honeys. Dangerous as yet because they are probably as fast as any aircraft in the world, and naturally in a new aeroplane a lot of faults crop up, but these things do, under good conditions, more than 300, and they just roar along without any nonsense.

Anyhow there won't be a war.

These ten pages are more than I've written for more than a year, Con, so I'm off. Give my best regards to Bob and to Sandra, and tell her she has a very noisy uncle who will shake her hand in a few years time ...

Love to all and thanks again

Pat

There were changes for 64 Squadron as 1938 wore on. Hawker Demons coming from the production line at the Boulton Paul Company were equipped with a hydraulically operated, segmented metal shield in the aft cockpit. The shield was introduced to give the gunner a measure of protection from the slipstream. A programme was implemented to modify the earlier machines to this standard retrospectively and they were then known as Turret Demons. Then in May there was a much bigger change when the squadron relocated from Martlesham Heath to Church Fenton near York. It was here that Pat discovered a familiar face from Point Cook days – Desmond Sheen. Sheen had been allocated to a fighter unit too and he was in 72 Squadron, which was also stationed at Church Fenton.

But Des Sheen was flying real fighters – Gloster Gladiators!

72 Squadron had been reformed on 22 February 1937 at Tangmere in Sussex out of a flight from 1 Squadron. The flight commander, Flight Lieutenant E. M. 'Teddy' Donaldson, had actually taken the pilots of his flight to Gloster's factory to collect the first production machines. After building the squadron up to full strength the unit moved Church Fenton, which became its home base. Here it was involved in working the Gladiator up into operational RAF service and it was the precursor of numerous Gladiator squadrons. Sheen had joined the squadron from 9 FTS at the end of June 1937. By the time of the Munich crisis, the Gloster Gladiator was the RAF's main single-seat biplane fighter but by then it was already obsolescent, if the reports concerning the Luftwaffe's new Me 109s and fast monoplane bombers were true.

And what of the RAF's fast new monoplane fighters? It was said that Hurricanes and Spitfires were coming into the squadrons, but where were they? First deliveries of Hurricane Mk Is had gone to 111 Squadron late in 1937, but only ninety-three of these new eight-gun fighters were available by September 1938. The first order for Spitfires had been placed in June 1936, barely three months after the prototype flew for the first time. Finished machines began trickling through to Fighter Command from June 1938 onwards, but at the time of Munich not one squadron of Spitfires was ready. The RAF's remaining 666 aircraft were outdated biplanes.

To have opposed Germany in September 1938 would have been suicidal. What had been made painfully clear was the fact that Britain's armed forces, and in particular those of the RAF, were not ready. Facing Fighter Command was the Luftwaffe's strike force of an estimated 1,200 modern bombers and rumour had it that the Hurricanes, without heating for their guns, were useless above 15,000 feet, even in summer!

After Prime Minister Chamberlain held up his scrap of paper from Munich and the world breathed its sigh of relief, the realities of the international situation actually became clearer – there was an almost inevitable drift to war. The Munich Agreement did at least have one positive effect. It stalled the inevitable. There was a breathing space in which Britain and France had precious time to plan and rearm.

British intelligence and a combined-services planning section compiled a list of potential targets that would be vital to any German war effort. The main assumption the planners made was that Germany would immediately commence operations in western Europe either with intense bombing raids on the British Isles or with a land offensive through France and Belgium. The assumption was flawed – no plans were put in place for the prospect of the Germans attacking in the opposite direction, towards Poland.

As for Fighter Command, after the September 1938 crisis Spitfire and Hurricane production (and indeed production of all types) was pressed forward so that if war should come the RAF would have defences revolving around at least 500 modern monoplane fighters. To defend Britain effectively, the Air Officer Commanding-in-Chief of Fighter Command, Air Chief Marshal Sir Hugh Dowding, calculated he needed fifty-three squadrons at his disposal. Given this number of squadrons he felt confident he could break Luftwaffe assaults on Britain, but with anything less ... More new squadrons were sorely needed.

No Hurricanes or Spitfires came to 64 Squadron, but new 'fighters' did begin to replace the Demons in December. They were Bristol Blenheim Ifs – more modified bombers!

In October 1938 the Air Ministry belatedly realised that there may be a need for a long-range escort fighter. Germany already had one in the final stages of development, its new Messerschmitt Me 110, and in the United States the USAAC had issued a requirement for such a type back in 1936. Britain had nothing – but there was the Blenheim light bomber. At this time, the twin-engined Bristol Blenheim was regarded as a modern aircraft with an outstanding performance. It was capable of easily overtaking the Gloster Gladiator, the RAF's main single-seat biplane fighter, and was, in fact, the only aircraft available that could be suitable. The Air Ministry ordered a crash conversion programme.

Browning machine guns had been designed in the USA as a 0.3-inch calibre weapon in 1916 for use in the First World War. Because of their reliability, and in the absence of any modern British machine gun, they were adopted by the Air Ministry in 1934. Production was carried out by the BSA Company after it acquired a licensing agreement in July 1935. These were the weapons for the eight-gun Hurricanes and Spitfires; they would be the guns for the Blenheim long-range fighters as well. Contracts were placed for over 1,300 packs of guns, each pack containing four .303-inch machine guns. The pack was bolted on under each Blenheim's bomb bay which stored four belts of ammunition, all containing 500 rounds. They were capable of twenty seconds' continuous firing. Other companies supplied reflector gunsights and extra armour to afford some frontal protection. The first contract was for kits to convert 200 Mk I Blenheim bombers into Mk If fighters, and these began to enter service in December 1938. Later contracts covered the similar conversion of the newer 'long-nosed' Blenheim Mk IVs into Mk IVf fighters.

The first Blenheim Ifs had gone to 25 Squadron. Now 64 Squadron was getting them too, but there is little to suggest that Pat was impressed! He was probably even less impressed when Squadron Leader Ron Lees, 72 Squadron's new CO, announced that his squadron would begin trading in its Gladiators in April for brand new Spitfires.

Ronald Beresford Lees had been born at Broken Hill, New South Wales, and attended Adelaide University. On 15 January 1930, he joined the RAAF and training at Point Cook before taking up a short service commission in the RAF in 1931. His commission was extended in 1935 and in June the following year he was granted a permanent RAF commission. After promotion to the rank of squadron leader in October 1938, he had been given command of 72 Squadron two months later.

A month after that, in January 1939, 64 Squadron changed leaders too. Victor Beamish left for a course at the RAF Staff Collage at Andover and his place was taken over by Squadron Leader J. Herber-Percy. With the arrival of Blenheim Ifs, the squadron began to concentrate more and more on night flying. In daylight, as 1939 wore on towards summer, Pat was only able to watch as Ronny Lees and Des Sheen paraded their brand new Spitfires, *real* fighters, in front of him.

Around this time Pat acquired a dog, an Airedale pup he called 'Pilot Officer Butch'. Butch's rank would rise each time that Pat's did, but the dog's rank would always be one below Pat's. When nobody was looking he took the pup flying in his Blenheim (it was one of those well-kept secrets that everybody knew about), and in his letters home to his mother Pat would tell her how many flying hours Butch had accumulated!

During March, the RAF introduced a system of squadron identification letters for in-flight aircraft recognition. These were large mid-grey letters painted on the fuselage of every machine. On the port side, two squadron identity letters were usually placed ahead of the roundel and the plane's identity letter aft of it. On the starboard side, the two squadron identity letters were placed aft of the roundel and the plane's identity letter ahead. From June, 64 Squadron's identifying codes were 'XQ' and 72 Squadron's codes were 'SD'.

In international affairs it became apparent that the Führer's next aim was to occupy the free city of Danzig which lay across the Polish Corridor. Hitler's blatant disregard for all of his assurances given at Munich led the British Government to offer guarantees of support to Poland in the event of attack but in practical terms it was difficult to see how the Poles could be helped. Poland was too far away. Its nearest point was 700 miles away from the RAF's bomber airfields. The only possibility was to establish a force close to the German border in France which would create the impression of threatening second front.

Plans were made for the army to send a British Expeditionary Force (BEF) to France if necessary. This force would have to have an Air Component under the operational direction of the commander-in-chief, Viscount Gort, and there would be an Advanced Air Striking Force (AASF) for short-range offensive operations across the German frontier.

On 23 August 1939 at the Berghof, Adolf Hitler's mountain retreat, the weather was peaceful and warm and the views across the mountain peaks superb. Military staff cars with fluttering pendants drove up the winding mountain road – a conference had been called by the Führer. The chief German commanders assembled and took their seats in a semicircle facing their leader. Standing behind his massive desk, Hitler announced exultantly that a treaty with Russia would be concluded in forty-eight hours. Germany's border in the east would be secure, and with political preparations complete, the way was open for action to be taken against Poland. He indicated that the probable date for launching hostilities would be Saturday 26 August.

That same day in Britain the government initiated various secret measures that had been put in place for an international emergency. In the evening, RAF units received orders to mobilise unobtrusively.

Next day, green envelopes bearing the word 'MOBILISATION' in large letters began to arrive at the homes of members of the RAF's Auxiliary Air Force and the homes of 3,000 Volunteer Reservists. For security someone tried in haste to stamp over the glaring word. At the Royal Air Force Club in Piccadilly the flood of telegrams threatened to engulf the entrance. So much for being unobtrusive! The VRs responded. They made their brief farewells and hastened off to mobilisation centres. Some who were on their annual training exercises had no need to travel.

On 25 August, the British Government's guarantees to Poland were confirmed by a binding official alliance between the two countries. France followed suit.

The Führer actually hesitated at the last minute. Appeals from Neville Chamberlain, or French Prime Minister Edouard Daladier, or US President

Franklin Delano Roosevelt, or even the Pope, did not concern him, but the new formal alliances with Poland did. It was now abundantly clear, even to Hitler and his foreign minister who had negotiated the pact with Russia, that an attack on Poland would mean a general war in Europe. At the same time, he learned that he would not automatically receive support from Mussolini. His Italian ally was not yet ready for a large-scale war.

The operation against Poland was postponed for a few days while the Führer made a hasty, superficial effort to secure his aims without resorting to war. The token attempt had no chance of success for the world knew by now the true value of his words. On 31 August, he sharpened his resolve and gave the order to march against Poland the next morning.

Early in the morning of 1 September 1939, Germany stepped into the abyss ...

That same day at Martlesham Heath, the Aircraft and Armament Experimental Establishment moved west to Boscombe Down in Wiltshire. With the outbreak of war, Martlesham Heath's days of experimental testing would be over and the station would become a forward aerodrome in No. 11 Group, RAF Fighter Command.

During the evening of 2 September, Britain's ambassador in Berlin handed an official final note to the German Government. It stated that unless Britain heard by eleven o'clock the next morning, 3 September, that Germany was prepared to immediately withdraw its troops from Poland, a state of war would exist between Britain and Germany.

The deadline came and went.

From the Cabinet Room at 10 Downing Street at 11.15 a.m., Neville Chamberlain began his announcement. Those gathered around their radios listened intently as the last few bars of orchestral music were followed by a BBC announcer introducing the Prime Minister. In a simple, flat voice he said:

I have to tell you now that no such undertaking has been received, and that consequently this country is at war with Germany.

In London's streets, men and women watched as barrage balloons climbed into the sky.

234 SQUADRON

It was generally believed that in the event of war the Germans would immediately launch an air attack on London. An air raid warning did sound shortly after Prime Minister Chamberlain made his announcement. Most of the Londoners went underground as they had been instructed but some escaped into nearby parks to see what was happening. It was the first of many false alarms.

Within a few days, some Australians, including several from the Point Cook class of 1936, were flying in France with the RAF's Advanced Air Striking Force and Air Component squadrons, but Pat was still at Church Fenton and still a member of 64 Squadron with its Bristol Blenheim Ifs. Three days after war was declared the air remained crisp with anticipation and tension. It was a time for making sure one's affairs were in order as there might not be another chance.

While he was waiting for instructions, Pat used the time to write letters to his family back home in Australia. One was to his brother, Bill:

Will,

I feel that I owe you a letter merely to let you know I'm still hale and hearty and not doing anything like hard work. I'm trying to get abreast of my correspondence now because in this first week we've got not much else to do except sit and wait till it breaks. I have written Mum, and today should see a letter for most of the family, as I'm just sitting out on the aerodrome with a lot of aeroplanes and guns and such with no place to go as yet ...

I had arranged to go to France with a chappie from the French Air Force for this month and just sit and swim but as you know old Adolf the Unwashed has rather been carried away in his old fashioned enthusiasm and now there's war in the land so to speak ...

Now that we have started I'm packing up a bit of stuff ready to ship it home if we move off to France or someplace but as far as I know we will stop in England on Home Defence, which promises to be livelier than anything else. Up till now nothing much has happened, except for a few sort of tentative prods from either side, but some of our coves did sling some good stuff into the Kiel Canal the other night. Rumours have just come through of the first raids on London, how true they are I don't know, but it's quite possible the fun has started in earnest at last.

If it has, Will, it will be an awful crack to start with because all of our chaps here are just sort of waiting now in a period of inaction, so that when it does break they will be damned hard to stop.

I haven't seen Peter, but he's got good aeroplanes and near London so he'll have some fun. [Peter Pettigrew was now in 151 Squadron; he was in the last Point Cook-trained group to come to England and join the RAF in July 1938.]

There's no use muttering about things Will, and to my mind the chances of living through it are equal anyhow, and that's all one can ask after all. The National Socialists in Germany have been bred and reared in a military atmosphere, and war is as much in their destiny as Xmas and plum pudding is in ours.

Until this has been going on for a while we won't be able to judge much about their men and machines or whether they fight well or indifferently, but one thing is certain both of these Air Forces are out to show just how bad the other one is, and how long it will take I'd hate to guess.

I've still got that silver cart wheel you sent me, and although its rather tarnished now from carrying it in my pocket and spilling ale on it, it still looks as if it will be going home in 1942.

This war has set the boys up in the marriage market, we've had about four in the last week and quite a few to come I'll wager, but so far I'm still rather footloose and dissolute, although in the last month I have acquired a rather dirty looking, but nevertheless fierce moustache. It's really good camouflage anyhow and more or less effectively hides the scowl I wear so often.

Well brother mine, after we've cleared these Huns from the blue skies of old England I'll come home to that tankard of old ale and the beach and forget that I've spent five years in fog and rain of Yorkshire.

Give my regards to all. See that you don't get married and be good.

Will write as soon as I can.

Yrs

Pat

P.S. We'll give 'em hell!!!!

Bill Hughes would keep his brother's letter for the rest of his life. Another of Pat's letters was to his sister, Constance.

Dearest Con,

I have gathered that you have moved into Strathfield a long time ago, but I don't know if I've got your new address or not so I'm sending this along to the family to forward to you.

By now you are no doubt an established mother and housewife and Bob has grown a beard, and Sandra must by now be of manageable state. However, I hope you don't let any of the attendant worries absorb too much of your time.

Except for a couple of parties in town last month we have been rather subdued lately.

I had lunch with Peter the other week, and except for sporting a pipe and confessing to being in the throes of a violent love affair or such nonsense he's still the same old chap.

Geoff has written to say he was definitely coming to England this year, sometime around October, but by now he'll probably have realised he'll be coming over a lot quicker now.

Celia Wilkinson called in on her way from the New York and had lunch and a gossip with me a month or so ago; but apart from her I haven't seen a soul from home for years it seems.

We spent a week on manoeuvres near Cambridge in August, and then a fortnight doing some practice gunnery on the Norfolk coast, so you can gather we have spent time rather pleasantly.

I had arranged to go to France with chap from the French Air Force for September, but Adolf the Unwashed has, as you know, allowed himself to be carried away in his own enthusiasm and the doctrine of his mailed fist nonsense, and so you see Sister mine, all the fun and games we play about at have suddenly fallen around our ears and now we don't play, but we are in damned deadly earnest.

There's no question whether we are worried about these affairs or not; and there'll be no letting up once we start until we have swept him right from the skies clean back to his own borders. How long it will take I hate to think and what it will do to the people in it who will live through it will be incredibly devilish.

We've known it was coming for quite a while and we'll try and give him an awful shock, but I suppose they are thinking the same about us, so it hardly matters except to win.

My dog 'Butch' has grown incredibly and now likes to fight as well as fly, although he doesn't yet display much intelligence.

Give my regards to Rob and a kiss to Sandra.

All the love possible dearest sister,

Pat[2]

*

For security reasons, within days of the declaration of war the RAF ordered that the large mid-grey identification letters of every aircraft in every squadron be changed. 64 Squadron's identifying codes went from 'XQ' to 'SH', and 72 Squadron's codes were changed from 'SD' to 'RN'.

Another security measure was the top-secret 'Scatter Scheme'. This was implemented when the war began in order to make the disposition of the RAF confusing to the enemy. Its squadrons started transferring to different airfields from those they had occupied in peacetime. This was a huge, unsettling logistical exercise. The first unit to move from Church Fenton was 72 Squadron. On 15 October, Ron Lees and Des Sheen took their Spitfires down to Leconfield near Hull, and Pat was sorry to see them go.

In the long run the bomber squadrons gravitated up to the Yorkshire area and left the London area to the fighter boys. The capital had to be heavily defended. Did the moves confuse the enemy? One cynic remarked that the Scatter Scheme actually confused no one but the RAF itself!

To defend Britain effectively against an estimated 2,000 long-range bombers that were expected to be launched in raids from Germany, Air Chief Marshal Sir Hugh Dowding had calculated that he needed at least fifty-three squadrons of fighters at his disposal. Forty-six squadrons were required for general defence, four to protect convoys sailing up and down the east coast, two to cover the big naval base at Scapa Flow in the Orkneys and one for Northern Ireland.

When war was declared, instead of the fifty-three squadrons that he deemed essential, Dowding had no more than thirty-five.

He began to pressure the Air Ministry for the immediate formation of twelve more fighter squadrons, but the realities of the situation were not encouraging. Hurricane and Spitfire production was crawling along at less than 100 aircraft per month – not sufficient to cover the estimated wastage in the existing squadrons, let alone enough to create a large number of new units.

The Air Member for Supply and Organization reported that two new fighter squadrons might be formed at most, not of Spitfires or Hurricanes but of Blenheims.

Confronted with this judgment, Dowding reduced his request to eight squadrons. At the same time, he complained bitterly that the four squadrons of fighters (Nos 1, 73, 85 and 87) set aside for France had been sent before the anticipated Luftwaffe offensive on England had been met and beaten off. As well, just before the war he had received orders to put six more Hurricane squadrons on a mobile basis. Although he had been assured that these would never be withdrawn from Fighter Command unless they could be safely spared, he queried how much reliance could be placed on such pledges. His fear was that attrition in France would drain away the entire Hurricane output. As for the demands of other commands, he put his opinion on record that:

The home defence organisation must not be regarded as co-equal with other Commands, but that it should receive priority to all other claims until it is firmly secured, since the continued existence of the nation, and of its services, depends on the Royal Navy and Fighter Command.

The Air Staff had far wider responsibilities. The Air Ministry was committed to building up a powerful force not of fighters but of bombers as its main contribution to victory. On top of this, the army, the RAF in France, and the French themselves all wanted more fighters sent across the Channel. It was impossible to satisfy everyone, but it was also clearly essential to create more fighter squadrons. German actions targeting the Royal Navy's new base at Scapa Flow and the emerging threat against Britain's east-coast sea traffic underlined the necessity.

Thanks principally to his persistence, and largely to the support and foresight of the Chief of Air Staff, Sir Cyril Newall, Dowding got what he wanted. It had already been acknowledged that it was possible to form two Blenheim squadrons. Dowding, who had a use for Blenheims as night fighters, requested that these might take the form of four half-squadrons which could be built up to full strength as occasion permitted. He also requested that an extra squadron previously approved for training and reserve should be made first-line, in the form of two half-squadrons.

Newall consented to both ideas but went further. He also agreed that two more squadrons should be formed as insurance against two of the mobile squadrons going to France. This gave Dowding his eight half-squadrons which, once established, had the potential to be built up quickly as the resources, men and machines became available.

October saw 152 Squadron formed at Acklington in Northumberland with Gladiators released by 603 Squadron; 263 Squadron formed at Filton with Gladiators formerly belonging to 605 Squadron; 219 Squadron formed at Catterick equipped with Blenheim Ifs; 229 Squadron at Digby also equipped with Blenheim Ifs; 92 Squadron at Tangmere, raised with Blenheim Ifs as initial equipment and a nucleus of pilots from 601 Squadron; 141 Squadron at Turnhouse with Gladiators; 145 Squadron at Croydon armed with Blenheim Ifs; and 253 Squadron born at Manston with Miles Magister trainers.

Cyril Newall went further still. He was convinced that the demand for fighters would soon become even more urgent, but it did not seem possible that more squadrons could be formed so soon. The entire output of single-engined fighters was already fully allocated. So too was that of the Blenheims, largely to cover the normal attrition in Bomber Command. Nevertheless, if more fighter squadrons could be formed, even if they were equipped with the wrong types of aircraft, they might be ready for action with the right types precious weeks earlier than if their formation were delayed until production increased – *if* it did increase, and *if* the enemy allowed the time.

Newall called a meeting of the Air Members and some of the Air Staff on 17 October. He announced first that Dowding's recently approved extra squadrons must be completed by the end of the month, and then declared that an additional ten squadrons must be formed over the following fortnight. After dropping that bombshell, he invited those present to suggest how this could be achieved.

It was achieved. At the end of the month a host of new units appeared, their motley array of equipment demonstrating a growing shortage of aircraft of any type with which to equip them. On 30 October, the following were all formed, or reformed having been First World War units: 234 and 245 Squadrons at Leconfield; 242 Squadron at Church Fenton; 264 and 266 Squadrons at Sutton Bridge; 235 Squadron at Manston; 248 Squadron at Hendon; 254 Squadron at Stadishal; and on 31 October, 236 Squadron also at Stadishal.

The struggle all of these squadrons would have to go through to become fully operational would be protracted and painful. Nos 235, 236, 248 and 254 were eventually transferred from Fighter Command to Coastal Command in January and February 1940. Manpower was needed too. So it was that at the end of October 1939, Flying Officer Paterson Clarence Hughes was posted from Church Fenton and 64 Squadron to join the newly forming 234 Squadron at RAF Leconfield.

When he reached Leconfield via Hull he expected to find the Spitfires of 72 Squadron again but he could not see the 'RN' identification letters anywhere. The squadron had transferred from Church Fenton to Leconfield a few weeks earlier. Pat was on the lookout for a couple of familiar Aussie faces too, but they were not there either. He had just missed them. Desmond Sheen, Ron Lees and 72 Squadron had moved again already, north to Drem in Scotland.

Pat noted the presence of a couple of Whitley bombers, some Fairey Battles, a few Miles Magister trainers and a number of old biplanes. When he asked what kind of station this was, he was told it was a bomber station, or it had been. Two Whitley squadrons had been stationed there before the war for operational training but they had moved out in mid-September under the Scatter Scheme.

He did spy a few Spitfires but they had unfamiliar 'YQ' squadron code letters. These had only just arrived and belonged to 616 (South Yorkshire) Squadron. This was an Auxiliary Air Force unit and it had only been at Leconfield for a week having transferred over from Doncaster. Its previous equipment had been Gloster Gauntlet biplanes with fixed wheels but it had been training on four Fairey Battles supplied to it in May to accustom the pilots to flying monoplanes with retractable wheels. The Earl of Portland was the squadron's Honorary Air Commodore and up to September 1939 its CO had been the Earl of Lincoln. The current CO, Squadron Leader Walter Beisiengel, was a well-known cricketer.[3]

Now, two new squadrons were to be created at Leconfield at the very same time, 234 and 245. On paper, they were all both supposed to be fighter units, but the way things looked to Pat, they could be anything!

Both 234 Squadron and 245 Squadron had their origins in the First World War. 234 Squadron had formed originally at Tresco on the Scilly Isles in August 1918 as a flying-boat unit for covering the Western Approaches. It had been formed from the RAF Seaplane Base there which had been already carrying out the task since February 1917. It stayed there until May 1919, when it was disbanded.

Likewise, 245 squadron first flew as a coastal reconnaissance unit on anti-submarine patrols over the Irish Sea from Fishguard in Pembrokeshire and it was disbanded there in May 1919. Both squadrons were reformed on 30 October 1939, at Leconfield with a variety of non-operational types.

The man appointed to command and form 234 Squadron was thirty-one-year-old Squadron Leader William Arthur John Satchell who had joined the

RAF in March 1930. After training, he had been posted to 54 Squadron at Hornchurch flying Bristol Bulldogs but he transferred to the School of Naval Co-operation at Lee-on-Solent on 16 December 1932. He was posted on 5 June 1937 to 204 (General Reconnaissance) Squadron, which was equipped with Saunders-Roe London flying boats at Mount Batten, Plymouth. The following year in October he obtained a staff position there. 234 was his first command.

Acting Flight Lieutenant John Graham Theilmann was given command of 'A' Flight. He had seniority over Pat having joined the RAF on a short service commission in January 1936 and receiving promotion to flying officer in July 1938, four months ahead of him. Theilmann's previous unit had been 41 Squadron at Catterick. It had been equipped with Hawker Fury IIs up until January 1939 when it converted to brand-new Spitfire Is. He, at least, had experience on what promised to be the best fighter in the world. Pat saw this as a promising sign – Theilmann, at least, was a fighter type!

A couple of pilots had arrived early. Pilot Officer Geoffrey Gout from Sevenoaks was a car enthusiast and had actually raced at Brooklands. He joined the RAF in February 1939 and was fresh from training. Pilot Officer Michael Boddington from Lancashire had flying experience having joined the RAFVR in December 1936. He had been one of the 3,000 Volunteer Reservists called up at the outbreak of the war.

The new squadron's start was far from auspicious. On 2 November, Bill Satchell was injured in a car accident and taken to hospital. When Pat arrived he was still in Hull Royal Infirmary where his condition was stable, but he was not able to return to his new command. He was replaced.

Satchell's position was taken over by Squadron Leader Richard 'Dickie' Barnett MBE. Barnett had graduated from Cranwell in December 1931 and joined 54 Squadron at Hornchurch. Posted overseas in September 1932, he joined 6 Squadron at Ismailia on 1 November. He went to the RAF Depot at Aboukir in July 1935. In the Coronation Honours List Barnett was made an MBE (11 March 1937) for operations in Palestine from April to October 1936. After returning to the UK he had been posted on 16 August 1938 to the Aeroplane and Armament Experimental Establishment at Martlesham Heath. He had gone with it to Boscombe Down in Wiltshire at the beginning of September before his rushed reappointment.

Pat would take command of 'B' Flight and with this would come his promotion to acting flight lieutenant. Of course, his devoted canine companion would henceforth be known as 'Flying Officer Butch'.

New pilots began to arrive for the squadron. One of the first was Sergeant Alan Harker from Bolton in Lancashire on 5 November. He had joined the RAFVR in 1937 and, like Geoff Gout, had been called up at the outbreak of war. After a course on twin-engined Avro Ansons, he had volunteered for night fighters. More confusion – what exactly was the newly forming 234 Squadron supposed to be?

The majority of the new pilots arrived the next day. It was raining as they were transported by truck from Hull. Among them was Pilot Officer Robert Doe who was originally from Reigate in Surrey. Bob Doe had started work as an office boy at the *News of the World*. In March 1938 he joined the RAFVR and began training at Hanworth, going solo on 4 June. He successfully applied for a short service commission and joined the RAF in January 1939. Before joining 234 Squadron at Leconfield, he did his elementary flying training at Redhill and then 6 FTS at Little Rissington. Doe recalled his arrival later:

No one knew what sort of squadron it was, or what it was equipped with, and on a wet day in November we arrived at Hull to be taken by lorry to Leconfield. On asking the driver what the squadron was, he didn't know, and we were eventually dropped at a wooden hut which turned out to be the officers mess. There we met the CO and the two Flight-Commanders, and they didn't seem to know, either.[4]

Among the others Pilot Officer Richard Hardy had joined the RAF on a short service commission a month after Bob Doe in February 1939. Pilot Officer Edward 'Ted' Mortimer-Rose was from Littleport, Cambridgeshire, and had been educated at Haileybury. He too had joined the RAF on a short service commission in February.

Sergeant William 'Bill' Hornby had been a junior civil servant before the war. He joined the Royal Auxiliary Air Force in 1936 as an aircraft hand and transferred to the RAFVR in April 1937. He did his weekend flying at Hanworth and later at Stapleford. Like Alan Harker he had been posted to 10 FTS at Tern Hill in September before he joined 234 Squadron.[5]

There were three New Zealanders. Pilot Officer Cecil Hight was from Stratford in the south-west of the north island where he was a car salesman. He began flying at the Western Federated Aero Club in 1937 and obtained his licence in August. Late that year he worked his passage to England, intending to join the RAF. Unable to first meet the educational requirements when he applied for a short service commission early in 1938, he studied maths and was provisionally accepted the next time he applied. After further training he was awarded his flying badge in early August 1939.

Pilot Officer Patrick Horton had been born in Dunedin but he had been educated at the Hutchings School in Hobart, Tasmania, and Wellington College after which he worked for the Mines Department in 1936. After being provisionally accepted for an RAF short service commission, he had sailed for England on 1 February 1939 in the RMS *Tainui*.

A fellow traveler aboard the *Tainui* for an RAF short service commission was Keith Lawrence, formerly a bank clerk in Invercargill. Pat Horton and Keith Lawrence remained together during training and they both joined the new 234 Squadron at Leconfield on 6 November.[6]

Altogether that day, fourteen new young pilot officers and four sergeant pilots arrived as well as Squadron Leader Barnett. As for equipment, like Dowding's other newly forming units, 234 Squadron did not have the up-to-date aircraft necessary to give the newly arriving pilots proper flying experience.

According to 234's Operations Record Book there were four Bristol Blenheims, apparently without gun belly packs; three Miles Magisters; two Avro Tutors; three Gloster Gauntlets, forerunners of Gloster's Gladiators; and one Fairey Battle trainer with dual controls. They would have to make do with this strange assortment of machines. The squadron's identifying letters were 'AZ' and its radio call sign was 'Cressy'.

A working routine commenced but from the outset flying had to be limited because of the desperate lack of aircraft. Pat and John Theilmann set about assessing the flying skills of their new charges whenever an aircraft was available and on whatever type it happened to be. The link trainer was put to good use. To the new young fliers a short trip in one of the Gauntlets was prized because it meant that they were in the air at last and nobody was looking over their shoulder or watching them from the co-pilot's seat.

The lack of flying time was due to lectures – many lectures. There were lectures on Fighter Command organisation; stripping and assembling Vickers and Browning machine guns; aircraft recognition, particularly the new German types; methods of fighter attacks; wireless; navigation; the organisation of the German Air Force; and so on.

To the new pilots Pat tended to stand out. For a start, he was easy to find and approach. He wore his distinctive, much darker Royal Australian Air Force uniform which immediately set him apart from the others in their RAF light blue. There was an air of confidence about him which made him seem older and more mature than most, even though he was only in his early twenties. Flying Officer Butch went with him everywhere, even into the air when the chance arose. He was not a remote figure like the other two senior officers and increasingly he was looked to for guidance and motivation.

Meanwhile, although 616 Squadron was envied because it was 'working up' on its Spitfires, the pilots seemed to be having a number of problems because of landing accidents. It was not unusual to see a Spitfire nose-up somewhere off the runway. Perhaps the speedy new machines were very difficult to handle.

On 15 December, 234 Squadron had its own accident, and it was costly. The squadron's official records reported:

P/O J. Hemingway (detailed as safety officer) and P/O C. B. Elsdon (carrying out the practises) engaged in instrument flying practise in Magister. It went into a spin and crashed both suffered fractured spines and detained in RAF Hospital Cranwell.

There was more it to than that. Historian Helen Doe looked closely into the episode:

On the face of it this is the report of an accidental but serious crash but it was carefully written up to disguise an unfortunate incident. Elsdon and Hemingway had decided to beat up a train between York and Darlington. They eventually overdid it and ended up in a field. Unluckily for them here was a Group Captain on the train who witnessed the event and who was called into the inevitable Court of Inquiry. Elsdon was posted away immediately to Bomber Command but Hemingway was removed from the RAF.[7]

Five days later, Geoff Gout crashed a Blenheim while taking off when he raised the undercarriage too soon and struck rising ground. He was not hurt but the aircraft suffered damage.

At the same time, it was noticeable that Pat and John Theilmann were doing the bulk of the flying; Squadron Leader Barnett was noticeable for his absence from the air. The positive leadership that was needed for the new men to gain skill and confidence was being provided by his two acting flight lieutenants. Dickie Barnett looked the part. He was dark-haired, in his mid-thirties, and in attitude was somewhat of the 'old school', as he had been trained. He sported a nice 'military' moustache but he was rather distant – but perhaps there were serious and necessary matters of administration that required his attention first.

*

With the onset of winter on the Continent, the German and Allied forces facing each other were settling down to the period that was labelled the 'Phoney War'. It was an uneasy peace, and it was false. What Pat probably did not know at this stage was that the Point Cook Class of 1936 had already suffered its first casualty of war.

John Allsop had been sent to Bomber Command and posted to 10 Squadron where he flew Armstrong Whitworth Whitleys. Back on the night of 1/2 October he and his crew carried out a 'Nickel' (leaflet-dropping) operation over Berlin. A message was heard from his aircraft at 0505 hours during its return flight. Its position was roughly 180 miles east of St Abb's Head, Berwickshire, Scotland. Then there was nothing. Despite an extensive search no trace of the aircraft or its crew was ever found. John had only recently married.

6

KATHLEEN

Most people cherished the hope that the war might be over by Christmas. That is what they had hoped for in 1914, too. They had been drastically wrong then, and now they were drastically wrong again. In the north of England, the end of 1939 was accompanied in rapid succession by snow, frost, fog and heavy rain. In Lancashire, showers of sleet held up trains. On the Yorkshire hills between Burnley and Harrogate the snow was so deep that a snowplough had to clear the roads.

With the New Year, the coldest winter for more than forty years crept all over the country. Everywhere, poorly protected pipes froze, expanded and burst, and the population shivered beside modest fires of rationed coal. Outside the small radius of heat these fires generated the houses and hotels felt as 'cold as the arctic poles'. At night, heavy mists and the blackout made normally familiar city streets dark and menacing. Posters throughout England warned the public: 'Children are safer in the country. Keep them there.'

Hovering over it all was the grim spectre of fighting which could break out at any moment. Early in January, rumours of a Nazi invasion of the Netherlands because her water defences were frozen startled Europe for several days.

The coldest day ever recorded in England up to then was 21 January 1940. In London, snow fell and lay deep, becoming as hard as iron beneath heavy frost. The Thames froze over at Kingston and ice extended for eight miles between Teddington and Sunbury. Twelve inches of ice covered lakes and reservoirs, and in Hyde Park people went skating on the Serpentine. Snow was still falling in mid-February.

At Leconfield, creating an efficient training programme for 234 Squadron was enough of a challenge given such weather conditions, but not knowing what type of aircraft it would finally end up with did not help at all. Officially, Leconfield was in Fighter Command so eventually the squadron might have Hurricanes, Spitfires, Gladiators, Blenheims or perhaps even new two-seater Defiants. Each type required different skills, including basic flying practice and formation flying.

By the end of January 1940 the squadron's flying personnel consisted of one squadron leader, two flying officers (acting flight lieutenants) and twelve pilot officers. Of the other ranks, there were eighteen senior NCOs, twenty-six corporals and 163 aircraftmen. The squadron was equipped with nine Bristol Blenheims, two Miles Magisters, two Avro Tutors and one Fairey Battle.[1] Given the numbers at this stage, Blenheim Ifs for long-range convoy cover or night fighting were becoming the strongest possibility – but there were no air gunners in the squadron, only pilots. Then, eleven men were despatched to train as air gunners. It had to be either Blenheims or Defiants.

From a distance a Defiant looked like a Hurricane. It had a humped back, a large radiator under the centre fuselage and evenly tapered round-tipped wings. It sounded like a Hurricane or Spitfire because it had the same Rolls-Royce Merlin engine. But the hump looked bigger than usual. On closer inspection, it wasn't a hump at all ... It was a gun turret! This was the RAF's latest fighter, but it was a throwback to the two-seater fighter designs of the First World War – pilot in the front, gunner at the back. Advocates of the layout pointed to such outstandingly successful machines as the Sopwith 1½ Strutter and Bristol F2B Fighter and argued for a similar type of aircraft to replace the Hawker Demon. The revolutionary Merlin engine was combined with what was thought would be the devastating firepower of a hydraulically operated turret with four Browning machine guns. In theory, the 360-degree traverse of this turret would give greater flexibility to the crew as the aircraft would not need to manoeuvre into a position behind the enemy in order to fire with fixed forward-aimed armament. So certain were they that that this concept would work, Defiants were designed with no forward-firing armament at all! Defiants would be the RAF's 'bomber destroyers'.

The possibility that the new Defiants would be for 234 Squadron was very unlikely. The assembly alone was slow and the first production examples of them were only going to only one unit, 264 Squadron. Hugh Dowding neither liked them nor wanted them, particularly with the outstanding and much needed Hurricanes and Spitfires coming into service at an improving rate.

Pat would have even settled for old Gladiator biplanes. He could only glance every day with envy at 616 Squadron and its Spitfires, but the pilots were still having difficulties taking off and landing. The pilots of 234 Squadron came out one morning and found no fewer than three of 616's Spitfires tilted up on their noses – a good way to bend propellers and break undercarriages! Meanwhile, 245 Squadron was in the same situation as 234 Squadron. It was still training with Blenheims and in January it received some Fairey Battles, but there was a rumour that there might be Hurricanes coming in March. There were always rumours. Anything could happen, but the poor weather was playing havoc with any proper practical training routine.

It was a tragic day for Leconfield on 21 February. 234 Squadron suffered its first fatality and 616 Squadron lost two Spitfires and a pilot. In the morning, 616 was ordered to escort a coastal convoy off Flamborough Head. As Flight Lieutenant A. Wilson led his section down through mist to locate the ships his wingmen lost contact. He simply disappeared. His aircraft crashed into the sea off Hornsea.

Another section was scrambled in the afternoon. Flying Officer John Bell, who was leading, brought the section to the end of the runway and began his take-off – but the runway was not clear. He had to avoid a stray Fairey Battle just before he was airborne but then struck a 234 Squadron Magister trainer taxiing onto the runway. Pilot Officer David Coysh in the trainer was taxiing around the corner of a hangar to reach the runway for a solo flight. He was unable to see the Spitfire racing along the runway on the other side. Apparently in the rush those in the control tower were unaware of what was about to happen too. No warning of the other's presence was given to either pilot. The long nose of the Spitfire obscured forward vision until the tail was raised during takeoff. Its spinning propeller ripped right into the Magister. Both aircraft were wrecked and Coysh was killed. Bell emerged unscathed.[2]

David Coysh's funeral was held three days later. He was described as a quiet and likeable young man and his unnecessary death cast a shadow of gloom over the squadron.

Aside from this, Pat's task of trying to weld the squadron into a cohesive unit capable of becoming operational was becoming all that much more difficult. It was always a relief at the end of the day when he could drive into Hull or visit a local pub to relax with his pilots and down a few ales.

Not that it was so easy to do. Nationwide every night an inky blackness descended over the country. The blackouts were far more rigorous than those of the First World War and the combination of blackout and snow hindered normal social life considerably. A story circulated about two pilots who decided one night in January to go to a cinema. They set off through the main gates of their base and down the road in a car but darkness and snow made it impossible to see through the windscreen. One man climbed out and walked beside the car with a torch as the other drove, inching forward as carefully as possible. Then, unexpectedly, they found something familiar – the main gates again! Somehow, without knowing it, they had turned around and gone back the way they had just come! There was no cinema for them that night.

In the cities, vehicles crept their way through the streets with masked headlights. Pedestrians by the thousands bumped into each other on the way home in the dark, yet vigorously cursed anyone who left a door or curtain open which cast a light. Road accident reports from the Ministry of War Transport showed that 4,133 people were killed in the last four months of 1939 compared with 2,497 over the same period in 1938, and in December alone there were 1,155 fatalities, the highest ever recorded.

Most of the victims were pedestrians, one person in five having had an accident in the blackout. People were advised that they would see better if there were adequate amounts of Vitamin A in their diets. According to this idea, experiments showed that Vitamin A improved the ability of the eyes to adjust quickly when going from light to dark – as when going outdoors into the blackout. Cod-liver oil capsules were recommended. Eating carrots was suggested. For greater safety when walking in the blackout advice was given to 'wear white at night' or to carry white objects such as newspapers. Small rear lights were made compulsory for cyclists to avoid them being run down from behind by other vehicles. Kerbs and tree trunks were whitened.

As for cars, with petrol restrictions the number of civilian cars on the road was already declining but motorists had to paint their bumper bars and running boards white. The comment was made that if deaths from road accidents continued at the same rate as they did in December, the losses in a year would resemble war casualties. Faint street lighting was permitted again. On 1 February a speed limit of 20 mph during the blackout was imposed. Just over three weeks later, on 24 February, 'Double Summer Time' was introduced, lengthening the safe daylight period by another hour.

Gradually, as days turned into weeks, and weeks into months, and still no violent war erupted, people in the major cities adapted to the blackout and began to resume their old pastimes at the pubs, theatres and cinemas. An odd, unrealistic quality about life settled over Britain. In city clubs and restaurants that were being patronised by young servicemen on leave, a new dance craze called 'The Blackout Stroll' became a favourite. Away from their homes, men were pleased to visit places where dancing partners – girls in evening dresses of chiffon, lace and taffeta – could be found. As they danced, the lights would go out and everyone had to change partners.

For some the blackout was good for romance.

They met at the Beverley Arms, a former coach house dating back to 1794. It was located opposite St Mary's church in the centre of Beverley, a medieval village half an hour from York and a fifteen-minute drive from the centre of Hull. The attractive, dark-haired girl he noticed was there with friends from the airfield when Pat walked in one evening. He found out that her name was Kathleen, Kathleen Broderick, but her friends called her Kay.

Her family lived in Hull, in James Reckitt Avenue. The daughter of a widowed mother, Kay was pert and pretty, and by her own admission a bit spoilt. She had her own car, attractive clothes and was never short of boyfriends.

Kay became very aware of Pat too the moment he walked in, tall, fair, with grey eyes and carrying an Airedale puppy he called 'Flying Officer Butch'. His 'handsome' good looks, moustache and smart dark blue uniform made him stand out. She was reminded of the Hollywood film star Errol Flynn, an Australian from Tasmania. Pat Hughes was obviously 'one of the boys', but he seemed so noisy and conceited. Flying Officer Butch, however, could win any heart![3]

As the night drew to a close, Pat asked her to telephone him, but she didn't. It was he who rang three days later and asked her out. (Don't let things happen to you – make them happen!)

*

The confusion over what 234 Squadron would fly deepened when on 10 March, after all their hours training on Blenheims, the squadron had to watch as their Blenheims began to be taken away. What now?

Five days later, after an armament practice camp at Catfoss, the pilots of 234 Squadron returning to Leconfield had a very pleasant surprise. 'This beautiful thing arrived,' Bob Doe recalled, 'We walked round it, stroked it. We took turns sitting in it.'[4] It was a Mk I Spitfire, the thoroughbred racehorse of planes. Even just standing there on the ground on its delicate, out-swinging undercarriage, it seemed to say, 'Come on! Let's go!' After training for so long on ex-bombers, slow trainers and biplanes, 234 Squadron was to be supplied with the latest and the best. More Spitfires began arriving and by the end of the month they had sixteen. For all the pilots, but particularly for Pat, it was sheer pleasure. He wouldn't be just flying 'crates' anymore; at long last he would be flying a real fighter. It was as if he had suddenly grown his own wings!

As well as new aircraft, new pilots were arriving too. In April Sergeant Bill Thompson reported in from 603 Squadron. He had applied to join the RAF as a trainee wireless operator in the 1930s but because there were no vacancies he became an armourer and was eventually promoted to LAC. He volunteered for pilot training and qualified as a sergeant pilot. Postings to the Armament School at Catfoss and then 603 Squadron had followed.

Flying Officer Charles Igglesden came from 41 Squadron, John Theilmann's old unit, where he had flown Spitfires. Thompson and Igglesden were both experienced and added extra to the skills of the squadron.

Another Australian joined the squadron on 12 April and he was quite a character. His name was Vincent Parker, but back in Townsville, Queensland, he was known as 'Bushy' Parker. In Australia, 'Bushy' was a nickname often bestowed on people, usually distinctive characters, who lived in the country areas away from the main towns or cities. (In fact, in Townsville they still know him as 'Bushy' Parker today.)[5] In 234 Squadron he quickly became known as 'Bush' Parker, although he had actually been born in England.

Jack and Edith Parker adopted their only son, Vincent, in 1920. The boy, originally Vincent Wheatley, was actually a son of Edith's sister. He had been born on 11 February 1918 in Chester-le-Street, County Durham, the youngest in a family of three sons. When he was a few months old his mother died, and Vincent was adopted by his aunt. In 1928, the Parkers emigrated to Australia and arrived at Bilyana in Queensland, a small fruit farming settlement midway between Townsville and Cairns. Unfortunately, the community was devastated by a cyclone just before they arrived but Jack Parker managed to obtain work with Queensland Railways and Edith became station mistress at Purono.

Vincent was educated at Bohleville State School, but after leaving he drifted in and out of several jobs (including as a magician) until he eventually obtained a billet as a steward on the passenger liner *Ontranto* voyaging to England and back. At this stage he read about and became interested in training in England and joining the RAF. After his second trip, he left the vessel and cabled his mother in Townsville seeking her permission and financial support. She agreed.

Once in England, Vincent stayed with his birth family while at civilian flying school at Gatwick, and on 22 July 1939 he was granted a six-year short service commission as a pilot officer on probation. His training began in August with No. 11 Fighter Training School at RAF Shawbury in Shropshire, where he gained his pilot's badge on 25 October. Vincent received a posting to 234 Squadron in Yorkshire on 10 April 1940, and when he arrived two days later he was placed into 'B' Flight. Pat Hughes was his flight commander. It may have been Pat who shortened his nickname from 'Bushy' Parker to 'Bush' Parker as it was his habit to give nicknames to most of the people around him like 'Morty' Mortimer-Rose, 'Hornpipe' Hornby, 'Bish' Owens, and so on.

Bush Parker nearly did not last very long. Two weeks after joining, he could have been killed while flying in a section of three Spitfires which were caught up in heavy fog and then a storm. Before long they were lost. With fuel running low, Parker tried to make an emergency landing in a field but as he was coming down a flock of sheep loomed in his path. Somehow he managed to avoid them, but the wheels of his plane caught in an unseen hole and the aircraft flipped over onto its back. Fortunately, he was not hurt. It was fortunate too that his Spitfire was only slightly damaged. A message was circulating in the squadron to the effect that anyone who crashed one of the precious Spitfires would be posted immediately! Parker was not transferred.

Shortly after the Spitfires arrived, Pat was sent on an air fighting course at RAF Northolt for a week. When he returned he intensified the training programme.

The authorities thought the most likely threat they would have to face would be air attacks by German bombers flying directly across the North Sea from Germany. These would be open to interception by fighters based in eastern England and in France or Belgium. Because of the distances involved they would be far beyond the range of escorting fighters to protect them, except perhaps from heavy twin-engine fighters like the Me 110s that could carry more fuel to extend their range.

In strict accordance with RAF regulations, the pilots were taught to fly their Spitfires in tight formations and carry out precise manoeuvres. In the RAF Training Manual of 1938, the chapter on 'Air Fighting Tactics' stated:

> Manoeuvring at high speeds in air fighting is not now practicable, because the effect of gravity on the human body during rapid changes of direction at high speed causes a temporary loss of consciousness.

The thinking was that dogfighting as it occurred in the First World War was a thing of the past. The manual went on to instruct that single-seater fighter attacks at high speed must be confined to a variety of attacks from the general direction of astern. It gave three text-book methods of attack with the basic fighter section being the standard vic of three aircraft.

In 'Fighter Command Attack Number One', on sighting an enemy bomber the leader would order his two wingmen into line astern. Diving to attack, the three fighters would drop just below the height of the bomber to avoid return fire from the rear-gunner. The fighters would close and in turn open fire from about 400 yards, then one by one break away outwards and down. They would then turn and regain height behind the enemy aircraft to reposition themselves for a possible further attack.

The German bomber types did not have a rear-gunner position in the extreme tail like RAF bombers. They had a dorsal gunner positioned more or less in line with the trailing edge of the bomber's wings. All the guns appeared to be on free-standing mounts and not in power-operated turrets like most RAF bombers.

'Fighter Command Attack Number Two' dealt with attacking an enemy bomber formation with two three-plane sections. The leader of the six fighters would orders his pilots into line astern to attack. Positioning themselves behind the target bombers and slightly below, the leading section would attack the right-flank bomber and the second section the left-flank bomber. As the attack went in, the sections, which would ideally be separated by about 200 yards fore and aft, would form a rear echelon formation. The leading three would go into a starboard echelon and the second three into a port echelon. After the attack, the leading section would break to the right and down, the second section to the left and down. They would all then pull up and around for the next attacks.

'Fighter Command Attack Number Three' was very similar to the Number Two attack, except that it was designed for a squadron using four vics of three fighters attacking a larger number of bombers. It was far more complicated and as the fight began the sections would endeavour to attack simultaneously from the rear, beam and rear quarter.

All of this became quite complex as the number of aircraft increased. Instinctively, some pilots in the squadron were beginning to feel that such rigid procedures that were out of date! The three attacks would only be effective if the German bomber pilots obligingly flew straight and level without taking much evasive action.

As Pat intensified the training programme, he found that he was shouldering the burden of more and more responsibility because of his seemingly indifferent CO. He had to walk a political tightrope, but it had to be so – a mere acting flight lieutenant could only do so much. At the same time, he had no choice but to support his commanding officer as the chain of command and discipline had to be maintained. Any desire to 'make things happen' had to be tempered with patience.

Even so, the other pilots were becoming aware of the situation. Years later Bob Doe recalled:

It was about this time also that we noticed that the CO and the 'A' flight commander didn't seem to do much flying. Our flying was supervised and led by

Pat Hughes, the 'B' flight commander who, being Royal Australian Air force, wore a royal blue uniform with gold rank badges. He was a good leader and we flew three to four sorties a day each, under his instruction.[6]

Away from the squadron Pat could relax. And there was Kay. Far from remaining 'rather footloose and dissolute', as he had written in his letter to Bill last September, a new romance was blossoming, and the two began to see each other at every opportunity.

Meanwhile, the war clouds were building. During the night of 16/17 March while attacking Royal Navy ships in Scapa Flow, German aircraft dropped bombs on British soil for the first time and killed a civilian, James Isbister, as he stepped outside his home at Bridge of Waithe in Orkney to help a neighbour. Seven others were wounded. A reprisal raid was ordered on the German seaplane base at Hörnum, on the southernmost tip of the North Frisian island of Sylt.

English newspaper headlines the morning after the raid blazed out: LAND TARGET AT LAST FOR THE RAF; TONS OF BOMBS DROPPED; SIX HOURS' ATTACK ON SYLT; HANGARS AND OIL TANKS ABLAZE; ADMIRATION IN U.S.; NIGHT SKY LIT UP! Reports on the BBC described it as a heavy raid and claimed extensive damage.

The story was told differently in Germany. Berlin's newspapers carried the headlines: 'BRITISH BOMB DENMARK!' The German High Command claimed that no damage had been caused despite the bombing going on for nearly seven hours. It seems that during the attack on the seaplane base a couple of bombs did fall on Danish territory and on orders from the German propaganda minister, Dr Goebbels, this was how it was reported.

Another member of Pat's Point Cook course was lost in France on 31 March. Like Britain, France was emerging from one of the coldest winters on record and with the warmer spring weather approaching the placid 'Phoney War' was expected to end, particularly in the air. Cec Mace was in 105 Squadron flying Fairey Battles. He and his gunner were flying on an anti-aircraft cooperation detail and did not have an observer with them when their plane crashed north of Champigneul. Both men were killed. Pat's wrestling mate, 'Grappler' Mace, with his endless supply of funny, spicy, stories, was no more.

On 9 April at dawn German forces invaded Denmark and Norway. The move into Denmark by land was almost uncontested and the country was occupied within hours. The attack on Norway was carried out by sea and air and it was opposed by the Norwegians.

On the night of 13/14 April, Bomber Command went gardening and carried out the first RAF mine-laying operation of the war. In future, such missions had the code name of 'Gardening'. Different areas to be mined were known by their own code names. Oslo was known as 'Onion', the Elbe area was coded 'Eglantine', and so on. Fifteen Hampdens took off and fourteen of them laid mines in the sea lanes off Denmark between the German ports and Norway.

The Handley Page Hampden was the only RAF bomber with a bomb bay that could be easily altered to carry sea mines. Each mine was like a large cylinder about ten feet long and eighteen inches in diameter with a parachute fitted into one end and an anchor into the other. They weighed approximately 1,500 lb.

One Hampden failed to return, an aircraft from 50 Squadron. Its pilot was Flight Lieutenant Bob Cosgrove from Hobart who had been Pat's first roommate at Point Cook. Bob's returning aircraft was detected by RDF as it approached England on its return flight but then it disappeared from the screen. It never crossed the coast. The Hampden apparently crashed into the sea off Mablethorpe, Lincolnshire. He and his crew were lost and their names are recorded on the Runnymede Memorial. Bob and his father never had the chance to reconcile.

Pat proposed to Kay in April. 'The war will be over in a year,' he said, as he put the diamond ring on her finger.[7] They agreed to marry when it was over. But time was running out.

On 17 April, after only six weeks with their Spitfires, the pilots of 234 Squadron flew to Church Fenton for exercises to assess whether or not they could be declared operational. The decision was delayed pending another test at Leconfield; apparently they were not quite ready. An officer from No. 13 Group HQ carried out this next test on 8 May. He was willing to pronounce the squadron fit for day operations ... and none too soon. Two days later the German army swept into France and the Low Countries.

7

ST EVAL
JULY 1940

On 10 May, the uneasy quiet on the Western Front suddenly ended when the Germans marched across the Ardennes plateau into neutral Belgian territory. In the early morning, the Dornier and Heinkel bombers of the Luftwaffe ranged over north-east France, Belgium and Holland and attacked a total of twenty-three airfields and destroyed most of their potential opposition on the ground. The battle for air superiority was almost over before it even started. Any resistance that the Allied air forces in France (and indeed from England) could mount now would only be piecemeal and lacking coordination, although at times it was desperately heroic. Stuka dive-bombers roamed the skies almost at will without fear of being seriously molested. They systematically destroyed anything that stood in the path of the advancing panzers.

Later that day, Neville Chamberlain resigned as Britain's Prime Minister. He was replaced by Winston Churchill who immediately formed a War Cabinet with members drawn from all political parties.

Now day operational, 234 Squadron began to carry out interception flights a few days later. Making successful contact was rare, but very early in the morning on the 28th Pat and his section, Bush Parker and Sergeant George Bailey (newly arrived on 4 May), intercepted a 'bogey' which turned out to be a friendly Whitley bomber probably coming home late from a night raid. The squadron also started night-flying training.

Meanwhile, the situation on the Continent went from bad to worse at an alarming rate. Casualties in the air and on the ground were heavy and included several of Pat's Point Cook classmates. On 14 May, four out of eight Fairey Battles from 142 Squadron failed to return from attacking bridges between Sedan and Mouzon. Flight Lieutenant Ken Rogers, who was from Toowoomba, was killed in action. The squadron leader in charge of flying, Squadron Leader John Hobler, also a Queenslander from Rockhampton, was shot down and injured. Despite serious facial burns, Hobler set fire to his plane, evaded the advancing Germans and led his crew back to safety. The squadron's other flight commander, Flight Lieutenant William 'Wiggly' Wight of Melbourne, another Point Cook classmate, took over Hobler's role of leading the squadron in the air.

On the 15th, the Dutch army capitulated at 11 a.m. That same day, F/O Bill Fowler from Adelaide went missing over France. His Hurricane flying at the rear of 615 Squadron's formation was bounced by Me 109s coming out of the sun. He shouted a warning to the others but his Hurricane was hit at the same time. Almost blacking out in a tight turn, he fired at a 109 which fell straight down but he was hit again by another Messerschmitt and his Hurricane burst into flames. He bailed out with his flying boots on fire but landed safely in the Ardennes Forest. Some French soldiers joined up with him but next day the whole group was captured near Namur. (Bill Fowler later earned the distinction of being one of the few Allied airmen to escape successfully from Colditz Castle.)

There were ten squadrons of Hurricane in France, and Hugh Dowding, in charge of Fighter Command, would not commit any of his Spitfire fighters.[1] The pressure to release more fighter squadrons built as the Germans rapidly advanced. Dowding maintained his stance and defended it in his now famous 16 May letter to the Air Ministry. He reminded the Air Council that 'the force necessary to defend this country was fifty-two squadrons and my strength has now been reduced to the equivalent of thirty-six squadrons'.

On the evening of 26 May, orders were given to commence Operation *Dynamo*, the evacuation of the trapped British Expeditionary Force from Dunkirk. Fighter Command was to provide an air umbrella, and for the first time Spitfires operating from England were involved in fighting over the Continent. 616 Squadron, which had been flying convoy patrols, was relocated to Rochford, a forward base near Southend in Essex and committed to patrolling over Dunkirk. It was a race against time. On the 28th, Belgium surrendered to the Germans with effect from 11 a.m. British and French troops just managed to plug the gap this created in the line in time to block the German army from reaching Nieuport and the beaches. Dunkirk was finally captured on 4 June but by then a total of 338,226 troops, including 112,000 French, had been successfully evacuated – but Operation *Dynamo* had been costly.

616 Squadron flew a final patrol over the Dunkirk area that day. It was deserted, littered with debris and abandoned equipment. On the return flight the weather deteriorated and while attempting to land at Rochford one Spitfire crashed and the pilot was killed. The others were diverted to Tangmere. After leaving behind 2,000 guns, 60,000 vehicles, 600,000 tons of fuel and 76,000 tons of ammunition, the British army was now practically unarmed. Nevertheless, Winston Churchill in the House of Commons defiantly declared, 'We shall fight on the beaches, we shall fight in the fields … we shall never surrender.'

Elsewhere, another disastrous campaign ended as British and French troops began evacuating from Norway.

Three days later, Pete Pettigrew, Pat Hughes' closest friend from his schooldays, disappeared while his unit, 151 Squadron, patrolled with 56 Squadron between Abbeville and Amiens. There was a brief clash with Me 109s, incorrectly identified as Heinkel He 113s, but no dogfight. All of the Hurricanes except Pettigrew's returned to Manston and nobody had the slightest idea what had happened to it. (Casualty lists show him as being wounded around this time. An unconfirmed story suggests he was shot down, hidden by French nuns and eventually smuggled back to England. Another says he escaped from a POW camp. Whatever actually happened, he did get back to England and by 1944 he was with the Aeroplane and Armament Experimental Establishment (A & AEE) at Boscombe Down but on 24 August 1944 he was killed in a mid-air collision. He had married an English girl.)[2]

Events accelerated. On 5 June, the Germans launched the final Battle for France with air and artillery bombardments along the Somme and the Aisne. Five days later Mussolini, eager for spoils, declared war on Britain and France. It was only a matter of time; the French could not last much longer. British evacuations began from Cherbourg on 15 June and continued over the next three days. There were more evacuations from St Malo, Brest, St Nazaire and Nantes, all leading to the successful recovery of 144,171 British troops and airmen. The French government requested an armistice on the 17th and Britain would defiantly declare herself 'alone'.

In fact, Britain was not completely alone – the Commonwealth was responding. Australian and New Zealand troops were diverted to England from the third troop convoy from Australia bound for the Middle East. They disembarked at Gourock on the Clyde on 17 June. Three liners in the convoy had transported around 8,000 officers and men and three other ships landed a similar number of New Zealanders.[3] Meanwhile, Canadian troops had already arrived and an RCAF fighter squadron was being formed in the RAF. An RAAF Sunderland squadron was already operational with the RAF at Mount Batten on Plymouth Sound.

New Zealand, for her size, was already making a major contribution in the air. By September 1939, there were some 550 New Zealanders serving in the RAF, more than from any other Commonwealth nation outside the British Isles. Aside from veterans who remained in the RAF after the First World War, increasing numbers of New Zealanders made their own way to Britain during the early 1930s so that by the end of 1935 about 100 were already serving with Britain's air force, mostly as pilots. Then in 1936, at the request of the British Government, a start was made with the selection of candidates in New Zealand to serve as pilots in the RAF. As soon as volunteers were accepted they went to England for training, the first party arriving in July 1937. Thereafter, groups of twelve to twenty sailed at approximately monthly intervals for the next two years, the total number reaching 241. Shortly afterwards, this scheme was supplemented by another under which men were given preliminary pilot training in New Zealand and sent to the RAF as 'trained cadets', as were the Australian cadets from Point Cook. Training began at Wigram in June 1937 and the first seven pilots left for England the following April. Altogether 133 men reached England under this arrangement, the last of them arriving early in 1940. They were enlisted into the RAF under the short service commission scheme, and the UK paid the New Zealand government £1,550 for each home-trained pilot. Those who went to Britain under the pre-war arrangements were classified as members of the RAF.

Likewise, there were already many Canadians in the RAF when the war commenced. These were the 'several hundred' volunteers of the so-called 'cattle boat brigade', air-minded young men who crossed the Atlantic independently and of whom the RCAF kept no records.

On 18 June, 234 Squadron received movement orders to transfer from Yorkshire to St Eval in Cornwall. It was the same day that Winston Churchill made what was probably his most famous speech:

> What General Weygand called the Battle of France is over. I expect that the Battle of Britain is about to begin ... The whole fury and might of the enemy must very soon be turned on us. Hitler knows that he will have to break us in this island or lose the war. If we can stand up to him all Europe may be free and the life of the world may move forward into bright sunlight uplands. But if we fail, the whole world, including the United States, including all that we have known and cared for, will sink into the abyss of a new Dark Age made more sinister and perhaps more protracted by the lights of perverted silence ... If the British Empire and its Commonwealth last for a thousand years, men will still say, 'This was their finest hour.'

234 Squadron's 'A' and 'B' Flights flew down to St Eval via Filton near Bristol with sixteen Spitfires, a Magister and two Avro Tutors. The remainder followed by train.[4]

Aviation in Cornwall had evolved since Percival 'P. P.' Phillips' early days. At the end of the 1936 he had finally closed his Cornwall Aviation Company, but he continued his aviation interests in other ways. By the end of the 1930s there were numerous airfields dotted around Cornwall and commercial passenger services had also expanded with the establishment of such companies as Western Airways and Great Western and Southern Air Lines. As the decade progressed the threat of another conflict with Germany emerged, and so during 1937 the RAF carried out the first surveys of possible sites for military airfields. The compulsory purchase of land for military uses, including new airfield construction, was introduced under the Emergency Powers (Defence) Act of 1939. By September 1939, plans were well ahead to utilise Cornwall's position and resources for what was coming.

Immediately following the declaration of war, British commercial aviation was drastically cut by legislation forbidding all civilian flights over the east of England and Scotland and special licences were required. The Land's End–St Mary's link was one of the few services permitted to continue. Special measures were taken. The aircraft were camouflaged, their windows painted were over to prevent passengers photographing shipping, and landing lights were masked out. Service departure times were varied to avoid a routine that would be noticeable to the enemy.

By then the first new Cornish military airfield was operational, though its work was generally undramatic. This was RAF Cleave, four miles north of Bude on the cliff-top near Kilkhampton village. The station was used for anti-aircraft gunnery training.

Autumn saw the opening of RAF St Eval, 234 Squadron's new home, around five miles north-east of Newquay. Planning for the airfield had begun two years beforehand when it was realised that aerial patrols off Cornwall would be needed. It was designed to accommodate two general reconnaissance squadrons. Work on the airfield began in 1938 when nine houses in the hamlet were torn down. The station opened on 2 October 1939 when twin-engine Avro Ansons of 217 Squadron arrived for anti-submarine work and convoy patrols over the English Channel and the Irish Sea.

The Anson squadron was reinforced by the addition of detachments of 58 Squadron Whitley bombers capable of carrying greater bomb loads. Later, Bristol Beaufort bombers and torpedo-bombers would arrive. When France fell in June 1940, Cornwall became vulnerable to the attention of the Luftwaffe so fighter defence was necessary. This became the responsibility of 234 Squadron which, when it arrived, was the only fighter squadron in Cornwall.[5]

The pilots found that St Eval was brand-new and close to the sea. It was in a very rural setting, home to a farming community, and an isolated old church was located right at the end of the runway. They were barely settled in when a French military aircraft, a Farman 222, landed unannounced the next day. Those on board were fleeing to England for sanctuary and to continue the fight. The squadron's intelligence officer, Pilot Officer Gregory 'Crikey' Krikorian, by birth an Armenian who spoke several languages, acted as interpreter. Next day the Farman was flown to Boscombe Down near Andover escorted by a section of Spitfires from 'B' Flight. Over the following weeks several more escaping aircraft would arrive.

Once established, 234 Squadron continued with the role it had begun in Yorkshire – convoy patrols and flights to intercept 'bogeys' (unidentified aircraft) – but no early contacts were made. Often, unarmed PRU Spitfires used St Eval as a base from which to conduct reconnaissance flights high above the Continent to photograph what the enemy was doing.

St Eval was being organised to be a Sector Headquarters in Fighter Command's new No. 10 Group which would cover much of England's south-west and up to the south of Wales. It was not yet fully operational. The Group Commander was AVM Sir Christopher Quintin Brand, a capable South African who had served with distinction as a fighter pilot in the First World War, and been awarded an MC, a DSO and a DFC. His headquarters were at Rudloe Manor in Wiltshire. The Sector HQ was under the command of Wing Commander Harvey. Basic operations commenced on 26 June and it became fully operational at the beginning of July. On 5 July, twelve WAAFs reported for duty in the operations room as air plotters.

With France out of the war, Britain in July 1940 had to concentrate solely on bolstering her immediate defences against almost certain invasion. Anything that could hinder such an event had to be used as a weapon. Barbed wire and minefields were planted along the southern coast and trenches were dug behind them. Obstructions of all kinds were erected in fields where gliders might be able to land. On the aircraft industry's test airfields old cars salvaged from rubbish-heaps were lined along the runways ready to be rolled into the paths of any invading enemy aircraft.

Civilians of the Local Defence Volunteers (LDV) armed themselves with shotguns, pikes and pitchforks. The LDV had been initiated back on 14 May, and men between seventeen and sixty-five who were 'capable of free movement' were asked to volunteer to be part-time soldiers to defend the nation from the threat of parachute troops. Although there was no pay for service, within twenty-four hours 250,000 had volunteered. In July the numbers swelled up to 1 million and Prime Minister Churchill gave them a new name: the 'Home Guard'.

Fighter Command's focus was on building up the strength of its squadrons. Before Dunkirk the pilot numbers in most units averaged about seventeen. By the second week in June most had been boosted to around twenty, but the drawback was these newcomers were new and inexperienced, fresh from training schools. They would have to gain their experience the hard way – if they survived long enough.

PRU pilots flying over occupied areas of Belgium and France and the coastlines of the Continent searched to see what was happening. They found the landscape changing. Strange scars in the form of huge strips of concrete were appearing in many places. The Germans seemed to be mixing the concrete with the bare earth after scraping off the turf. It became obvious that they were making runways for new airfields. Large army camps were appearing all over the countryside too. In other areas the canals seem to have disappeared but close inspection of photos revealed they were still there covered by camouflage netting. Underneath were increasing numbers of large barges. Railway sidings had appeared, roads were being extended and bomb and fuel dumps established. There was little doubt these were preparations for an invasion.

At the end of June, German troops landed unopposed on the island of Guernsey in the English Channel, and within twenty-four hours, on 1 July, the BBC announced that communication with the Channel Islands had ceased.

It was the next day that Adolf Hitler ordered his Armed Force Supreme Command, the *Oberkommando der Wehrmacht* (OKW), to make provisional plans for an invasion of England. Two weeks later Field Marshal Walter von Brauchitsch, commander-in-chief of the German army, and General Franz Halder, his chief of staff, submitted ambitious proposals for the operation. Hitler approved despite serious doubts expressed by the navy and he directed them to begin active preparations, but at the same time he stressed that attaining air superiority was the indispensable prelude to carrying out a landing.

On 2 July, the *OKW* issued its first operational instructions to the Luftwaffe. There were two basic tasks:

1. The interdiction of the English Channel to merchant shipping to be carried out in conjunction with German naval force by means of attacks on convoys, the destruction of harbour facilities and the laying of mines in harbour areas and approaches.
2. The destruction of the Royal Air Force.

Two *Fliegerkorps* were assigned to establish air superiority over the English Channel and close it to British shipping: General Bruno Lörzer's *II Fliegerkorps* based on the Pas de Calais and General Wolfram Freiherr von Richthofen's *VIII Fliegerkorps* near Le Havre. Clearing the Straits of Dover of ships was not considered to be difficult so Lörzer did not think it necessary to commit his whole force. A small battle group under Oberst Johannes Fink, Kommodore of the Dornier Do 17-equipped *Kampfgeschwader* 2 based at Arras, was given the job.

In addition to the Dornier bombers, Fink had two Junkers Ju 87 Stuka *Gruppen* and two Messerschmitt Me 109 *Jagdgeschwader* based on the Pas de Calais at his disposal. The fighter component was formidable, *JG26* being led by the flamboyant, cigar-smoking Major Adolf Galland and *JG53* by the much more serious and philosophical Major Werner Mölders, two highly distinguished commanders. Adolf Galland had developed the Luftwaffe's ground support techniques during the Spanish Civil War and Werner Mölders had emerged as the Cóndor Legion's top ace. Mölders was highly respected by his men who nicknamed him '*Vati*' (Daddy); it was he who pioneered the new techniques of air fighting that were standard in the Luftwaffe. As a basic element, Mölders had his fighters fly in pairs, called a *Rotte*. About 200 yards separated each plane and the main responsibility of the wingman, or number two, was to cover the leader from quarter or stern attack. The leader looked after navigation and covered his wingman. Two *Rotten* made up a *Schwarm* (flight) of four aircraft. This combination improved a flight's all-round vision, combat flexibility and gave mutual protection. Two or three *Schwärme* made up a *Staffel* (squadron). By flying their loose formations the Germans found many advantages: they could easily maintain their positions in combat; they could keep a better look-out; and by flying at separated heights they could cover each other and scan a greater area of sky.

For achieving the task of air superiority over his allotted area, Johannes Fink's battle group had at its disposal about seventy-five bombers, sixty plus Stuka dive-bombers and some 200 fighters. Fink was given an impressive title: *Kanal-Kampführer*, or Channel Battle Leader. He established his command post in an old bus on top of the cliffs at Cap Blanc Nez close to a statue of Louis Bleriot, which had been erected to commemorate the French pioneer's conquest of the English Channel thirty-one years before in July 1909. From the windows of the bus he could follow the progress of his aircraft and if the visibility was good enough he could watch the British through powerful binoculars.

Wolfram von Richthofen did not marshal any of *VIII Fliegerkorps'* twin-engine bombers from Le Havre. His Stukas, supported by fighters, were presumed capable of establishing air superiority and clearing shipping from the area between Portsmouth and Portland.

Flying conditions over most of England on 2 July were poor, cloudy and rainy, and there was only limited aerial activity. Fighter Command shot down only one enemy aircraft, a Dornier Do 215 reconnaissance plane. The next day, small groups of German bombers, covered by roving fighter patrols, were out hunting for ships. A Dornier suddenly dived out of cloud and attacked No. 13 EFTS at Maidenhead. Half a dozen men were injured and one was killed, while six Tiger Moth biplane trainers were destroyed and twenty-five damaged.

The weather in the Channel was better on 4 July and this enabled von Richthofen to strike a decisive blow. Convoy OA178 was an Atlantic Convoy made up of large merchant ships. It had come through the Straits on the 3rd and was off Portland on the 4th, where it came under heavy attack by two Stuka *Gruppen* unhindered by RAF fighters. Four ships were sunk and nine damaged, some by fire. A third *Gruppe* of twenty Ju 88s attacked Portland, damaging two ships. During the night German E-boats found and mauled the convoy again sinking one ship and damaged two more. Out of approximately ninety bombers deployed, the cost was just one aircraft shot down by the convoy's AA guns. It was a major blow because after this the Channel was closed to all ocean-going ships using the Port of London. These had to be diverted either to Britain's west-coast ports or sent around Scotland. Henceforth, the only convoys to risk using the English Channel would be made up of small coasters, mainly colliers. They would gain renown as 'The Coal-Scuttle Brigade'. Elsewhere, two enemy aircraft penetrated as far as Bristol. One was shot down by Spitfires from 92 Squadron at Pembrey near Swansea but the RAF obviously had to extend its role to offer a protective umbrella for shipping.

These first encounters over the Channel made it obvious to British leaders that the country's RDF (radar) network could not detect German aircraft soon enough for defending fighters to intercept. They simply could not scramble, climb and position themselves fast enough. From this day on, too, a flight from each RAF sector station was dispatched to operate from its forward landing grounds close to the coast to fly convoy patrols. These patrols could last up to two hours at a time with the pilots searching the grey sky around a gathering of ships on a grey ocean – boring and full of tension all at the same time.

At St Eval, Pat Hughes and four of 234 Squadron's other pilots who were deemed 'night operational' were rostered for night scrambles over Plymouth as well. On a typical night the pilot on duty would sleep on a notoriously uncomfortable camp bed in the dispersal hut. If needed, the telephone near the bed would ring and he'd be told to take off and patrol the 'GIN.A' or 'GIN.B' lines around Plymouth at a specified height. He would grab his parachute, carry it out to his plane, shout for his ground crew to start up, and order the flare-path crew to go out and light the runway's Glim Lamps. These lamps had been introduced recently because it was thought they could not be seen from above 2,000 feet. 'There were times,' recalled Bob Doe, 'when you couldn't see them from a lot less than that!'

After the Spitfire taxied out and took off, the pilot had to tell his controller immediately he was airborne. He would then set the throttle to minimise the sparks from the exhaust stacks, which were on both sides of the engine, just in front of his eyes. If he throttled back too quickly, it caused a sheet of brilliant sparks to flare past the cockpit, blinding his night vision for the next few minutes. Later, covers were put over the exhaust stubs so it was easier to see at night. As he neared Plymouth flying through the darkness, the pilot found himself entirely on his own as radio control instructions from the ground did not reach that far, and there was no other station he could call up. That fault had to be rectified as soon as No. 10 Group could organise itself. On arrival in the area, he would then spend his time watching the searchlights, hoping they would catch an enemy aircraft, a target, in the beam – and carefully watching the status of his fuel. Finally, there would be the flight back home in the darkness and landing on the Spitfire's narrow undercarriage guided by the dim Glim Lamps. With convoy patrols by day and scrambles at night, these pilots were often deprived of vital sleep which could in turn potentially lead to the danger of excessive fatigue, but somehow most coped.[6]

On Sunday, 7 July, the weather in the south and west of England consisted of scattered rain showers with widespread low cloud. Nevertheless, German aircraft probed the western area looking for shipping. To Pilot Officer Ken Dewhurst fell the honour of having 234 Squadron's first brush with the enemy when he encountered a Junkers Ju 88 over Plymouth early in the evening. It was a brief engagement but Dewhurst claimed to have inflicted damage before it escaped.

Next day, 8 July, weather conditions were mostly clear but there was plenty of cloud, ideal for convoy attacks. Fighter Command was kept busy flying cover. A section of three Spitfires from 54 Squadron ran into trouble tackling a formation of Me 110s that crossed the coast at Dungeness. The Spitfires were about to intercept when they were attacked from above by Me 109s. Two Spitfires were shot down and the third was damaged before it could escape. Fortunately, the pilots survived, but one had been wounded and would be out of action for several weeks. The Spitfire pilots had been caught by surprise because they were employing the outmoded, compact formations and tactics that had been taught before the war – parade ground stuff and dangerous! Such set-piece manoeuvres could be disastrous.

Eventually the RAF would begin imitating the Germans by flying in a formation of two pairs. They called it a 'finger-four' because each plane flew in a position corresponding to the finger-tips of a hand seen in plain view. The leader was represented by the longest finger, the number two by the index. Numbers three and four took up the positions of the third and little finger-tips. Number two always flew on the sun side of the leader scanning down-sun – he positioned himself slightly below so that the other pilots could see him well below the glare. That left two pairs of eyes stepped up down-sun of the leader scanning the danger area. When fighting, each pair worked as a unit like the German *Rotte*. But that was in the future. The tactics the Luftwaffe had revealed over France and Dunkirk had not been fully studied and digested. In the opening phase of the Battle of Britain, these lessons had yet to be absorbed and applied.

Operating from Exeter, Hurricanes from 87 Squadron damaged a twin-engine German aircraft identified as a Do 215. The elusive Dornier escaped back into the clouds.

At 3.40 p.m., 79 Squadron found trouble. Nine Hurricanes were scrambled from Hawkinge to cover a large convoy which had put out from the Thames Estuary. They were attacked off Dover by Messerschmitt 109s. Two Hurricanes and their pilots were lost in a short, sharp encounter.

Just before teatime, 234 Squadron met the enemy for the second time. Blue Section, three Spitfires led by Pat, was scrambled to fly a convoy patrol. Pat's wingmen were the New Zealander, Pilot Officer Keith Lawrence as Blue 1, and Sergeant George Bailey as Blue 3. At 6.15 p.m., twenty-five miles south-east of Land's End they intercepted a Junkers Ju 88 flying at 2,000 feet just above a layer of cloud. Lawrence attacked first and, as he broke away, Pat closed in from astern, opening fire with only slight deflection. He wrote later in his formal Combat Report:

Blue 1 intercepted E/A on top of cloud layer, after Blue 2 had attacked it and broken away. Blue 1 attacked E/A from astern using slight deflection. E/A climbed steeply into cloud. Blue 1 followed and continued firing at range between 30–50 yards until enemy emerged from cloud. Blue 1 gave 2 short bursts as E/A went into shallow dive & then broke away to port and downwards. Rear gunner continued firing throughout this engagement.[7]

Pat had fired a total of 2,494 rounds of ammunition mostly using two second bursts, starting at 150 yards and closing in at times to as close as 30 yards. In the process his Spitfire (P9366) was hit by return fire – just a single bullet which went through the leading edge of the starboard wing. On landing, Pat chided his wingmen for opening fire from too far out – 400 yards was too far away to hit anything. According to Luftwaffe records researched after the war, two Junkers 88s were apparently lost on this day. This may have been the machine from Stab/LG1. The squadron's Operations Record Book (ORB) noted down the Ju 88 as 234 Squadron's first confirmed victory, but it had taken a lot of shooting to do the job.

For Pat and the men of 234 Squadron battle had been joined successfully at last, albeit while using the formal pre-war tactics. The anticipation of more action in the immediate future was palpable. It boosted adrenalin and heightened the senses!

Before the war, on the orders of Fighter Command's officer-in-charge, AM Sir Hugh 'Stuffy' Dowding, the guns of the RAF fighters were harmonised to give a widely spaced bullet pattern at a range of 400 yards. This spread of bullets was intended specifically to destroy bombers and because of Dowding's nickname, it became known as the 'Stuffy Spread'.

While the method certainly gave a new or average pilot a greater chance of scoring some hits on the target, early engagements had shown that it was unlikely enough damage would be caused to actually bring an enemy plane down! A concentrated and accurate burst of fire gave far better results. Although Dowding's order to spread the field of fire was still standard procedure, squadrons with combat experience were harmonising their guns on a single point 250 yards in front of their aircraft. Going in close seemed to be another way of preventing the 'Stuffy Spread' from scattering bullets too far and wide. Obviously, the closer a fighter could be positioned behind, the closer together the pattern would be and the more certainty there was of making a kill. Effective perhaps, but obviously dangerous. But wasn't war dangerous anyway?

Before the fighting intensified, one nervous young pilot reportedly asked Pat, 'What do I do if I miss?'

'What do you do if you miss?' came back his deliberate reply, 'Listen mate ... you get as close as you can and you can't miss!'[8]

Meanwhile, there was someone Pat was really missing, especially since the squadron had moved to St Eval. He telephoned Kay and told her that, in spite of them agreeing to marry after the war, he had changed his mind. They should marry right away. She should come down to him in Cornwall. They could be married at the register office in Bodmin. He would organise leave and make the arrangements. It was a tantalising idea. Kay was twenty-three years of age and did not need to ask for permission but she did discuss it with her mother. She recalled her mother's reaction was strongly in favour. 'My mother said I should grab whatever happiness I could as no one knew what was going to happen.'[9] Kay's answer to Pat was a joyful, 'Yes!'

Mid-afternoon on the 12th, a lone Ju 88 suddenly appeared over the aerodrome, dropped some bombs in a hit-and-run attack and swiftly made off out to sea. Keith Lawrence was up at the time with a newcomer, the Scotsman Pilot Officer Bill Gordon, and they gave chase, damaging it before it escaped.

Just over two weeks passed before 234 Squadron's next engagement. During that time the Luftwaffe created havoc. Fink's bombers showed that merchant ships were worthwhile and vulnerable targets. On 13 July two convoys were attacked off Harwich, as was another convoy off Dover the following day.

Pat and Blue Section were detailed to go on the 13th to the sector's new advanced base, a grass airstrip at Roborough in Devonshire, where for a week it would operate under St Eval's Fighter Sector Control. This was to improve communications, carry out extra patrols over the Plymouth area and test whether or not the airstrip would be a safe place to use Spitfires. As yet it was primitive. There was no accommodation and facilities were very limited. Pilots and personnel on site had to be billeted out. Another squadron was to be formed there, but the judgement was that Roborough's grass airstrip was not suitable for high-performance Spitfires. The new unit's equipment would need to be something slower, Gloster Gladiators perhaps.

Pat and Blue Section returned to St Eval on the 20th.

Meanwhile in the east, shipping between Ramsgate and Deal had been heavily attacked on 18 July.

On the 19th another convoy was hit off Dover in an area that was earning the nickname of 'Hellfire Corner'. Some of the sea and air battles were reported live on radio and were even caught on film. That day, a news cameraman spotted a burning aircraft in its last seconds and followed with his camera as it came whining down over Dover and blew up in a spectacular rupture of flame and smoke. The sequence was shown in a newsreel that would become famous, with the commentator screaming out, 'There goes another Messerschmitt.' His identification was tragically wrong. Nine two-seater Boulton Paul Defiants of 141 Squadron had taken off from Hawkinge, but only three returned. It was the Messerschmitts that had shot the Defiants out of the sky in the squadron's first and last action over Dover. The RAF was being drawn into a war of attrition it could not afford – precisely what the Luftwaffe wanted.

Day after day throughout the month coastal convoys that ventured gamely out were attacked and suffered casualties. Convoy CW8 which sailed from Southend on the morning of 25 July consisted of twenty-one merchant ships escorted by two armed trawlers. By the time the sun went down five were on the bottom of the Straits, six were crippled on the water and the convoy was scattered. Two destroyers that came boldly out of Dover to help were heavily damaged. E-boats emerged from Calais to complete the destruction during the night. Under the cover of darkness they successfully attacked the surviving ships, sinking three. In all, the convoy suffered 50 per cent losses, many of them witnessed by thousands of people on shore.

Since 10 July, the Channel convoys had lost 24,000 tons of shipping sunk by air attack alone. One vessel in every three that sailed had become a casualty. There was no other choice for the Admiralty but to cancel all sailings of merchant ships through the waterway.

Fink and Wolfram von Richthofen had carried out the first of the OKW's 2 July directives successfully and won a tactical victory. After 4 July, all large-ship convoys on the world's trade routes in and out of the port of

London had been driven away from the Channel; after 25 July, all coastal convoys had been stopped. On 28 July the destroyers were forced to withdraw from Dover, and after 29 July the use of destroyers in the Channel by day was forbidden. In daylight the English Channel was now the front line up to the island's very shores, and the British were losing.

Late on the 25th, 234 Squadron lost the quiet and popular Geoffrey Gout on night patrol. His aircraft, Spitfire P9493, crashed near Porthtowan at about 11.45 p.m. The reason was never discovered. Was it excessive fatigue from flying day and night? He was buried in St Eval Churchyard four days later on the 29th. In a letter on 3 August, the squadron adjutant, Flying Officer E. C. 'Bish' Owens, wrote to Gout's mother expressing the squadron's sense of loss. Gout's green sports car was sent to her and the personal effects she did not want were auctioned with the proceeds going to charity.

It was on Saturday 27 July, shortly after 3.00 p.m., that Pat Hughes and his Blue Section found another Ju 88. His wingmen this time were Flying Officer Frank Conner and Sergeant George Bailey. Pat was flying Spitfire N3280. The Spitfires had been ordered to patrol the coastal area off Land's End at 10,000 feet but when radar picked up a 'bogey' they were then instructed to climb to 23,000 feet. Hauling their Spitfires up to that height and heading south-east, they soon spotted the Junkers still higher up twenty-five miles south-east of Land's End. Apparently the German crew saw the three British fighters coming. Inexplicably, the enemy pilot decided to leave the safer high altitude and dive vertically, possibly hoping that his built-up speed would keep them safe from harm. He was wrong.

Pat was after the Ju 88 quickly, closing to 200 yards in a screaming dive, and he clearly noticed its brown and green camouflage patterns. His Spitfire was severely buffeted about by the slipstream. The German rear-gunner began to fire at the Spitfire as Pat opened up with a two-second burst from dead astern. Tracer bullets zipped back at him from the Ju 88's top and ventral gun positions. As in his first encounter back on the 8th, his fighter was hit by a single bullet, this time in its mainplane.

I attacked from astern using deflection and followed the enemy aircraft down onto water. I fired three bursts – both rear guns were put out of action. Glass perspex was seen to fly off the top cockpit and parts of aircraft fell from both engines. I finished all my ammunition and broke away to port. Estimated speed of enemy aircraft 300 mph.[10]

Just after Pat ran out of ammunition and broke to the left, the Ju 88 was observed still diving. They were only fifty feet up by then. In his combat report, Pat claimed the destruction of 'one Ju 88 (unconfirmed)'. Confirmation came later that the German machine had gone into the sea, twenty-five miles off Land's End.[11]

It was 'B' Flight's turn at dawn readiness the following Sunday morning. At the ungodly hour of 4.25 a.m., Blue Section was scrambled to investigate an enemy aircraft over Plymouth Harbour.

As Pat and his wingmen, Pilot Officers Ken Dewhurst and Pat Horton, another Kiwi, arrived over the harbour town they saw a 'large amount of AA fire' bursting in the morning sky and then spotted yet another Ju 88. It was diving steeply towards an object on the land. Like the previous Junkers, this one was camouflaged green and brown and the forefront of its nose section was painted red. Pat went down after it.

I waited till the enemy aircraft pulled up and opened fire at 100 yards, closing to 50 yards and holding this position, firing off short bursts. The enemy aircraft carried out slight turns to either side. Smoke as from oil, and grey-yellow in colour, started to pour from the starboard engine, and then a red-hot object appeared to fall from this engine. Aircraft continued course at low altitude where it was attacked in turn by Blue 3 and 2. Aircraft finally climbed slightly, then starboard engine caught fire and the aircraft slowly turned to starboard and hit the water. The aircraft sank in 10 secs, but no crew were seen to escape. Rear gun fire was experienced throughout the engagement – tracer bullets were used.[12]

Fire from the German rear-gunner had hit Pat's Spitfire (N3239) with a single bullet yet again. This one punched a hole in the radiator fairing.

This Ju 88 came from II/LG1 and had been flown by Leutnant Pfanf and his crew. Although the Spitfire pilots did not see anyone escape before the plane sank, there actually was one survivor. One NCO who had been wounded was rescued from the water, but Pfanf and his two other companions, both NCOs, were lost.[13]

Three Ju 88s had been claimed destroyed for 234 Squadron in three weeks and Pat had led all three attacks. He had gone in close. That was definitely the answer.

George Bailey would recall years later,

Amongst some of his [Pat's] efforts towards the war effort – frowned upon and stopped by higher authority [Squadron Leader Barnett?] – painting of the spinners of our Spitfires bright colours in competition to the yellow nosed 109's. Use of incendiary bullets in all guns and bringing the concentration of fire power from the eight guns down to the minimum distance that could be obtained from the mountings ... about 50 yds less than that recommended by the A.M.[14]

Pat would do it again and again.

8

THE IDES OF AUGUST

Despite three successful combats, all without loss, and the enthusiasm they generated, 234 Squadron was a long way from being a happy unit. Something was not quite right and, in fact, seemed to be getting worse. The commander of 'A' flight, John Theilmann, gave the impression to the others of being 'remote' and having some difficulties. He was flying less often than usual, perhaps blaming asthma, and as for the CO – Barnett hardly flew at all! In effect, it was Pat who was leading the squadron – the young pilots looked to him for guidance rather than anyone else. It was his squadron! Bob Doe recalled: 'Hughes was the one who taught me everything in the air. We respected him, listened to him. But he was not a remote figure like the other two; he was one of the lads as well. He was the real power behind the squadron.'[1]

Meanwhile, during the latter part of July a flight of Gloster Gladiators was installed at Roborough to create the nucleus of a new squadron. Roborough's two grass strips that formed a 'T' shape had been deemed too small for 234 Squadron's high-performance Spitfires, so another alternative was worked out. Formerly the Fighter Flight, Sumburgh, it was ordered to move from Sumburgh as it was being replaced by Hurricanes from 3 Squadron, the Flight's five Gladiators left for Roborough on 21 July and assembled in Devon, where on 1 August it became 247 Squadron.

The airstrip was suitable for the Gladiators but there was still no accommodation and facilities remained very limited. Pilots and personnel were continuing to be billeted out. The new squadron's parent station was Mount Batten, Coastal Command, home of 10 Squadron RAAF. A few tents and some transport vehicles were obtained from Mount Batten and a small amount of hangar space was made available there for major inspections on the aircraft by the officer commanding Roborough.

247 was passed for day operations immediately but was allowed a fortnight to settle in properly and become conversant with its new sector and patrol lines. For operational flying it was a unit of 10 Group under the direct control of Headquarters Fighter Sector St Eval. As all R/T communications came from St Eval, and night operations were to be made from there as well, it was

arranged for an officer from 234 Squadron to assist with the organisation on a temporary posting from 1 August – Flight Lieutenant Pat Hughes.[2]

It was the opportunity Pat and Kay had been waiting for. As soon as Kay had gained her mother's approval to be married, Pat went ahead with the necessary arrangements as there was much to do in the days beforehand. This meant a break from operations, and the Register Office at Fore Street, Bodmin, was en route to his appointment. Married, they could set up house nearby before his temporary posting came to an end. They stopped at Bodmin on 1 August and were married with strangers as witnesses on the same day that 247 Squadron became a reality.

According to Francis K. Mason in his book, *Battle Over Britain*, published in 1969, during this period one of 247's Gladiators, N5585, became emblazoned with an emblem below its cockpit consisting of a map of Australia with a standing kangaroo superimposed upon it. Printed alongside were the words 'ANZAC ANSWER'. Below these, there was a victory emblem in the shape of a miniature swastika. The origin of the motif has been a puzzle over the years. There was no Australian shown in squadron records as a pilot in either the Fighter Flight or 247 Squadron at this time.[3] A tenuous possibility comes out of the fact that 247's task was to provide air cover for the naval base at Plymouth and this was also the home of 10 (Sunderland) Squadron RAAF at Mount Batten. Roborough, in fact, was a satellite airfield for Mount Batten and was often used by landplanes coming to and from the flying boat base. Australian personnel therefore frequently used the field and Australian ground crews may have been 'borrowed' to assist in setting things up in the early stages. As well, 10 Squadron had played a major part in successfully sinking a German submarine, the U-26 on 1 July, only the second submarine victory of the war for Coastal Command. It was a matter of pride for the squadron – pride which might have manifested itself in the painting of a symbol of defiance on the side of one of 247 Squadron's Gladiators. Could it be that the 'ANZAC ANSWER' swastika referred to a submarine kill, not to an aircraft kill?[4] Most unlikely.[5]

Far more likely was Pat's temporary attachment to 247 Squadron. Pat's Record of Service shows him to be in the right place at the right time and such was his imposing, outgoing character that it does not stretch credibility to see him as being responsible for an emblem like this – if the aircraft was allocated to him. The swastika on the 'ANZAC ANSWER' can be linked to 234 Squadron's gratifying first victory, the Ju 88 on 8 July in which Pat played the major role. In the middle of July when Pat visited Roborough with Blue Section, 234 Squadron had only this confirmed success to its credit at the time. Pat's wingman was Keith Lawrence, a New Zealander who had actually made the initial attack in the encounter before Pat closed in to 'finish it off'. It really was an 'Anzac Answer'!

Pat was apparently with 247 Squadron for around a week, but if he believed that his temporary stay was actually to be longer, or even permanent to go with his promotion from 'acting flight lieutenant' to 'flight lieutenant' (to be gazetted on 3 August), then he may have arranged to reserve Gladiator N5585 for his own use. To have an aircraft set aside and decorated in this fashion does suggest that someone at least thought his stay would be for some time, otherwise why go to the trouble of doing it? It certainly would have been a grand welcoming gesture – perhaps worthy of the Flight's new commanding officer? The person who did take over the Flight was of flight lieutenant rank, Flight Lieutenant George Chater, an experienced flying instructor at Cranwell. Perhaps someone mistakenly thought it was going to be Pat. Were there mixed messages, conflicting orders? Pat and Kay may have thought so. They did start to set up house at Treyarronn Bay in Cornwall. Perhaps the 'Temporary Duties' shown in Pat's record of service were actually going to be 'Flying Duties' and the orders were altered. If so, and the orders *were* changed, something may have been happening to draw him back to 234 Squadron again. With the realisation that someone other than the Australian would be using the plane, the motif was undoubtedly quickly removed.

Because of the state of Roborough, 247 Squadron initially had only day 'stand-by' there and was held at 'night readiness' at St Eval, although it was recognised that its patrols would be at a disadvantage against the enemy's faster bombers. The Gladiators also flew regular convoy patrols off the coast covering the approaches to Plymouth.

247 Squadron expanded to twelve Gladiators for day and night fighting, and became fully operational as part of 10 Group on 13 August – the same day as *Adler Tag*.

*

In Germany on the first day of August, Adolf Hitler had issued his Directive No. 17 dealing with the conduct of air and sea warfare against England. An invasion, code named *Seelöwe* (Sea Lion), was to be prepared ready to launch on 15 September.

On the 6th, Reichsmarschall Göring instructed his commanders to be ready by 10 August for the main assault on the RAF – *Adler Tag* (Eagle Day). The main assault would be spearheaded by *Luftflotte* 2 and *Luftflotte* 3 operating from bases in France, Belgium, Holland and Germany, and *Luftflotte* 5 would fly from Norway and Denmark to threaten north-eastern England and Scotland. From the 10th, all that was required to start was a forecast of three or four days of suitable weather.

Two days later German bombers and E-boats ambushed Convoy *Peewit*. The convoy was decimated. Out of twenty-three ships, seven were sunk and six – plus six escort vessels - were heavily damaged. Pilot Officer John Curchin, an Australian in 609 (Spitfire) Squadron operating from Middle Wallop, destroyed one Me 110 and damaged another.[6]

Because of unfavourable weather forecasts on 10 August, Göring postponed *Adler Tag*, but the following day his Luftwaffe struck at Portland, the Royal Navy's principal base near the proposed invasion area. Heavy fighting ensued.

On the 12th, the Luftwaffe attacked RDF stations, forward airfields and two small convoys in the Thames Estuary. German radio announced later that heavy damage had been caused on the British mainland and claimed the destruction of seventy-one RAF aircraft. The day's aerial battles were obviously a foretaste of what was to come, although German claims for the day were optimistic. Of the fighter airfields attacked, all were operational again in a matter of hours with the exception of Manston which was out of action for twenty-four hours, and Ventnor RDF station which was out of action for several days. Then with predictions of fine weather, Göring ordered *Adler Tag* for the 13th.

Next morning, the weather on this fateful day was mainly fair but with widespread early mist and drizzle. A last-minute signal from Göring's Headquarters postponed the main attack until the afternoon in the hope that the weather would clear. There was some fighting in the morning because some units did not receive the signal in time. After a lull until just beyond midday, *Adler Tag's* planned attacks took place between 3.45 and 5.00 p.m. with raids on Portland, Southampton, Kent and the Thames Estuary. The last German aircraft disappeared off British RDF screens around 6 p.m. Luftwaffe claims were for eighty-four RAF fighters destroyed and the British claimed sixty-four German aircraft shot down. In fact, both of these were exaggerated but on the ground the RAF had a further forty-seven aircraft destroyed, only one a fighter.

Widespread dive-bombing attacks had tragic results. At Detling, the messes and cookhouses were all destroyed and all the hangars set on fire. Twenty-two aircraft were destroyed and sixty-seven people killed. However, the Luftwaffe had made a mistake with this particular target because Detling was not a Fighter Command airfield so none of the planes destroyed were fighters. Fighter Command's loss of thirteen fighters in the air was bad enough.

The main assault was only beginning, and the situation could only get worse.

Pat seems to have arrived back at 234 Squadron during the 6th as he flew a night patrol late that night and another very early the following morning. Much had happened in his absence. A Coastal Command Blenheim squadron, 236 Squadron, had started to arrive from Thorney Island, its first flight landing on the 3rd. The acting CO was familiar – Dick Power from Pat's old Point Cook days! It was a chance to catch up again but some of the news Dick had was harrowing. Dick's CO was missing and so too was Bryan McDonough, another Australian. Bryan McDonough was Peter McDonough's cousin – Peter who had lived in the room next door to Pat at Point Cook early in 1936.[7]

Power explained what happened. At the beginning of the month, PRU Spitfires had reported a large concentration of German aircraft at Cherbourg.

Grasping the opportunity to strike first, the RAF ordered a bombing raid for thirteen Blenheim IV bombers from 59 Squadron with an escort of ten Blenheim long-range fighters from 236 Squadron.

The escort was divided into three parts. First off was Dick Power leading a section of three. Five minutes later two more Blenheims took off, the first flown by the CO, Squadron Leader Peter Drew, and the second with Bryan McDonough at the controls. There was supposed to be three planes in this section but one was late taking off. These two sections were to follow 59 Squadron in and strafe the aerodrome after the bombs were dropped. The last section was to wait one or two miles off Cherbourg to cover the withdrawal.

Low cloud blanketed the French coast causing Power and his section to miss Cherbourg completely but shortly afterwards a break in the clouds appeared and the bombers attacked. Following this, Drew led McDonough and a third Blenheim in for the low-level strafing but only the last machine emerged and it was heavily damaged. Missing after the expensive raid were Peter Drew and Bryan McDonough and their crews as well as the CO of 59 Squadron, Wing Commander Weld-Smith and his crew.

It was recorded in 236 Squadron's ORB that:

Squadron Leader Drew commanded the squadron from the time it was reformed on 31st October 1939 and the loss of such a much loved leader is a bitter blow to the entire squadron. P/O McDonough who is an Australian was also another original member of the squadron, a pilot of great dependability and the utmost determination.

Dick Power was placed in temporary command to bring the squadron to St Eval.

Meanwhile, 234 Squadron was having its own internal problems as Luftwaffe activity heightened over the Channel and south-east England. On 31 July, Flight Lieutenant Cyril Page, who had been with 234 since early July, was posted out to 145 Squadron and Sergeant William Thompson had crashed into a stone wall on landing after a routine night patrol. He was badly injured and was currently in the Royal Cornish Infirmary. He would not fly again.

It was becoming apparent that, as the intensity of fighting increased, 234 Squadron could be shifted to relieve one of those squadrons that had suffered heavy losses. As it was, AVM Keith Park's No. 11 Group was bearing the brunt of it in the south-east, but AVM Sir Trafford Leigh-Mallory's 12 Group in the Midlands and Sir Quintin Brand's new 10 Group had to provide essential support. Park's tactics were born out of necessity. He had to get his squadrons up quickly, singly or in pairs, to intercept the incoming raids as early as possible rather than lose precious time forming them up into larger numbers. On the 5th, Brand relieved some of the pressure on 11 Group by taking over one of its bases, Middle Wallop in Hampshire.

234's problems reached a crisis point on 7 August when two pilots were removed from flying duty. One was Flight Officer Charles Igglesden, but what triggered his departure remains uncertain. He had been one of the few experienced pilots to join the squadron. He had come from 41 Squadron, where he had flown Spitfires with John Theilmann. (He would resign his commission in the RAF in September 1941 and afterwards join the Royal Navy.) The second man to go was Flight Lieutenant John Theilmann himself. He relinquished command of 'A' Flight and was categorised as non-effective 'because of sickness'. Theilmann was diagnosed as suffering from asthma, but despite such a health problem he had regularly led his section in the air throughout June and July, until the beginning of August. His last recorded flight was for just twenty minutes. Perhaps the increasing exposure to cold and pressure at high altitude, dry air, smoke and fumes were causing him to wave breathing difficulties and an increasing number of asthma attacks. Clearly he could not continue.

That two men should go on the same day pointed to symptoms of discontent that were worsening, exacerbated by an underlying problem – a commanding officer that did not fly. The records show that Squadron Leader Barnett flew just four times early in July, but never with the squadron, he always went alone. His last was a 'patrol' on 9 July to Land's End. AVM Douglas Strath Evill, who was Dowding's SASO, had visited St Eval a few weeks earlier so Barnett's lack of air time and other limitations, which caused so much unpopularity with his pilots, were apparently known to the chief of Fighter Command – but what could be done about it? Two pilots being removed from duty in one day probably provided the necessary impetus to act.

On 11 August, Sir Quintin Brand visited St Eval, first calling in on Wing Commander Harvey, the Fighter Sector CO. After spending time in 234 Squadron's mess that night, the AOC interviewed Barnett next morning in private. Whatever was said behind closed doors led to Barnett suddenly resigning his command the next day. That was on 13 August, *Adler Tag*, the day the Battle of Britain erupted.

Most of the pilots in 234 Squadron were happy to see Barnett go. Alan 'Budge' Harker remarked, 'He was a hopeless CO. He did all his flying in the hangar. I was delighted to see the back of him.'[8] Others felt Barnett's case was one of LMF (lack of moral fibre), but some were more charitable, Keith Lawrence commenting, 'He was a nominal CO. Don't think he had very good health either.'[9] (Barnett resigned his commission on 11 August 1941, a month before Charles Igglesden resigned in September.)

Pat now found himself in the position of being 'the last man standing' until a new CO could be found. His temporary command came at a drastic time. Because of the severe air activity of 11 and 12 August, Dowding ordered three of his most devastated squadrons to quieter areas. From Middle Wallop, 238 Squadron, with its CO wounded and both of its flight commanders killed in action (they were both Australians, Stuart Walch from Tasmania and

Jack Kennedy from Sydney), was ordered west to St Eval; 234 Squadron was instructed to transfer east to Middle Wallop as its replacement. The standard routine of day and night patrols, convoy escort and intercepting lone enemy raiders was about to change.

The move from St Eval to Middle Wallop on 14 August could have been disastrous. With dawn there was a thick wet mist rolling from west to east making flying impossible. They could only wait. As the morning went on it did break and the weather was good when the squadron took off. A factor overlooked was that the mist was rolling to the east and the squadron would catch up to it! It did. Before reaching Middle Wallop, the Spitfires were flying in tight formation through the mist. Bill Hornby remembered, 'Dark shapes loomed everywhere and it was a miracle that there were no collisions.'[10]

During the day the Germans continued attacking RAF airfields. Late that afternoon *Luftflotte 3* launched nine scattered and relatively small raids designed to spread 10 Group's defences. As they advanced on the south coast over a 100-mile front, AVM Brand's squadrons were obliged to scatter to meet the oncoming bombers. Inevitably, some groups avoided the British fighters and reached their targets, one of which was Middle Wallop.

When 234 Squadron arrived it was found that it shared the airfield with 609 Squadron and 604 Blenheim night fighter Squadron but it was 234's turn to be on 'Readiness'. The newly arrived Spitfires were being refuelled when Middle Wallop was attacked.

Three Heinkel He 111s appeared over the airfield and unloaded their bombs. Then a single Ju 88 conducted a dive-bombing attack. In the same instant three airmen, realising that the thirteen-ton steel doors of 609 Squadron's hangar were open, ran to close them to protect the Spitfires inside. They were cranking them shut when the hangar was struck by a bomb which blasted the doors down, killing them instantly. Two others were wounded, one having his foot blown off and the other losing his arm at the shoulder. Inside the hangar, three Blenheims and several Spitfires were destroyed. One of 234's new pilots, Joseph Szlagowski, ran for shelter in a nearby wood and threw himself flat. The trees ahead of him erupted in flames, exposing a hidden ammunition dump! Bob Doe was on a lorry taking some of the pilots to the mess when he heard bombs exploding and turned around to see the huge doors blown off the hangar.[11]

While the bombs were falling two 609 Squadron Spitfires managed to take off. They overtook the Heinkels and shot down the leading bomber. Another 609 pilot, already airborne, tackled the Ju 88 which crashed and exploded near Romsey.

For the young men of 234 Squadron, it was a worrying welcome to their new home, and so particularly was the heavy mantle of responsibility that had fallen on Pat's shoulders as 'the last man standing', who was so suddenly put in command! What would happen next?

Nightfall brought small scattered raids over southern England but, following the interception of German radio signals, the British defences were keyed up for a possible heavy attack on Liverpool. The RAF's counter-measures included patrols by Blenheim night fighters, some of them carrying new, experimental airborne radar, and several single-seat day fighters.

Pat flew a night patrol at 10 p.m. The expected raid did not eventuate.

9

15 AUGUST 1940

Because German forecasters predicted poor weather for Thursday 15 August, Göring summoned his senior air corps commanders to a meeting to analyse the *Adler Tag* attacks. With daylight the predictions seemed to be correct as German bomber crews returning from night and early morning sorties reported that there was extensive cloud over England. Later in the morning, however, the skies cleared and conditions also improved over northern France as well. Orders were issued for all *Luftflotten* to come to readiness in accordance with plans that had been outlined the previous day.

At Middle Wallop, the remainder of 234 Squadron arrived, completing the transfer from St Eval.[1] The other Spitfire squadron at the base had another Australian in it. John Curchin had been born in Hawthorn, a suburb of Melbourne, but his family moved to Enfield in Middlesex while John was young. He was educated at Merchant Taylor's School and applied to join the RAF in June 1939, at which time his address was Grange Park, London. His posting to 609 Squadron at Northolt came in June 1940, when the squadron was replacing losses suffered covering the evacuation of the BEF from Dunkirk. The squadron had transferred to Middle Wallop on 5 July and been involved in much of the heavy fighting.[2] There was little indication of the huge air battles about to take place.

At 11 a.m. a two-pronged attack was picked up on RDF. The first, consisting of sixty Junkers Ju 87 Stukas escorted by Messerschmitt 110s, made a heavy dive-bombing attack on the forward airfield at Lympne, putting it out of action for forty-eight hours.

The second raid of twenty-plus Stukas headed for Hawkinge with a strong escort of Me 109s of *JG26*. Before the British fighters could intercept, the Stukas were already diving on the airfield and inflicted heavy damage. The unplanned severing of power cables put the Dover RDF system out of action and posed a very serious problem for the defences. As the dive-bombers withdrew the British fighters pounced and claimed seven shot down. *JG26* responded by engaging the interceptors and the RAF lost two Spitfires and two Hurricanes.

Believing RAF Fighter Command to be almost exclusively concentrated in the south, the Germans launched a two-pronged daylight assault in the north. What they did not realise was that several experienced fighter squadrons were in 13 Group in the north 'resting' at Acklington and Church Fenton.

At 10 a.m., sixty-three Heinkel He 111s from *KG26* took off from Stavanger/Sola in Norway. Their main targets were the northern British airfields of Dishforth and Asworth, with secondary targets listed as Newcastle, Sunderland and Middlesbrough. Their escorts, twenty-one Messerschmitt Me 110s of *I/ZG76* stationed at Stavanger/Forus took off shortly afterwards. Further south, fifty unescorted Junkers Ju 88s of *KG30* were flying from Aalborg in Denmark, heading for RAF Station Driffield.

Just after midday, RDF detected the northernmost raid. Five minutes later the controller scrambled a Spitfire squadron from Acklington. Numerical estimates by RDF at this stage of the war were far from accurate. Each time the controller guessed at the size of the raid, he presented a more dramatic picture. At first reported as ten bandits, a few minutes later this jumped to thirty and then to fifty. The true picture was further confused by a diversionary mock attack further north by Heinkel He 115 seaplanes. The enemy was sighted some thirty miles east of the Fame Islands and the aircraft in the big broad-fronted formation were identified as Heinkel He 111s followed by Junkers Ju 88s with Messerschmitt Me 110s bringing up the rear. The Spitfires had in fact encountered the force from Norway containing Heinkels and Messerschmitts, but no Ju 88s – these were coming from Denmark to a target a hundred miles further south. Meanwhile, knowing that a large raid was taking place, the controller called more units into action. A Hurricane squadron intercepted raiders approaching Newcastle. Again aircraft recognition was faulty and Dornier Do 215s were identified as well as the actual He 111s. The unescorted Heinkels were badly mauled.

Twelve Spitfires and six Hurricanes engaged the Ju 88s from Denmark when they swept over the Yorkshire coast.

Out of the 134 aircraft despatched from Norway and Denmark, *Luftflotte 5* lost sixteen bombers and seven fighters and many others were damaged. These losses were so severe that *Luftflotte 5* would never again make a major daylight attack on the north. The cost to the RAF was just one Hurricane.

The battle switched back to the south. At midday, twelve Messerschmitt 110s swooped down on Manston airfield in a hit-and-run attack, raking it with cannon and machine-gun fire. Two Spitfires were destroyed and there were sixteen casualties. It was the beginning of a series of attacks in the early afternoon in which the defending British fighters found it almost impossible to engage the bombers because of the size of the fighter escorts.

A raid on Rochester was highly successful. Over 300 bombs rained down on the airfield and the Short Bros factory where production was under way on the RAF's newest heavy bomber, the huge four-engine Stirling. Six completed aircraft and the spare parts store were destroyed. Although this was serious, the Luftwaffe had not hit a Fighter Command target and therefore had not taken a step towards achieving air supremacy.

Around 5 p.m., two more raids materialised, this time in the south-west. One force of forty Ju 87 Stukas escorted by sixty Messerschmitt 109s and twenty Messerschmitt 110s was detected on the way to Portland. The second raid of over sixty Junkers Ju 88s of *LG 1*, escorted by forty Me 110s, was on a heading for Middle Wallop.

The two Hurricane Squadrons at Exeter, Nos 87 and 213, were ordered up, as was 234 Squadron at Middle Wallop. Thirteen Spitfires took off. Pat Hughes in the extra Spitfire was Cressy Leader at the head of 'A' Flight. They were ordered to patrol Swanage and await instructions.

Shortly afterwards, 609 Squadron still on the ground at Middle Wallop was brought to 'Readiness'. Minutes later the Ju 88s of the second raid split up, half diverting for an attack on Worthy Down while the rest continued on. At 5.50 p.m., 609 Squadron was scrambled. The Spitfires were hardly airborne when the bombers appeared overhead. Two stranded pilots ran to parked planes which had been earmarked for maintenance and took off just before the bombs began raining down.

In sharp contrast to the previous day's raid just after 234 Squadron had arrived, very little damage was done to the airfield. Likewise at Worthy Down and Oldham damage was negligible. On the other hand, 609 Squadron's pilots claimed one Ju 88 and four Me 109s destroyed plus three Ju 88s probables.

While this was happening, 234 Squadron had continued patrolling south of Swanage, flying in its usual formal tight formation of four sections in vics of three. The only person who did not have to concentrate on staying in position was Pat in the lead. Bob Doe was Pat's Number Two. They flew at the same height that they had been told the enemy was flying and proceeded to patrol up and down sun. Because of their lack of combat experience they were 'following the book' just as they had been trained. They did not yet realise that by doing so they were not only heading for the enemy in an inflexible, cramped formation; they were also leaving themselves open to attack from above and behind.

The inevitable happened. Coming around in another turn they suddenly became conscious that there were only nine Spitfires, not twelve! The rear vic of three, Red Section, had vanished. Then almost by surprise, they were in the middle of the German escort fighters, twin-engine Messerschmitt 110s and some stray Me 109s.

Pat, followed by Doe, turned after a 110 and, seizing a fleeting chance, he fired a short burst and broke away. To Doe it seemed to have little effect but then he closed in and fired in his turn. The rear gunner replied but the Messerschmitt was hit. With its engines alight the big fighter turned over and dived down towards the sea. Doe followed in the dive and when the fire coming from the engines seemed to wane he gave it another burst from 100 yards away, seven seconds this time. The gunner kept up his return fire until at around 1,000 feet he decided it was time to bail out. Doe kept watching the 110 until it plunged into the water.[3] He zoomed up again heading towards three Me 110s he spotted diving through thick haze at about 4,500 feet. Closing on the nearest aircraft, he fired the remainder of his ammunition and saw pieces fly off it as he broke away. Another Spitfire appeared, sweeping in to engage the same 110 which Doe had attacked. It was Blue 1 – Pat. The big heavy fighter caught fire and, like the other, it too crashed into the sea.[4]

It became a fast and brutal running battle as the Germans retreated out to sea. Budge Harker's Spitfire was hit in the tail before he could fire his guns in anger. He managed to nurse his damaged fighter back to Middle Wallop, some twenty-five miles, and land without further difficulty. Szlagowski's plane was also slightly damaged, but the Pole made it home as well.

In ones and twos the others returned, but some didn't. Mortimer-Rose was the only one back out of Red Section. Altogether, three were missing: Cecil Hight, one of the New Zealanders; Richard Hardy; and the Australian Bush Parker. Perhaps they had landed at another field. All that Pat and the others could do was await news of them. A report did come in about Cecil Hight, the leader of 'A' Flight's Yellow Section. He had been killed. He had run into trouble over Bournemouth and his Spitfire crashed at Walsford Road, Meyrick Park. About the other two, there was nothing. They had to remain as 'missing'. Nothing would be known about them for months.

In the running fight, Red Section had been overwhelmed by the enemy fighters. The Spitfire of Richard Hardy, Red 1, was hit probably by a cannon shell which hit struck the fuselage just behind the pilot's seat. Hardy was wounded in the shoulder. Short of fuel and far out to sea, he headed for France where he managed to land safely on Cherbourg-East/Theville airfield, much to the shock of those on the ground. He struggled out and surrendered to Hauptmann Rolf Pingel, *Staffel* Kapitan of 2/JG53, and was taken prisoner. Hardy would remain a POW until the end of the war. Red 2, Bush Parker, chased a Messerschmitt 110 low over the Channel and apparently fell victim to his intended target. Unteroffizier Willy Lehner, the radio operator/gunner to Leutnant Siegfried Hahn of *Stab II/ZG76*, reported he had shot down a Spitfire off Cherbourg before they themselves had to crash-land their damaged machine at Cherbourg-West. Parker bailed out into the sea near Cherbourg. He was rescued by a German boat after hours in the water.

Against these losses 234 Squadron claimed five Messerschmitt Me 110s destroyed and one Me 109 damaged. Pat Hughes and Bob Doe were credited with one Me 110 destroyed apiece and they shared the third; Mortimer-Rose destroyed one Me 110; Janusz Zurakowski, another new Polish pilot who had joined the squadron early in August, also destroyed one Me 110; and Ken Dewhurst damaged an Me 109.[5]

But the day's fighting was not over. A large force of Dornier Do 17s in several small formations aimed for Biggin Hill. It flew in over the coast of Kent at 6.20 p.m. with covering Messerschmitt 109s following.

To defend Biggin Hill 610 Squadron had eight serviceable Spitfires and 32 Squadron had nine Hurricanes. The controller ordered 610 Squadron off first and ten miles south-east of Biggin Hill they met the Dorniers and shot several down. Those that continued on attacked West Mailing by mistake. At the same time 32 Squadron was ordered up to orbit the airfield. From this position the Hurricane pilots could see a pall of smoke and dust to the west. Croydon was under heavy attack and they rushed there as fast as possible. Fifteen Messerschmitt 110s escorted by eight Me 109s made a highly effective hit-and-run attack on Croydon, the home of 111 Squadron. Sixty-eight people were killed, almost 200 injured and numerous buildings were damaged. Luckily, the nine Hurricanes of 111 Squadron had taken off moments before the bombing. They clawed for height and counter-attacked the German fighter-bombers which immediately formed a defensive circle.

At the same time 32 Squadron arrived and took on the 109s. Down below the 110s decided to make a run for it and broke out of their circle into small groups heading for cloud cover. It was the chance that 111 Squadron had been waiting for and they dived to give chase. Seven Me 110s were claimed shot down. Meanwhile, 266 Squadron from Hornchurch fell victim to Me 109s over Maidstone. One Spitfire was shot down and a second severely damaged.

Claims of the aircraft destroyed on this day were greatly exaggerated by both sides. The RAF claimed to have shot down 182 German aircraft while the Luftwaffe claimed eighty-two Hurricanes and Spitfires, five Curtiss Hawks and fourteen others. Clearly aircraft recognition was a problem for both sides. While in some areas RAF pilots saw Ju 88s and Dornier 215s where none were flying, the Curtiss Hawks claimed by the Luftwaffe did not exist. Post-war figures would put Luftwaffe losses at seventy-five and Fighter Command losses at thirty-four, with seventeen pilots killed and sixteen wounded. German airmen would remember this day as 'Black Thursday'.

Hermann Göring and his commanders had remained in conference for most of the day. At their meetings he demanded better bomber protection from his fighters, especially for the Stukas. He also suggested that there was not much value in continuing with attacks on the RDF sites because apparently none of them had been put out of action. This decision would prove to be a costly error.

*

It had all happened so suddenly. 'We're on the move again,' Pat had said on the phone. 'Lock up the house and get to the White Hart. Be there, now.'[6]

Kay Hughes had driven from Cornwall to meet him at the cosy little White Hart Hotel at Andover, not far from Middle Wallop airfield. It had been sad to leave the quiet seaside house near St Eval where they were to have spent their honeymoon. Pat had not even slept there a single night. He had only managed twenty-four hours' leave before he'd had to report to the squadron again. After they were married in the Bodmin Register Office at the beginning of August, they'd had their wedding night at a hotel in Newquay and then, for some reason, he'd had to go back.

Pat had not even been able to have a meal there. For Kay it was a lonely time. On a few occasions he had phoned ahead that he was bringing some of 'the boys' over, 'put the coffee on and get out a few beers.'[7] There would be a precious hour or two of fun, but then he would be gone again.

At least at the White Hart they could be together, but it had been a 'Black Thursday' for 234 Squadron too. Kay knew they had lost someone and could not hide her concern. 'Don't be so upset,' Pat had pleaded, 'it'll never happen to me.'[8]

10

16 AUGUST 1940

German air activity overnight was limited after Thursday's maximum effort, but incendiary bombs were dropped close to Middle Wallop aerodrome near the camp of the 18th Infantry Brigade, Australian Striking Force. There was no damage.

Troops of the Australian 6th Division, 2nd AIF, had been diverted to England from the third troop convoy from Australia bound for the Middle East. They had disembarked at Gourock on the Clyde on 17 June 1940. Three liners, the *Queen Mary*, *Mauretania* and *Empress of Canada*, carried around 8,000 officers and men, and three other vessels had transported a similar number of New Zealanders.

The following day, Major-General H. D. Wynter was appointed to command the Australian force in Britain, to be known as Australforce, as advanced units began to reach Salisbury Plain in southern England where they were to establish a base camp. The troops were transported from Gourock overnight by train. By 4.00 a.m., they were travelling through the Midlands – to pinpoint exactly where they were was impossible because the station signs had been painted over. Sometimes other troop trains passed going in the opposite direction. When they halted beside one stationary train, the Australians leaned from the windows to question the Tommies on board. One man who had recently returned from Dunkirk said he had not even seen a German soldier, only endless dive-bombers. His words gave the Australians a great deal to think about.

Wynter's headquarters was set up in Amesbury Abbey and Australforce was initially allocated several responsibilities: protection of Middle Wallop and Andover aerodromes from attack by German paratroops; local protection of the Salisbury Plain area; and creation of a mobile striking column in case of invasion.

On 13 July, just after 8 a.m., the Australians had their baptism of fire when a low-flying bomber, identified as a Dornier, strafed the 18th Infantry Brigade's camp. There was little damage and just one casualty, Private Albert Webb of the 2/10th Battalion who was wounded. He was shot through the buttock and groin. From Prospect, South Australia, Webb survived with the dubious honour of being the AIF's first battle casualty of the Second World War.

Recently, Wynter had received clarification of Australforce's role. The 18th Brigade, with artillery, the machine-gun battalion and other attached troops, would become the 'Southern Command Striking Force', should a mobile striking force be needed. His 25th Brigade would continue in the role of local protection in the Salisbury Plain area.[1]

The morning weather on Friday 16 August was fine and sunny but the Luftwaffe delayed launching attacks until 11 a.m., taking time to build some of its units which had suffered casualties back to strength. Several light raids were despatched against airfields in Norfolk, Kent and Greater London. Of these, only an attack on West Mailing airfield achieved any success.

In France, after spending the night at Cherbourg, Bush Parker was flown to *Dulag Luft* at Operursel. Here the Germans interrogated him and handed him false Red Cross forms to fill in. In accordance with the Geneva Convention, the Australian gave only his number, rank and name. He was then taken to the cells.

He would remain a prisoner until the end of the war, winding up incarcerated in Colditz Castle because of his many attempted escapes. In his book, *The Latter Days of Colditz*, Patrick Reid wrote of Bush Parker:

He might equally well have been called 'Fingers' Parker, for his wits and hands were as quick as lightning. He learned to handle locks with consummate skill. Bush was a colourful character ... Colditz would not have been quite what it was if Bush had not been there.

Colditz was the Australian's home for three years almost to the day. Liberated after the war, he decided to remain in the RAF having been promoted to flight lieutenant while a POW. Sadly, while serving with No. 56 Operational Training Unit at RAF Millfield, he was killed in a flying accident when his Hawker Tempest crashed at Felkington Farm, Duddo, near Berwick-upon-Tweed on 29 January 1946.[2]

*

Around 12.25 p.m., three heavy attacks built up. The first, a raid of fifty aircraft consisting of twenty-four Dornier Do 17s plus escorting Messerschmitt 109s, headed for the Thames Estuary. The second, comprising 150 aircraft, appeared off Dover while a third, estimated at one hundred aircraft, built up over Cherbourg and set course for the Portsmouth–Southampton area.

The first raid, apparently making for Hornchurch, was intercepted by Spitfires from 54 Squadron and turned back. The second raid crossed the coast near Dover and split up into several formations. To meet these widespread threats three squadrons of RAF fighters were scrambled. British tactics were for Hurricanes to engage the bombers while the Spitfires kept the escorts busy. The two Hurricane squadrons found several groups of Dorniers and charged in, using highly dangerous head-on attacks. For 111 Squadron it was a standard tactic to break enemy formations. The Hurricanes spread out in line abreast and charged, firing wildly. Several bombers were hit but there was a wrenching collision as a Hurricane and a Dornier met at a closing speed well over 500 mph! Both planes and their dead occupants crashed in flames.

266 Squadron found themselves trapped by Me 109s and outnumbered two to one. Five Spitfires were shot down and a sixth crash-landed near Faversham, but the bombing by the Dorniers was scattered and inaccurate.

The third raid consisted of over 100 Junkers Ju 87 Stukas and escorting Messerschmitt 109s followed by twelve Junkers Ju 88s and a *Staffel* of eighteen Me 110s. Over the Isle of Wight the Stukas split into four groups, the largest continuing on to Tangmere airfield while the others headed for Ventnor, Lees-on-Solent and Gosport. The Stukas approached Tangmere from the east and peeled off for a textbook attack but 601 Squadron was airborne and intercepted. The Hurricanes dived on them at well over 400 mph but serious damage was inflicted on Tangmere. Two hangars were destroyed and the other three were damaged. The station's workshops received direct hits. Six Blenheims of the Fighter Interception Unit (FIU) were destroyed on the ground and seven Hurricanes and one Miles Magister were damaged. Bristol Beaufighter R2055 of the FIU was damaged. It was the first night fighter of this type to be delivered to the RAF. Forty motor vehicles were either destroyed or damaged, and twenty people killed.

At the height of the attack a burning 601 Squadron Hurricane crash-landed on the aerodrome. Before the pilot could scramble out, the plane became an inferno. Courageous ground crewmen carried him to safety but his injuries were such that he died the next day.

As the Ju 87s tried to escape they were made to pay dearly. Many were shot down by the defending fighters. The CH radar station at Ventnor was practically flattened. Barely recovered from an attack on the 12th, it would be out of action for seven more days.

The last raid of Ju 88s and Me 110s headed for another naval airfield at Gosport. The force was met by three Hurricanes of 249 Squadron. The British fighters were overwhelmed by the escorting Messerschmitts.

In the late afternoon Kesselring's *Luftflotte* 2 and Sperrle's *Luftflotte* 3 launched three major bombing raids combined with 'free chases' by Messerschmitt 109s.

It was 65 Squadron's turn to operate from Manston. Near Deal they sighted sixty Ju 88s in close lines of six abreast 2,000 feet higher up. Around these were an estimated 200 German fighters. Deciding that it was impossible to attack the bombers, 65 Squadron climbed to a favourable position to engage the fighters. A twisting dogfight developed but suddenly the radio warned that enemy aircraft were over Chatham so some Spitfires set off in that direction. The same large formation of enemy bombers was still pressing relentlessly.

Eight Me 109s paid Manston yet another visit. They hurtled across the airfield, raking buildings and parked aircraft with cannon and machine-gun fire. One Spitfire and a 600 Squadron Blenheim night fighter were destroyed and a second Blenheim damaged.

The Hurricanes of 32 Squadron were airborne for their fourth patrol and at 5.30 p.m., over Biggin Hill, they encountered over thirty Ju 88s escorted by Me 110s, all flying in the opposite direction. They sprayed as many bombers as they could with bullets until their ammunition was used up. After their four patrols the squadron was able to claim nine enemy aircraft destroyed.

The twelve Spitfires of 234 Squadron were scrambled again at 5.25 p.m. and Pat was Cressy leader. At 6.15 p.m. they were patrolling south of the Isle of Wight when Pat spotted about fifty Me 109s circling 4,000 feet above. They were in a dangerous position. Ordering his sections into line astern, he led them up to attack. The 109s formed a circle. Pat fired a deflection shot at the nearest which was on the tail of another Spitfire. It immediately caught fire and blew up in front of them.

Suddenly his plane was jolted and, reacting quickly, he threw it into a sharp turn to find a 109 on his tail. Pat chased after it as it tried to climb away right in front of him. This only succeeded in presenting the Australian with an easy target. His burst struck the 109 behind the cockpit and the German fighter burst into flames and crashed into the sea. Immediately afterwards Pat found four Ju 87s heading south and set off in pursuit. As he attacked, his Spitfire shuddered again as its tailplane was heavily damaged by cannon fire from yet another Messerschmitt. His Spitfire went into a dive and his attacker overshot. Pat was able to turn onto its tail and fire but after only a quarter of a second his machine guns fell silent. Out of ammunition! He broke away and fortunately his Spitfire was still flyable. He'd had a lucky escape.

Back at Middle Wallop Pat was credited with two Me 109s destroyed. After inspection his plane, Spitfire R6896, was pronounced able to be repaired. The squadron claimed six destroyed altogether for the loss of two, but this time both of the pilots were safe. Credited with victories besides Pat were Bob Doe with an Me 109 and a stray Dornier Do 18 he'd encountered low over the Channel; Pat Horton (the New Zealander from Dunedin who had been partly educated at the Hutchings School in Hobart), one Me 109; and Zygmunt 'Ziggy' Klein, another of the new Polish pilots, one more Me 109. Dewhurst had bailed out over Gosport and landed safely near Widley, and Connor had parachuted over the sea during a dogfight with 109s off Portsmouth. He was rescued by a naval launch and taken to Haslar Naval Hospital. He would not be returning to the squadron as he would remain there in hospital for two months – but at least he was safe.[3]

Nightfall brought much needed rest for both sides. After 'Stand Down' at Biggin Hill, the pilots on learning that two captured German aviators were being held prisoner in the guard room decided to entertain them. They were brought into the mess for a drink. At first one German remained aloof and somewhat angry because he, an officer, had been imprisoned under the command of a sergeant of the RAF police. After a few drinks he began to relax.

The airmen of 266 Squadron at Hornchurch were not in the mood for celebration. They had lost five Spitfires and a sixth was badly damaged. The commanding officer and two others had been killed and two more injured.

At Middle Wallop, although 234 Squadron had been shaken up by the events of the past two days, in the bar of the White Hart the pilots were tired but full of bravado: 'Good show, Pat! How many did you get today?'[4] Pat had been affected more than he showed. His plane had been shot up, and he had missed death by inches. That night privately to Kay he said as if joking, 'In case of accidents make sure you marry again.'[5]

Across the Channel, the Luftwaffe was licking its wounds too. Replacement aircraft and personnel were urgently needed. After the maximum effort and strenuous combat of the last few days, the crews needed rest. Because of this German night raids were greatly reduced.

In contrast, RAF Bomber Command was very active overnight. One hundred and fifty bombers were dispatched to targets in Germany and Holland.

11

18 AUGUST 1940

It was 1.59 p.m. when Poling RDF station near Littlehampton on the south coast picked up the first echoes. They were coming from north of Cherbourg. Soon a slow-moving formation estimated at a strength of 'eighty plus' was reported incoming – obviously the bombers. There were smaller groups of 'twenty plus', 'twelve plus' and 'nine plus' moving along with it. Another formation of 'ten plus' aircraft was plotted coming from Le Havre. The smaller ones had to be the escorting fighters. Altogether, the RDF operators estimated that the incoming raid was made up of about 150 aircraft. They were wrong. Within minutes these plots were passed through the Fighter Command filter room and then to the operations rooms of the commands defending England's south coast: No. 10 Group at Box in Wiltshire and No. 11 Group at Uxbridge in Middlesex. It looked like the raiders might be moving towards the Solent to repeat the attack made on Tangmere airfield two days ago when the Stukas had caused so much damage.

To meet the threat, the two fighter group controllers now sprang into action to deploy their squadrons. In the No. 10 Group area:

152 Squadron from Warmwell with eleven Spitfires was ordered to patrol over Portsmouth and wait for instructions;

From Exeter, 213 Squadron with twelve Hurricanes was ordered to move eighty miles to the east and patrol over St Catherine's point; and 234 Squadron up from Middle Wallop with twelve Spitfires was directed to move south of the Isle of Wight to meet the incoming raiders.

In addition, 609 Squadron's twelve Spitfires were to remain on the ground in reserve at Middle Wallop, their pilots waiting impatiently for an order to scramble.

In No. 11 Group's area, eleven Hurricanes from 601 Squadron from Tangmere were already airborne on patrol over their home base. To reinforce them:

Nine Hurricanes from 43 Squadron, which was also based at Tangmere, were scrambled and ordered to patrol over the Coastal Command airfield at Thorney Island and await instructions.

602 Squadron with twelve Spitfires was instructed to patrol over its base at Westhampnett. After five days almost continuously at readiness for sixteen

hours per day, this squadron had been released from operations for the afternoon, but just as the pilots were settling down to relax they were ordered to take off again as soon as possible! Now they too were waiting for the next instructions.

*

The weather that Sunday had been fine early on, but as the day progressed it clouded over. Fighter Command had already been busy although not in 10 Group's area. At first, the Luftwaffe had sent over a few high-flying reconnaissance aircraft to check on conditions and discover which RAF forward airfields were still occupied by fighters. The real action had started just after midday in the south-east when Dover RDF reported a huge build-up of enemy aircraft.

No. 11 Group brought every serviceable fighter to 'Readiness'. Airfields to the south and south-east of London were being targeted. These included Kenley, Croydon, West Malling and Biggin Hill. The intention of the Luftwaffe was to deliver a one-two punch in their attacks. Trying to catch the defences by surprise, two groups of bombers, one flying at medium altitude and a smaller formation coming in fast and low, were to hit the targeted airfields almost simultaneously. Fighters still on the ground at Kenley were ordered off in a 'survival scramble'. Aircraft able to fly but not fight were directed northwest to safety. Twelve Hurricanes from 111 Squadron already airborne from Croydon were ordered to assemble over Kenley and provide cover.

The German plan miscued. Two raids of escorted Dornier Do 17s came in at 1.30 p.m., but the fifty bombers at medium altitude meant to strike first were late. 111 Squadron intercepted the low formation and a frantic full-throttle chase ensued. German and British aircraft all hurtled into the light flak and machine-gun fire from the airfield's defences. One Hurricane was hit – return fire from Dornier gunners or flak, who could tell? It crashed. The other Hurricanes hastily broke away to clear the ground fire and sped to the northern side of the airfield to catch the bombers as they emerged. One Dornier attracted concentrated anti-aircraft crossfire and crashed. A second bomber fell too and most of the others suffered damage. When the Dorniers cleared the flak, 111 Squadron swept in again. A frenzied low-level chase began. More were shot down until, one by one, the British fighters ran out of ammunition and turned back. Three Hurricanes were lost.

As the Dorniers were attacking Kenley, sixty Heinkel He 111s supported by forty Me 109s made a bomb-run on Biggin Hill untroubled by either defending fighters or flak. Shortly beforehand, 32 and 610 Squadrons had been scrambled so they were already well clear and clawing for height. One bomb fell squarely on the airfield's motor transport sheds and another exploded close to a Bofors gun, killing one man and wounding others. After a mad head-on attack through the Heinkels, the British fighters pulled up steeply, turned back and gave chase. The withdrawing Germans had to run a gauntlet of angry Hurricanes and Spitfires ordered to cut them off, but the weather was in their favour. Thickening haze made it difficult for the British fighters to make a concentrated counter-attack.

With the Biggin Hill raid over, personnel were organised to fill in the many bomb craters pockmarking the field. Unexploded bombs were marked with red flags until a bomb disposal squad could arrive. The effort was only briefly interrupted as the returning fighters landed carefully, snaking their way between the craters and red flags.

Kenley had suffered most. The damage to Biggin Hill was superficial and only a few bombs had been dropped on West Malling and Croydon.

It was now south and south-west England's turn to face the onslaught – and an onslaught it was. The attack was made up of the largest concentration of Junkers 87 Stuka dive-bombers so far deployed: the whole of Dive Bomber *Geschwader 77*, four *Gruppen* strong with a total of 109 aircraft. Their targets were the airfields at Gosport, Ford and Thorney Island, and the radar station at Poling. Each Stuka carried a 550 lb bomb under the fuselage, plus four 110 lb bombs under the wings.

The Stukas were crossing the English Channel in one huge formation, supported by no fewer than 157 Me 109s. Acting as close escorts were seventy Messerschmitts from *JG 27*, and thirty-two from *JG 53*. In addition, fifty-five Me 109s of *JG 2* were coming independently from Le Havre for a sweep over the Portsmouth area to catch the flushed out British fighters.

To face this formidable total array of 266 enemy aircraft, not the 150 estimated, the RAF deployed sixty to seventy Hurricanes and Spitfires. Added to them from the Coastal Command airfield at Thorney Island, a detached flight of Blenheim If fighters from 235 Squadron was scrambled to assist. There were two Blenheim units stationed here, 59 Squadron with bombers and the detached flight from 235 Squadron.

Realising the main weight of the German attack was coming in east of the Isle of Wight and over Selsey Bill, Tangmere Control ordered 601 Squadron there. A few minutes later part of the Stuka formation with its escorting fighters broke away and headed north-west. This was the *Gruppe* making for Gosport. As the main Stuka formation reached Selsey Bill, another *Gruppe* broke off for the attack on Thorney Island. The remaining two dive-bomber *Gruppen* swung north-east, heading for Poling and Ford. To bomb accurately, the Stukas had to attack directly into wind which was blowing from the south-west. They had to split up to come in from north-east of each of their targets.

Around the dive-bombers, the escorting Me 109s began accelerating to fighting speed. To avoid overshooting and speeding away from their charges, they had to zigzag to maintain their relative positions. Meanwhile, the fifty-five Messerschmitts from Le Havre were moving in for their free hunt.

By 2.30 p.m., it was all happening: thirty-one Ju 87s were in the process of bombing Poling RDF station; twenty-eight Ju 87s were bombing the airfield at Ford, but the Spitfires of 602 Squadron had sighted them and were moving in to attack; twenty-eight Ju 87s had started their attack on the airfield at Thorney Island, but they and their escorting Me 109s had been intercepted by Hurricanes from 43 and 601 Squadrons and were involved in a running fight; the *Gruppe* comprised of twenty-two Ju 87s was moving into position to attack the airfield at Gosport, but their Me 109 escorts were about to pounce on the Spitfires of 234 Squadron; and the Spitfires of 152 Squadron were moving across to the Isle of Wight to be in a position to engage the raiders as they withdrew.

234 Squadron had a new commanding officer. Squadron Leader Joseph Somerton O'Brien DFC had taken over just the day before. Previously, he had been attached to 92 Squadron at Pembrey in South Wales. Joe O'Brien's father had been an army officer, a major, who was killed in France in 1917, and as a young man Joe had actually sought a career in the Merchant Navy. He did spend several years at sea before joining the RAF on a short service commission in January 1934. After his flying training, he was posted to 3 Squadron at Kenley on 16 March 1935. The squadron flew Bristol Bulldogs and deployed to the Middle East in September where it was stationed in the Sudan during the Abyssinian crisis. It returned to the UK in August 1936. Meanwhile, O'Brien had been transferred to 23 Squadron which he joined at Wittering in Northamptonshire on 9 July 1936. The squadron had a mixture of Hawker Harts and Demons but in December 1938 began to convert to Bristol Blenheim Ifs.

On 9 June 1940, O'Brien was ordered to take charge of the Operations Room at RAF Pembrey, north-west of Swansea, as a newly promoted squadron leader. It was while here that he had joined 92 (Spitfire) Squadron as a supernumerary on the first day of July. The *London Gazette* of 30 July recorded that he had been awarded the DFC. He was married and the father of a young daughter.[1] It was O'Brien who led 234 Squadron's twelve Spitfires off from Middle Wallop at 2.20 p.m. on the afternoon of 18 August. Pat, in command of 'B' Flight, led Blue Section in Spitfire X4036. As they climbed they were ordered to move out south of the Isle of Wight to intercept the incoming raid.

At 2.55 p.m., as they flew over the Isle of Wight at 16,000 feet, they spotted around twenty of the escorting Me 109s above, apparently stalking them. The German fighters held all the advantages: superior numbers, greater height, and the sun at their backs. For the Spitfires it was a case of either facing the enemy and counter-attacking, or waiting to be attacked. There was no hesitation. The Spitfires climbed to face the 109s and by doing so they presented the Germans with the smallest possible targets – targets that were bristling to fight back.

Pat opened fire at a Messerschmitt from about 150 yards but did not cause any obvious damage. He was not able see what happened to it next because another pair of aggressive Me 109s turned their attention onto him. Suddenly he was much too busy to keep tabs on the first German fighter. One of the two Messerschmitts shot at Pat from extreme range so he turned and counterattacked this machine, sending off an aggressive two-second burst. This time the result was immediate – the 109 caught fire. As it fell burning, Pat could not watch this plane go down either because the second German in the pair immediately launched his own attack. After firing, this second attacker zoomed up and away and then, apparently assuming he was safe, began to dive.

Pat followed until the 109 started to level out. By now they were down to about 10,000 feet. The instant he saw his chance, Pat pounced. He went in close again as usual and pressed the firing button twice to deliver two-second bursts from just thirty yards away. The German fighter caught fire; with his aircraft crippled, the German pilot jumped. His parachute opened and floated down onto the Isle of Wight. A few seconds later the burning Me 109 crashed nearby. As Pat circled watching, he noticed flames and another cloud of smoke rising a short distance off the island that appeared to be the wreckage of the first Messerschmitt he had sent down burning.[2]

A short time later all of 234 Squadron's Spitfires were back on the ground at Middle Wallop – no losses. It was a brilliantly satisfying day for the squadron and a gratifying first combat mission for the new CO. The keeper of the Operations Record Book recorded:

One interception scramble by 12 aircraft against large raid approaching, S/Ldr O'Brien claimed 1 Me 109 probable, F/Lt Hughes destroyed 2 Me 109, P/O Doe 1 Me109 confirmed and 1 Me 109 damaged, P/O Mortimer-Rose destroyed 1 Me 109 and destroyed another. P/O Gordon and Sgt Bailey each damaged 1 Me 109, Sgt Harker destroyed 2 Me 109.[3]

While 234 Squadron battled the Messerschmitts, the Stukas were being mauled by the other British fighters. Altogether, the RAF fighter squadrons claimed thirty-four of these gull-winged dive-bombers destroyed and the anti-aircraft gunners claimed two more. After the war this figure was revealed to be greatly exaggerated. Of the 109 Stukas involved in the four attacks, fifteen had been lost and one was damaged beyond repair. Another six Stukas returned to France with varying degrees of damage but they could be repaired. Eight Me 109s were shot down with three of the pilots killed, three taken prisoner and two rescued from the sea. For these results in the air, Fighter Command lost five aircraft and seven were damaged. Two pilots were killed and three wounded. The magnitude of the achievement, although much less than that it was thought at the time, was still significant. Because of their vulnerability when confronted by serious opposition like Hurricanes and Spitfires, the Luftwaffe was forced to reassess the chances of its Stuka dive-bombers surviving in English skies.

However, despite their losses in the air, the Luftwaffe's bombing did cause considerable damage and many casualties on the ground. The attack on Ford rendered the airfield practically out of use until it was handed over to the RAF in September. At Thorney Island and Gosport the airfields were still able to be used, but with reduced facilities. The long-range warning RDF station at Poling was put out of action.

Tactically, however, the raids this day did not contribute to the enemy's primary aim of knocking RAF Fighter Command out of the air as the necessary prelude to mounting an invasion. None of the airfields that were attacked were used by Fighter Command. In that sense, it had been a wasted effort at terrible cost.

Gosport housed an RN torpedo development unit. The airfield at Thorney was Island Coastal Command, where three aircraft on the ground were destroyed and a visiting Wellington bomber damaged. Its flight of Blenheim fighters had been scrambled and was unscathed. The Fleet Air Arm Station at Ford, HMS *Peregrine*, where there had been only six post-mounted Lewis-guns for defence, had suffered the greatest damage, but it was actually the base at which 829 Squadron was working up with their new Fairey Albacore torpedo-bomber, the latest to enter service for RN aircraft carriers. It was also the home of the navy's air observers' training school.

As for the long-range warning RDF station at Poling, its loss was only temporary and caused relatively few problems. The Chain Home Low (CHL) RDF station which was also located there for detecting incoming low-flying aircraft was still operational and it could 'see' out over the English Channel almost as far. Moreover, seventy miles along the coast on either side of Poling there were six other RDF stations providing interlocking coverage. The enemy had failed to punch a hole in the network through which German aircraft could slip by undetected. Within a couple of days a mobile RDF station was erected in the nearby woods and this supplemented coverage of the area until the main set at Poling could be repaired.

A final Luftwaffe assault for the day developed in the south-east around 5 p.m., but it involved neither 234 Squadron nor No. 10 Group. RDF detected five separate German formations converging on Kent but for the most part they were engaged successfully by Hurricanes from North Weald and Spitfires from Hornchurch. The bombing was reported to be inaccurate and was widely scattered over Kent and Surrey.

What was becoming an increasingly more serious problem for Fighter Command was the mounting pilot losses – men put out of action, either killed or wounded. More pilots were being lost than could be replaced and many of these men were veterans with invaluable combat experience. To boost numbers, the pilot training programme was shortened, but this resulted in replacements coming through inexperienced and therefore more vulnerable – and there were not enough of them. The Air Ministry had already circulated a request throughout the other RAF commands calling for volunteers to fly fighters. These men were beginning to arrive, some of them veterans who had flown Fairey Battle light bombers during the fighting in France. But the question was: would there be enough of them to redress the balance?

That night, to maintain the pressure, the Luftwaffe sent about fifty bombers over England to carry out widespread nuisance raids. They also laid mines in the Thames Estuary and Bristol Channel.

12

26 AUGUST 1940

With the arrival of fine weather on Saturday 24 August, both sides readied for the main event. Most historians agree that this day marked the beginning of the most critical phase of the Battle of Britain. It was time for the Luftwaffe to devote its entire energy into the destruction of RAF Fighter Command if it was to gain air supremacy before the invasion.

The early morning was fine and cloudless. At 11 a.m., a large build-up of aircraft was detected moving from Cap Gris Nez but the Germans were adopting a new tactic to keep the British guessing. About twenty miles out to sea they turned and maintained a constant stream of aircraft flying parallel to the Sussex coast. Occasionally these planes turned in towards England but they were only feints to attract the RAF fighters up from their bases and make them waste precious fuel. These feints then turned quickly back to leave the British planes hopelessly out of position. Then, while the Hurricanes and Spitfires were returning to base to refuel, a real attack began.

Out of this confusing mass, a raid by forty bombers escorted by over sixty fighters materialised and dropped bombs on Dover. The fighter escort was packed so tightly around the Dornier Do 17s and Junkers Ju 88s that British fighters that did intercept had great difficulty breaking through. The Germans retired almost unscathed.

Meanwhile, the British made their own tactical blunders. Defiants of 264 Squadron were deployed into Hornchurch, a Spitfire base in 11 Group. There were no personnel there who were experienced in maintaining Defiants and no stores or spare parts for them. Over Dunkirk 246 Squadron had achieved outstanding results but at the time its Defiants had been mistaken for Hurricanes and been attacked from behind directly into their power-operated four-gun turrets.

Mistake followed mistake. The squadron was ordered forward to operate from, of all places, a patched-up Manston airfield, where the least warnings, wild scrambles, and zooming, full-throttle climbs for height were the expected norm. Defiants were slow-climbing two-seaters requiring time for the crew to board and, once aloft, time to form up for a formation attack. They were simply not suitable for such a place.

Just after midday the Defiants were being refuelled when a warning was given of enemy aircraft approaching. Nine of the turreted fighters scrambled, the last leaving the ground as the first bombs exploded. Caught low, they were at the mercy of the escorting Me 109s. Three Defiants were lost before (fortunately for them) a Hurricane squadron operating in the area intervened. The survivors made their way back to Hornchurch.

At 3.30 p.m. another large raid built up over Le Havre, crossed the Channel and bombed Manston again. The Germans found so much smoke and dust had been created by the first bombing wave that they were unable to clearly identify their target. Nevertheless, to the hardworking ground personnel trying to affect repairs after the earlier attack, this new bombing was the last straw as the grounds were rendered virtually useless.

At the same time, another large raid winged its way to targets north of the Thames Estuary where Hornchurch and North Weald came under attack. The commander of 11 Group, AVM Keith Park, realised that because all his squadrons were engaged his airfields were vulnerable. He requested air cover from 12 Group but, apart from six cannon-armed Spitfires from 19 Squadron, no help arrived.

At Hornchurch, the Defiant crews had just finished lunch when they were ordered to scramble as they had at Manston a few hours before. Again, the last plane was just airborne as the bombs began falling. Unable to form up for their own defence, the Defiants had no chance of reaching the bombers at 12,000 feet. While Hornchurch was under attack, about twenty bombers arrived over North Weald and unloaded. Nine people were killed and ten wounded.

Keith Park was bitterly angry over 12 Group's failure to arrive. AVM Leigh-Mallory had ordered his squadrons up but they had instructions to assemble into a wing over Duxford first. In doing so they lost precious time and arrived too late to help.

At 3.40 p.m., Ventnor RDF station, now repaired with new equipment but experiencing teething difficulties, plotted enemy aircraft approaching the Isle of Wight. The British fighters were scrambled late, due in part to the Luftwaffe's confusing patrolling tactics. An error in judging the enemy's height caused controllers to order their interceptors to fly too low in anticipation of meeting Stuka dive-bombers once again. They were unaware that the Ju 87s had been withdrawn from the fighting.

Up from Middle Wallop, 609 Squadron found itself over the Isle of Wight, 5,000 feet directly below the enemy aircraft. Fortunately, the German escorts were not particularly aggressive and 609 managed to extricate itself from the situation with only two Spitfires damaged.

Likewise scrambled late to intercept the raid approaching Portsmouth, 234 Squadron clashed with the escorting fighters. The CO, Joe O'Brien; Bill Gordon, a Scotsman from Aberdeen; and one of the Poles, Ziggy Olenski were all credited with Me 109s destroyed, and Kiwi Keith Lawrence damaged an Me 110.[1]

A flight of three Blenheims from 235 Squadron led by Fred Flood from Roma, Queensland, in his usual machine, 'Buskarlet's Brig', was up to defend its base at Thorney Island but the German bombers, fifty Ju 88s of *LG1*, continued to Portsmouth and dropped over 200 bombs, causing considerable damage to naval installations and the city. 104 civilians were killed and 237 injured. There were fifty casualties among the naval personnel.

Just after 5.00 p.m., Flood's three Blenheims were patrolling over the Solent when they were suddenly attacked by fighters and faced with the shocking realisation that their opponents were Hurricanes. A patrol from 1 Squadron RCAF had mistaken the Blenheims for Ju 88s – not a difficult thing to do because from some angles the two types looked similar. One Blenheim was riddled by bullets and its crew killed – it plummeted down into the sea. A second had to crash-land. Through violent evasive manoeuvres, Flood managed to evade the Hurricanes and escape with his aircraft only slightly damaged.[2]

The British defences were heavily punished. Results in the air for the Luftwaffe showed that, while providing close escort for the bombers was unpopular with the fighter pilots, it had been successful in creating difficulty for the British to break through. The downside was that although bomber losses had lessened fighter losses were correspondingly higher. The Luftwaffe had lost thirty-eight aircraft to RAF Fighter Command's twenty-two.

Damaging for the RAF was the defeat of the Defiants. They had been revealed again to be useless as front-line, anti-bomber day fighters. Worse still, there were signs of a serious rift developing between the British commanders. Keith Park was highly critical of 12 Group's inability to back up his 11 Group.

An event occurred overnight that would have great significance later. In the evening the Luftwaffe continued its pressure by sending over more than 150 bombers to various targets in Kent, Sussex and Surrey. Some were directed to bomb Rochester and the Thameshaven oil tanks. Because of a mistake in navigation, bombers instructed to hit the oil tanks strayed over London and dropped their bombs on the city itself. Adolf Hitler had specifically ordered that London was not to be bombed. This, the first raid on the British capital since 1918, although unintended, set in motion a chain of events that would completely change the course of the battle.

On Sunday 25 August, fine weather continued over southern and eastern England. The Luftwaffe continued its tactic of flying formations of planes along the coast and making occasional feints to keep the RAF on its toes, but this time it did not initiate any major raids. All the squadrons of 11 Group had to be held at 'Available'.

It was not until mid-afternoon that a change in the enemy's pattern of operations was detected. Ventnor RDF picked up several groups of aircraft building up west of Cherbourg Peninsula. It reported a raid of over 100 aircraft approaching Weymouth Bay. So that the previous day's mistakes would not be repeated – the defending fighters being caught too low – the squadrons at Tangmere, Exeter, Warmwell and Middle Wallop were scrambled as early as possible.

There were actually over 300 German planes in the air. As they arrived over Weymouth, the German force split into three major formations to target Portland, Weymouth and Warmwell.

The Portland force was met by twelve Hurricanes of 87 Squadron across from Exeter and twelve Spitfires of 609 Squadron. The Hurricanes attacked the bombers while the Spitfires took on the fighters. John Curchin sent a Messerschmitt 109 down in flames.[3] Meanwhile, 234 Squadron was held back to patrol over Middle Wallop in case the airfield was a target. It was not touched.

Only seven bombers managed to reach Warmwell but they did cause heavy damage by hitting two hangars and the sick quarters. They also scored an unseen tactical success with almost all of the telephone lines being severed – communications would not be restored until midday the next day – and again the presence of an overwhelming number of escort fighters effectively reduced bomber casualties. Of the twelve planes lost by *Luftflotte 3* only one was a bomber.

After dark, 103 aircraft from RAF Bomber Command carried out raids on Germany and France. For half of these the nominated target was Berlin. The previous night's bombing of London had provoked Prime Minister Winston Churchill into ordering an immediate reprisal raid. It was a hasty and ill-conceived attack involving return flights of up to eight and nine hours for the bomber crews. On reaching the target, they found Berlin covered by thick cloud, making bombing highly inaccurate. Most crews saw no results because of the murk below. Records for that night indicate that just two people were slightly injured. On their homecoming flights, the bombers encountered strong headwinds that particularly affected the Hampdens which were operating at the furthermost limit of their range. Six were lost, three of them running out of fuel and having to ditch into the sea.

However, like the bombing of London the previous night, despite the raid's lack of military success its political consequences would be far-reaching.

Weather conditions were still good for flying the following day, Monday 26 August, and the Luftwaffe continued flying bogus sorties up and down the English Channel to keep the RAF guessing. The first real raid was directed against Biggin Hill in Kent and Kenley in Surrey at 11 a.m. It crossed the coast north of Dover. While the main group continued westward, a small force broke away and bombed Folkestone. At the same time, a few Me 109s carried out low-level strafing attacks on targets of opportunity in East Kent and others shot up the Dover balloon barrage.

More than seventy British fighters were scrambled to intercept. Spitfires of 616 Squadron from Kenley were suddenly bounced by thirty Messerschmitts. The squadron was taken completely by surprise and its two weavers were shot down. Overwhelmed by the odds, five Spitfires were lost.

The Defiants of 264 Squadron were hard hit again. While taking on a formation of twelve Dorniers over Herne Bay they were jumped by the escorting Me 109s. Two Defiants were shot down, a third crash-landed and a fourth was badly damaged but managed to land safely.

This time, the Defiants of 264 Squadron and the Spitfires of 616 Squadron were not sacrificed in vain because their engagements had drawn away the German escort fighters. Hurricanes and Spitfires from other squadrons were able to break into the main bomber force, inflicting casualties and turning it away from Biggin Hill. The Germans jettisoned their bombs as they withdrew towards France.

The second German raid was in the early afternoon with orders to attack the Essex airfields at Hornchurch and Debden. Judging by its size and direction that the attack would be very heavy, AVM Park again requested 12 Group to cover his northern airfields, and ordered up all of his own available squadrons. Park's squadrons engaged the escorts early and succeeded in drawing them away from the bombers, leaving many without cover.

The bombers split into two groups. One group of forty Do 17s and forty Me 110s headed for Debden while the remainder turned towards Hornchurch. As each proceeded to its target, more British fighters pounced and the flak became heavier. The harassed Me 109s were already running low on fuel and began turning back. The Hornchurch force found itself virtually without cover and several Dorniers were shot down. Realising they would be cut to pieces if they continued, the entire formation wheeled around and withdrew. The other Dorniers heading north for Debden met heavy flak too and also ran into a barrier of defending Hurricanes and Spitfires. They too were obliged to turn back, except for a dozen or so that did manage to reach the airfield. This two-pronged attack had been foiled.

Meanwhile, Park was furious that Leigh-Mallory's 12 Group had failed again to protect his airfields. Spitfires from Duxford that were meant to cover Debden did not arrive until long after the Dorniers had gone.

At 4 p.m. *Luftflotte 3* despatched fifty Heinkel He 111s against Portsmouth and Warmwell aerodrome in Dorset. Escort was provided by over 100 Messerschmitt Me 110s and Me 109s. Park's 11 Group sent up five squadrons while AVM Brand scrambled another three from his 10 Group.

234 Squadron took off from Middle Wallop with Pat again as Cressy leader. Once airborne it was ordered to Portsmouth. Thirty minutes later, over the south of the Isle of Wight, the Spitfires met eight Me 109s at 16,000 feet but they could also see another group of thirty others about 2,000 feet higher up and three miles behind. Were the eight in front intended as decoys?

Pat ordered his section into line astern and attacked the leading eight, all of which appeared to have red spinners. The Messerschmitts immediately split up into sections of two. Pat closed in on the leading pair until he was a distance of fifty yards from the rear machine before he pressed the button on his spade grip for five seconds. The 109 caught fire under the concentrated deluge of .303 bullets and plunged down vertically.

The leading Me 109 had meantime gained height quickly but Pat was fully prepared for it as it attacked him from above. When he turned tightly to face it, the German fighter immediately dived away. Pat followed. As it pulled out of its dive, Pat caught up and fired a long burst from dead astern. The Messerschmitt started to burn but still managed to keep flying. Although he was now out of ammunition, Pat continued to follow and a few minutes later he saw the pilot bail out. The German pilot splashed down near what appeared to be an auxiliary launch. It was painted dark grey and blue and opened fire at Pat's circling Spitfire. At the same time it moved to recover the man in the water. Pat climbed away to return to Middle Wallop but then spotted more Me 109s heading towards him fast. They were probably low on fuel and intent on reaching home. As the gap between them closed rapidly, one Messerschmitt fired a snap burst from maximum range but missed. Pat could not reply. They loomed up in front and then hurtled past on their way back to France.[4]

While this was happening, three squadrons of Hurricanes and Spitfires intercepted the German bombers and, after shooting down at least four Heinkels, succeeded in turning them back.

As well as Pat's brace of Messerschmitts, Bob Doe, Bill Hornby, Pat Horton and Edward Mortimer-Rose had all accounted for one Me 109 apiece, and better still there had been no losses.[5]

That night, the Luftwaffe carried out scattered raids around Bournemouth and Coventry, and approximately fifty bombers made a sustained assault on Plymouth. The bombing lasted for seven hours but RAF Mount Batten, located on Plymouth Sound and home to 10 Squadron RAAF, was not damaged. Many bombs fell into the Sound itself but none of the Sunderland flying boats moored there were hit.

Across in Cornwall at St Eval, a decoy aerodrome had been constructed and several German bombers were attracted to the spot by a false flare path. They dropped sixty-two bombs onto open heath.

Tuesday morning broke dull and hazy. Central and eastern England had light rain with cloud in the English Channel and haze over the Straits of Dover. No major raids developed. Action by the Luftwaffe was devoted to small attacks and photographic reconnaissance missions mainly from Southampton to Portsmouth by single aircraft at very high altitude to assess the damage done so far.

Taking advantage of the lull, AVM Park issued more instructions to his controllers. He began by thanking AVM Brand's 10 Group for its help in covering the Portsmouth area but then followed up with an attack on 12 Group for its lack of cooperation. On two occasions when 12 Group had been requested to cover 11 Group's aerodromes, they had failed to do so and the airfields had been bombed. He directed that from now on 11 Group controllers were to put their requests for 12 Group's assistance to the Fighter Command controller. These orders brought the friction between himself and AVM Leigh-Mallory into the open. Leigh-Mallory fostered the idea of operating a large wing against large-scale enemy raids instead of using Park's tactic of sending squadrons up singly or in pairs. In fact, Park's tactics were the result of necessity. He simply did not have time to assemble three or more squadrons into a wing before vectoring them after the enemy – an enemy that would already be spreading out in various directions. This big wing argument would be expressed with increasing bitterness as the battle progressed.

The German tactics of splitting their formations once they passed the English coastline were difficult to counteract because they consistently confused the defences as they spread out. The outward-facing RDF could no longer track their progress. From then on the defences had to rely solely upon reports from the Observers' Corps. It became practically impossible to guide defending fighters onto the enemy formations the further they dispersed. Often up to two-thirds of the fighters did not manage to engage. Park instructed his squadron leaders and flight commanders who did make contact to pass a proper sighting report back to their controllers before they engaged.

Another warning issued by Park was not to engage in battle unless there were bombers in the enemy formation. The RAF could not afford to lose fighters and pilots wastefully in fighter versus fighter combat. When battle was joined, ideally the higher performance Spitfires were to engage the escorting fighters while the Hurricane squadrons attacked the bombers.

With over 80 per cent of the Luftwaffe's Messerschmitt Me 109s now concentrated in the Pas de Calais area under Kesselring's command, there was always a likelihood that raids from this direction could be fighter sweeps to be avoided.

In the evening scattered enemy raids came in from Cherbourg. The RAF replied with patrols by Blenheim night fighters, two-seater Defiants and even single-seater fighters. At Middle Wallop, 234 Squadron's pilots with night-flying experience were rostered for 'cat's eyes' patrols in their Spitfires. Spitfires, and to a slightly lesser extent Hurricanes, were not good for night fighting. Flames from the engine exhaust stacks in front could too easily render the pilot's night vision almost useless and some felt that they had an uncomfortably long landing run which seemed even longer at night.

Every evening underlined the ineffectiveness of the British night defences. On 28/29 August, out of five Blenheim night-fighter squadrons that flew more than eighty sorties, only one Blenheim even sighted an enemy raider. The pilot pushed the throttles wide, manoeuvred into position behind the German bomber and fired a long burst. The startled bomber immediately dived away. It was too fast for the poor old Blenheim to catch. All the night-fighter pilot could do was watch as it quickly melted into the dark.

Liverpool received the first of four consecutive night raids. It was the city's heaviest attack so far and the dock area suffered widespread damage. There were more than 470 casualties.

During the day, the few remaining Defiants of 264 Squadron left Hornchurch bound for Kirton-on-Lindsey. They were being withdrawn from day fighting and were led out by a twenty-year-old pilot officer, the only experienced man remaining. The effects of combat and stress were clearly evident.

Across the Channel, German intelligence noted that the English fighters were avoiding combat and deduced that the RAF was weakening.

Meanwhile, the night raids were having an effect on British industry which may not have been wholly anticipated by German planners. Almost 70 per cent of the towns along the flight paths of the bombers were placed on a 'Red' warning (raid likely or imminent). The sirens sent thousands of people to air-raid shelters and at the same time the lights of the factories, railway stations and the like were extinguished for lengthy periods of time. Industrial activity and production schedules were disrupted.

On Friday 30 August, with weather conditions likely to remain fine for several days, the Luftwaffe chiefs were determined to intensify the pressure.

13

4 SEPTEMBER 1940

With thirty-nine aircraft written off on the last day of August, Fighter Command suffered its heaviest losses in one day of the Battle of Britain so far. Despite this, aircraft attrition was not 'Stuffy' Dowding's major cause for alarm. The output of Hurricanes and Spitfires for the month exceeded the projected estimates by 69 per cent. It was the loss of aircrew that was far more critical. This was Fighter Command's most serious problem. Of forty-six squadron commanders who began the battle of Britain early in July, eleven had been killed or wounded. Of ninety-seven flight commanders, twenty-seven had been killed, twelve seriously wounded and seven promoted to take command of squadrons. To compensate, the training programme had been cut, volunteers had been obtained from other commands and Czech, Polish and Canadian squadrons, previously held in reserve, had been ordered into battle. Even so, Dowding and Park were coming to the dreadful realisation that they were not winning.

With unrelenting pressure mounting day by day, the fight for survival was reaching its most dangerous period.

For Desmond Sheen, Pat Hughes' mate from Point Cook days, and the men of 72 Squadron, the first day of September was very busy. Because of the damage inflicted on Biggin Hill, the squadron was moved to Croydon while 79 Squadron stayed put for air defence.

After being slightly wounded in an engagement early in December 1939, Sheen had spent a month in hospital before rejoining the squadron in January. The following April he had volunteered to fly 'something very fast' but secretive and been transferred to 212 Squadron, Photographic Development Unit. He found that this unique unit was equipped with specially modified Spitfires for high-altitude photographic reconnaissance. It had been formed by the highly inventive, entrepreneurial Sidney Cotton, formerly of Queensland. He moved to France with a detachment attached to the AASF on 12 May 1940, three days after his DFC was gazetted. He recalled:

I flew down to the south of France and Corsica with Sidney Cotton in his Lockheed 12 (uncamouflaged) ... prior to PR operations over Italy ... At Bastia we were met by bayonet-fitted rifles surrounding the aircraft as it was thought we might be Italians who had yet to enter the war ... Operations over Italy started mid-May initially from Le Luc, a French fighter base not far from St Raphael and then from Ajaccio in Sardinia to give a bit more range. We were there when Italy entered the war and next morning found the airfield completely obstructed. With some difficulty we persuaded the French to clear enough for us to fly off back to Le Luc.

The PR Spits ... were stripped of guns, ammunition and radio, the weight being replaced by additional fuel tanks and cameras. They were normally flown at full throttle at around 30–32,000 feet, depending upon the tropopause as it was essential not to leave a persistent contrail. The average sortie was about two and a half to three hours and the longest I recorded being about three and a quarter hours at a maximum height of 34,000 feet.

Minor physical problems were the cold, and we found that three loose layers of clothing were the most effective, and mild attacks of the bends were found at altitudes after a long period but nothing could be done about that. The special bubble hoods to facilitate downward vision were (predictably) patented by Sidney Cotton who was ... quite a character.

Another small problem in the south of France was that the airfields had long grass and with our fairly long take offs, grass tended to block the pilot head. The only solution was to fly the sortie without an airspeed indicator and thus burn up the fuel before landing.[1]

After Italy entered the war, the Le Luc airfield was bombed by the Italian Air Force. Fortunately, the precious Spitfire was unharmed but the support Hudson, which was not camouflaged, was destroyed. The Spitfire was sent home and the remainder of the small RAF party, including Des Sheen, left Toulon on the 17 June. Upon his return to England, Sheen continued photographic reconnaissance work over Germany and Holland until 29 July when he rejoined 72 Squadron, by then based at Acklington. His old CO, Ron Lees, was no longer there. Lees had finished his two years in charge and with the rank of Acting Wing Commander had been posted to the Headquarters of 13 Group for Air Staff Operations Training duties. He'd handed the squadron over to Squadron Leader Anthony Collins who was transferred from Coastal Command. Collins had led the squadron down from Acklington to Biggin Hill on 31 August, swapping places with 610 Squadron which was being rested. As he landed at Biggin Hill, Sheen was shocked by the condition of his new surroundings.[2]

Biggin Hill had been hammered by the Luftwaffe. It had been hit particularly hard the day before. Just after 1 p.m., instead of having a couple of hours respite between attacks, Kesselring began an assault sending waves of bombers and fighters over the south coast of Kent at twenty-minute intervals. It seemed that the Germans were building up toward their ultimate goal – invasion.

Twenty-two Fighter Command squadrons were in action that day, some of them as many as four times and almost all of them at least twice. At 4.00 p.m., again without pause, the third and perhaps heaviest group of raids began to build up. During the next two hours large and small formations of enemy aircraft flooded in over Kent and the Thames Estuary. The Junkers Ju 88s that appeared over Biggin Hill at 6 p.m. were only in a small attacking group of nine planes, but the havoc caused by their bombs was far worse than that of any previous attack.

The airfield was taken completely by surprise. Six of 79 Squadron's Hurricanes managed to scramble and escape before the bombs started to fall, but what followed was wholesale destruction as the workshops, cook houses, sergeants' mess and WAAF quarters were wrecked and 90 per cent of the station's transport was damaged or destroyed. All electricity, water and gas mains were cut and two parked aircraft were reduced to scrap. The airmen's shelter was pulverised by a direct hit and all those who had crammed in a few moments earlier were killed. Another bomb hit the airwomen's shelter causing the concrete walls to cave in, crushing and smothering those inside. Everyone outside started digging furiously to try and free the trapped women. Ambulance and stretcher parties stood by waiting. One-by-one they were carried out. Some were barely recognisable because of the dirt and blood on their faces. Others were dazed and bruised but all, except one, were alive. Corporal Lena Button from Tasmania was the only WAAF killed.[3] Altogether, thirty-nine personnel perished and twenty-six were injured.

It was the results of this bombing that had shocked Desmond Sheen as he landed at his new surroundings. This was also why 72 Squadron was moved to Croydon.

Taking advantage of cloudless conditions on the 1st, the Luftwaffe began building up its first raid around 10.20 a.m. After the usual diversionary feints, sixty bombers escorted by sixty fighters advanced on Dover where the force split into two groups. The German plan was for each to split up again so that four targets could be hit: Biggin Hill, Detling, Eastchurch, and London docks.

In a scramble from Croydon, 72 Squadron was directed onto a formation of Dorniers coming in south of the Thames. Over Beachy Head, Des Sheen lined up one bomber but before he could fire, a glance behind revealed that six Messerschmitt 109s were after him. The situation was the same for all of the 72 Squadron pilots and in the frantic dogfight that took place three Spitfires were shot down. One pilot was killed and one wounded. Two other Spitfires had to forcibly land.

One of the aircraft shot down was that flown by Desmond Sheen. In a twisting, turning encounter he managed to break free of the six 109s but not before his engine was hit by a cannon shell and caught fire. The Australian bailed out. As he floated down, Sheen was high enough to survey a vista that would live in his memory forever. On his right he could see explosions from bursting bombs in the Dover area with answering anti-aircraft fire from the defences. On his left he could see bombs falling on the London docks. The air was pungent with the acrid smell of cordite and it throbbed to the engines of the bombers. This was punctuated by the whining, straining sounds of fighters as they dived, climbed and twisted somewhere above. Not far off an Me 109 fell in flames. A parachute blossomed out but its harness must have been faulty because the airman dangling beneath suddenly disconnected and fell. Another 109 turned towards him but there was a Spitfire on its tail. Both planes curled away and merged into the panorama. Sheen landed lightly in the middle of a field.[4]

At Biggin Hill, the funeral of those killed in the earlier raids was held in the small cemetery beyond the airfield. There were over fifty coffins beside the newly dug graves but not enough flags to lay over them all. Even as the ceremony was being conducted, the air raid sirens wailed and Biggin Hill suffered its fifth raid in forty-eight hours. As the noise of the bombing faded away, the dead were finally laid to rest.

The airfield's runway was so pitted and scarred by craters that the returning Hurricanes of 79 Squadron had to be diverted to Croydon. It was out of service until late afternoon but even then it was not left alone.

The Luftwaffe's last wave of operations began around 5.30 p.m. when several formations swept in over the coast of Kent. They were mostly fighters and, following AVM Park's instructions, the RAF fighters avoided contact. However, there were small groups of bombers among them and fifty aircraft bombed Hawkinge and Lympne while a small formation of Dorniers bombed Biggin Hill again, its third raid in one day. Nevertheless, effective communications were re-established within an hour, and by working through the night the airfield was made operational again the next day.

Up until midnight the Luftwaffe was relatively quiet but after that over 100 bombers carried out widespread single and small-scale attacks. The most spectacular German success occurred between Swansea and Neath where six 10,000 ton oil storage tanks were set ablaze.

Early the next morning, the Luftwaffe built up a heavy raid behind Calais. RDF indicated formations of thirty and forty aircraft and shortly afterwards the Germans came in swiftly over Dover, with forty Dornier Do 17s closely escorted by Messerschmitt 110s and high-flying Messerschmitt 109s. This was a change of tactics. Prior to this, early morning German sorties had been confined to single reconnaissance aircraft. Many sector controllers were caught by surprise because, as usual, they only had standing patrols up over their airfields. The incoming raiders broke up to make separate attacks on Eastchurch, North Weald, Rochford and Biggin Hill.

No. 11 Group despatched eleven squadrons altogether but only five of these made contact. Consequently, as nine Spitfires from 72 Squadron, which Tony Collins had led forward to Hawkinge satellite airfield for the day, were heavily engaged over Maidstone, nine Dorniers slipped through and carried out a sharp, low-level thrust at Biggin Hill.

Shortly afterwards, 72 Squadron's former CO, Ron Lees, turned up flying his own Spitfire. He had kept track of the squadron's activities and now, with a week of leave from his duties at 13 Group HQ, he had decided to join it for the day. During heavy engagements through the day, Collins was wounded (for the second time in two days) and Lees took over. Unfortunately, as Lees was leading the squadron in the afternoon on his first sortie, he too was wounded. He crash-landed back at Hawkinge with a lacerated thigh. Although his aircraft, Spitfire K-9840, was damaged, it was able to be repaired. Instead of spending his leave with his companions, Lees spent time in hospital.[5]

Pressure from the Luftwaffe continued all day. At 3.15 p.m., yet another large raid was detected over Calais. Again 250 German aircraft came in over Dover and fanned out over Kent to various targets. Biggin Hill was hit again and so were the airfields at Detling, Kenley, Eastchurch and Hornchurch.

One potential target of special concern to Hugh Dowding and Keith Park was Brooklands airfield where the Hawker and Vickers companies had factories. The two commanders were worried about the possibility of an enemy move to bomb aircraft factories as the next stage of the offensive. To meet this potential threat, Park and Brand maintained a standing patrol of fighters from Tangmere and Middle Wallop along a line from Weybridge to the south coast over Guildford.

On this day the duty fell to 234 Squadron, but the squadron's Operations Record Book gives conflicting information concerning the activity. The Form 450 'Summary of Events' sheets state that one security patrol was carried out over Guildford by twelve aircraft, and also during the day there was one interception scramble by two aircraft. On the other hand, the Form 451 sheets 'Detail of Work Carried Out' list two separate patrols by twelve aircraft in two flights, one in the morning and one in the afternoon. Pat Hughes in his usual aircraft, Spitfire X4009, led both, taking the six aircraft of 'B' Flight off first at half-past ten to patrol Guildford at 15,000 feet. 'A' Flight followed five minutes later led by Flight Lieutenant Cyril Page who had rejoined 234 Squadron at Middle Wallop back on 19 August. The squadron was back on the ground just after midday.[6]

They were up again at 2.45 p.m. patrolling Brooklands to Kenley at 'Angels 10'. On this occasion they were ordered forward to tackle the enemy aircraft fanning out over Kent, but unfortunately this left enough of a hole in the defences for enemy raiders to break through to Brooklands airfield for the first time. The Germans had been briefed to attack the Hurricane factory but instead their bombs fell on the Vickers works where Wellington bombers were being assembled. Damage was described as moderate but to Dowding and Park this was an ominous sign of what could be ahead.

Elsewhere, the force sent to raid Hornchurch was so successfully disrupted by RAF fighters that fewer than a dozen bombs fell within the airfield's boundaries. The story was far worse at Eastchurch, which suffered badly when its bomb dump was hit and the resulting explosion demolished practically every building nearby. Water mains and sewers were smashed, five aircraft were destroyed and the communications system was put out of action.

Meanwhile, 234 Squadron landed back at Middle Wallop between 4 and 4.15 p.m. after a frustratingly ineffective search for enemy aircraft.

The hammering of 11 Group continued. Around 5 p.m. a fourth major attack appeared over Dungeness. The Germans were after the airfields again;

Eastchurch was struck a second time and a hangar was destroyed. Casualties for Eastchurch for the day were four killed and twelve wounded. Detling received approximately 100 bombs that wrecked a hangar and rendered the airfield unusable for two hours.

Soon afterwards 72 Squadron was up again, heavily involved in combat over the Thames Estuary. The squadron's records noted that it had been 'a hell of a day' but on the credit side it could claim eighteen victories.

Darkness brought some respite for the defences until 1.30 a.m., when individual raiders were plotted coming in over East Anglia. Seventy-five bombers from *Luftflotte 3* flew over with impunity during the next few hours, approximately half of them carrying out mine-laying operations while the rest conducted scattered raids on Liverpool, the Midlands and south Wales.

The weather conditions next day, Tuesday 3 September, were dark and overcast but in the south it became fine and warm as the day progressed. As usual, it was Park's 11 Group that bore the brunt of the assault, but this time most of the heavy fighting took place over Essex, north of the Thames and the Thames estuary, well away from 234 Squadron at Middle Wallop.

During the morning action, Richard Hillary of 603 Squadron, the son of an Australian diplomat, had his Spitfire shot up by an Me 109. Despite being trapped, his cockpit erupting into a mass of flames and the canopy jamming as his Spitfire fell in a spin, Hillary finally managed to bail out and pull the ripcord after a desperate, painful struggle to escape. The parachute brought him down into the sea near the seaside resort at Margate. Observers on shore had seen him fall but the Margate lifeboat had difficulty finding him. It searched for three hours in vain. The crew was about to give up when one man spotted the floating parachute. Hillary was drifting in and out of consciousness. He was finally lifted to safety but he had suffered cruelly; once a handsome young man, he had been grotesquely mutilated by the fire.[7]

Another Australian, Desmond Fopp from Adelaide, suffered a similar fate. While flying with 17 Squadron from Debden, a Messerschmitt 110 put a cannon shell into the radiator of his Hurricane and it blew up. He was immediately surrounded by flames. In severe pain he succeeded in escaping from the blazing machine and fell several thousand feet before pulling his ripcord. As he floated down he realised that his vision was impaired but he could see that his uniform was smouldering. Suddenly he crashed through the leaves and branches of trees. He had come down into a wood in Essex. Freeing himself from his parachute harness, Fopp staggered blindly through the trees until he reached a clearing. He was at once confronted by farm labourers armed with pitchforks. They were ready for anything and Fopp was in such a state that they were unable to tell whether he was British or German. The vigour of his language dispelled their doubts but he was close to exhaustion and by now hardly able to see. Gentle hands covered his burns until an ambulance arrived.[8]

Besides Desmond Fopp's Hurricane, 17 Squadron lost one other aircraft and its pilot. On the credit side, claims were lodged for the destruction of two Me 110s and two Do 17s plus two Me 110 probables.

Another attack developed in the afternoon but it was smaller than the morning raids and successfully beaten off. For 10 Group and 234 Squadron at Middle Wallop the day was quiet and no actions were recorded.

So ended the daylight fighting on this day that marked the first anniversary of the start of the war. It was twelve months ago that Neville Chamberlain had made his solemn declaration. On this day, too, Desmond Sheen's promotion to flight lieutenant was recorded in the *London Gazette*.

Although low cloud at night hindered German operations, about sixty raiders reached London and other scattered targets. The General Aircraft Company at Feltham in Middlesex was damaged.

On Wednesday 4 September, the weather was fine and warm over the south of England while in the north there was occasional rain accompanied by strong winds. Several squadrons from 12 Group moved southwards closer to 11 Group to act as reinforcements for the units around London.

In accordance with the Luftwaffe's Operations Staff Orders which had been issued on 1 September, the targets for *Luftflotte* 2 were divided between sector airfields and aircraft factories, the latter to try and halt the seemingly endless flow of fighters and equipment to British squadrons.

The first major raid in the morning concentrated on the airfields, with the Germans coming in via Dover and the Thames Estuary. Dover's barrage balloons received their usual harsh treatment and Lympne airfield was strafed. At Eastchurch, bombs made six large craters on the runway and destroyed ration stores.

Large concentrations of German aircraft were detected by RDF around noon. By 1 p.m. about 300 enemy planes crossed the coast at Beachy Head, Hastings, Folkestone and Dover. Fourteen RAF fighter squadrons were scrambled and out of these nine made contact. The squadrons on the edge of the danger zone were ordered up to cover the sector stations.

Near Testerton, Spitfires from 72 Squadron encountered two formations of German escort fighters but almost immediately they formed defensive circles. Desmond Sheen checked that there were no other enemy aircraft above before he attacked a Messerschmitt 110 about to join one of the circles. As he fired, smoke came from the 110's port engine but Sheen was closing in too fast and he had to break away. As he climbed again for height he looked around for other aircraft but there were none to be seen. One instant the sky had been a mass of planes, now ... nothing.

Patrolling over Tangmere, the twelve Spitfires from 234 Squadron led by Pat Hughes had spiralled up to 15,000 feet by 1.20 p.m. Down below on the airfield, the Hurricanes of 601 Squadron were taking off. Pat spotted two groups of German aircraft. About fifty twin-engine Me 110s were coming in over the coast while fifteen others were already circling over Haslemere lower down. Detailing Red, Yellow and Green Sections to attack the larger formation, he led Blue Section down after those over Haslemere. As soon as the Spitfires were sighted the 110s formed their usual defensive circle. Pat attacked the leading Messerschmitt head on, firing two short bursts. His aim was deadly. The 110 reared up and another short burst struck its fuselage, causing it to erupt in flames. It crashed just north of Brighton. Seconds later the Australian came in directly behind another 110 and fired briefly twice, as usual closing right in from 100 to twenty-five yards. The heavy escort fighter rolled over onto its back and crashed, diving vertically into the ground and blowing up about ten miles north-east of Tangmere.

Suddenly Pat realised he was being surrounded by three more Messerschmitts and noticed a fourth 110 slipping behind him into a firing position. Manoeuvring wildly, he fired three snap bursts to break up their circle and this caused one to dive away. He pounced after it and emptied the remainder of his ammunition into it. With one engine appearing to catch fire, it turned slowly towards the coast. Both engines were now burning. It could not get far. As if to make sure, a stray Hurricane appeared on the scene and delivered a short burst into it just before it hit the water.

The German escort fighters had suffered badly on this day and 234 Squadron alone claimed a record fourteen Me 110s and one Do 17 destroyed plus seven Me 110s damaged for only one damaged Spitfire. It was the squadron's best day so far. Bob Doe kept up with Pat as he too claimed three Me 110s destroyed; Mike Boddington two; Zbigniew Olenski one; Alan Harker one; Zygmunt Klein one; Pat Horton one destroyed and one damaged; Bill Hornby one destroyed and three damaged; Jozef Szlagowski one Me 110 destroyed and the Do 17 destroyed; George Bailey two damaged; and Keith Lawrence one damaged. Olenski's was the damaged Spitfire but he was uninjured.[9]

However, although the RAF fighters were successful in the air, a formation of bomb-carrying Me 110s reached Brooklands again and dropped six bombs on the Vickers works. The Wellington bomber assembly sheds were destroyed and there were 700 casualties inflicted, among them eighty-eight dead. It was an unintended success for the Germans because they had been after the nearby Hawker factory, which escaped unscathed. Another raid reached Rochester, where the Short Brothers factory, who were producing new, four-engine Stirling bombers, was also damaged. Although these were significant blows, neither of them contributed directly to the strategy of gaining superiority in the air by knocking out Fighter Command.

With the day's air fighting obviously over the support squadrons from 12 Group returned to their bases in the early evening.

That night in Germany, Adolf Hitler addressed an audience of nurses and social workers at the *Sportpalast* in Berlin on the opening of the *Kriegswinterhilfswerk*. His address was, of course, well covered by the German press. Among other things in his speech, he accused the RAF of indiscriminate bombing.

The first year of the war ended in these last days. The second began and with it the new *Kriegswinterhilfswerk*. The successes of the first year, my *Volksgenossen*, are unique, so unique in fact that not only our enemies had not envisioned the course of history in this manner, but many in the German

Volk were hardly able to comprehend the greatness of the occurrences and the rapidity of events ... People in England today nosily inquire: 'Well, why isn't he coming?' Calm yourselves: he is coming!

Nothing frightens us. We German National Socialists have graduated from the toughest school conceivable. First we were soldiers in the Great War, and then we were fighters in the resurgence of Germany. What we had to suffer in these years made us hard. Thus we cannot be intimidated by anything and nothing can surprise us.

Mr Churchill is demonstrating to us the use of his invention: the nightly air raid. He does not do this because air raids at night are particularly effective, but because his Air Force cannot penetrate German airspace during the day. While the German pilots, the German planes, fly over English land day by day, no Englishman has yet managed to as much as cross the North Sea by daylight. That is why they come at night and drop their bombs, you know it well, indiscriminately and without plan on civilian residential centres, on farmsteads, and villages.

Wherever they see a light, they drop a bomb ... And should the Royal Air Force drop two thousand, or three thousand, or four thousand kilograms of bombs, then we will now drop 150,000; 180,000; 230,000; 300,000; 400,000; yes, one million kilograms in a single night. And should they declare they will greatly increase their attacks on our cities, then we will erase their cities.

His were no idle threats but while he was speaking the night sky over England was quiet, ominously so. The deceiving calm lasted until 1.30 a.m. when RDF plotted individual raiders on their way across to East Anglia. Seventy-five bombers from *Luftflotte 3* were active during the following few hours, about half of them carrying out mine-laying operations while the rest made scattered raids on Liverpool, the Midlands and south Wales.

14

5 SEPTEMBER 1940

The stress of sustained battle was showing on airmen and machines on both sides of the Channel but Thursday, 5 September would bring no respite. Once again the weather was ideal for air fighting.

Beginning around 10.00 a.m. *Luftflotte* 2 launched numerous raids over southern England. There were at least twenty-two separate formations dispatched although two were larger than the others. Kesselring targeted the airfields of Croydon, Biggin Hill, Eastchurch, North Weald and Lympne.

Biggin Hill was still only capable of operating one squadron, 79, while 72 Squadron, Desmond Sheen's unit, which was already down to nine serviceable Spitfires, remained at Croydon. 79 Squadron was scrambled to cover Biggin Hill and broke up a raid of thirty bombers and their escorts. Six Hurricanes met the Dorniers at 15,000 feet and scattered them so effectively that their bombing was well off target. It was obviously going to be a very busy day so reinforcements from the adjacent groups were alerted to reinforce Park's 11 Group.

After the raid on Biggin Hill, the CO, Group Captain Grice made an aerial inspection of his airfield. One hangar, although it was only a burnt-out shell, appeared from the air to be undamaged. This, he reasoned, was why the enemy persisted with attacks. Grice arranged to have explosive charges placed in the hangar so that when the next raid occurred they could be detonated and the building brought down.[1]

Just after lunch, RDF tracked another large concentration of aircraft sweeping in over the Thames Estuary at extremely high altitude. These were Heinkel He 111s and Junkers Ju 88s which bombed the oil storage facility at Thameshaven and caused serious fires.

RAF fighter squadrons were scrambled from everywhere. Clawing for height over Kent, the Spitfires of 72 Squadron climbed as fast as they could. They were flying in their usual tight vic formations of three with the rear section providing two 'weavers' while the leader flew in the box position at the rear. It was the duty of the weavers to guard the others against being surprised by German fighters but this time the warning came too late.

Over Canterbury, Desmond Sheen heard a shout in his earphones but, before he could react, he was bounced from behind. His Spitfire shuddered from a heavy burst of cannon and machine-gun fire and flying metal struck his leg, hand and face. As he passed out, the stricken Spitfire, with large pieces missing from its port wing, heeled over into a vertical dive. Fortunately, Sheen regained consciousness just seconds later. His plane was still hurtling straight down. He tried the controls but they did not respond. He had no idea how close he was to the ground but he sensed that it could not be far away. Releasing the harness pin to rid himself of his straps, he was instantly sucked out of his seat but did not fall free. His feet were caught, stuck somehow at the top of the windscreen. Pinned by the slipstream against the top of the fuselage, he struggled with all his strength, but in vain. He was trapped; helpless and streaking down at tremendous speed.

Suddenly, for no obvious reason, his feet were released and instinctively he pulled the ripcord without even waiting to ensure that he was clear of the aircraft's tail. With a bone-jarring snap the parachute opened at what he found out later was only about 800 feet. Sheen had only a split-second glimpse of trees beneath him before he started to crash through boughs and branches. The crown of a tree caught the top of his parachute and acted as a brake. His fall was slowed rapidly and miraculously he ended up with a simple, light landing. Physically, apart from the wounds in his leg, hand and face, he had suffered just a few extra scratches and bruises. A moment later, he noticed a policeman on a bicycle riding towards him. Upon reaching the Australian, he produced a flask and asked 'Why didn't you bail out earlier?'[2]

Sheen was taken to Queen Mary's Hospital in Sidcup. This time he would spend six weeks in hospital and on sick leave before being able to return to his squadron on 13 October.

Meanwhile, twelve Spitfires from 234 Squadron had been scrambled from Middle Wallop. Pat Hughes was Blue Leader, his section being positioned behind Red Section at 20,000 feet. Anti-aircraft fire was sighted about forty miles off over Gravesend so they headed in that direction. The section leaders scanned the sky for bandits, but they didn't see them in time. Suddenly, without warning, they were bounced from out of the sun by Me 109s. There seemed to be three of them – fast black shapes with white wing tips and white spinners. The squadron had been caught down-sun again!

As Pat broke into the attack, he spotted twelve more Messerschmitts flying up the Thames Estuary. They appeared to be flying in two 'V' formations, one of seven aircraft and the other of five. At this juncture he was joined by two Hurricanes and together they launched an attack on the advancing 109s. In the ensuing dogfight, Pat seized a fleeting chance and fired a full deflection burst, four seconds worth, at one German fighter which blew up.

Next, he went after another vic of three more 109s, selected a new victim and gave chase from dead astern. A sustained burst of fire, six seconds, caused oil from the Messerschmitt's ruptured oil tank to splatter all over his wings. The 109 dropped away and force-landed in a field about fifteen miles south-west of Manston. The German pilot was climbing out of his cockpit as Pat departed.[3]

Waiting at Biggin Hill for the usual 6 p.m. raid, Group Captain Grice was almost disappointed when the Luftwaffe did not turn up. The Royal Engineers had set their charges and he could wait no longer to give the signal to demolish the burnt-out hangar. With what was probably the loudest explosion ever heard at Biggin Hill, the hangar crumbled. From the air, the destruction of the base now appeared to be complete. As he predicted, Biggin Hill did not suffer from another major air raid. Whether this was the result of Grice's action or changing German tactics was open to conjecture.

The 5th had been another day of tenacious fighting by both sides. German losses amounted to twenty-three aircraft, although British claims were for thirty-nine at the time, while the Fighter Command lost twenty. Five Me 109s were claimed by 234 Squadron without loss. The Operations Record Book noted two victories for Pat Hughes; Bob Doe scored one; Mike Boddington one; and Jan Zurakowski one.[4]

According to Francis K. Mason in his remarkably detailed book *Battle Over Britain*, the dazed German pilot who climbed out of the cockpit of the downed Me 109 on that September afternoon was Oberleutnant Franz von Werra, who was the adjutant of *II/JG3* and the only German aviator to escape from British custody and return to fight for his country. The bravado von Werra displayed among his comrades as an audacious fighter ace remained with him as a POW. He proved difficult to hold and made numerous escape attempts, on one occasion bluffing his way onto an RAF airfield and trying to take off in a Hurricane! Eventually, he was transferred to Canada with other POWs. In Nova Scotia the prisoners were transported by rail from Halifax to their new camp, but en route von Werra forced open a window and jumped from the moving train. This time he succeeded in making good his escape by crossing the nearby border into the USA which at that stage was still neutral. After returning to Germany, von Werra eventually became commanding officer of *1/JG53* on the Russian front. He shot down thirteen Russian aeroplanes to bring his tally to twenty-one before his unit was withdrawn from that front and transferred to Holland. On 25 October 1941, the engine of his Me 109 failed and the aircraft plunged into the sea near Vlissingen, where he drowned.

Mason declared that von Werra was shot down by Pat Hughes at 3.25 p.m.[5] His book did not give a description of the action but the claim was repeated elsewhere in other publications including *Target England – The Illustrated History of the Battle of Britain* by Derek Wood, which was outstanding for its time. Earlier, Derek Wood had also been the originator and co-author with Derek Dempster of *The Narrow Margin,* the first detailed, day-by-day account of the Battle of Britain, which in turn formed the basis of the classic all-star film, *The Battle of Britain*. All of these works were groundbreaking for their time and were the forerunners of the brilliant studies existing today.

Just about every aspect of the Battle of Britain, one of world history's pivotal campaigns, has been studied and dissected over the years. The books by Mason, Wood and Dempster, being early works on the subject, have been subjected in-depth analysis and scrutiny, and inevitably some unintended inconsistencies have been found and provoked criticism, sometimes most unfairly. Mason's claim that von Werra was shot down by Pat Hughes contradicted an earlier account of the German ace's capture. Franz von Werra's story was first told in *The One That Got Away* by Kendal Burt and James Leaser, published in 1956, thirteen years before Mason's book. It was also the basis of a film of the same name. There has been much confusion concerning the combat that resulted in von Werra's fall into British hands.

Pat Hughes estimated that his Me 109 had come down about fifteen miles south-west of Manston in Kent but he may have erred in his estimate of the position because von Werra's damaged fighter actually landed at Winchet Hill, Love's Farm, Marden, also in Kent but some forty miles from Manston. That he force-landed at Winchet Hill cannot be disputed as his aircraft and the crash site were photographed many times and are well known. Bert and Leasor stated in *The One That Got Away* that von Werra was shot down shortly after 10 a.m. by Flight Lieutenant John Terrence Webster DFC of 41 Squadron. Webster was a veteran of operations over Dunkirk and by 5 September, he had been credited with the destruction of fourteen German planes.

John Webster's combat report stated:

I was leading Blue Section 41 Squadron when large enemy formation was sighted to the port. I followed Mitor leaders ['Mitor' was 41 Squadron's radio call sign] in and Blue Section delivered an attack in line astern on ME 109 attacking on the beam from above. I fired a 3 sec. burst at an 109 and saw the bullets going into the engine. This a/c dived away steeply. I then attempted to attack the rear bomber formation again using a diving quarter. I tried three successive attacks but each time was followed in by 109 and forced to break away before getting a good deflection. I did not fire at the bombers. I then dived away from the bombers and ran into several HE 113's [sic]. I attacked these and saw one burst into flames after a 3 sec. burst from astern and directly above, using just over full deflection. After this attack I pulled up steeply and looked around.

I saw a Spitfire diving steeply chased by 3 ME 109's. I chased after these and one broke away after a short burst from directly astern. I lost the Spitfire but followed another 109 down to ground level when I managed to get in a good burst from 48 degrees astern and saw the a/c roll on to its back and crash into the ground near Maidstone. I then returned to base.[6]

The Heinkel He 113 (He 100) mentioned in John Webster's combat report was a type never actually accepted for service use by the Luftwaffe, even though it appears on numerous occasions in RAF records. Only twelve production models were built, and in a ploy to mislead Allied Intelligence these were repainted over and over with different insignia to give the impression that the type was in widespread use. Many propaganda photographs were distributed. The ruse was successful and the type featured in Allied aircraft identification leaflets, books and lectures. During the frenzy of a dogfight, the error of mistaking a normal Me 109E for a He 113 would have been easy for any pilot to make.

Was von Werra shot down in the morning or the afternoon? Fighting that morning centred on mid-Kent, around Maidstone and Ashford, while that in the afternoon appeared to be located further east over the Thames Estuary. An inquiry on this was directed to the *Bundesarchiv* but the reply received indicated that German records on this period were not available at that time. However, it was known that *JG3* lost six aircraft and their pilots on 5 September, some in the morning and some in the afternoon. Mason suggested that 41 Squadron actually engaged *JG54* that morning and named Unteroffizier Behse and Hauptmann Ultsch as the Luftwaffe pilots killed in the action. If von Werra was shot down in the afternoon, possibly one, or both, of these may have fallen to John Webster's guns.

Characteristically, von Werra's own accounts of what happened were not reliable because he tended to 'colour' his version of events to suit his audiences. On one occasion, he claimed to have shot down three British planes before colliding with another Me 109 and being forced down. Another time he claimed to have destroyed only the fighter that had attacked him. He always maintained that his plane had caught fire when it crash-landed and was gutted, but it was actually captured in a relatively undamaged condition.

Photographs of the downed machine at Winchet Hill show quite clearly that Messerschmitt Me 109E-4 (1480) did not 'roll on to its back and crash into the ground' as described by John Webster. Nor could it have been the He 113 that 'burst into flames', but it might have been the 109 that had 'bullets going into the engine' and 'dived away steeply'. However, the 109 did go down near Maidstone, Winchet Hill being miles away. On the other hand, details in Pat Hughes' combat report, which stated the time of attack as being 3.45 p.m. over Eastchurch, line up well with other information:

I was Blue Leader. We were behind Red Section at 20,000 feet and going towards Gravesend where we had seen A.A. fire when we were attacked out of the sun by 3 Me. 109's. As I turned to attack I saw 12 Me. 109's in two vics of 5 and 7 coming up the Estuary. I turned and dived and was joined by 2 Hurricanes. A dogfight ensued over Eastchurch. I fired a full deflection shot at one Me. 109 and hit his ammunition tanks. He blew up and spun down. I then attacked a vic of 3 Me. 109's, singled out one and chased him attacking from dead astern. I must have shot his oil tank away as there was oil all over my wings to the tips. E/A force landed in a field 15 miles S.W. of Manston.

He also added some extra details:

Note
These 12 ME 109's were all silver with red spinners. The others I saw were black with white curves on wing tips and white spinners.[7]

Pat Hughes' description of his combat tallies more closely with the scenario worked out by Burt and Leasor in *The One Who Got Away*. They also mentioned the vic formation of the German planes when they noted that leading the formation was 2/*JG3*'s commanding officer, Hauptmann Erich von Selle, who had on his immediate left and right two staff officers, Leutnant Heinrich Sanneman and Oberleutnant Franz von Verra, respectively. Could it have been these three that Pat attacked when he chased the Me 109 that he caused to eventually force-land? It was unusual for German fighters to fly in an element of three. The standard fighting unit was a pair.

To further complicate matters, von Werra's low-flying aircraft was fired on by a Lewis gun at a searchlight battery site just before it crash landed. A claim was submitted by the gunners. Von Werra at no time mentioned being hit by ground fire but during the last moments of his desperate chase and forced-landing he may not have even noticed it. However, it was most unlikely that he would have been flying so low as to come within range of a Lewis gun at all had he not been pursued, or his aircraft not already damaged.

The favoured opinion in the 1980s and early 1990s was that von Werra was downed in the afternoon. Mr A. E. Munday of the Air Historical Branch (RAF), Ministry of Defence wrote on 14 February 1983:

Modern research seems to indicate that Werra was shot down in the afternoon, rather than the morning of 5 September 1940. The No 41 Squadron operations Record Books throw no light on the subject and I feel, having been interested in this subject, that Flt/Lt Webster shot down someone other than Werra in the morning of 5 September 1940.

The book 'The One That Got Away' was written some years ago when a number of relevant papers were not available for consultation. Most modern writers and the 109 historians agree that Werra belly landed his ME109E sometime after 3pm at Winchet Hill, Curtisden Green, near Marden, Kent. (The place of landing is not disputed).

The fighting in the morning centred around mid-Kent (Maidstone–Ashford), whilst that of the afternoon appeared to centre slightly further north over the Thames Estuary. From there, as the Germans made their way home, it could have drifted southward toward the South Kent Coast as the raiders crossed out over the Channel. In terms of flying time, the journey from the Thames Estuary to Marden would take only a few minutes; if Werra received damage over the river or North Kent and turned onto the most direct route home, he would eventually have landed at the place he did, near Marden.

I do not think that the question of who shot Werra down will be resolved now. According to Winston Ramsey, *JG3* lost 6 aircraft and pilots on this day, some in the morning, and some in the afternoon.'[8]

John L. Stitt of East Grinstead, West Sussex, communicated on the matter in August 1990. In his account, he wrote:

In 1940 I was an Auxiliary Airman with 500 County of Kent Coastal Command Sqdn (Ansons) based at Detling and had a grandstand view of the Battle of Britain. Detling had virtually been destroyed on the 13th August and by 5th September we had all become one hundred per cent better at aircraft recognition and above all – alertness!

I was a member of 'B' Flight, dispersed at the NE edge of the airfield on the Stockbury Road. We enjoyed a panoramic view of the Isle of Sheppey and the Thames Estuary.

On this particular afternoon an air battle was raging to the north of our position and we were manning a slit trench armed with .303 rifles and a Lewis Gun (NOT FIRED).

Suddenly someone shouted 'Look!' and pointed to the NNE. We saw two low flying aircraft beyond coming towards us. Less than 400 feet. The front one was soon recognized as an Me 109 hotly pursued by a Spitfire. As they passed over our heads the Spitfire pilot was firing his guns and I distinctly recall a yellow/green haze coming from the 109. They flew over the airfield and were lost to vision over the Downs.

Now at the time, my late father was the Adjutant (Captain William Wallace STITT) at the Maidstone Barracks, Depot of the Queen's Own Royal West Kent Regiment, and nearly all German airmen shot down in the area passed his through his hands whilst awaiting collection from the Royal Air Force, London.

That evening we swapped stories and he told me that the A/C we had seen crashed at Marden. It was not until after the war when Werra had become world famous that he told me that the German pilot who had passed through on that day was in fact *Oblt* Franz von Werra!

I have drawn a line on an ordnance survey map which runs from Sheerness, over our dispersal at the Stockbury Road, finishing up at Winchett Hill, Marden and found it marked exactly the course flown by Werra and the Spitfire!

Hughes said in his report that 'EA force landed in a field, fifteen miles SW of Manston'. I believe he wrote 'fifteen miles SW of Maidstone', which is the correct distance.

A few years ago, I was based in Hull with an international company. We would celebrate office birthdays and promotions at a pub in Sutton. One lunch time the landlord told me there was an airman buried in the churchyard opposite the pub. I walked over and found Pat Hughes' grave.

Werra, as you will know, finally went missing off the coast of Holland, not far from Sutton 'as the plane flies'.

What a waste of two good men.

John Webster was killed in action between 3.25 p.m. and 3.30 p.m. that afternoon. The Spitfires of 41 Squadron had engaged Dornier 17s and their escorting Me 109s over the Thames Estuary, and during the melee two of the British machines collided over the Thames Estuary. Both John Webster and his CO, Squadron Leader Hilary Richard Lionel Hood, were killed around the same time that Pat Hughes was engaging in combat.

Although in the 1980s and 1990s there seemed to a general acceptance that these events occurred in the afternoon, the bulk of later research focuses on, and favours, the morning action.

In that case, John Webster was not the only possibility. Another scenario, now widely accepted, suggests that von Werra's Me 109 may have been damaged by Pilot Officer George Bennions of 41 Squadron and then pursued and finally shot down by Pilot Officer Basil Gerald Stapleton of 603 Squadron. By far the best references for this are Winston Ramsey's, *The Blitz – Then and Now Vol. 1* and Nigel Parker's *Luftwaffe Crash Archive Vol. 3*. In both, the time given is 10.10 a.m., which lines up with that given by Kendal Burt and James Leaser.[10] David Ross, in his biography of Richard Hillary, accepted this latest scenario and presented a convincing case in support of Gerald Stapleton's claim.[11]

Gerald 'Stapme' Stapleton was a tough South African. He had joined the RAF on a short service commission in January 1939 and had been posted to 603 Squadron the following October. George Bennions was an experienced flier, having joined the RAF as an aircraft apprentice at Halton in 1929, and in 1935 he completed his pilot training. In January 1936, he joined 41 Squadron at Khormaksar, Aden. Promotion to flight sergeant followed in November 1938 and he was commissioned in April 1940. By September, he had at least two enemy aircraft to his credit.[12]

However, how possible is it to be absolutely certain beyond a reasonable doubt of the events occurring within a whirling, confusing dogfight and a hectic chase? The question has to be asked: if it wasn't Franz von Werra that Pat Hughes brought down on 5 September 1940, who was it? Nigel Parker's *Luftwaffe Crash Archive* series records that four Me 109s force-landed in relatively good condition in Kent that day, three in the morning and one in the afternoon. These were:

Me 109E-4 (Wn.1985) 'White 6' of 1/JG53 which came down at Banks Farm, Aldington, at 10.10 a.m., the pilot was Leutnant Heinz Schnabel;

Me 109E-4 (Wn.1480) of *Stab II/JG53* which came down at Winchet Hill, Love's Farm, near Marden, at 10.10 a.m., von Werra's machine;

Me 109E-4 (Wn.750) 'Yellow 7' of 3/JG3 which came down at Wichling at 10.30 a.m., the pilot was Unteroffizier Heinz Grabow; and

Me 109E-4 (Wn.5375) of *Stab JG53* which came down at Monkton Farm, near Manston, at 3.45 p.m.

The pilot of the Messerschmitt brought down in the afternoon near Manston was fifty-one-year-old Hauptmann Wilhelm Meyerweissflog, a veteran of the First World War who had served then as an observer in the German Air

Force. In this new war, he became an administrative officer attached to the staff of *JG 3*. On the evening of 4 September 1940, he returned late from a period of leave apparently to *JG 53* at a place (he thought) was near to Boulogne. Shortly after lunch next day, the 5th, he saw his pilots preparing to depart for a mission over Britain so he decided he would do the same. He reportedly 'jumped into his Messerschmitt,' and 'flew vaguely in the direction of England', apparently by himself, or so his story goes. Over England, he was shot up by a British fighter and had to make a forced landing.[13]

This time Pat Hughes was in the right place (near Manston) at the right time (3.45 p.m.), and much of the other information about Me 109E-4 (Wn.5375) lines up with details in his combat report. 'I must have shot his oil tank away as there was oil all over my wings to the tips,' recorded Pat. A number of .303 inch bullet strikes were found in the oil cooler of this Messerschmitt's Mercedes Benz engine. These obviously caused the oil to drain out therefore making the engine overheat and fail. Pat had chased the 109 and attacked it from dead astern, firing from very close range as usual. This, no doubt, was the reason that his Spitfire was covered in oil. Pat recorded that the second group of twelve Me 109s he encountered 'were all silver with red spinners.' The camouflage of Me 109E-4 (Wn.5375) was light navy grey with white wing tips and rudder which, within a whirling dogfight, would very likely give the appearance of being all metallic silver. Its propeller spinner was half red, half white, and there was a twelve, inches, wide red band painted around the engine cowling.

However, Pat stated he had attacked a vic of three Me 109s, 'singled out one and chased him attacking from dead astern'. According to Hauptmann Wilhelm Meyerweissflog, he was flying alone.[14] It will be remembered that the basic element flown by Luftwaffe fighters was a pair, called a *Rotte*. Two *Rotten* made up a *Schwarm* (flight) of four aircraft. Two or three *Schwärme* made up a *Staffel* (squadron). Although Hauptmann Meyerweissflog may have taken off after the others, it is likely that he met up with a *Staffel* of his comrades in the air after he had. To come into the formation, he would have joined a *Rotte* of two aircraft, thereby changing it into a vic of three.

In the tightly regulated military and civil aviation of modern days to simply decide to take off and join in on a raid over enemy airspace in such a manner is inconceivable, but in 1940 it was actually done by rare individuals on both sides. Another such character in the Luftwaffe was Theo Osterkamp who became an ace in both wars and was known affectionately as 'Uncle Theo' by 'his boys'.[15]

One like individual on the RAF side was Pat's old CO from 64 Squadron days, the Irishman Victor Beamish who persistently indulged in such extracurricular activities. Promoted to wing commander at the beginning of March 1940, Beamish took command of RAF North Weald, a fighter station in Essex, on the following 7 June. His own Hurricane was always ready to take off with 'his boys' or he would take off just afterwards and catch up with them in the air. He did it regularly, and sometimes he would fly alone and find his own trouble – with considerable success. Already an iconic figure, his latest exploits were becoming the stuff of legends. Interestingly, his philosophy on air fighting was also to get in close so he couldn't miss.[16]

To fly alone in a hostile sky was to invite trouble, and on this September afternoon trouble certainly found Hauptmann Meyerweissflog. When matched with Pat Hughes' combat report, his Messerschmitt force landed in the right vicinity at around the right time.

*

With darkness the German Air Force stepped up its nocturnal activity and London experienced its longest night alert so far. It was not just London, targets were spread all over England. Although Sperrle's bombers could be tracked by RDF following their precise courses from Cherbourg, RAF night fighters were again not equal to the task of locating them, and bringing them down.

At the same time from the British side, RAF Bomber Command despatched eighty-two aircraft to various targets ranging from Turin to Stettin, and Berlin was raided again for two hours. Three Hampdens and one Wellington were lost.

15

6 SEPTEMBER 1940

Overnight in London the air raid alert lasted a record seven and a half hours.

Daylight on Friday 6 September brought with it fine weather again, and the British commanders, particularly Hugh Dowding and Keith Park, knew that the Luftwaffe would not allow any respite. Numerous early morning reconnaissance sorties by single German aircraft suggested to Park that, as well as 11 Group's airfields and sector stations, the vital factories at Weybridge could be under threat. He requested AVM Brand to divert fighters to cover them and the task was allocated in rotation to 234 Squadron and 609 Squadron at Middle Wallop.

The first large RDF plots appeared on screen at 8.30 a.m. Ten minutes later, twelve aircraft of 234 Squadron led by Spike O'Brien were ordered to take off and patrol Brooklands at 'Angels 10'. Pat Hughes in Spitfire X4009 was at the head of 'B' Flight as Cressy Blue 1, as usual. Well into their patrol, the Spitfires were directed to head east to Beachy Head and climb to 24,000 feet. Meanwhile, 609 Squadron was scrambled to cover Brooklands.

North of Beachy Head at about 9.30 a.m., 234 Squadron engaged a large formation of escorted enemy bombers – Dornier 17s escorted by Messerschmitt 109s and 110s. They were high over Dover when Pat saw he was in an ideal position above a group of Me 109s just below. Ordering his section into line astern, Pat launched an attack and the victim he selected was mortally hit with a long burst as he closed in from 150 to fifty yards and pursued it down. He saw that it 'crashed on landing approx. 5 miles west of Littlestone'.[1]

Littlestone-on-Sea is a small coastal village that was established in the 1880s as a resort for 'the gentry' close to New Romney. Old Romney village, situated two miles inland from New Romney, was the original settlement site on what was once an island in the former River Rother estuary. The Romney Marsh proper lies north of a line between New Romney and Appledore and is a sparsely populated wetland area of Kent and East Sussex covering about 100 square miles. It is flat and low lying, with areas below sea-level. In case of invasion in 1940, plans were afoot for the marsh to be flooded and covered with oil, ready to be set alight when the invaders arrived.

Old Romney is within the range of 'approximately five miles west of Littlestone' estimated by Pat in his combat report and, according to the *Luftwaffe Crash Archive*, a Messerschmitt 109 did come down in that area during the morning. This was Me 109E-1 (Wn.3877) of 7/JG26 which reportedly crashed on Swamp Farm, Old Romney, at 10.40 a.m., cause not known.[2]

Pat could well have been the cause, but there is an anomaly with the times recorded. The timing is open to question. Pat's combat report has the time of his attack as '09.30–10.00', and according to 234 Squadron's Form 451 sheets 'Detail of Work Carried Out' in the Operations Record Book, Pat was landing back at Middle Wallop at 10.40 a.m. – the same time as that recorded for the crash. However, 234 Squadron's Form 451 sheets are erratic in their layout and may possibly be just as erratic with some of their recorded times (given the circumstances of those days, not too surprising). Just how and when the time of the crash of Me 109E-1 (Wn.3877) was actually noted down may also be open to question, especially considering the circumstances of what happened next, which was absolute horror. By the time soldiers arrived on the scene the crashed fighter was burning fiercely. Flames had enveloped the machine and the pilot was trapped inside the cockpit! He was being burnt alive before their eyes! He could not escape and they were helpless to do anything to save him. There was only one thing that could be done – an act of mercy. To end the tormented man's agony, he was shot dead. After the flames were finally extinguished, his body was removed but identification was impossible. His remains were buried as 'Unknown' in the Folkestone (New) Cemetery.[3]

After seeing that the 109 'crashed on landing', Pat hauled back on his controls to regain height. He would have been well away before any soldiers arrived.

At 10,000 feet above Dover, Pat found five Me 109s escorting a damaged Messerschmitt 110. Seeing an opportunity, he stalked them from behind. The 110 had one engine on fire and just past Dover he saw the crew bail out. The burning 110 plunged down into the sea.

Pat's account tallies with what happened to Me 110C-4 (Wn.2145) 3U+CA of *Stab ZG 26 (Horst Wessel)* flown by Oberleutnant Friedrich Viertel and his wireless operator Unteroffizier Rudolf Roth. Viertel was the *Geschwader's* Technical Officer and frequently had to fly different aircraft. The pair had taken off at 8.50 a.m. to escort bombers and had just reached the coast of Kent without meeting any opposition when an electrical fault caused a fire in one engine. Friedrich Viertel managed to bail out but suffered injuries. The body of Rudolf Roth was not recovered from the sea until 30 October.

As the 110 fell, Pat positioned himself directly behind the last 109 and opened fire, but at the same time he was aware of three more Messerschmitts diving at him from the beam. Determined to finish off his victim, he kept the button down until he ran out of ammunition. Oil splattered over his windscreen. The 109 was badly hit, apparently with a ruptured oil tank. It was trailing heavy smoke and losing height when he last saw it. Breaking off at the last possible second, Pat turned swiftly into the three 109s, faked an attack and gave himself a chance to escape in the opposite direction.[4]

Meanwhile at Middle Wallop, they waited. It was always an anxious time waiting for the Spitfires to return.

First back was 'A' Flight at 9.50 a.m., but somebody was missing. There were only five of them. Spike O'Brien, Bob Doe, Alan 'Budge' Harker, Cyril Page, and Jozef 'Slug' Szlagowski were there but Bill Gordon had been shot down by a 109. On the credit side, O'Brien claimed two Me 109s shot down; Bob Doe destroyed one Me 109 and damaged three Do 17s; and Alan Harker destroyed two Me 109s plus probably one more.

'B' Flight had been scattered all over the place in the fighting but they began turning up in ones and twos five minutes later. First to arrive were the two sergeants Mike Boddington and Keith Lawrence, the New Zealander. Boddington claimed another Me 109 which made four kills in three days for him, and gave him a total of five altogether. Twenty minutes later, after another nervous wait, two more Spitfires arrived – the two Poles Zbigniew Olenski and Jan Zurakowski. Olenski, a former test pilot, had landed at Hawkinge for fuel before returning to Middle Wallop. Zurakowski's Spitfire, N3279, had been damaged by an Me 109 over Beachy Head. He made a shaky approach and overturned while landing. He emerged uninjured and cheerfully added to the tally by informing everyone he had shot down a 109.

Pat Hughes was the last to turn up at 10.40, twenty-five minutes after everybody else. He was late because he had landed and refuelled at North Weald before flying back. Why North Weald? His old CO, Victor Beamish, happened to be the station commander there. It is very likely that after escaping from the three Messerschmitts, Pat found himself over Essex low on fuel, realised he had the opportunity to drop in on an old friend and seized it. When he did return to Middle Wallop, he announced that he had one Me 109 definite and a probable he did not see crash although it was obviously badly damaged.[5] As a result of the engagement, 234 Squadron claimed eight Me 109s destroyed, two Me 109s probably destroyed and three Do 17s damaged, but there was no time to rest on its laurels.[6]

The day was far from over. As rapidly as possible, the Spitfires had to be refuelled and rearmed. There was just time for the pilots to grab some quick relief, a cup of tea and some sandwiches while the ground crews tended to their charges. Then they were at 'Readiness' once more.

The Luftwaffe was back early in the afternoon, about 200 aircraft divided up into four formations with orders to target the southern airfields again. 'A' flight took off at 12.25 p.m. led by Spike O'Brien, closely followed five minutes later by 'B' Flight with six machines led by Pat Hughes. Jan Zurakowski, insisting that he'd suffered no ill effects from his landing mishap in the morning, was up again in another Spitfire, N3279. Ted Mortimer-Rose in Spitfire P9319 had replaced Bill Hornby but shortly after takeoff, he had to abort and he landed back at Middle Wallop after only thirty-five minutes in the air.[7]

The remaining eleven Spitfires were instructed to patrol at 'Angels 15' over RAF Warmwell in Dorset. Shortly before 1.40 p.m., 'A' Flight's Yellow Section was vectored after a Ju 88 off Portland. Junkers 88s were fast and dangerous opponents, and this time the Spitfires came off second best. New Zealander Pat Horton in Spitfire N3061 was shot down in the clash. He bailed out over the sea and was rescued shortly afterwards by a navy launch from Weymouth. He had only been slightly injured.

'Zig' Klein in Spitfire P9508 was the first to return to Middle Wallop followed five minutes later by Spike O'Brien and Bob Doe. Pat brought his five Spitfires in straight afterwards. There had been no other encounters.[8]

The same highly efficient routine of refuelling and rearming the Spitfires as quickly as possible began all over again. It was the same for the pilots too – tea and refreshments, then again 'Readiness' and the waiting. The weather was good and the Germans could come again, but before then there was the wretched waiting. Mostly the pilots just lounged about as they tried to stay as calm as possible – they would read, doze, some played cards or chess; from time to time there would be snippets of conversation. Had anyone actually seen what happened to Bill Gordon or Bill Hornby? Did you hear? Jerry managed to get through and bomb Brooklands while 609 Squadron was back on the ground refuelling! What was on at the cinema? The telephone could ring at any the time.

At least if they were scrambled again the squadron would be at full strength once more thanks to the hard working erks. For 'B' Flight, Jan Zurakowski was rested, George Bailey taking his place as Pat's Number 3 in Spitfire P9320. Ken Dewhurst was replacing Mortimer-Rose. Dewhurst was fully recovered from his parachute escape from a burning Spitfire back on 16 August.[9]

As for Pat, he was worried about Kay. The previous day he had told her, 'We're getting so much trade that I want you to go home to Hull for a while.'

'I'll fetch our things from Cornwall, first, and stay at the White Hart on Saturday night,' she had said.

On Saturday nights rooms at the White Hart were in great demand, but as Kay and Pat had spent almost all of their married nights there, the landlord knew them very well. He'd promised her that he would try to keep them a double. She was driving to Cornwall today and would probably there by now – at least she would be safer over there than in Hampshire.[10]

The Germans did come again. At 5.35 p.m., there was another scramble and this time the squadron was ordered to patrol Brooklands at 'Angels 15'. Cyril Page was back leading his section, replacing Pat Horton in 'A' Flight.

The raiders, 150 aircraft strong, came in over the Thames Estuary towards Thames Haven ranging from 10,000 feet upwards, with escorting Me 109s flying up to 25,000 feet – one formation of 109s was even encountered at 31,000 feet.

This time the action was far to the east of 234 Squadron's patrol line, but Pat's old CO, Victor Beamish, was at it again. He took-off alone in his Hurricane at 6.00 p.m. behind 249 Squadron which had relieved

151 Squadron at North Weald. On the 1st, 151 had been moved to Digby in 12 Group for a rest. Climbing hard, he reached 15,000 feet and could see that 249 Squadron was high above him. There was smoke haze up to 10,000 feet but as he looked down he could see fires at Thames Haven blazing in three places and something else. There were eight German dive-bombers half-hidden in the haze – Ju 87 Stukas! They had just attacked Thames Haven, coming in unexpectedly from the west to surprise the defences, and by remaining in the haze they were staying out of sight of the British fighters flying higher up. Beamish dived after them, going in close as usual. His Hurricane was hit by return fire as he closed in, but he ignored it as he caused a Stuka to burst into flames and spin away. He manoeuvred behind another dive-bomber, fired another long burst into it, and left it trailing smoke and losing height.[11]

By that evening of the 6th, it was obvious to the British commanders that their situation was grim. Between 24 August and 6 September, Fighter Command losses amounted to 295 fighters destroyed and 171 badly damaged. During the same period 103 pilots were killed and 128 wounded. The average pilot strength of each squadron was down from twenty-six to sixteen. To counterbalance this, they had received only 269 new and repaired Hurricanes and Spitfires. Material damage was widespread and so severe that, in terms of communications and facilities, crisis point was at hand. AVM Park reported that the German bombing attacks on his aerodromes and sector stations had caused extensive damage to five forward airfields and six out of seven sector stations. Mansion and Lympne were out of action temporarily, and Biggin Hill was so appallingly battered that only one squadron could use it at a time. No. 11 Group was being crushed.

At Middle Wallop, the news was sombre. Bill Hornby did not return. His Spitfire, X4183, had been shot up and exploded over Quickbourne Lane, Northam, with the wreckage falling in flames. Hornby had managed to bail out although suffering badly from burns and facial injuries. After four days at the Casualty Clearing Station at Benenden, he would be moved to Hollymoor Hospital in Birmingham. He did eventually rejoin the squadron but by that time it had been withdrawn from Middle Wallop and was back at St Eval.

Bill Gordon of 'A' Flight had been killed. He was the squadron's first fatality in three weeks. His Spitfire, X4036, had crashed at Howbourne Farm, Hadlow Down. Arrangements needed to be made for him to be buried in Mortlach Parish Churchyard in Banff, Scotland, but before then more tragedy was waiting for 234 Squadron ...

Too many of the veteran pilots who had been caught up continually on duty and in combat over the past weeks were reaching the end of their endurance. That evening at Middle Wallop, 234 Squadron's intelligence officer, Gregory Krikorian, who tended to be a 'father confessor' to some of his young pilots, had an unexpected visitor — Pat Hughes. Pat looked tired ... very tired. The Australian was obviously unsettled and he confided that spots were appearing before his eyes while he was flying. Krikorian tried to reassure him and pretended that he was simply tired and depressed because he'd had too much to drink.[12]

As they talked, Krikorian had the chance to look carefully at the man who was regarded by everybody as the real driving force behind the squadron. He'd had to be. Pat had, almost alone, made it into a formidable fighting force. He had the ability to make things happen, to get things done; he didn't just wait for things happen to him. In the air, he was tough and uncompromising, setting an example by leading from the front; on the ground, he was still the leader but also still very much 'one of the boys'. He brought out the best in the others.

Pat Horton, the New Zealander, had developed into an excellent pilot; so had 'Budge' Harker, and Bob Doe was now a highly proficient fighter pilot who was matching Pat victory for victory; if anything, he was becoming overconfident. The early lack of leadership in 234 had had gone completely.

With the arrival of Spike O'Brien, the squadron had the right mixture – Pat's inspiration combined with O'Brien's competence and even-handed influence. As a result it now had sixty enemy planes to its credit. Pat had contributed at least six to the total in the last three days alone, but at great personal cost. Although outgoing and confident in front of the others, Krikorian was aware he was watching a different Pat Hughes – a man with his guard down, a man on the edge. Although the squadron had gone from strength to strength, relentless nervous tension and high anxiety, towering adrenalin-pumping peaks and deep cavernous troughs of constant stress had brought Pat to the brink of exhaustion.

*

Throughout the night the Luftwaffe was not as active as usual. Only single raiders were despatched to strategic areas of England to keep the air raid sirens screaming and the people confined to shelters. Most fighter controllers felt that the Germans were resting after their sustained effort and heavy losses over the past fortnight but some suspected a more sinister reason for the relative quiet. Aerial reconnaissance had revealed that more invasion barges had arrived in the captured French ports. Heavy concentrations of troops were already nearby. Were the Germans about to unleash their forces for the final blow … invasion?

Headquarters Home Forces issued its preliminary Alert No. 3: 'Invasion probable within three days.'

16

7 SEPTEMBER 1940

At Treyarronn Bay in Cornwall, Kay Hughes had packed all night. At dawn she set off to drive to Middle Wallop. There, she would pick up Pat and they would go to nearby Andover to stay again at the White Hart.

She felt sad driving away from the lonely seaside house near RAF St Eval where she and Pat should have spent their honeymoon, but so far Pat had not slept there a single night. He'd never even had time to eat there. A few times he'd phoned, saying, 'Put the coffee on, and get out a few beers for me and the boys.' Then there would be just time for a wildly happy hour or two. So far, they had only had eleven nights together, their wedding night in a hotel at Newquay and ten more in the little White Hart Hotel at Andover.[1]

It was a beautiful day for the drive east. Things seemed peaceful for once.

The period of relative calm continued overnight and into Saturday morning, but with sunrise there was an oppressive stillness over south and south-east England. Apart from a few isolated sorties by German reconnaissance aircraft, the first half of the day dragged on quietly, slowly.

During the morning, the latest reports of increased barge concentrations in the French ports, the building of new airfields close to the French coast, construction of new heavy gun emplacements, and rumours of bomber group deployments and information from captured airmen came in and were passed on to the British Chiefs of Staff (COS). Together with these, there was a forecast received that moon and tide conditions would favour a Channel crossing and landing on the English coast between 8 and 10 September. There was a heightened possibility of invasion. A COS meeting headed by Lieutenant General Alan Brooke, the commander-in-chief of home forces responsible for the army's anti-invasion preparations, was scheduled for 5.20 p.m. to discuss whether or not 'Alert No. 1' (invasion imminent and probable within twelve hours) should be issued.

Meanwhile at 11 Group HQ in Uxbridge, AVM Keith Park instructed his controllers and squadron commanders to follow orders 'exactly' and 'without modification' from Group Operations. This statement had been made necessary as his squadrons were too often being positioned too high to successfully intercept the German bombers. Because of this, they were instead becoming embroiled with the escorting fighters. To avoid being 'bounced' from above by the German fighter escorts, some squadron commanders were indeed consistently adding 'a few thousand feet' extra to the heights at which they were ordered to intercept. Two days earlier, Park had also instructed that, wherever practical, two squadrons were to operate together, with Spitfires, because of their better performance at high altitudes, engaging the escort fighters while Hurricanes attacked the bombers. He had emphasised that it was vital to harass and destroy as many bombers as possible. Bearing in mind the Luftwaffe's continuous pressure on his airfields and sector stations, Park issued his orders for the deployment of his squadrons before he left Uxbridge to attend a conference that had been called by Dowding at Fighter Command Headquarters, Bentley Priory.

The oppressive lull continued. RDF screens remained empty and sector controllers relaxed their fighter states, but for many the quiet was nerve-racking.

After the midday meal at Tangmere, the pilots of 43 Squadron took the opportunity to 'relax' in deck chairs outside the officers' mess. Someone produced a camera and took photographs of them. Little was it realised that from a group of eight men in several of the pictures, two would be dead within a few hours.

Just before 4.00 p.m., a marker was placed on the huge map-table at Fighter Command Headquarters. RDF had detected a build-up of enemy aircraft, twenty plus, over the Pas de Calais. The German air force was beginning to move.

On the cliffs near Calais, the Luftwaffe's commander-in-chief, Reichsmarschall Hermann Göring, stood posing and waiting for an incredible passing parade. With him were Albert Kesselring, commander of *Luftflotte* 2, and Bruno Lörzer, commander of *Fliegerkorps II*, an entourage of high-ranking officers and a following of war correspondents and reporters. Göring had arrived earlier in his special VIP train for the purpose of personally commanding the assault against London. He posed for the press, looking skywards through his binoculars as 348 bombers and 617 fighters, almost 1,000 aircraft, the largest aerial armada so far assembled, thundered overhead on their way to bomb London in daylight for the first time.

The rationale for the attack was that the few remaining RAF fighters should be drawn into the air to defend the capital of the British Empire and be destroyed by the escorting fighters.

It would also carry out the promises which Hitler had shouted to his audience in Berlin's *Sportpalast* a few days before:

In England they're filled with curiosity and keep asking: 'Well, why isn't he coming?' Calm yourselves: he is coming!

*

On his arrival at Bentley Priory, Keith Park found that, besides Dowding and an NCO shorthand typist to record the minutes of the meeting, there were four others present. These were Sholto Douglas, assistant chief of the Air Staff, a group captain from the Air Ministry, AVM H. Nicholl of Fighter Command and AVM D. C. S. Evill, Senior Air Staff Officer (SASO).

As he spoke, Dowding painted a grim picture. Up to now his policy had been to concentrate most of his squadrons in the south-east with supporting units just outside 11 Group to be brought into action upon Park's request when needed. As squadrons become fatigued they had so far been rotated out of the combat area and replaced by fresh squadrons drawn from the surrounding groups, but if the present scale of attack continued this procedure could not continue. He was after a decision on the best measures to be adopted so that a rapid recovery could be made should the situation change.

Strath Evill, who had been born at Broken Hill in the west of New South Wales, had figures to confirm the worsening situation. Disregarding accidents and illness, total pilot casualties for the four weeks ending 4 September amounted to 348. During the same period the three OTUs had turned out only 280 fighter pilots, resulting in a decline in numerical strength of sixty-eight. Park added that the casualty rate in 11 Group was nearly 100 per week.

Everyone knew that there was a big difference between a pilot fresh out of an OTU and a seasoned combat pilot. Park suggested that new pilots should go from the OTUs to squadrons in the north for extra training, and that his squadrons should only receive fully trained pilots from the north to replace those lost. It was agreed that a few fresh squadrons must be kept ready to relieve Park's most tired units when necessary, and that the importing of individual airmen would come into effect when a squadron's strength fell to only fifteen pilots.

For this purpose, the squadrons were to be re-classified:

Class A: All squadrons which based in 11 Group and those in 10 and 12 Groups which might be called upon by AVM Park were to provide first line reinforcements.

Class B: Squadrons of all groups (other than 11 Group) fully established in men and machines, which the southern Groups could call into action with consideration of fatigue or lack of combat experience.

Class C: All remaining squadrons which, although possessing combat experience, had suffered crippling losses in action and were obviously overdue for rest and the training of new pilots. Experienced airmen would be 'milked' from these squadrons after a short rest to provide replacements for those in Class A and Class B.

These would not be popular measures among the pilots and particularly with such 'resting' veteran units as 32, 65, 85, 145, 151 and 615 Squadrons whose members had achieved much and paid a heavy price. There were strong bonds between the survivors.

While the meeting continued, British RDF operators were chilled by what they were detecting. This was not just another raid on the airfields, sector stations or factories. An armada was coming, and it was coming in one direction – towards London. At 4.17 p.m., Park's controllers scrambled eleven squadrons; fifteen minutes later every fighter squadron within seventy miles of London was airborne or preparing to scramble.

The COS meeting at Whitehall began at 5.20 p.m. As it proceeded, the first bombs whistled down on London's dockyard areas of Woolwich and the Isle of Dogs. The attack was concentrated because the leading bombers had arrived unmolested. British defences were caught on the wrong foot, most of Fighter Command's squadrons having been deployed to counter the usual airfield attacks. They were hurriedly redirected, but there was no time for coordination. They were only able to arrive piecemeal, one by one, to confront masses of German planes.

Typically, nine Hurricanes from 43 Squadron had been scrambled at 4.35 p.m. and the controller had urgently given them new directions. They found twenty-five Dornier Do 17s escorted by large numbers of fighters crossing the coast near Folkestone. Coming into view at the same time were two other similar sized groups of bombers and fighters.

The Hurricanes tackled the front formation, climbing until they were 1,500 feet above it. Leaving one section to try and keep the fighters off, the other two sections dived on the Dorniers. They swept around in a coordinated attack from astern, firing for all they were worth, and then broke away to make individual attacks. Time and again they darted in until most were out of ammunition but at the same time three of their number fell to the escorting Messerschmitt 109s.

Over the Thames Estuary, 73 Squadron encountered twenty-five bombers escorted by thirty Messerschmitt 110s. The three Hurricanes of Blue Section had the job of blocking the fighters but they had little chance to gain enough height, so they attacked the bombers instead. Each plane fired a short burst from about 350 yards without any obvious effect and then zoomed up into the sun. As they climbed, a *Staffel* of Me 110s in a defensive circle loomed into view. After a series of diving attacks on this formation the Hurricane pilots claimed two Messerschmitts destroyed and one damaged.

Below was a scene of devastation. A huge cylinder of black smoke from burning warehouses near the docks was billowing steadily up into the clouds. The streets were full of the noise of racing fire engines and the shouts of running men. The docks and warehouses were ablaze as London's East End was hammered. 20 per cent of the bombs carried by the He 111s and Ju 88s were incendiaries and 30 per cent were delayed-action bombs.

The sinking sun glinted on the wings of the bombers as they turned, followed by flak. Smaller planes were darting in and out of the enemy formations but the sound of fighting overhead was drowned out by the noise in the streets. The German air fleet was being scattered but there were so many planes that it was impossible to stop.

Like so many others, the squadrons coming all the way from Middle Wallop were directed away from their usual patrol lines to try and intercept the raiders. The Spitfires of 609 Squadron caught a formation of enemy bombers as it turned south-west of London. John Curchin manoeuvred his Green Section to engage a group of Dornier Do 17s from the beam, but at the last instant the Germans turned so that a coordinated assault became impossible. Curchin instructed his men to break up and make individual attacks while he went after the leading Dornier. He turned in, closing fast, and fired a four-second burst before diving underneath and swinging around for a second attack from the other side. Again he fired for four seconds. The leading Dornier seemed undamaged but suddenly the second bomber in the formation broke away and fell in a dive. As Curchin turned off, he spotted a single Messerschmitt 109 ahead and below. He followed it through the thick smoke billowing over the Thames and finally caught up over the Estuary. He fired for three seconds. The 109 was hit and Curchin closed to fifty yards as he fired for the last time. Pieces of the German fighter were torn away before it crashed into the water.

South-east of Folkestone, 234 Squadron ran into an estimated sixty German aircraft consisting of Dornier Do 17s and escorting Messerschmitt 109s. Initially instructed to patrol over the airfields at Kenley and Biggin Hill at 'Angels 10', Spike O'Brien took his twelve Spitfires up to twice that height until they were above hoards of bandits all heading south on their way home. They were harried as they went by angry, stinging Hurricanes and Spitfires.

Pat Hughes was leading Blue Section in Spitfire X4009 as usual. O'Brien told Pat to go after the bombers while his flight covered the 109s. Ordering his wingmen to follow suit, Pat plunged after the bombers. He was well ahead of the others as he closed in on a straggling Dornier.

Blue 2 followed the Australian down and saw him make a quarter attack on the German machine. Large pieces flew off the enemy plane, then a wing crumpled and it went down spinning. An instant later, Blue 2 saw a Spitfire spinning down with about a third of its wing broken off ... a collision?

Above at the same time, O'Brien and his Red Section were attacked by yellow-nosed Me 109s. In the ensuing dogfight, Red 2 just managed to evade an aggressive Messerschmitt with a white spinner, but 234 Squadron's commanding officer of only just over three weeks, Squadron Leader 'Spike' O'Brien DFC, was shot down and killed near Biggin Hill.

The British fighters, their ammunition exhausted and fuel tanks almost empty, landed back at their airfields in ones and twos. Weary pilots climbed out of their cockpits in grim silence, carrying in their minds the unforgettable spectacle of the seemingly impregnable bulk of the German formations and of the terrible firestorm in London. They had hit back as hard as they could.

For 234 Squadron, 'Budge' Harker had destroyed two Me 109s and damaged another; Bob Doe destroyed a Heinkel 111; 'Zig' Klein probably destroyed an Me 109; and Pat Hughes may have accounted for a Do 17, but he was not back yet. In fact, three Spitfires were not back. As well as Pat and

Spike O'Brien, Blue 2, Keith Lawrence, was missing. The New Zealander had, in fact, landed at Croydon and would not return to Middle Wallop until the next day when he added to the tally by declaring he had destroyed an Me 109 and damaged a Do 17.

In the capital, flames spread furiously along the waterfront, rows of houses were obliterated and granaries and warehouses collapsed, falling into the river or crashing down into the streets. Every firefighting appliance for miles around was sent to the area. A huge pall of smoke prematurely darkened the sky but as night fell the glow was hellish.

London's agony was far from over. The first of 318 German bombers were approaching, guided to the target by the huge fires. It was the start of a series of violent attacks destined to go on for fifty-seven consecutive nights — the Blitz was beginning.

Against the incoming stream of German planes, the British night defences were almost powerless, having to rely almost solely upon the 264 anti-aircraft guns ringing the city. There were only two squadrons of Blenheim night fighters available and one of these, No. 600 Squadron based at Hornchurch, was unable to take off through the thick smoke swirling across the airfield.

All night the Germans cruised over London, a target impossible to miss, dropping 330 tons of high explosive and 440 incendiary canisters to stoke the inferno below. By morning, 306 civilians were dead and 1,337 badly injured.

*

It was late in the afternoon a few miles from Andover when Kay Hughes stopped and phoned the Mess at Middle Wallop. She asked for Pat. Instead, Flying Officer E. C. 'Bish' Owens, the fatherly squadron adjutant, came to the phone. 'Come right over,' he said, 'I'll meet you at the gate.'

For a second she wondered, why? Then, instinctively she knew. She clutched the gold charm bracelet Pat had given her. She knew he was dead.

True to his word, Bish and some of Pat's boys met her at the gate. They told her that Pat was missing – there was some hope but the chances were not good.[2] Then they took her to the White Hart. 'I've got your double,' the landlord said greeting her with a wide smile. That was before he realised something was wrong.

The boys took him to one side and told him.

At 8.07 p.m., Lieutenant General Alan Brooke issued the code word 'Cromwell', Alert No. 1, to his Eastern and Southern Commands. The signal was received in some places with panic. A number of Home Guard and army units ordered the ringing of church bells, the universal signal that an invasion was taking place already.

The 'Cromwell' alert came into Headquarters, Australian Striking Force, at Amesbury Abbey at 9.30 p.m. and all units were placed at one hour's notice to move. The 18th Infantry Brigade was handicapped by its incidence of leave, with almost 50 per cent of its personnel absent. Many of the men of the

1. Pat Hughes after graduation from Point Cook. (Bill Hughes, Dimity Torbett, Stephanie Bladen, David Hughes, Laurence Lucas)

2. Point Cook, Wednesday 11 March 1936, Pat Hughes' diary entry about his first solo. 'I went mad, whistled, sang and almost jumped for joy.' (Stephanie Bladen)

3. Point Cook, Tuesday 21 April 1936, Pat Hughes' diary entry about his first crash. 'Positively an unlucky day … I careered down to the deck and turned up on my nose in A7-40. I have requested permission to obtain damaged propeller.' (Stephanie Bladen)

4. Point Cook, Thursday 7 May 1916, Pat Hughes' diary entry about low flying and camera gun practice. 'Just imagine sitting on a chap's tail pouring a stream of hot lead into him and seeing his plane catch on fire. Makes out that I'm a pretty bloody fellow. I'm not.' (Stephanie Bladen)

Left: 5. A portrait of Kathleen. Pat Hughes met her at the Beverley Arms. He found out that her name was Kathleen, but her friends called her Kay. (Dimity Torbett, Stephanie Bladen)

Right: 6. A copy of Pat and Kay Hughes' Marriage Certificate. The couple were married in Bodmin Register Office on 1 August 1940 with strangers (except for Flying Officer Butch) as witnesses. (Bodmin Register Office)

7. Spitfires claw for height over an incoming raid, striving to climb above the bombers and take on the German escort fighters. As the Battle of Britain progressed, RAF tactics revolved around the faster Spitfires engaging the escorting Me 109s and Me 110s while Hurricanes attacked the bombers. A painting by Gordon Olive. (Rick Olive)

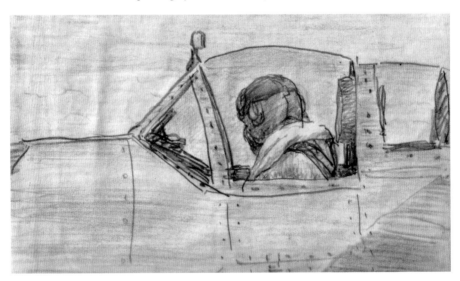

8. Looking for the enemy. A pencil sketch by Pat Hughes' Point Cook classmate, Gordon Olive. The need for vigilance was drummed into every pilot. 'Never stop looking around', they were told. 'Many pilots shot down never saw the enemy fighter that got them. Out of every five minutes on patrol four should be spent looking over your shoulders. Whether you are by yourself or with a hundred others, never stop looking around.' (Beryl Olive)

9. Spitfires carrying out a formal No. 1 Attack, diving line astern into a web of tracer bullets. The thin, dead straight, white pencil line streaks of tracer could have a curious negative effect as they flashed across in front leaving their trails – even the old trails could somehow seem lethal. A painting by Gordon Olive. (Maria Marchant)

10. Richard Hardy's captured Spitfire. In the running fight on 15 August 1940, 234 Squadron's Red Section was overwhelmed by enemy fighters. Hardy's Spitfire was hit and he was wounded in the shoulder, probably by a cannon shell which hit struck the fuselage just behind the pilot's seat. Injured, short of fuel and far out to sea near the French coast, he headed for the nearest land where he managed to touch down safely on Cherbourg-East/Theville airfield, much to the astonishment of the Germans on the ground. (ww2images.com)

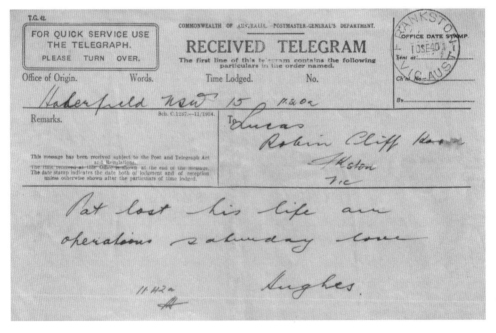

IN MEMORY OF
FLT.LT.P.C.HUGHES D.F.C. R.A.F.
AN AUSTRALIAN PILOT.
WHO FELL IN THE GARDEN HERE,
IN THE DEFENCE OF BRITAIN
7 SEPTEMBER 1940

Left: 11. Pat Hughes' grave, carefully tended over the years by Mr Bert Knowes, Norman and Margery Shirtliff of Hull and also by Mrs Jean Holmes of Barton-on-Humber, apparently on behalf of the Spitfire Society. Both Margery and Jean corresponded for many years with Pat's closest sister, Constance Torbett, until her death at the age of ninety-five in 2010. Constance remained very grateful to them for their care and for the fresh flowers they laid there. (Dimity Torbett, Stephanie Bladen)

Above: 12. The memorial plaque on the wall of the house identifying where Pat Hughes fell into the backyard garden. The resident in 1940 was William Norman. (Malcolm Booth)

13. The telegram sent to the Lucas family informing them of Pat Hughes' death. (Laurence Lucas)

14. Pat Hughes' medals. Bill Hughes donated his brother's DFC and campaign medals to the Australian War Memorial for display. A photograph of them was placed on the dust jacket cover of *A Few of 'The Few' – Australians and the Battle of Britain*, the book published by the Australian War Memorial to mark the fiftieth Anniversary of the battle. (Author's collection)

15. Lost for many years, Pat Hughes' posthumous Distinguished Flying Cross and service medals eventually came into the possession of his closest brother, Bill (mentioned as Will), who donated them to the Australian War Memorial in Canberra. Bill is shown here displaying them at his Beacon Hill home in Sydney in 1988. (Author's collection)

Thanksgiving Service for Paterson Clarence Hughes D.F.C. and Dedication of Stone

Saturday 23rd August 2008

Left: 16. The cover of the Pat Hughes Memorial Stone Service of 23 August 2008. Dedication of the Memorial Stone and the Memorial Stone Service were carried out by Shoreham Aircraft Museum in Sevenoaks on the initiative of the curator, renowned aviation artist Geoff Nutkins. (via Stephanie Bladen)

Below: 17. The Pat Hughes Memorial at Cooma NSW. This memorial was dedicated to him in Monahan Hayes Place in 2006. It is in the form of a glass topped font which contains the model of a Spitfire and a picture of Pat's last photograph. (via Stephanie Bladen, Laurence Lucas)

Above left: 18. Pat Hughes' parents: Caroline Christina (*née* Vennel) and Paterson Clarence 'Percy' Hughes. (Dimity Torbett)

Above right: 19. Family snap: Pat Hughes (right) with his brother William. William, of course, was usually called 'Bill' by his friends and relatives, but in his letters Pat addressed him as 'Will'. (Dimity Torbett)

Below: 20. Family snap: Pat Hughes with his sisters Marjorie (left) and Constance. (Dimity Torbett)

COURSE "A" – JANUARY 1936 ENTRY.

Cadets PAINE ROGERS ROBINSON CPL. DILLON LAC. COOPER AC1s. JACKSON SLADEN Cadets FOWLER KINANE GOOD CAMERON

Cadets COSGROVE YATES HULLOCK HUGHES ARMSTRONG WIGHT GREY-SMITH GILBERT POWER KELAHER SHEEN BROUGH

Cadets JOHNSON KAUFMAN McDONOUGH U/Os. BOEHM ALLSOP HARTNELL OLIVE MARSHALL Cadets MACE CAMPBELL EATON.

Above: 21. 'A' Course January 1936 entry at RAAF Point Cook. Left to right, back row: Cadets Paine, Rogers, Robertson, Dillon, Cooper, Jackson, Sladin, Fowler, Kinane, Good and Cameron. Centre row: Cadets Cosgrove, Yates, Hullock, Hughes, Armstrong, Wight, Grey-Smith, Gilbert, Power, Kelaher, Sheen and Brough. Front row: Cadets Johnson, Kaufman, McDonough, Boehm, Allsop, Hartnell, Olive, Marshall, Mace, Campbell and Eaton. Most subsequently had distinguished careers of in the RAAF and RAF. Of them, Pat Hughes, Gordon Olive, Desmond Sheen and Dick Power flew in the Battle of Britain. (RAAF Museum)

Left: 22. Pat Hughes at Point Cook. (Dimity Torbett)

23. Pat's mother, Pete Pettigrew, Marge and Bill at Pat's departure for England. (Bill Hughes)

24. Pat aboard the RMS *Narkunda* as the ship departs from Wharf No. 21 Pyrmont, Sydney, 9 January 1937. (Bill Hughes)

25. At sea: Desmond Sheen (right) and Bob Cosgrove in the swimming pool on the RMS *Narkunda*, photographed by Pat Hughes. (via Dimity Torbett)

26. Pat Hughes in a quiet mood at Uxbridge. (Bill Hughes)

27. Hawker Hart, photographed by Pat Hughes. (via Dimity Torbett)

28. Hawker Hurricane prototype K5083, photographed at Martlesham Heath by Pat Hughes. One of the Hawker test pilots who flew this machine regularly was South Australian, Richard Carew Reyell, who was killed in action on the same day as Pat. (via Dimity Torbett)

29. Vickers Wellington prototype K4049, photographed at Martlesahm Heath by Pat Hughes. The Wellington was one of the classic RAF bombers of the Second World War. It carried the lion's share of Bomber Command's night offensive until the introduction later of the four–engined Short Stirling, Handley Page Halifax and Avro Lancaster heavy bombers and was still in front line service at the end of the war. (via Dimity Torbett)

30. Pat Hughes at Martlesahm Heath carrying out some repairs to his normal mode of transportation. (Stephanie Bladen)

31. Pat Hughes (right) with 64 Squadron pilots. (Bill Hughes)

Right: 32. Pat Hughes in front of tent. Two of Pat's nephews later served in the RAAF: the late Air Vice Marshal. H. A. (Bill) Hughes of Canberra; and the late Wing Commander John Hughes of Perth, Western Australia. (Stephanie Bladen)

Below: 33. Pat Hughes in his RAAF uniform in the UK. George Bailey and Keith Lawrence recalled that Pat made a point of normally wearing his original dark blue RAAF uniform with gold stripes. Australian pilots serving in the RAF under the pre-war Short Service Commission Scheme were permitted to wear their RAAF uniforms, and most chose to do so. (Laurence Lucas)

34. Bristol Blenheim If fighter. Note the belly pack of four .303-inch Browning machine guns. The pack was bolted on under the Blenheim's bomb bay which stored four belts of ammunition, each containing 500 rounds. (IWM via John Hamilton)

35. Bristol Blenheim Mk.I bomber in flight with no gun pack. Pre-war, the twin-engine Blenheim bomber was regarded as a modern aircraft with an outstanding performance. It was capable of easily overtaking the Gloster Gladiator, the RAF's main pre-war single-seat biplane fighter. (RAAF Museum)

Above left: 36. Pilot Officer - later promoted to Flying Officer – Butch. 'My dog "Butch" has grown incredibly', Pat wrote home, 'and now likes to fight as well as fly, although he doesn't yet display much intelligence.' (Stephanie Bladen, Dimity Torbett)

Above right: 37. Pat with Butch. (Bill Hughes)

38. Butch on top of the fuselage of a Blenheim next to the gun turret. When nobody was looking Pat took the pup flying in his Blenheim (it was one of those well-kept secrets that everybody knew about) and in his letters home to his Mother, he would tell her the many flying hours Butch had accumulated. (Bill Hughes)

Above left: 39. Vincent 'Bush' Parker after his release from Colditz. After the war he stayed in the RAF but on 29 January 1946 he was killed in a tragic accident when the Hawker Tempest he was flying crashed into a hillside, cause unknown. He was deservedly Mentioned in Despatches the following 13 June. (Colin Burgess)

Above right: 40. Ron Lees, the Australian CO of 72 Squadron. He remained in the RAF after the war and on 3 February 1966, after thirty-five years of distinguished service, he retired as Air Marshal Sir Ronald Beresford Lees KCB, CBE, DFC & Bar. (RAAF Museum)

41. Desmond Sheen seated in the cockpit of his Spitfire. Out of the twenty-four RAAF cadets who chose to journey to England to join the RAF early in 1937, just three flew Spitfires during the Battle of Britain: Pat Hughes; Gordon Olive; and Desmond Sheen. This particular aircraft was Spitfire Mk. I, K9959/RN-J of 72 Squadron, Sheen's regular machine until he joined the Photographic Reconnaissance Unit (PDU) in April 1940. His personal emblem was a brown boomerang in a white circle. (Desmond Sheen)

42. Junkers Ju 88s. In 1940 the Ju 88 was the latest and fastest German bomber. Originally designed as a dive-bomber, it proved to be one of the most versatile types in the Luftwaffe arsenal and was always regarded by those Allied pilots who encountered it as a formidable opponent. (MAP)

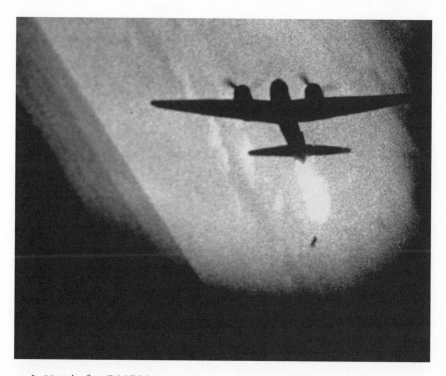

43. Ju 88 under fire. (RAAF Museum)

44. Tally ho! At 6.15 p.m. on 8 July 1940, the three Spitfires of Blue Section, 234 Squadron, led by Pat Hughes intercepted a Junkers Ju 88 twenty-five miles south-east of Land's End. Pat's two wingmen were New Zealander, P/O Keith Lawrence as Blue 2, and Sgt George Bailey as Blue 3. (AWM)

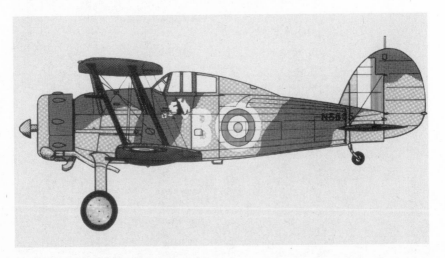

45. Gladiator N5585 of 247 Squadron depicted with the 'Anzac Answer' emblem. The sketch is based on the diagrams in Francis Mason's book, *Battle Over Britain*. (Dennis Newton)

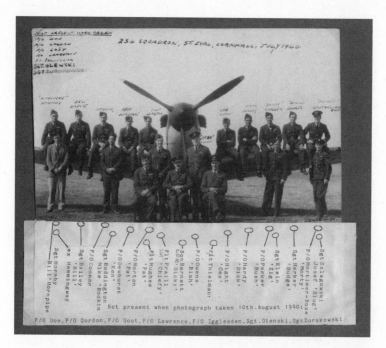

Within the top photo, handwritten annotations:

234 SQUADRON, ST. EVAL, CORNWALL, JULY 1940.

NOT PRESENT WHEN TAKEN
P/O DOE
P/O GORDON
P/O GOUT
P/O LAWRENCE
F/O IGGLEADEN
SGT.OLENSKI
SGT ZUROKOWSKI

Not present when photograph taken 10th. August 1940:

P/O Doe, P/O Gordon, P/O Gout, P/O Lawrence, F/O Igglesden, Sgt.Olenski, SgtZurakowski

Names (left to right):

Sgt.Hornby 'Bill' Hornpipe
ex Hemingway 'Bill'
Sgt.Bailey 'Bill'
F/O Connor
Sgt.Boddington Mike 'Bodkin'
P/O Dewhurst 'Ken'
P/O Horton 'Pas'
P/O Hughes 'Pat'
Flt.Hughes 'Pat'
Sgt.Chisely
Flt.Prail 'Chiefy'
Sgn.Barrett S/LDR 'Dicky'
P/O Owens 'Bish'
Flt.Thielmanr
P/O Hight 'Dick'
P/O Hardy 'Dick'
P/O Parker 'Bush'
Sgt.Klein 'Zig'
Sgt.Harker 'Budge'
P/O Mortimer-Rose 'Morty'
Sgt.Siarowski Josef 'Sus'

46. Pat Hughes and 234 Squadron at St Eval. The extra details on the photograph were added by Keith Lawrence who, with Pat, took part in 234 Squadron's first credited victory on 8 July 1940. He was also flying with Pat when the Australian was killed in action during the first huge daylight attack on London on 7 September 1940. Pat is seated on the left. (Keith Lawrence)

47. Pat Hughes at dispersal, as usual wearing his dark blue Royal Australian Air Force uniform. (Dimity Torbett)

48. Messerschmitt Me 109E. The Me 109 and Me 110 aircraft referred to by the Allies were actually the Bf 109 and Bf 110 respectively. (MAP)

49. A Messerschmitt Me 109E damaged to the extent that its port undercarriage has dropped down. Me 109s made up the majority of Pat Hughes' victories. (AWM)

50. Messerschmitt Me 110. Although fast and well armed with two 20 mm cannons and four 7.9 mm machine guns in the nose firing forward and one flexible 7.9 mm machine gun in the rear cockpit, it failed as an escort fighter when confronted by Fighter Command's fast and far more nimble Hurricanes and Spitfires. Later in the war the type was developed into a highly dangerous night fighter. Pat Hughes claimed three Me 110s in his most successful combat on 4 September 1940. (AWM)

51. Pat Hughes with a couple of pilots from 234 Squadron's 'B' Flight. (Stephanie Bladen)

52. Pat in happier times at a picnic at St Eval in August 1940, before he found himself in the position of temporary commander of 234 Squadron. Pat led 234 into some of the heaviest fighting of the Battle of Britain. (Bill Hughes, Dimity Torbett)

Left: 53. Pat Hughes photographed the day before he was killed in action. Despite the smile, it seems evident that he was feeling the effects of stress and fatigue by this stage. In the intense, bitter fighting three days before 7 September 1940 he was credited with destroying six, possibly seven, enemy aircraft. (Bill Hughes, Keith Lawrence)

Below: 54. F/Lt Dick Reynell, the other Australian pilot killed in action on 7 September 1940, was shot down by Me 109s. His parachute also failed to open. (Marjorie Horn)

55. Dornier Do 17s over London on 7 September 1940. The curved road on the left is Silvertown Way where it becomes North Woolwich Road. West Ham Speedway is directly underneath the bombers. The first bombs fell on the capital's dockyard areas of Woolwich and the Isle of Dogs at around 5.20 p.m. (AWM)

56. The London docks area ablaze late on the afternoon of 7 September 1940. That night, the code word 'Cromwell', Alert No. 1, was issued. This was the alarm signalling that the anticipated German invasion of England had begun. Fortunately, it was a false alarm. (AWM)

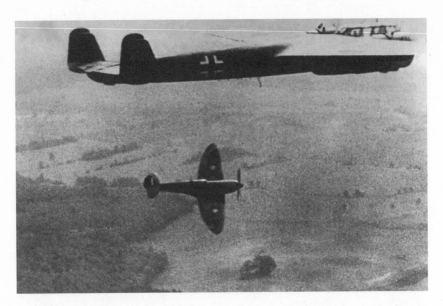

57. A Spitfire breaks away from an attack on a Dornier Do 17. The mission that day for the crew of Dornier Do 17Z (2596), F1-BA, of *Stab KG 76* was to photograph the bombing of London docks. Its crew was Lt Gottfried Schneider, Ofw Karl Schneider, Fw Erich Rosche and Uffz Walter Rupprecht. On the return flight, the Dornier was attacked repeatedly by RAF fighters. Among these may have been the Spitfire of P/O Ellis Aries of 602 Squadron who claimed a Do 17 destroyed, and a Hurricane flown by F/O George Peters of 79 Squadron. (ww2images.com)

58. The site of Pat Hughes' grave in the churchyard of St James' Church of England in the parish of Sutton-on-Hull. (Stephanie Bladen)

59. Dornier Do 17Z (2596) crashed down into a stream at Sunbridge near Sevenoaks at around 6.00 p.m. on 7 September 1940. The tail fin was found some distance from the main wreckage. (*After the Battle Collection* via Winston Ramsey)

Left: 60. The flying helmet of Fw Erich Rosche, wireless operator of Dornier Do 17Z (2596). Erich Rosche managed to bail out and was captured but the rest of the crew perished. At his capture, Rosche was relieved of his flying helmet and oxygen mask, items which became the highly prized souvenirs of a Sevenoaks resident, or residents. (*After the Battle Collection* via Winston Ramsey)

Middle: 61. Tool kit found at the crash site of Dornier Do 17Z (2596). (*After the Battle Collection* via Winston Ramsey)

Right: 62. Dornier engine cowling clasp with a .303-inch shell casing embedded in it. Over the years two excavations were carried out at the site of the Dornier crash and they made numerous remarkable finds. (*After the Battle Collection* via Winston Ramsey)

Left: 63. Portrait of Kay Hughes *c.* 1942. By then Kay was a WAAF. (Stephanie Bladen)

Right: 64. Kay when she was presented with Pat's posthumous Distinguished Flying Cross at a ceremony in June 1942. (AWM)

65. Pat Hughes' name in the Australian list on the Battle of Britain Memorial, London. (Author's collection)

66. Pat's memorial plaque on the stone wall at the front of All Saints Church, Kiama, New South Wales. It was placed there by his sister Muriel 'Midge' Tongue. (Author's collection)

10th Battalion who were due back from leave were unable to get away from London because of the bombing.

War correspondent Kenneth Slessor, who was stationed at the abbey, was awakened at 11 p.m. with the news that the Germans had landed on the south coast and that everyone had been ordered to stand by for an immediate move. Although this was unconfirmed, he noted that everyone appeared to accept it as correct. General Wynter, who was absent when the signal arrived, was now back in his office. The abbey had become a hive of activity and all available troops paraded in full battle dress. One guard muttered to Slessor, 'I'll be glad when the bastards come.'

With the passing of time the bustle gradually diminished as they waited tensely for orders. By midnight the men were allowed to return to their tents and sleep but were told to be ready to move at one hour's notice. The signal would be two or three blasts of a whistle. Some listened to the midnight news on the radio and learned that London had been under heavy attack and fires in the East End were still out of control.

Overnight for the first time, RAF Bomber Command's main effort was concentrated on the enemy invasion barges being assembled in the Channel coastal ports.

*

In her single room at the White Hart, Kay Hughes had confirmation during the night that Pat had been killed. He had bailed out, she was told, but a German fighter had followed him down, riddling him with bullets. It must have been over in seconds.

She asked about Flying Officer Butch, but the dog was missing too. He had run out of the Mess and disappeared.

Kay cried into the night and consumed double brandies. She wept uncontrollably until there were no tears left.[3]

17

WHAT REALLY HAPPENED?

Over the years, many accounts, sometimes conflicting, have been written about Pat Hughes' fate. They assert: he was shot down by Me 109s; he rammed the Dornier; the Dornier crashed into him; the Dornier blew up; wreckage from the Dornier struck his Spitfire; he didn't bail out; he did bail out; he was shot up in his parachute; his parachute didn't open; and even that he was a victim of friendly fire.

It must be remembered when looking into such issues that what happened took place in a short, intense space of time – just a matter of seconds – more than three-quarters of a century ago. In the hope of reaching a valid decision on what actually transpired, eyewitness accounts (bearing in mind that the senses can deceive) and substantiating physical evidence have to be considered.

In the Form 450 sheets of 234 Squadron's Operations Record Book it says that:

S/Ldr O'Brien and F/Lt Hughes were both shot down and killed in the engagement – It was reported that F/Lt. Hughes had destroyed 1 Do.17 before being sent down himself.[1]

The combat report of Blue 2, Keith Lawrence, inferred rather than stated that the Australian had collided with the Do 17:

As Blue 2 I followed Blue 1 into an attack on the Do 17s. Blue 1 was well ahead of me and I saw him go down to make a quarter attack on a straggling Do.17 below the rest of the formation. I saw large pieces fly off the E/A then a wing crumpled and the E/A went down spinning. Immediately after I saw a Spitfire which I assumed to be Blue 1 spinning down with about $^1/_3$ wing broken.[2]

In 1980, as part of an article to commemorate the fortieth anniversary of the Battle of Britain, Kay Hughes was interviewed for *Woman* magazine by journalist Joan Reeder. It was published in the November 15 issue. By then Kay was Mrs D. Wray, aged sixty-four, living just outside Hull. At one point in the article Kay related that when Bish Owens and the boys had taken her to the White Hart they told her, 'Pat had bailed out, but a German fighter followed him down, riddling him with bullets. It must have been over in seconds.'[3]

In 1990, at the time of the fiftieth anniversary of the Battle of Britain, I wrote an article about Pat Hughes that was published in the September 1990 issue of *FlyPast* magazine. In response to it, Desmond Hall of Sundridge, Sevenoaks, Kent, wrote to me via Ken Ellis, the editor of the magazine at that time. He wrote:

Since I was a boy of ten in 1940 I have been interested in the Battle of Britain and in the action in which Hughes lost his life in particular. This action took place over the area of our village and the description in your article coincides with eyewitness accounts from that time of people from the village. Accounts from other publications do not. The following may be of interest to you.

Our family home was and still is situated in this village, alongside the A25 opposite a then electricity generating plant which was itself alongside a water pumping station.

On September the 7th 1940 my mother and I were visiting my grandmother at the other end of the village. Around 5 p.m. the air raid warning sounded and we took cover under the stairs. Consequently I did not see any of the ensuing action, just heard the fighting, the machinegun fire, culminating in the awe inspiring scream of falling aircraft at full power, followed by a thunderous roar as they hit the ground. After the 'all clear' it was realized that one of the planes crashed near to our home and we cut short the visit and hurried home to see if all was well.

In answer to our excited but fearful questions, my father who in company with neighbours had been watching the fighting said (and I quote as best as memory serves me), 'We thought we were finished. A German plane has been rammed by a Spitfire. The Gerry was spinning down straight for us but a wing came off and it veered away. It's crashed behind the waterworks. The Spitfire pilot jumped out but his parachute did not open. They think he was a Pole.'

That was the scene as described by my father.

We boys of course visited the crash sites both the German and British. The piece that fell off the Dornier 17 came to earth in Chipstead and turned out to be the port rudder and fin. It was stored in a builder's yard there and we boys, peeping through the cracks in the door, were thrilled to see it, its swastika seeming to our minds to be almost luminous.

Years later I asked the builder what had become of it, and to my pleasure he took me to his home and gave it to me much damaged (by his two sons, he said). In turn I gave the fin to the author and historian, Dennis Knight, who I believe still has it.

The Spitfire crashed at Bessel Green beside Dry Hill Lane and the pilot who was P. C. Hughes fell to his death in the garden of a bungalow alongside the A25 at Sundridge.

The resident of the 'bungalow' referred to by Desmond Hall was William Norman, as John Day of No. 8, Main Road, Sundridge, recorded in October 2006:

I think one of my clearest memories of the Battle of Britain took place on a Saturday in September 1940.

A Spitfire fighter and a Dornier German bomber collided in mid-air to the east of Sundridge Village. I did not see the actual collision of the two aircraft but I remember the following events.

Mr William Norman, an elderly neighbour who lived at No. 16 Main Road called at our address, No. 8 Main Road. Mr Norman who was in a distressed state asked my father if he would go back with him to see the body of a young man laying on the lawn of his back garden.

Later we learned the body of the brave young man was in fact the Australian pilot of the RAF crashed Spitfire.

The mission that day for the crew of Dorner Do 17Z (2596), F1-BA, of *Stab KG 76* was to photograph the bombing of London docks. The crew was Leutnant Gottfried Schneider, Oberfeldwebel Karl Schneider, Feldwebel Erich Rosche and Unteroffizier Walter Rupprecht. On the return flight, the Dornier was attacked repeatedly by RAF fighters. Among these may have been the Spitfire of Pilot Officer Ellis Aries of 602 Squadron who claimed a Do 17 destroyed, and a Hurricane flown by Flying Officer George Peters of 79 Squadron.[4]

The Dornier's final encounter was with Pat Hughes. From this it went out of control and at 6 p.m. crashed down into a stream at Sundridge near Sevenoaks, east of Bessels Green where Pat's Spitfire came down. One of the tail fins was found some distance away. The wireless operator, Erich Rosche, managed to bail out and was captured but the others perished. At his capture, Rosche was relieved of his flying helmet and oxygen mask, items which became the highly prized souvenirs of a Sevenoaks resident, or residents.[5]

Desmond Hall expanded his account when writing a letter to a Herr Bauman, who was a relative of Erich Rosche, the only survivor of the Dornier crew:

To those of us who were then 10 years old or thereabouts, the summer days of 1940 were filled with exciting hours spent watching the great air combats which came to be known as the Battle of Britain. I do not remember fear at first or my friends being afraid, the village was never the target and we in our young innocence felt immune and secure in the knowledge that our airmen would always win (such innocence). The fighting almost always took place at great height, the machines just glinting pinheads and weaving vapour trails, sometimes near the end of the battle there would be the odd smoke trail, may be a parachute floating distantly, and aircraft returning to Biggin Hill aerodrome 6 or 7 miles distant. To we boys it seemed a battle between machines with little thought of the men crewing them, when we thought of it at all. Germans in our imagination were a sort of automen (propaganda, I suppose).

The seventh of September changed all that.

It had been a quiet morning and afternoon, I remember my Grandfather saying, 'They are not coming today.' Around 4.30 p.m., the warning sirens sounded for the first time that day, people thought, 'It won't be much', and carried on with afternoon tea, at approximately 5 p.m. a distant hum of aircraft engines grew louder and nearer, the planes lower, there were bursts of machine gun fire which grew more intense that we had ever heard before, spent bullets and cartridges falling like hail. Then according to my father and other witnesses two aircraft, a Spitfire and a Dornier 17, appeared to collide. As they began to fall two men took to parachutes, one of which failed to operate, and the wearer, the Spitfire pilot, died among the flowers in the garden of a bungalow alongside the main road (A25) his aircraft fell in a meadow close by. The other parachutist was Hauptman Roche [*sic*] from the Dornier 17, he was taken prisoner in another village, I believe.

The Dornier came through the sky with an awesome wail of racing engines which I can still call to mind even now, the aircraft narrowly missing the water pumping station, came to rest in a stream (the infant River Darenth) alongside a birch plantation. For what seemed a long time after the crash but must have only been minutes there was silence, then people began to run to the scene, rescue vehicles arrived but there were alas no survivors. An armed guard was mounted to keep people away until the ambulance men removed the German airmen to a place of rest.

At the end of the day when darkness had fallen and the night bombers were droning towards London the neighbours gathered to sit with us in our air raid shelter. Before going in we paused to look at a scene never to be forgotten, the sky to the north was alight with a warm red glow, search light fingers swept the heavens, sometimes they focused on one place, then there were sparks of anti-aircraft fire, great pools of light were drifting down as bombers dropped flares to see their way. I saw many raids later but nothing to compare with this. We guessed (correctly) that London was on fire and the red sky was from the flames.

Sitting in the cosiness of the shelter everyone was of course talking of the day's events. Mr Cook who was the first on the scene at the Dornier crash described the attempts to rescue the men. From what he said they were dead anyway and must have died quickly. Someone said, 'Poor blighters.' Another, 'They were only flesh and blood like us.' A mother remarked, 'They were someone else's sons after all.' This seemed to be the mood of most people in the village on that day and after.

During the night church bells which had been silent since the surrender of France were heard to ring the signal for invasion! My father and Mr Cook along with other members of the defence volunteers 'stood to' next day, and on the Monday went about their work armed, but luckily for us it was a false alarm, no invasion fleet had sailed.

On Sunday morning, the 8th, we boys went to the crash and we stood by the birch trees, the silence of the morning broken only by the ripple of the stream. We looked at the broken green and blue wreckage and the violence in the world seemed all wrong, and my friend said sadly, 'Just think Des, yesterday these Germans and our pilot were alive and now they are gone.' This was a moment which made a great lasting impression on me and has stayed with me over the years.

The following Tuesday or Wednesday, I am not sure which, they were given a military funeral and laid to rest in our churchyard among village people. The father of Mrs Wells who keeps a village shop was a carpenter and he made the coffins for the men. Flowers were placed upon the grave, there was a touching posy from two little girls who lived near the scene of the crash, a white painted cross was placed, it was simply inscribed:

> Schneider
> Schneider
> Ruprecht
> German air force
> 7-9-40

During the years they lay in our churchyard flowers were placed, from time to time the grass was trimmed and the cross repainted, no one owned to doing these things but they happened.

These are my memories of a day seen through a ten-year-old's eyes. Ever since then I have wondered about these men, what they looked like, what manner of people they were, etc. They are not forgotten, certain people still remember on the day and spare them a thought.

A few years ago the men were exhumed and taken to an official war cemetery at Cannock Chase in Staffordshire, England. When this happened some people were indignant and thought they should remain in the village over which they fell. I felt that way at first but on reflection it is better perhaps to be in an official burial place where their names will be seen for all time. I expect they would have eventually passed into obscurity in our church yard.

From books on the subject of the Battle of Britain I have learned the target that afternoon was the London docks. The raid apparently was a complete success for the Luftwaffe. The RAF were taken off guard by a change of tactics and the bombers were on the way out from London going home when they were intercepted.

The pilot who died with the Germans was claimed by the RAF so was not buried in the village. It is now known that he was an Australian, Flt Lt Hughes of 234 Squadron RAF operating at that time from Middle Wallop, Hampshire.

That seems to be all I have to say, except I wonder what became of Hauptman Roche and if Herr Schneider Senior ever heard from him after the war.

*

But what really happened to Pat Hughes? Was he shot down by Me 109s?[6]

This has to be a distinct possibility. Certainly there were plenty of German fighters about. Precise figures for the armada, according to most accounts, have been put at 348 bombers and 617 fighters, which meant there were nearly two fighters for every bomber. In this particular battle, 'Budge' Harker claimed two Me 109s, Keith Lawrence one Me 109, 'Zig' Klein probably destroyed a 109, and Spike O'Brien was shot down and killed by Me 109s near Biggin Hill.

However, Keith Lawrence made no mention of any Me 109s at the point in his combat report when Pat was attacking the Dornier. Nor did Desmond Hall's father. Desmond related 'according to my father and other witnesses two aircraft, a Spitfire and a Dornier 17, appeared to collide' – no Messerschmitt. It would seem, then, that Me 109s were not involved just at that moment, but perhaps they should not be completely ruled out. Desmond Hall's father was undoubtedly more concerned with the Dornier 'spinning down straight' on top of him than looking around for other planes, and Keith Lawrence was busy too. As the old saying goes: 'it's the one that you don't see that gets you.'

*

Kay Hughes had been told that 'Pat had bailed out, but a German fighter followed him down, riddling him with bullets'.[7]

This can be discounted. According to Desmond Hall's father, the Spitfire pilot jumped out but his parachute did not open: 'Then according to my father and other witnesses two aircraft, a Spitfire and a Dornier 17, appeared to collide. As they began to fall two men took to parachutes, one of which failed to operate and the wearer, the Spitfire pilot, died among the flowers in the garden of a bungalow alongside the main road (A25). His aircraft fell in a meadow close by.'

It would have been a well-nigh impossible shot for any fighter pilot to try and hit a falling figure, probably with a streaming parachute attached if the ripcord had been pulled and its canopy failed to open. To waste time and precious fuel on such a fleeting target, one that was obviously doomed anyway, was pointless. In any case, the Me 109s were operating at close to the limit of their range. In the circumstances, to waste time and precious fuel chasing after and firing on a man at the end of a parachute would increase the risk of having to ditch in the Channel. And would it have been possible to tell if the falling aviator was British or German? The man on the parachute was Erich Rosche!

But perhaps Pat was hit, or injured, as he tried to bail out. Perhaps he was not able pull the ripcord. Perhaps the parachute itself was damaged.

The witnesses did not mention a streaming parachute. Nor did John Day mention a parachute in his account when his father was asked by William

Norman to inspect Pat's body on the lawn in the back garden of No. 16 Main Road, Sundridge.

According to some accounts Pat's aircraft went down spinning wildly and he had no chance to bail out.

In January 1984, George Bailey, who was then living in Albany, Western Australia, wrote:

Whilst in 234 (F) Sqn. [Pat] wore his dark blue uniform with gold stripes, the original RAAF uniform. Had he not been killed 7/9/40 trying to save his a/c instead of jumping when damaged he could easily have been one of the outstanding figures in the record books.[8]

This was clearly not the case. Desmond Hall's father was positive that as the Dornier and Spitfire began to fall two men, Erich Rosche and Pat, tried to parachute to safety. Pat's parachute failed to operate and he died among the flowers in the back garden of No. 16 Main Road, Sundridge, where William Norman found him and John Day's father inspected his body. Pat's Spitfire, X4009, crashed at Dark's Farm, Bessels Green west of Sevenoaks. He was not found in the wreckage.

In 1968, Ken Anscombe and a number of colleagues, collectors of Second World War relics, decided to explore the area with a metal detector. Small aluminium fragments were located and the point of impact established. After obtaining permission, a dig was organised and some aircraft remains were recovered including a small information plate from the tail fin. Serial numbers found on the relics identified the aircraft as Spitfire X4009 – Pat's machine.

*

Did Pat's Spitfire ram the Dornier, as stated by Desmond Hall in his September 1990 letter?

Pat's intention would not have been to deliberately ram another aircraft – that was not his way. His way was to go in close and blast them! His way when out of ammunition and confronted by three Me 109s was to pretend to make a head-on attack so that he could escape in the opposite direction. He was a survivor. Pat had too much to live for; but there was another possibility.

Pat could have seriously misjudged his attack. Keith Lawrence's combat report revealed that he was well ahead of the others in his dive to chase after the bombers. Gregory Krikorian had time the night before to observe the Australian's stress and fatigue. Later he blamed himself for making light of Pat's depressed state of mind when told he was seeing spots before his eyes while flying. Pat's ability to estimate speed and distance could have been seriously compromised when he plunged down to make his usual close-in attack on the lagging Dornier.

Desmond Hall modified his account in his letter to Herr Bauman. He said simply that the two aircraft 'appeared to collide', which in itself implies that his father may not have actually seen Pat's Spitfire ram the Dornier at all.

*

Was it the Dornier that crashed into Pat's Spitfire?

According to some, this may well have been the case. Statements have ranged from 'the Dornier was attacked at 16,000 feet by fighters, which killed the pilot and the aircraft went into a dive',[9] to the Dornier 'went out of control and collided with Flight Lieutenant Hughes of 234 Squadron'.[10] This suggests that the Dornier went out control when the pilot was hit *during* Pat's attack. On the other hand, Keith Lawrence clearly stated that a wing crumpled, which would obviously cause loss of control, and it went down spinning.

The aircraft was under control before Pat attacked, although it was straggling below the rest of the formation. Possibly the pilot may have already been wounded or the aircraft had already been damaged in earlier encounters with other RAF fighters. It may have been struggling to get home when Pat attacked. Was this loss of control a dying effort by the Dornier pilot to evade Pat's line of fire?

Maybe the Dornier lagged back in order to photograph the bombing of London's docks – it would have been at the rear of the formation for this duty – and was in the process of trying to catch up to the other bombers for safety as they all raced for home. Regardless of whether or not there was a wounded pilot aboard, or damage to the aircraft, Pat's attack clearly delivered the *coup de grâce*.

*

Did the Dornier blow up 'with such force that it wrecked his Spitfire'?[11]

If such an explosion had occurred, particularly while the Dornier was being attacked at a height of around 16,000 feet, wreckage including bodies and body parts would probably have been spread all over the place. This was not the case. Keith Lawrence did not mention a big explosion. What he described was a sequence: he followed Pat down; saw him make a quarter attack; large pieces flew off the German bomber, then a wing crumpled; and it went down spinning.

Desmond Hall wrote that the Dornier came through the sky with an awesome wail of racing engines, which

> I can still call to mind even now, the aircraft narrowly missing the water pumping station, came to rest in a stream (the infant River Darenth) alongside a birch plantation. For what seemed a long time after the crash but must have only been minutes there was silence, then people began to run to the scene, rescue vehicles arrived but there were alas no survivors, an armed guard was mounted to keep people away until the ambulance men removed the German airmen to a place of rest.

A man named Mr Cook who was the first on the scene of the Dornier crash described attempts to rescue the airmen. From what he reportedly said, those still in the aircraft were dead anyway and must have died quickly. The next day Desmond Hall and his friends went to the crash and stood nearby looking at 'the broken green and blue wreckage'.

Clearly, the Dornier did not 'blow up', it came down relatively intact. Desmond Hall's father thought he and his friends were finished when the German plane was spinning down straight for them 'but a wing came off and it veered away'. This 'wing' was apparently the tail fin which was found some distance away.

The wreckage was intact enough for rescuers to arrive and try to recover survivors, and for a guard to be mounted to keep people away until the bodies were removed.

*

Did wreckage from the Dornier strike Pat's Spitfire?

This seems obvious, as Keith Lawrence's combat report stated clearly that he saw large pieces fly off the bomber, a wing crumple and the Dornier go down spinning. An instant later, after glancing away to seek his own target, he saw a Spitfire, which he assumed was Pat's, spinning down with about a third of its wing missing. The impression given is that the Dornier's wing must have smashed into the Spitfire's wing.

He did not report that he saw the two planes actually crash into each other, or their wings touch or them touch each other in any way, but there was definitely debris *before* the wing gave way (presumably outboard of the engine as Desmond Hall recalled hearing 'an awesome wail of racing engines' – plural – so they must have been still attached).[12] With Pat making his usual style of close-in attack, to have some debris or the part-wing strike his Spitfire is the strongest of possibilities.

Desmond Hall's father saw the German plane 'spinning' straight down before what he thought was a wing (the tail fin) come off and it 'veered away'. In his modified account, he said simply that two aircraft 'appeared to collide', which means perhaps his father may not have seen Pat's Spitfire actually ram the Dornier at all.

Keith Lawrence's combat report also stated the height of the enemy to be '17,000 approx'. So Pat would have attacked the straggling Dornier at about 16,000 feet. From the ground at that distance, smaller pieces of wreckage flying off would have been invisible to the naked eye. What those on the ground so far below would have seen, if indeed they were watching from the very beginning, was two planes come extremely close together, so close that they *might* have touched.

The sound of Pat firing as he attacked would not have reached them until a second or so later (sound travelling slower than light) and possibly not much at all depending upon wind direction and other noise. By then, their attention would have fastened onto the larger machine losing part of a wing and going into a spin, followed an instant later – almost instantaneously – by the smaller plane falling with part of its wing gone too! Then, two men jumped for their lives and one parachute opened as they realised the larger plane was coming down on top of them – all of this happening in a matter of seconds!

The sound of an explosion as the two planes came close together, or just after, was not mentioned by those on the ground. Could that have been what drew their attention to the two aircraft in the first place? But then, how much other sound was there in the air with the straining engines of the bombers racing for home and of fighters darting in and out, all mixed in with the rattle of gunfire? So much was going on, all at the same time!

*

Were the circumstances of Pat's death caused by friendly fire?[13]

Unfortunately, friendly fire incidents happen in warfare far too often. Witness the fate of the three Blenheims back on 26 August because of faulty aircraft recognition. They were patrolling over the Solent when they were suddenly attacked by Hurricanes mistaking them for Ju 88s. One Blenheim plunged into the sea, the second crash-landed and the third escaped with minor damage.[14] Witness how Me 109Es were misidentified so often as non-existent Heinkel He 113s.[15] At one point, 'Budge' Harker, as he was about to attack an Me109 firing at a Spitfire, realised at the last instant it was actually a Hurricane, and it *was* firing!

Consider then the combat report of a Spitfire pilot from 222 Squadron, Pilot Officer Brian van Mentz, who was caught up in the same chase over the same general area. He submitted the following account:

I followed A Flight into an attack on a formation of Dornier 215's.

As I was manoeuvring for position, a yellow-nosed ME 109 flew between me and my target aircraft. I therefore gave him a long burst and saw glycol or petrol start pouring from his engine. He turned on his back and disappeared. I continued my attack on the 215 and saw his port rudder come adrift. As I broke away I was hit by one bullet which punctured my glycol pipe. I landed the aircraft without further damage at Hornchurch.[16]

From Johannesburg, Brian van Mentz was accepted for a short service commission in the RAF in October 1937. In May 1940, he joined the Hurricane-equipped 504 Squadron which moved to France on the 12th, straight into action. He claimed three confirmed victories and one unconfirmed in France before the unit evacuated back to the UK after ten days of heavy fighting and heavy losses. Straight after his return he was posted to 222 Squadron at Hornchurch and during the summer fighting over Britain he claimed three more victories. The South African's claims on 7 September 1940 were for one Me 109 probably destroyed and one Do 215 damaged.

Externally, the Dornier Do 17Z and Dornier Do 215 aircraft were almost identical. The most obvious difference was the engines. Do 17Zs were powered by two Bramo 323 air-cooled radial engines whereas Do 215s had a pair of Daimler-Benz liquid-cooled inline engines. To fighter pilots attacking from above and coming from behind, the different power-plants would hardly be noticed.

But why would the pilot of a Messerschmitt 109 do that – fly between a Spitfire and its target? Wouldn't he attack the Spitfire rather than place himself in harm's way – unless, of course, in the twisting, turning fight he just happened to unintentionally fly into that patch of sky?

Perhaps Pat Hughes' fatigue caused him to make a fatal error of judgment – that of diving in much too close, much too fast – and it has been suggested that the yellow-nosed Me 109 which suddenly 'flew between' van Mentz and the Dornier he was attacking may, in reality, have been Pat's Spitfire. If so, the South African was likely to have brought them both down. He only had split seconds to react and he obviously did so instinctively.

Concentrating on his target in front, van Mentz would not have seen Pat's Spitfire coming from above and behind, or from high on the beam, until it flopped in front of him. Likewise, as Pat came fast from above and behind, van Mentz's aircraft would have been in the blind area under the wings of his Spitfire as he too concentrated on the Dornier.

If Pat suddenly realised as he was making his attack that he was being fired on from behind or the side, he may have instinctively jerked on the controls in a bid to evade but careered into the Dornier instead. The theory has credibility.

Looking again at van Mentz's combat report, he did say that he 'gave him [the apparent Me 109] a long burst and saw glycol or petrol start pouring from his engine. He turned on his back and disappeared.' No explosion – and no collision! There was no mention either of the yellow-nosed fighter losing a third of its wing, but he may not have seen it as he continued after the Dornier once more.

According to his report, he saw the Dornier's 'port rudder come adrift' and then he broke away. He did not mention the German plane going into a spin, or falling or a collapsing wing. Desmond Hall's father saw the German plane 'spinning' straight down *before* what he thought was a wing come off but this apparently turned out to be the tail fin which was found some distance away.

One standout feature in the South African's report is the description 'yellow-nosed'. It is important. Presuming his snap observation to be correct, this eliminates the possibility of the aircraft being an RAF fighter. In the Second World War, yellow was a colour reserved mainly for RAF training aircraft. RAF day fighters over Britain at this stage of 1940 mostly had brown-green upper camouflage with sky blue, or duck-egg green, undersides. Identification letters were grey. The red, white and blue roundels were edged with a yellow band around the circumference, but these were on the fuselage between the cockpit and tail, not emblazoned on the nose or engine cowling.

The yellow-nosed fighters over southern England in 1940 were the Me 109s of *JG* 2. For van Mentz to have seen the yellow, the 109 must have actually come from the side and across in front of him in some manner as even such a bright colour would not have been readily seen from behind. He was also a veteran of the fighting over France *and* Britain with Me 109s to his credit so he was familiar with them – his aircraft recognition would have been more trustworthy than most others.

Picture Brian van Mentz closing in behind the Dornier, concentrating on lining up the target in front of him when the other fighter suddenly came into his peripheral vision. A splash of yellow – Fire! It was possibly a full deflection shot, or close to it, so the incoming fighter would fly through a shower of .303-inch bullets. It rolled onto its back then and disappeared from sight emitting white glycol or fuel, or perhaps pulling vapour. All of this would have happened in an instant.

If glycol or petrol started pouring from his victim's engine, there must have been some physical damage. This has reportedly not been backed up by physical evidence from the Spitfire's wreckage or crash site. But how much evidence would there be – a bullet, or bullet hole, or holes? How obvious would a .303-inch bullet hole be amid such wreckage?

Interestingly, as van Mentz broke away a bullet punctured the glycol pipe of his own Spitfire but he managed to land safely without further damage. Presumably it was return fire coming from the damaged Dornier's gunner, or possibly from another gunner in the bomber formation. Perhaps the plane that van Mentz caused to stream glycol or fuel managed to land safely too.

Two excavations were carried out at the site of the Dornier crash over the years and they turned up many remarkable finds. Among numerous other relics there was a cowling fastener with a .303-inch cartridge case lodged in it, a Bramo radial engine, and a propeller boss with a damaged blade still attached, but damaged by bullet holes. Obviously the bullets responsible had been fired from a British gun, or guns, but whose gun, or guns? Were they from the guns of Ellis Aries of 602 Squadron; George Peters of 79 Squadron; Pat Hughes of 234 Squadron; Brian van Mentz of 222 Squadron; or somebody else yet again?

If it is accepted that the Dornier 17 was under control before Pat attacked, although straggling below the rest of the formation, there is little doubt that it was Pat who delivered the final death blow. When the physical evidence of the cartridge case being found lodged in a cowling fastener is considered with the propeller blade damage, it tends to confirm that Pat's firing was concentrated on an engine and wing, causing them to shed debris until the wing outboard of the engine finally collapsed.

When the outer wing *did* collapse, it became the largest piece of debris flying back at the attacking Spitfire – Pat's attacking Spitfire, not van Mentz's attacking Spitfire. It sliced like a blade into the Spitfire's wing shearing a third of it away.

Is that really what did happen that fateful day?

*

Pat's funeral was held six days later in Hull on 13 September. He was buried by the RAF in the churchyard of St James' Church of England in the parish of Sutton-on-Hull.

A week later, Kay realised she was pregnant, but she still could not stop crying …

18

AFTERWARDS

In Berlin on Sunday 8 September, all the morning papers carried the headlines: 'BIG ATTACK ON LONDON AS REPRISAL.'[1]

The bombing of London stopped at 4.30 a.m. local time. After the twelve-hour ordeal, people emerged, shell-shocked and silent, from their shelters. The air was full of fumes and smoke as the fires along the dock areas burned freely. Hundreds were dead and injured and many homes had been reduced to rubble. The stark horror and reality of total war had been driven home. Air raid wardens, rescue workers and volunteers, including many Australian soldiers on leave, dug amongst the ruins searching for the injured. Three main railway stations, including London Bridge, Waterloo and Victoria, were out of action.

Unconfirmed rumours of invasion were rife – but there was no invasion. Early morning reconnaissance planes revealed that no fleet of German barges had crossed the English Channel or even set sail. Nevertheless, anti-invasion patrols were stepped up all along the coast as far north as the Shetland Islands.

The weather was fair early and in the late evening but the Luftwaffe made only a few minor raids on airfields.

During the morning Keith Park flew in his Hurricane over the smoke-shrouded British capital. His immediate reaction was one of anger but at the back of his mind he saw a glimmer of hope. If the Germans continued to strike at London and left his airfields unmolested there just might be a chance ...

*

In Australia, the Secretary, Department of Defence Co-ordination, received the following message on the teleprinter from the Secretary of the Prime Minister's Department on 9 September 1940:

Cablegram from the Under Secretary of State Air Ministry London dated 8/9/1940. 7.23 p.m., received 9/9/1940:

IMMEDIATE FROM AIR MINISTRY P.933 8/9/1940:

Regret to inform you that Flight Lieutenant Paterson Clarence HUGHES is reported as having lost his life as a result of air operations on 7th September, 1940. Please inform father, Paterson Clarence Hughes, 43 Kingston Street, Haberfield, New South Wales.

F/Lieutenant Hughes' wife has been informed.

As a result of this message, the following telegram was drafted and sent to Pat's father on 9 September:

Deeply regret to inform you that your son Flight Lieutenant Paterson Clarence Hughes is reported as having lost his life as result of air operations on Seventh September (.) The Air Board joins with the Air Ministry in expressing profound Sympathy in your sad bereavement (.) His wife has been informed.

The Hughes family was stunned by Pat's death. His cousin, Lawrence Lucas, who was still living at Frankston in Melbourne on Port Phillip Bay, recalled that his mother 'went to pieces' when she received the news that her brother had been killed. It came via a telegram sent by other members of the family.[2]

The afternoon the telegram came I was playing football in a sandy lay-by off our street when a member of our class rode up to us on a red PMG bicycle. During the course of the conversation he said he had a telegram for the Lucases. He refused my offer to take it to my mother on the grounds that it had to be handed personally to a responsible adult. I accompanied him to our home where the telegram's contents were revealed. My sister was visiting friends, and our father was not yet home.

With my mother in a state of almost collapse, and with one eye on the main chance of being allowed to return to the game, I asked if she was all right and could I return to my mates. I don't think she even heard me, but I took her expression as permission and left the house.

Although only eleven, in hindsight, I know that I had been tried and found wanting.

I also know that if it had been Pat and his mother, he would not have asked. He would have stayed. That's the difference.

But Pat's death was not the only shock. 'His wife has been informed' – the family was not even aware that Pat had married!

One of Pat's sisters, either Constance, Marjorie or Valerie, wrote to the Royal Air Force to find out more, and Percy wrote to the RAAF authorities in Melbourne seeking further information.

4th October 1940

Dear Sir:

I am writing respecting the death of my son Flight-Lieut. Paterson Clarence Hughes who was reported as having lost his life during air operations in England on the 7th September 1940.

In the official communication it was announced that 'his wife has been informed'.

The fact of my son's marriage has come as a complete surprise and I have no details regarding his wife, with whom I am anxious to get in touch.

I will be obliged if you could furnish me with any details regarding the date of marriage, the name and age of the wife and her present address.

Certain business matters have to be attended to and it is necessary for me to have this information for their completion.

Thanking you in anticipation of your early reply.

Yours faithfully,
P. C. HUGHES

Percy's letter was acknowledged on the 11th but three more weeks passed before a final reply arrived:

23 OCT 1940

Dear Sir,

With reference to your letter dated 4th October, 1940, and my reply there to dated 11th October, 1940, relative to your late son's wife, I now desire to inform you that information has been received stating that her maiden name was Kathleen Agnes Brodnick [*sic*] and her address 'The Buck' Treyarronn Bay, Cornwall. Her age is not known.

Yours faithfully,
(Sld.) N. T. Goodwin
Squadron Leader,
OFFICER IN CHARGE OF RECORDS.

The following month, another letter arrived. It was sent to Pat's sister and the family by Bish Owens, 234 Squadron's Adjutant.

Dear Miss Hughes,

I have your letter of the 23rd September 1940. First of all, may I express to yourself and your Mother, my sympathy and the sympathy of the Squadron in your sad bereavement. Your Brother had been serving with me in this Squadron since last November, and words are almost inadequate to express our feelings at his loss. By his heroic work and brilliant leadership he helped to bring the Squadron to the unique position in which it was placed on his death; we now have to our credit 80 enemy aircraft.

He was always enthusiastic on the job of work to be done, and in the work of leading his Flight, and at times the Squadron, he was always there, ever keen that his colleagues should do their best and follow his wonderful example. In his personal relations and influence with all the members of the Squadron he was an inspiration whose memory we shall always cherish. It will scarcely be possible to replace such a gallant leader and lovable colleague and friend. As some measure of reward and recognition, your Brother was awarded the D.F.C.

With reference to your enquiry I have to inform you that your Brother was married on the 1st August 1940 at the Register Office, Bodmin to Kathleen Agnes Brodrick. Her present address is 384 James Reckitt Avenue, Hull, Yorkshire.

I am enclosing herewith photograph of some of the members of the Squadron.

Thank you for your good wishes and I shall be most happy to hear from you again. Please let me know if there are any further particulars I can let you have.

Kind regards to yourself and your Mother.

Yours sincerely,
F/O and Adjutant.

While this exchange of letters was going on, changes took place for 234 Squadron in England in accordance with Hugh Dowding's edicts of 7 September. On 11 September, four days after Pat and Spike O'Brien had been killed in action, a much depleted 234 Squadron was moved back to St Eval where it was quieter. Alan 'Budge' Harker recalled, 'Only about three pilots and five aircraft from our original squadron had survived to return to St Eval. I was quite twitchy myself by then.'[3]

Cyril Page had been placed in temporary command with 'Morty' Mortimer-Rose and Keith Dewhurst acting as officers commanding 'A' and 'B' Flights while the squadron waited for replacements. The squadron had to be regarded as Class C. It had suffered such losses in action that made it obviously due for rest and the training of new pilots. A number of experienced pilots were 'milked' from the squadron to provide replacements for those units about to go into action or already in action.

Zbigniew Olenski transferred across to 609 Squadron at Middle Wallop before 234 Squadron left. Keith Lawrence, the New Zealander, was posted to 603 Squadron at Hornchurch on 9 September, and the next day George Bailey followed him there. Staying with squadron for its return to St Eval were Bob Doe, Mike Boddington, Ken Dewhurst, Alan Harker, the other New Zealander, Pat Horton, and Ted Mortimer-Rose of the originals, plus the other Polish fliers, Zygmunt Klein and Jozef Szlagowski. Bob Doe did not stay for long. He was posted to 238 Squadron and went back to Middle Wallop on 27 September. Nor did Zig Klein stay. He was posted to 152 Squadron at Warmwell on 5 October. Jozef Szlagowski was posted to 152 Squadron a couple of weeks after Klein but the pair were not together for long as Klein was reported 'Missing' on 28 November.

The threat of invasion had been a false alarm. The invasion didn't come the night Pat Hughes and Spike O'Brien died – but it seemed that it had to come soon.

By 14 September the Luftwaffe commanders had noted erratic British defences over the previous few days. The English seemed to be weakening. The RAF must be running out of fighters. Actually, the Luftwaffe's pre-occupation with bombing London and its failure to continue attacking the RDF sites and Fighter Command's airfields was helping the RAF to recover.

Next day, 15 September, the Luftwaffe launched two massive attacks on London. They were beaten off with heavy losses. The BBC claimed 185 German planes had been destroyed. Post-war figures were put at sixty-one German aircraft destroyed for thirty-one British fighters lost. This would become known as 'Battle of Britain Day', marking a pivotal shift in the fortunes of the Third Reich.

Two days later, although PRU photographs showed that despite RAF bombing there were 600 invasion barges assembled at Antwerp, 266 at Calais, 230 at Boulogne, 220 at Dunkirk, 205 at Le Havre and 200 at Ostend, Hitler postponed Operation *Seelöwe*. The RAF had obviously not been defeated and adverse weather, unsuitable for launching an invasion, was forecast for the coming week.

The Führer had missed his chance.

*

When Kay realised she was expecting she was so pleased, but at nearly four months she suffered a miscarriage. She and Pat would have had a son, but it was not to be. 'After that I didn't care about anything except getting drunk,' she said when interviewed years later, 'and playing Pat's favourite record, *Where or When*, tears streaming down.'[4]

Eventually the crying did stop and she realised she had changed – from a romantic girl into a woman. There would be no more tears. She did not even cry when she was presented with Pat's posthumous Distinguished Flying Cross at a ceremony two years later in June 1942. 'The King gave me Pat's DFC. Other widows were crying. I wasn't, every tear in me had poured out in 1940. I still feel dreadfully upset but no tears have come since.'[5]

By then she was a WAAF. Kay had returned to Hull to live with and care for her Mother. When the city was bombed she volunteered to drive an ambulance, and after that she joined up because she hated the Germans and wanted to serve.

Pat had told her to marry again and after the war she did. She met an army officer who had been a prisoner-of-war and for three or four years there was happiness and two lovely children, both sons. Then came adversity when he left the country. She and her sons were stranded and penniless. She had to seek a divorce. A third marriage which proved loveless also led to divorce.

It was early in 1949 that Kay was visited in England by two of Pat's sisters, Valerie Hughes and Muriel (Midge) Tongue. Their expensive trip had been planned by the family for quite some time. Valerie was single and an accountant who paid her own way, but Midge was a Kiama housewife and was reputed to have saved for years by placing threepences in old fashioned, wide-necked milk bottles to achieve about £20 per bottle. Laurence Lucas recalled, 'The other sisters helped out with Muriel's expenses. I know my mother did. It was considered a joint tribute; if you couldn't go, you could contribute.'[6] They had arrived by ship, the SS *Arcades*, and were anxious to meet her at last.

Pat's brothers, Fred, Charlie and Bill, had joined the Australian army during the war and served against the Japanese: Alfred (Fred), a sergeant in 2/12 Field Company in Malaya; Charlie, a private in Australia; and William (Bill), a corporal No. 3 Wireless Section in New Guinea. Fortunately, all survived but for some time little was known about Fred's fate because he was captured with the fall of Singapore in 1942 and was a POW for three years, including toiling on the dreaded Burma railway. After the tragic loss of Pat so early, Fred's disappearance was of grave concern for the whole family, but it was a special hardship for their stoical mother, Caroline. The tangible relief when news finally came through official channels that he was alright may have been too much for her. Caroline died shortly afterwards at the Anzac Memorial Hospital in Katoomba, New South Wales on 27 September 1945.

For Valerie and Midge, the journey to England was a pilgrimage. They wanted to know and see everything, and especially to visit Pat's grave. Kay obliged. When the sisters departed to return to Australia they carried with them photos and precious souvenirs. Kay presented them with Pat's DFC for the family. It was something she would regret later.

Kay eventually became the deputy, then the matron, of an aged care home and she was content in doing that. It was her profession for fourteen years.

In her later years, Kay felt that she had given the DFC to Pat's sisters out of a sense of misplaced guilt because of the circumstances of the marriage. She made determined efforts to recover it. One of the people she contacted in her quest was Pat's old Point Cook classmate and close friend, Geoff Hartnell, who was now living in Canberra. In reply to her first letter, Geoff wrote on 22 October 1980:

How good to hear from you after such a long time. I think of you often as Pat still has a particular place in my heart and his photo is located where I can see him even as I write this letter. His nephew, incidentally, is now an air vice Marshal and an impressive successor to his uncle. He also was a fighter pilot and earned a DFC in Korea. I retired some 12 years ago as an AVM myself. They kicked me out a little early as I developed some heart trouble but my health seems to have improved steadily ever since.' He added that Pat's 'name is now on the Remembrance Wall of the Australian War Memorial.[7]

It had taken nearly forty years to get Pat's name on the Remembrance Wall of the Australian War Memorial. Geoff wrote later:

There was some debate about the rights and wrongs of Australians, like Pat, having their name there but he and a number of others were in an unusual position in the Royal Air Force ... They were, in effect, posted to the RAF from the RAAF for a period of five years at the end of which, having completed their short service commissions, they were under an obligation to return to the RAAF reserve. As the war was on when the five-year period was up, even those who were still alive continued to serve in the RAF until the end of the war.[8]

It so happens that Henry Hughes (Pat's nephew) is stationed in Canberra so I had a chat to him about Pat's DFC. I waited a few weeks while he made inquiries but he seems to be running into difficulties ... Although his name is Henry he is known as Bill ... Unfortunately Midge died a few years ago.[9]

Kay contacted Henry Hughes about the DFC in December 1980, and he replied just before Christmas: 'As you are aware Val and Midge are dead, as is my father and several other of Pat's brothers and sisters.' He went on to suggest that Pat's eldest brother, Jack

may be in possession of the DFC – but I am not sure because there is one other brother and sister still alive with whom I have no contact at all ... I am pursuing with the RAF, and various museum authorities Pat's records and other memorabilia. He deserves a place in RAAF history (he trained at Point Cook) and I am determined that he becomes properly recognised in Australia.[10]

Kay contacted Jack, who replied on 30 March 1981:

I apologise for the delay in replying, as I have been trying to seek information on the whereabouts of the medals. As you ceased corresponding with my sister Midge a long time ago, I regret to tell you that my sisters Valerie and Midge have passed away and as far as I know Pat's medals could be either in Australia or England.[11]

In the meantime, Henry Hughes was instrumental in having an identification plate belonging to Pat's Spitfire placed in the RAAF Museum at Point Cook. In 1968, Ken Ascombe, a collector of Second World War relics, had explored a field at Bessel's Green near Sevenoaks in Kent with a metal detector. He found aluminium fragments, one of which carried the serial number X-4009. This was identified as belonging to the Spitfire Pat had flown on 7 September 1940. It had, in fact, been his regular aircraft. Ken Ascombe and his colleagues had rediscovered the historic crash site. Placement of the relic in the RAAF Museum at Point Cook was done with Kay's approval.

Henry thanked her in a letter dated 12 May 1982, but there was also sad news:

Geoff Hartnell died about a year ago. He was given a service funeral in which I, along with many of his associates, participated. His widow is still living in Canberra.

Midge's married name was TONGUE. Tom, her husband, came originally from the Midlands. To the best of my knowledge, Pat's DFC was in Midge's keeping until she died. Since Tom survived her for a while, the decoration remained in his keeping. On his death, we believe, the DFC somehow went into the possession of his family.[12]

Things seemed to have gone full circle. The medals might be back in England! Kay attempted to trace them, even placing a notice in local newspapers including the *Hull Daily Mail*, but all to no avail.

In fact, they were still in Australia. Pat's closest brother, Bill, who he called 'Will' in his letters, was the 'the last brother standing' and by 1988 when I interviewed him the medals had somehow come into his possession.

*

I first wrote about Australians in the battle of Britain in 1982 in *Australian Aviation* magazine. While I was researching I was amazed by the lack of primary source information and knowledge about these men. The Battle of Britain was a pivotal battle in world history, a turning point of the war, and Australians were there, but who knew about them in their own country? Where were the plaques and memorials? There did not seem to be any around at all. Records held by the Australian War Memorial, where they existed, consisted only of some thin manila foolscap folders with just a few sheets of paper in them, perhaps containing a standardised form dating back to 1942 or 1943. These were often only partially filled in by someone other than the person named.

Because of the deadline imposed, the information for the article had to be gleaned hurriedly from secondary sources available at the time, from such ground-breaking publications as *The Narrow Margin* by Derek Wood and Derek Dempster and Francis K. Mason's *Battle Over Britain*; a few unit histories like Tom Moulson's *The Flying Sword* (601 Squadron, 1964) and Frank Ziegler's *Under The White Rose* (609 Squadron, 1971); some biographies; and a few recent overview books such as Peter Townsend's *Duel of Eagles* (1970), Marcel Julian's *The Battle of Britain* (1967) and Richard Collier's *Eagle Day* (1968) – all from England.

In Australia, the four-volume official RAAF history of *Australia in the War of 1939–1945* contained little more than a couple of pages on the Battle of Britain; and a thin, vintage, long-out-of-print book *RAAF Over Europe* edited by Frank Johnson (published in 1946) but this too was from London. This had in it a Battle of Britain chapter but named just six pilots - Gordon Olive, Desmond Sheen, John Cock, John Curchin, Clive Mayers and lastly a short paragraph on Pat Hughes.

The article was written using these sources, but clearly the situation was unsatisfactory. There did not even seem to be any clarity in Australia over how many Australians were actually involved. The Battle of Britain was one of the turning points of the war, and Australians were there, but officialdom did not seem to know or care! Clearly, something had to be done about that. It was necessary to probe further.

The end result after seven years of additional research was the book published by the Australian War Memorial in 1990 for the fiftieth anniversary of the Battle of Britain, *A Few of 'The Few'*. While researching I had the privilege of meeting, interviewing and corresponding with many of the still surviving veterans of the battle and their relatives and friends. This was how and why I met Bill Hughes, truly one of nature's gentlemen.

When I visited Bill at his Beacon Hill home, he made me most welcome. After we had almost talked the afternoon away, he asked if I would like to see his brother's medals – and there they were! At the time I was unaware of the drama that had been going on over them. He asked quietly what I thought should be done with them and Pat's other memorabilia. I suggested that if there were no relatives who would appreciate them, perhaps it would be appropriate to donate them to the Australian War Memorial or the RAAF Museum at Point Cook.

Bill did both. He donated his photo album to the RAAF Museum and at the same time also donated the propeller from a Sopwith Scout into the hub of which he had assembled and installed a clock. The whole piece was designed to be mounted like a trophy on a wall. This was one of his hobbies, particularly later in life, and it was a carryover from his modelling days with Pat when they were young. He donated Pat's DFC and campaign medals to the Australian War Memorial for display, and although he did not say so, I think that Bill also did that because of the forthcoming book. They were photographed and a picture of them was placed on the dust jacket cover of *A Few of 'The Few'*.

*

I have been reminded of a story told to me by Dimity Torbett, one of Pat Hughes' nieces. In 2005, Dimity was passing through the town Aberdeen in northern New South Wales when she saw a furniture and book emporium and decided to stop. It was sixty-five years after the Battle of Britain and Pat's death.

As she chatted to Myra Baines, the owner, Dimity put money in the tin hat Myra used to collect donations for Legacy. Myra had told her about the number of Legacy widows in the district. Dimity commented that one of her uncles had survived the Burma railway, adding, 'And Uncle Pat was in the Battle of Britain'. Myra came out from behind the counter to where Dimity was sitting, fell to her knees and, grasping her hand, said: 'I'm not talking to the niece of Paterson Clarence Hughes, am I?' It was an extraordinary moment and the beginning of a lasting friendship.

Myra Baines was a remarkable Englishwoman who came to Australia in the 1970s. Born in the East End of London, Myra spent her childhood there during the Blitz and was wounded in one eye when flying shrapnel came through her bedroom window. At the age of seven she went missing when she used her pocket money to travel by herself across the Channel to France to visit the First World War battlefields and the Menin Gate which she had heard so much about.

She owned the emporium, continuing with it after her husband died until 2012. Her poor eyesight did not deter her from acquiring an encyclopaedic knowledge of both world wars, amassing a vast military library and rooms full of wartime memorabilia. She was a dedicated fund-raiser for Legacy and as an author and poet she had written many biographies commissioned by families in the district of their fathers, sons and brothers who took part in various wars.

But of all wartime participants, Pat Hughes was her particular hero – 'because of his bravery and his sacrifice' – ever since she read about him decades ago (I like to think perhaps in *A Few of 'The Few'*). Every year on his birthday and the anniversary of his death while she lived in Aberdeen she would cross the highway, braving the trucks hurtling around the corner by the war memorial, to put flowers there in his memory, as she also did every Anzac Day and Remembrance Day.[13]

Myra is a symbol. As Geoff Hartnell pointed out, for too long Pat Hughes and others like him were overlooked by officialdom in Australia. They were only remembered by individuals, the members of families and friends – and sometimes, just sometimes, by a few who never knew them.

But I digress.

*

Kay married for a fourth time after she retired from being the matron of an aged care facility. There was a difference of eighteen years in their ages. When she was sixty-four, her new husband was eighty-two.

We married for companionship. He visits his wife's grave regularly, knowing I understand. He understands, so do my sons, that when I die I want my ashes put with Pat. It's always been in my will.

I've this idea that the first person I'll meet will be Pat, not grown old or changed at all. Don't know what he'll make of me but he'll understand everything, just as he always did, and we'll have time together, at last.[14]

Kay died on 28 June 1983 at the age of sixty-six. Her sons buried her ashes in accordance with her wishes.

19

PAT HUGHES NIGHT

Neil Marks is an accomplished writer whose works include *Tales from the Locker Room*, *Tales for All Seasons* and *Australian People Australian Tales*, books motivated by his passion for Australian sport and Australian personalities, particularly from cricket and rugby. He played first-grade cricket himself at the age of fifteen and went on to represent New South Wales at the age of twenty-two, before a serious heart condition limited his prospects on the field. After retiring from a successful insurance brokerage business, he began to write about sport, the people he had known and the stories he had heard, emphasising the personalities, idiosyncrasies and foibles of many Australian characters.

After reading *A Few of 'The Few'* on Australians in the Battle of Britain, he became intrigued by the deeds of Pat Hughes, and ended up contacting Pat's only living brother, Bill, who told him stories of Pat's childhood and early manhood.

Pat was one of twelve children, coincidently the same number of children as their forefather from the 'First Fleet', John Nicholls, fathered. Pat's own father was a postman in Cooma who achieved a minor sort of fame at the time by being recognised as the best bush balladist in the Snowy River area of NSW. Bill showed me some of his father's verses which were indeed excellent and deserving of greater exposure.

When Neil and his wife, Kay, travelled to the UK in the early 1990s, he contacted a number of Battle of Britain pilots who had flown with Pat or who knew of him. They were unanimous.

The one thing in absolutely no doubt was Pat's ability as a fighter pilot. Everyone with whom I spoke was adamant that Pat Hughes was the greatest they had ever seen.

Particularly helpful was Bob Doe. He and Kay shared a wonderful afternoon with Bob and his wife, Betty, looking out on their magnificent garden in West Sussex. The couples became close friends over the ensuing years.

Bob Doe had had a distinguished career in the RAF. After he had been posted to join 238 Squadron back at Middle Wallop on 27 September 1940, he claimed an Me 109 destroyed on the first day of October and a Ju 88 on the 7th, but then his good luck ran out. His Hurricane was shot up three days later and, wounded in the shoulder and leg, he had to bail out. While recovering, he was awarded a DFC on 22 October and a Bar to it a month later on 26 November. At the end of December he rejoined 234 Squadron but was injured during a heavy crash-landing on 3 January 1941. After this he served as a flight commander with 66 Squadron and then with 130 Squadron later in the year. Posted to the Far East, he formed the Indian Air Force's 10 Squadron in December 1943 and commanded it all the way through the Burma campaign. For this he was awarded a DSO in October 1945, an exceptional honour. He returned to England in September 1946 and retired from the RAF as a wing commander on 1 April 1966.[1]

Neil determined he would write his own tribute to Pat. 'I had intended to write my story of Pat Hughes in prose – but I was fascinated by the examples that Bill Hughes had shown me of his father's verse. So I chose that route.' The result was *The Best of A Few*.

Kay and Neil would visit the UK every three years or so and they phoned each other regularly. On one occasion, Neil said that:

I received a call from Betty and Bob which told me of a recent reunion of 234 Squadron (lovingly called Pat Hughes Night). Bob then told me that my verse (doggerel) about Pat was read out and was a highlight. He went on to say that he couldn't read it as his accent was 'too Pommy' and so they dredged up some Aussie to do it. According to Bob, the Aussie went well, 'Even though his accent wasn't as rough as yours, Old Boy.'

The Aussie 'dredged up' was the Australian Air Attaché at 234 Squadron Association's annual reunion in 2004. *The Best of A Few* is a fitting tribute to Paterson Clarence Hughes DFC, and I sincerely thank Neil Marks for allowing it to be placed here.[2]

THE BEST OF A FEW

I stopped at a pub down in Cooma,
(I'd just spent five hours in my car),
While buying a beer from the barmaid,
I spoke to a bloke at the bar,
As happens, we soon started yarning,
Like blokes in a pub often do,
I talked of my days in the city
And dropped famous names that I knew.

I spoke of known heroes and legends
And boorishly bashed on his ear,
He let me continue my boasting,
Stayed silent and sipped on his beer.
I talked of Les Darcy and Melba,
Our first settlers' lives of travail,
I then paused for breath – he grinned wryly
And told me this wonderful tale.

'You think you know real Aussie heroes,
Explorers and legends of sport,
Burke, Wills, Henry Parkes and Don Bradman,
Ned Kelly and Margaret Court?
You could name me others, you say, sir?
Well for you do I have some news
Of one you may never hear mentioned,
A bloke by the name of Pat Hughes.

'You scoff at my rash declaration?
Well we all have differing views.
You say I've had too much to drink, sir!
Let me tell you the tale of Pat Hughes.
Young Pat Hughes was dashing and handsome,
He looked a bit like Errol Flynn,
Pat was … hold on now, I'm digressing …
I'll go back in time and begin.

'A man by the name of John Nicholls,
Accountant in old London Town,
Engaged in a bit of embezzling,
So jury and judge sent him down.
But this was the seventeen hundreds,
For minor crimes men had to pay,
So the Crown transported John Nicholls
And bound him for Botany Bay.

'So John was shoved down in the dungeon
Of a boat, with chains round his feet,
Sailed with Captain Phillip's flotilla,
(Old ships – later called "The First Fleet").
And John stepped ashore at Port Jackson,
As Albion's flag was unfurled,
Not knowing that one day his grandchild,
Would help save old Albion's world.

'John served out his time as a convict,
He found a nice girl whom he wed,
Was granted some acres at Prospect,
Toiled hard on his farm and then bred.
Like Nicholls, his children were clever,
The Lord forgave John for his sins,
And Pat Hughes was Nicholl's great-grandson,
And that's where my story begins.

'Pat Hughes first saw daylight in Cooma,
But didn't stay long in the cold,
The Hugheses then moved up to Sydney,
A town for the robust and bold.
Young Pat shone at surfing and rugby,
But life often springs a surprise,
For Destiny's diary was calling,
And Pat's heart was high in the skies.

'He attended Air Force Staff College,
Though outdated, Pat didn't care,
He flew only tortoise-like bi-planes,
But Pat Hughes was up in the air.
In London the "RAF" was recruiting,
He applied in May thirty-eight,
And then he set off for old England,
That moment Pat settled his fate.

'Pat was a natural-born flyer,
Knew tactics, manoeuvres and bombs.
Instead of Pat learning from others,
He found he was teaching the Poms!
His uniform never was British,
He always wore Aussie-style blue,
His accent was typically Sydney,
Not, "pip-pip old chap, toodeloo".

'A dog, name of Butch, was Pat's mascot,
He followed his mate everywhere,
And sometimes when no-one was watching,
Pat took old Butch up in the air.
But training and fun days were ending,
In Europe the Nazis had won,
Then Hitler's eyes turned upon England,
The Battle of Britain begun.

'Soon Pat became surrogate leader,
Though no braid was sewn on his arm,
To Hell men would follow this Aussie,
A skipper with toughness and charm.
He led by his own brave example,
He bent them like slaves to his will:
("If we lose there'll be no tomorrow,
The name of the game is to kill.")

'"Get close to the bastards, I tell you,
So close that propellers can kiss,
Then give 'em your whole ammunition,
I promise you boys, you can't miss.
For we have the home-ground advantage,
The Spitfire's the very best plane,
But if by some chance you should crash it,
Then bail out, and go up again."

'The future of freedom was doubtful,
For three months the world held its breath,
As daring lads soared into battle
And flew with their co-pilot, Death.
They fought without thought of survival
Limbs weary, nerves tattered and torn,
Not knowing if they'd be returning,
Or if they'd be dead the next morn.

'T'was high over verdant south England,
The stage where this drama was played,
The sky was alight with the carnage,
And down on the ground people prayed.
Pat moved his plane closer and closer,
He looked his foe full in the eyes,
The gun would deliver his message,
Pat Hughes was the king of the skies.

'The Luftwaffe started to worry,
They'd not lost a battle before,
They started to learn what defeat meant,
There's no second prize in a war!
"They've run out of planes," said H. Goering,
(Though he was a bit of a clown),
"Must be ghosts up there," said his airmen,
'Cause somebody's shooting us down!"

'While battle was raging Pat married,
Sweet Kathy caused Pat's heart to sing,
They both lived their lives for the moment,
Who knew what tomorrow would bring?
Though Pat was the idol of females,
His pretty young bride didn't mind,
With Pat on her arm she'd go strolling,
While dear old Butch trotted behind.

'But even the toughest feel pressure,
When playing a game they daren't lose,
And rumours were constantly flying,
"The Doc reckons Pat's on the booze!"
Pat had a few beers, that's admitted,
I guess you and I'd do the same,
When each single sortie spells danger,
And killing's the name of the game.

'But Pat never cared about rumours,
He continued as he began,
And his squadron cheerfully followed,
The kid that they called "the old man".
In eight weeks he'd shot fourteen Germans,
This grand "old man", aged twenty-four,
Of all the RAF's publicised heroes,
Pat Hughes was on top of the score.

'On September seventh, a battle
Saw Pat up and into the chase,
"Get close to the bastard," he whispered,
But "the bastard" blew up in his face.
He nose-dived, cartwheeling and turning,
"Hey, Pat's going down," someone cried.
The Spitfire spun round in its torment
Smashed deep in the ground and Pat died.

'Pat's wife had a bad premonition,
When that morning Butch disappeared,
Then later that day Kathy heard it,
The news that she always had feared.
The squadron looked hard for the Airedale,
They called and they whistled in vain,
That day they lost leader and mascot,
For Butch was not heard of again.

'The battle went on 'til November,
A Czech was claimed No. I Ace,
Though Pat died in early September,
He still ended up in third place.
The tide to the British was turning,
The Germans were now on the run,
Then Hitler's hate turned towards Russia,
The Battle of Britain was won.

'You quiz me on who was the greatest!
That's something we'd all like to know.
The Ace of the Battle of Britain —
The Czech, Bader, Townsend, or Doe?
When I posed this question to vet'rans,
They seemed to have total recall,
With no, hesitation they answered,
"Pat Hughes was the best of them all".

'Pat's medal from Buckingham Palace,
Was awarded posthumously,
He lies in a churchyard in Yorkshire
And lives in the hearts of the free.
You ask me what happened to Butch, sir?
A riddle I cannot explain.
P'haps he died of a dog's broken heart,
Or perished with Pat in the plane.

'The rest, as they say, sir, is hist'ry,
Misty times, six decades ago,
Now rockets can fly without pilots,
And Spitfires are only for show.
But if you should journey to Britain,
I'll tell you, sir, what you will see,
A land green and cold – but it's lovely,
A sky often grey – but it's free.

'I hope Pat is somewhere up yonder,
Above in the heavenly blue,
And knows his account is in credit,
That many owe much to so few.
So let's lift our glass up to heroes,
Great people, whomever we choose.
We'll then have a toast to Australia!
And let's have a beer for Pat Hughes.'

I had one more drink then I left him,
For I had some clients to phone,
I stood in the cold Cooma evening
And felt very sad and alone.
We often feel we are important
We think times are tough, though they're not,
For compared to those gone before us,
Our deeds hardly matter a jot.

'Our lives were not meant to be easy',
A saying oft-used though profound,
For some life is lengthy but boring,
They stay with their feet on the ground.
For others adventure is calling,
They gamble; they win or they lose,
We can stay on safe terra firma
Or fly to the stars – like Pat Hughes.

NEW SOUTH WALES: THE ANCESTRY OF PAT HUGHES

In the early 1900s, to be a fifth-generation Australian of British descent was rare. You belonged very much to a minority group. Paterson Clarence Hughes, born on 19 September 1917, was one of those rare few – but he was rare in more ways than one.

Pat Hughes' ancestor was John Nichols (sometimes spelt 'Nicholls' or 'Nicholds') who had arrived in New South Wales in 1788 with the historic 'First Fleet' from England. He'd had no choice in the matter. He was a convict.

As far as the Hughes family is concerned, Pat's story began in London at the Old Bailey on 21 April 1784 when John Nichols, estimated age twenty-nine, was accused of 'Theft: Simple Grand Larceny'. It was alleged he stole merchandise from his employers to the value of £15 0s 6d.

Much of the world that John lived in was violent, callous and crude. This was Georgian England, the turbulent realm of 'sad, mad' King George III. Dirt and disease flourished amid the trappings of elegance and luxury. London was a metropolis polluted by slums where crime, cruelty, filth and sickness abounded. Such conditions were accepted by most as part of the nature of existence, like the weather or the four seasons of the year. Londoners were hardened to it. Some were even entertained by such sights as the insane in Bedlam Asylum and the whipping of half-naked women at the Bridewell; or the hangings at Tyburn, where the corpse of a young boy or girl might be seen dangling from a rope between the bodies of a highwayman and a murderer. Penalties for even minor crimes were harsh and uncompromising. They could range from death to transportation to distant colonies.

With one word – 'Guilty!' – John Nichols was sentenced to transportation to Africa for seven years.[1]

England lost her American colonies early in King George III's reign. For a century beforehand, surplus criminals had been shipped to Virginia, the Carolinas and Georgia, but that changed in 1776. The American Revolution brought the convict transportation system to North America to an abrupt halt. Afterwards, the newly constituted United States of America refused to tarnish its principles by returning to the practice. As a result, the English gaols became pitifully overcrowded.

For an expedient short-term solution to the problem, until something more permanent could be resolved, the British Parliament passed the Hulks Act of March 1784. More and more convicts were 'temporarily' incarcerated in ships moored along the River Thames, in Portsmouth Harbour and elsewhere. These 'hulks' were mostly old ex-navy vessels that were no longer seaworthy. At first they were operated by private contractors. The numbers detained on them varied with their size and capacity but averaged from 275 to 300 per vessel. The first Thames hulks were moored off Woolwich and on the bank opposite. In the eighteenth century, there were marshes along the northern shore and few people lived there. On the southern side was the 'Woolwich Warren', a hotchpotch of workshops, timber yards, foundries, warehouses, barracks and firing ranges. Despite their growing numbers, the hulks were soon overcrowded. By the time John Nichols was sentenced, overcrowding in the gaols and on the hulks had already become so serious that Parliament decided to renew the transportation system. But to where?

A House of Commons Committee looking at alternatives concluded that criminals might be transported firstly to those parts of Africa that belonged to the Crown; secondly, to the provinces and islands still subject to the Crown in America; or lastly, to other parts of the globe that would not violate the territorial rights of any other European power. Courts were encouraged, therefore, to condemn convicted criminals to sentences of transportation to Africa at almost every session. John Nichols' destination was to be Cape Coast Castle in West Africa, despite the fact that an experimental transportation of 300 prisoners there in 1782 had ended disastrously when more than half of them died. Even so, preparations for transporting convicts to Africa were still going on at the end of 1784.

John never went to Africa.

The African solution was doomed to failure and John was imprisoned instead on the penal hulk *Censor*. This was an old frigate purchased from the Admiralty by Duncan Campbell in 1776, the first of his hulks on the Thames. She initially housed 183 prisoners but Campbell successfully contracted to accommodate 240 on her from October 1784. Likewise, another of his hulks, the *Justitia*, originally housed 125 but this was increased to 250. As well as prisoners, each ship had around twenty officers and guards on board.

As convict numbers increased, so did the number of floating prisons. Like a floating shantytown, hulk after hulk, hung with bedding, clothes, and rotting rigging, lined the river. On hot, still days the stench of the prisoners contaminated the air from bank to bank.

Because of the hulks' isolated position, convicts were less able than prisoners on shore to have special treatment, particularly visits from relatives and friends. Normally they were stationed on the south shore of the river, but sometimes because of unrest they were anchored off the north side to make escape attempts more difficult. Escapes to the more populous Woolwich waterfront were more common than to the north shore through the forbidding marshes. Few convicts tried for freedom that way.

Whether John was sent directly to a prison hulk or first to a gaol is not known, but he is erroneously recorded as being aged twenty-four (rather than twenty-nine) and on the *Censor* from at least 11 July 1785.

Around the same time, major dredging of the river was needed to overcome a drift of the channel toward the centre. John may have been a member of a chain gang clearing the river by raising sand, soil and gravel, or in another gang working to build docks, quays and yards for the Royal Arsenal at Woolwich.

Meanwhile, the authorities were urgently reassessing how to deal with their overcrowding dilemma. They were down to their last alternatives. One suggestion was to establish a convict colony on the other side of the world at Botany Bay, about a seven-month voyage away from England on the east coast of New Holland.

As early as 1779, Sir Joseph Banks, who had sailed nine years earlier with James Cook aboard the *Endeavour*, had recommended this as a likely site for a penal colony to a House of Commons Committee. Then in 1783, a plan for resettling colonists who had remained loyal to England during the American War of Independence came to the attention of the Home Office, presided over by Viscount Sydney, the Secretary of State for Home Affairs in His Majesty's Government. It was realised that, rather than being for free American loyalists, Botany Bay could be an excellent destination for the mushrooming number of convicts sentenced to be transported.

A decision was finally made and on 18 August 1786, Lord Sydney wrote to the Lords Commissioners of the Treasury:

> I am ... commanded to signify to your Lordships his Majesty's pleasure that you do forthwith take such measures as may be necessary for providing a proper number of vessels for the conveyance of 750 convicts to Botany Bay, together with such provisions, necessaries, and implements for agriculture as may be necessary for their use after their arrival.[2]

Lord Sydney's letter finally set in motion the organisation of the historic 'First Fleet', which was destined to give birth to a new nation.

Commodore Arthur Phillip, a retired naval officer, was placed in charge of the enterprise. Born in London on 11 October 1738, Phillip had joined the Royal Navy as a midshipman in 1755, seen active service in the Seven Years' War, and then retired on half-pay. After some years as a farmer he later served, with the Admiralty's permission, as an officer in the Portuguese navy. He rejoined the Royal Navy in 1778, and then retired again in 1784 on half-pay. Now, two years further on, he was chosen not only to form a fleet and establish a penal settlement at Botany Bay, but also to act as governor of the new colony.

Phillip dealt methodically with the numerous problems before him. During the remaining months of 1786, the personnel and vessels for the expedition were gradually assembled. The Navy Board chartered five transports – the *Alexander, Charlotte, Friendship, Lady Penrhyn* and *Scarborough* – and three victuallers (stores ships) – the *Borrowdale, Fishburn* and *Golden Grove*. It soon became obvious, however, that these eight vessels and the two warships, HMS *Sirius* and HMS *Supply*, would not be adequate, and a sixth transport, the *Prince of Wales*, was added to the expedition. Of the six transports, the *Scarborough* had been built in 1782 at the port from which she derived her name; the *Alexander* at Hull in 1783, the *Charlotte* in 1784 on the Thames and the *Friendship* at Scarborough the same year; and the *Lady Penrhyn* and the *Prince of Wales*, both in Thames yards, in 1786. Of the three storeships, the *Fishburn* and the *Golden Grove* had been built at Whitby in 1780, the *Borrowdale* at Sunderland in 1785.[3]

Meanwhile, convicts nominated for transportation at Woolwich were employed raising ballast for the voyage, and those on board the prison ships at Portsmouth and Plymouth had the task of picking oakum and spinning rope-yarn. Those from other parts of Britain were moved in preparation to the hulks at Bristol, Leith, and Harwich.

On 24 February 1787, after spending almost three years on the *Censor*, John Nichols was transferred to Portsmouth prior to being loaded aboard the *Scarborough* with 207 other male convicts. Among these men were James Ruse, who had been sentenced to death for stealing, but this had been changed to transportation for seven years; William Thompson, convicted for stealing clothing to the value of 5s; Philip Farrell, a pickpocket accused of stealing a handkerchief valued at 1s; and Thomas Griffiths convicted of stealing items to the value of 80s.

The *Scarborough* was a two-decked, three-masted vessel, rigged as a barque, having an extreme length of 111 feet 6 inches, an extreme breadth of 30 feet 2 inches, and a height between decks of 4 feet 5 inches. Only the *Alexander* was slightly larger. The *Scarborough* was the first transport to reach the fleet's assembly point at Portsmouth but she had not been ready to receive prisoners. It was found that her security hatches were faulty so on 12 January carpenters were employed to make the appropriate alterations.

The first convicts had already been embarked at Woolwich, males on the *Alexander* and females on the *Lady Penrhyn*, on 6 January 1787. The *Charlotte* and the *Friendship* embarked their prisoners at Plymouth, and the *Prince of Wales* and the *Scarborough* at Portsmouth, where the fleet assembled in March. A few late arrivals were also added to those aboard the *Alexander* and the *Lady Penrhyn*.[4]

An article appearing in *The Times* of 30 March 1787, before the First Fleet was due to sail from Portsmouth, recorded:

> The transportation to Botany-bay has the advantage of the former mode of transportation to America, in securing the kingdom from the dread of being again infested with these pernicious members of society. From the mortality which has already taken place on board the transports, it is supposed not more than one in five will survive the voyage; and should the remainder live to the expiration of their sentence, they can never pay the expence of a passage home.

Expectations at the time, therefore, were that the majority of those transported would survive the 15,000-mile voyage, with those that did manage to see out their sentences never affording the passage back to England.

Mortality was an issue even before sailing. The government intended that the convicts should be embarked in good health. This was mostly the case, but on the *Alexander* many prisoners arrived from different gaols already suffering 'malignant disorders'. Despite receiving fresh provisions, their confinement handcuffed together in the prison space below deck led to outbreaks of illness. By 15 April, eleven men on the *Alexander* had died. While lighters took off some of the prisoners temporarily, the ship was thoroughly cleaned, smoked, sponged with oil of tar, and white-washed. These measures proved only partially effective for, although the prisoners began to recover, there were five more deaths prior to sailing. The vessel was down to 195 convicts out of the 211 originally embarked. Meanwhile, one woman died of fever aboard the *Lady Penrhyn*.

There were 101 remaining female prisoners aboard the *Lady Penrhyn*. One of them was Mary Carroll, a former dressmaker. Reportedly, she was born Mary Randall in 1752 but was married to a James Carroll at the time of her trial. She had specialised as a mantua maker – a mantua being a loose wedding dress or ball gown fixed open at the front to show an underskirt. It was a favoured garment worn in the seventeenth and eighteenth centuries. Mary had been convicted at the Old Bailey on 25 October 1786 for stealing linen to the value of 15s. Like John Nichols, her sentence was transportation for seven years.

The number of convicts embarked was reportedly 586 men and 192 women, but two men later received pardons and were returned to shore and freedom. This was further reduced by the deaths aboard the *Alexander* and the *Lady Penrhyn*, but the other transports sailed with their full complements of prisoners.

Inconsistencies exist in the returns regarding prisoner numbers, but the most reliable evidence indicates that the six convict ships sailed with 568 male and 191 female convicts – an overall total of 759. At the anticipated survival rate of just 20 per cent, around 600 of them were expected to perish. In addition to the prisoners, the transports carried marine guards, some with their wives and children; there were other children belonging to the convicts, various officials, and of course the crews. The decks were cluttered with water casks, animal pens and caged birds. Stowed below decks were large quantities of stores and provisions. By modern standards, but not by those of the eighteenth century, they were woefully overcrowded.

Many female criminals were difficult to control. On 19 April, five of the *Lady Penrhyn's* prisoners were put in irons for prostitution and the ship's second mate was dismissed. Similar trouble occurred aboard the *Friendship* and probably on the *Prince of Wales*. Despite rigorous efforts to prevent it, keeping the women and seamen apart proved to be impossible. Neither the *Alexander* nor the *Scarborough* had this problem because their convicts were all male.

At last all seemed ready, although clothing for the women had not yet arrived despite Captain Phillip's appeals. Phillip had spent most of this time in London attending to the countless details connected with the expedition. He joined HMS *Sirius* on 7 May, and on the 12th, when the escort frigate, HMS *Hyaena,* arrived, he made the signal to sail but there were delays until very early next morning. The eleven ships of the First Fleet departed on their historic voyage on Sunday 13 May 1787, with a fresh breeze from the south-east. With the fleet at sea, Captain Phillip ordered that the convicts could be unchained and allowed fresh air and exercise, except for those under punishment.

A potentially dangerous surprise was not discovered until after sailing. The navy's notoriously inefficient Ordnance Office had neglected to deliver the expedition's small-arms ammunition! Naturally, except for those who needed to know, this was kept a closely guarded secret for fear that the prisoners might find out. If they knew they might mutiny.

On 20 May, the fleet was some 200 miles west of the Scilly Isles, and Phillip gave orders for the *Hyaena* to return to Plymouth with his despatches. The weather was fine but such a high sea was running that Phillip, experienced seaman though he was, found it difficult to sit at the table. The swell delayed the *Sirius* sending a boat around to the transports to collect their returns relating to the prisoners, but eventually this was done. Phillip had just sealed his despatches when word reached him of trouble brewing aboard the *Scarborough*, the vessel carrying John Nichols.

John Marshall, the *Scarborough's* master, had reason to believe a serious plot existed among the convicts to seize his ship! An informer even named the ringleaders. Given the shortage of small-arms ammunition, and Phillip's earlier direction that the irons of the convicts could be removed, the report had to be taken seriously. The alleged ringleaders were transferred to the *Sirius* where each was given twenty-four lashes and then sent heavily ironed aboard the *Prince of Wales*. Phillip wrote a hasty report of the incident before his despatches were finally placed aboard the *Hyaena*. Then, after exchanging three cheers with the First Fleet, *Hyaena* departed for Plymouth.

Most of the prisoners suffered from acute seasickness during the early part of the voyage, but in general their health improved once at sea. For the time being, the majority were too dejected and lethargic to cause problems.

Apart from the alleged near-mutiny aboard the *Scarborough*, they gave little trouble.

By ten o'clock on the heavily clouded morning of 20 January 1788, the entire fleet lay at anchor in Botany Bay. Some vessels had arrived earlier over the previous couple of days, but it had been a gruelling expedition and an amazing voyage. The passage from Portsmouth had taken thirty-six weeks. Of the 212 marines, only one had been lost; and of the 759 convicts who had departed from England, only twenty-four had perished while at sea. Given the prior expectations for the voyage, this had to be judged an outstanding success and a remarkable achievement. The newspaper's judgement of a 20 per cent survival rate was completely wrong. Altogether, from the time before departure when the convicts were loaded onto the transports, thirty-six men and four women had died. There had been eight other deaths – a marine, a marine's wife, a marine's child and five children belonging to convicts. The total number of deaths, therefore, was forty-eight – a long way short of 600.

As for John Nichols and the others confined on the *Scarborough,* all of whom had been embarked in good health, Death had not visited them at all.

One hundred and forty nine years later, John Nichols' great-great-grandson, Pat Hughes, made the voyage in reverse. He departed from Sydney Harbour in January 1937. For him, the voyage was the start of the adventure of his life. It was a journey of his choosing, and it took just six weeks. There were no deaths – not on his passage to England anyway.

John Nichols, Mary Carroll and the other convicts had not had a choice. They were forced to leave their homeland on a perilous journey, and on that January day in 1788 they had arrived at an unknown, perhaps hostile place. The voyage had started the adventure of their lives. Even more than before, it was a matter of survival.

What was ahead of them now?

Botany Bay was not suitable for a settlement. The terrain was too open to the elements and there seemed to be only a scanty supply of fresh water. As well, the soil was poor, not suitable for crops. Before attempting to carry out his instructions to establish a colony, Captain Phillip decided to search along the coast for a better site. He knew of an inlet to the north which James Cook had seen as the *Endeavour* sailed along the coast in 1770. Cook had charted it merely as a boat harbour and named it Port Jackson. With a few officers and some marines Phillip set out in three open boats and proceeded northwards. They passed numerous precipitous rocky cliffs until, after having run about three leagues, they were abreast of some high sandstone cliffs at the northern extremity of which appeared to be a promising inlet. The entrance was flanked by two steep bluffs – the present day North Head and South Head.

Phillip and his party had the satisfaction of finding what he called 'the finest harbour in the world, in which a thousand sail of the line may ride in the most perfect security'. In his despatch to Lord Sydney, Phillip continued,

The different coves were examined with all possible expedition. I fixed on the one that had the best spring of water and in which the ships can anchor so close to the shore that at a very small expence quays may be made at which the largest ships may unload.

This cove, which I honoured with the name of Sydney, is about a quarter of a mile across at the entrance, and half a mile in length.

He made the obvious decision – the fleet would transfer from Botany Bay to Sydney Cove.

Arthur Phillip's Secretary, David Collins recorded:

Jan. 1788. The governor, with a party of marines, and some artificers selected from among the seamen of the *Sirius* and the convicts, arrived in Port Jackson and anchored off the mouth of the cove intended for the settlement on the evening of the 25th; and in the course of the following day sufficient ground was cleared for encamping the officer's guard and the convicts who had been landed in the morning. The spot chosen for this purpose was at the head of the cove, near the run of freshwater, which stole silently along through a very thick wood, the stillness of which had then, for the first time since the creation, been interrupted by the rude sound of the labourer's axe, and the downfall of its ancient inhabitants;—a stillness and tranquillity which from that day were to give place to the voice of labour, the confusion of camps and towns.[5]

John Nichols may have been a member of the first work party to go ashore for clearing trees. It has also been suggested that he may have carried on his back the first Royal Marine officer to go ashore, but that is unlikely. The officer carried ashore was Lieutenant George Johnson, and the convict that carried him and almost dropped him in the shallows was James Ruse, another convict transported on the *Scarborough*.

On 26 January 1788, when the Union Jack was raised to the masthead in the first clearing made at Sydney Cove to allow the unloading of the ships, there were two main causes for celebration. First, it marked at last the real ending to the long voyage from England, and secondly, half of this unknown continent was formally claimed for the British Empire. The ceremony was formal and simple. A detachment of marines fired three volleys and Phillip proposed a toast to the health of His Majesty and the royal family. Then there was another toast for the successful future of the new settlement.

Much needed to be done. The Englishmen had a slender foothold on a vast unknown land. There were enough rations to tide them over for the first few months but beyond this there was no way of knowing whether or not they could scratch out even a subsistence existence. As well, the new arrivals were surrounded by a native people who gave no indication that they would help them through their first agonising years to extend and consolidate their precarious foothold. Rather, the possibility was they might hinder and endanger their efforts. Causing additional concern on top of all this was the unexpected appearance of French ships in Botany Bay as the British were in the process of leaving. Captain Lieutenant of Marines, Watkin Tench, described the ant-like activity at Sydney Cove:

> The landing of a section of the marines and convicts took place the next day, and on the following day the remainder were disembarked. Business now sat on every brow, and the scene, to an indifferent spectator, at leisure to contemplate it, would have been highly picturesque and amusing. One party was cutting down the woods; a second was setting up a blacksmith's forge; a third was dragging a load of stores or provisions; here an officer was pitching his marquee, with a detachment of troops parading on one side of him, and a cook's fire blazing up on the other. Through the unwearied diligence of those at the head of the different departments, regularity was, however, soon introduced, and, as far as the unsettled state of matters would allow, confusion gave place to system.
>
> Into the head of the cove, on which our establishment is fixed, runs a small stream of fresh water, which serves to divide the adjacent country to a little distance, in the direction of north and south. On the eastern side of this rivulet the Governor fixed his place of residence, with a large body of convicts encamped near him; and on the western side was disposed the remaining part of these people, near the marine encampment. From this last two guards, consisting of two subalterns, as many Serjeants, four corporals, two drummers, and forty-two private men, under the orders of a Captain of the day, to whom all reports were made, daily mounted for the public security, with such directions to use force, in case of necessity, as left no room for those who were the objects of the order, but to remain peaceable, or perish by the bayonet.[6]

Among the many problems Captain Phillip had to face anew was the morality of the male and female convicts.

Phillip was proclaimed Governor on 7 February 1788, to the acknowledgement of another 'triple discharge of musquetry'. The new Governor thanked the soldiers and then turned to address the convicts. He promised that the full rigour of the law would certainly be applied against offenders and particularly drew attention to the illegal intercourse between the sexes as an offence which 'encouraged a general profligacy of manners, and was in several ways injurious to society'. To prevent this, he strongly recommended marriage, and promised every kind of assistance to those who, 'by entering into that state, should manifest their willingness to conform to the laws of morality and religion'. The new Governor's speech obviously had some effect. During the ensuing week, the Chaplain of the Settlement, the Reverend Richard Johnson, was kept busy with some fourteen marriages among the convicts.

Shortly after that, on 24 March 1788, Reverend Johnson also joined in matrimony Mary Carroll and John Nichols. John, who could not read or write, placed an 'X' on the register in lieu of his signature.

*

After nearly five years in the colony Watkin Tench was ready to go home, but before departing at the end of 1792 he had to carry out another survey. By now in his early thirties, Tench was more than just a military officer. Described as a cultivated and good-natured man and a person enthused by scientific curiosity, he rendered more than just reliable service in the fledgling settlement. He took part in a number of useful explorations into the bush, and kept journal records of his experiences which he had published in England. They came in the form of two books, namely *A Narrative of the Expedition to Botany Bay*, first published in 1789, and *A Complete Account of the Settlement at Port Jackson*, first published in 1793. Like many of his contemporaries, Tench was well aware he was part of history in the making. Indeed, his first book appeared in print before his return to England, the manuscript having been taken back by the first ship home from the voyage to Botany Bay. Suddenly, Port Jackson and Sydney Cove were in the news. Exciting accounts of the colony were splashed all over the press. Tench's book went into three authorised editions within a year, plus another in Ireland. In the same year it was translated into French twice and into German and Dutch.

Back at the ceremony of February 1788, when Arthur Phillip was proclaimed Governor of the new colony, Watkin Tench's account added details as to what took place. Phillip made his first efforts at crop growing on nine acres of land adjoining what was therefore called 'Farm Cove.' They were a failure. So were his attempts to establish vegetable growing on Garden Island, a beautiful place in the harbour. The rocky ground around Sydney yielded little success.

He turned his attention inland to an area that seemed to have potential. He named the place 'Rose-hill', after Sir George Rose, a secretary to the Treasury. Later, in June 1791, he renamed the growing settlement 'Parramatta' after he found out the aboriginal name meaning either 'head of the river' or 'the place where eels lie down'.

By June 1789, the year following settlement, Rose Hill was a useful base from which to explore. On the 26th, Captain Tench, now in charge of the Rose Hill outpost:

Accompanied by Mr. Arndell, assistant surgeon of the settlement, Mr. Lowes, surgeon's mate of the *Sirius*, two marines, and a convict, I left the redoubt at day-break, pointing our march to a hill, distant five miles, in a westerly or inland direction, which commands a view of the great chain of mountains, called Carmarthen-hills, extending from north to south farther than the eye can reach ... we found ourselves on the banks of a river, nearly as broad as the Thames at Putney, and apparently of great depth, the current running very slowly in a northerly direction. Vast flocks of wild ducks were swimming in the stream ... Having remained out three days, we returned to our quarters at Rose-hill, with the pleasing intelligence of our discovery.

When Tench reported his finds to the governor, Phillip named the new river the 'Nepean'. The hill from where he saw the 'Carmarthen-hills' (later to be called the 'Blue Mountains') was given the name of 'Tench's Prospect Hill'; this title was later shortened to 'Prospect Hill' and later still to 'Prospect'. Governor Phillip formed a farming settlement at Prospect Hill in 1791 by granting land to time-expired convicts.

It was by the end of April that year that John Nichols finished serving the full term of his seven-year sentence. As a free man, he now had the choice of trying to return to the life he led back home by working his passage to England, or attempting to settle in the colony. The first emancipated convict to settle was James Ruse, a fellow transportee on the *Scarborough* with John.

Ruse was one of the few in the colony who had some farming experience. As a twenty-two-year-old, he had been convicted of stealing in the Cornwall Assizes at Bodmin on 29 July 1782 and sentenced to death, but this was changed to transportation to Africa, like John, for seven years. He actually spent almost all of the next five years aboard the hulk *Dunkirk* in Plymouth harbour before being put aboard the *Scarborough*. In July 1789, he claimed his sentence had expired and requested a grant of land for farming. This placed Governor Phillip in an awkward position. He had no paperwork detailing the length of the convicts' sentences, or the dates of their convictions. The masters of the transport ships had left the papers with the agents in England! The situation was still unresolved two years later.

Ruse was given one and a half acres at Rose Hill on 21 November 1789, and the area of this 'Experimental Farm' was increased to thirty acres a few months later because of his good behaviour. Early in 1791 he seemed to be succeeding and actually declined assistance from the public stores. He did not need it, he said, he could live on the produce of his holding.

Phillip noted that, of those convicts who claimed their sentences were up, very few wanted to become settlers. John was one of the few expiries who took up the offer of a grant of land. His was the twentieth grant given in the colony.

For clearing and cultivating the land, each person, whether man or woman, was supplied with a set of tools: a hatchet, a tomahawk, two hoes, a spade and a shovel. A number of cross-cut saws were distributed for sharing between them. To stock their farms, they all received grain to sow and plant for the first year and two sow pigs were promised.

On 18 July 1791, at Prospect Hill west of the Rose Hill settlement, by now renamed Parramatta, John and twelve others took possession of their allotments. By the end of August they were working their properties, but there was trouble.

When Watkin Tench arrived in the area the following December to conduct his final survey, he found that:

> To give protection to this settlement, a corporal and two soldiers are encamped in the centre of the farms; as the natives once attacked the settlers, and burnt one of their houses. These guards are, however, inevitably at such a distance

from some of the farms, as to be unable to afford them any assistance in case of another attack.[7]

The original land grants had been spaced apart, which gave the aborigines cover for any attack. To counter this, Governor Phillip decided the vacant land between should be settled too by extending the existing boundaries. This gave John an extra thirty acres on top of his original forty. Tench noted John down as a 'Gardiner' who had two acres under cultivation, but neither he nor the others had so far received their promised pigs.

The hardships the settlers were living under were obvious. 'Most of them were obliged to build their own houses; and wretched hovels three-fourths of them are.'

And Tench continued: 'Of the 13 farms 10 are unprovided with water; and at some of them they are obliged to fetch this necessary article from the distance of a mile and a half. All the settlers complain sadly of being frequently robbed by the runaway convicts, who plunder them incessantly.'

John's property was bounded by those of Thomas Martin to the north and William Butler to the south. He happened to be one of those enviable settlers having a creek flowing through his land. This gave him an easily accessible, continuous supply of water. Today, the site of his grant is intersected by the Great Western Highway, and is portion of the Commonwealth Scientific and Industrial Research Organisation (CSIRO) land and Fox Hill Golf Course.

Tench also noted there were five married couples on the thirteen properties at Prospect Hill, two of the pairs having children, but John and Mary were not among them. Mary was not there at all.

Mary Nichols (*née* Carroll, nee Randall) was not even in the colony.

*

Situated some 940 miles out to sea to the north-east of Port Jackson and with a coastline of approximately twenty-two miles, Norfolk Island was also discovered and named by James Cook. When he visited there on 10 and 11 October 1774, he noted that flax plants and pine trees were growing plentifully on the island.

When the First Fleet sailed from England in 1787, the British Government, still smarting over the loss of its American colonies, gave instructions to Arthur Phillip that, as the first governor of New South Wales, he should also establish a settlement on Norfolk Island. Inspired by Cook's report, the pines were of particular interest to the Admiralty because there was a shortage of shipbuilding materials. It was hoped too that cultivation of the flax would provide a staple product for any future settlers (wrongly as it turned out because of the inferior quality of the plants that were found).

Phillip formally assigned Lieutenant Philip Gidley King, who had been second lieutenant in HMS *Sirius*, as Superintendent and Commandant of Norfolk Island and gave him written instructions outlining his task. King was to travel there in the *Supply*, the brig-rigged sloop of only 170 tons that had been a naval escort of the First Fleet. The vessel was under the command of Lieutenant Henry Lidgbird Ball. King departed at 7 a.m. on 14 February with probably the smallest band to ever establish a British colony. His group of twenty-three included a surgeon, a carpenter, a weaver, two marines, eight male convicts, and six female convicts. Apart from the convicts, all of whom had been transported for minor offences, most of the settlers were volunteers.

They took two weeks to reach their destination and on the way they passed another island where they saw giant turtles. Its position was about 1,000 km east of Sydney and roughly the same distance south of Norfolk Island. Ball afterwards named it Lord Howe Island, after one of the lords of the Admiralty.

For the next two years on Norfolk Island, King explored, built and organised the clearing of land, all the time struggling against crop-destroying grubs, rats and heavy weather. Unfortunately, at times he had to deal with troublesome convicts. The sound of the lash was heard in this paradise for the first time. One of the marines, John Batchelor, stole rum from a cask in King's residence. All of the supplies were limited and precious. Careful rationing was needed for survival. King made the punishment for this theft especially harsh in the vain hope that it would be a deterrent for the future. He sentenced Batchelor to be led around in a halter and then given three dozen lashes.

Tragedy struck the island for the first time on 15 June when Batchelor was on an early morning fishing expedition in the only row boat on the island. It was swamped by the heavy sea and he was washed overboard and drowned. The boat was damaged on the reef and nobody had the necessary skill to repair it.

Among the convict women who had been taken to Norfolk Island was Ann Inett, who became Philip King's housekeeper and lover. She had been convicted in 1786 in the Worcester Court of stealing clothing, with a total value of a little under £1. Initially condemned to be hanged, her sentence was commuted to transportation for seven years. Ann would have two children with King, both boys, who would be named Norfolk and Sydney.

Meanwhile, Governor Phillip was optimistic about the Norfolk Island settlement. He decided to send the store-ship *Golden Grove* there in October with more settlers and provisions for another eighteen months. The *Golden Grove* arrived at the island on the 13th. Forty-two settlers were aboard including a sergeant, a corporal, five marines, two gardeners, twenty-one male convicts and eleven female convicts; a carpenter from the ship volunteered to stay. One of the female convicts on board was Mary Carroll.

It was a common practice for the men to take de facto wives. Although Mary had married John Nichols at Sydney Cove just the previous March, she lived with the convict William Thompson on Norfolk Island. Thompson had, in fact, been transported with John on the *Scarborough*. His trial for stealing clothing to the value of 5s had been held at the Old Bailey on 26 May 1784.

Sentenced to transportation for seven years, he was aged about thirty-one at the time *Scarborough* left England.

Back in Sydney Cove, Governor Phillip was faced with desperate food shortages and an unruly convict population. He decided again to offload many of his convicts to Norfolk Island. He was also hopeful that the island would be able to provide food for the mainland colony.

Unaware of the governor's plans, King continued with his assigned duties. His convict population already far outnumbered the free inhabitants, including military personnel, but with a total of sixty-two people on the island he was able to make good progress.

Although he treated the convicts with a certain respect and looked after their welfare, on 24 January 1789 King learned from an informant that there was a plot to seize the island. King, the free settlers and the military were to be captured and imprisoned. There might even be loss of life. Then, when the *Supply* returned, the convicts intended to possess the ship and sail to Tahiti. Acting quickly, King was able to thwart the scheme. Two of the ringleaders were put in irons. The others were cautioned to appreciate their privileges, and at the same time he introduced severe new restrictions on their movements and gatherings. Because of the plot, the fragile trust and goodwill that had been nurtured and grown between the authorities and the convicts evaporated. Instead of becoming valuable members of a pioneer settlement, the convicts turned into a troublesome, resentful burden.

On 26 January 1789, just when the mutiny scare was over, Mary Carroll's partner, William Thompson, was discovered stealing corn. The penalty was fifty lashes but this did not deter others. It was the start of a spate of similar incidents and punishments.

King's first tenure on Norfolk Island ended suddenly. On 13 March 1790, the *Sirius* and *Supply* appeared in bad weather which obliged them to anchor off shore. The excited settlers thought that the two ships had brought fresh supplies and news from Britain, but they were wrong. The two ships were to land 186 convicts, an army detachment including Captain Johnson, five lieutenants and several non-commissioned officers, a meagre supply of food, and Lieutenant-Governor Robert Ross who had been Governor Phillip's deputy at Port Jackson. Ross carried Phillip's orders to King, instructing him to turn over his command. Phillip wanted King to be his emissary to the home government.

The procedures of the command transfer, including the checking of the island's stores, were begun immediately while the convicts and soldiers were landing. As usual, the weather imposed great difficulties. The ships were buffeted by strong north-east winds. The *Sirius* under Captain John Hunter hove into the bay on 19 March to lower her boats and help with the unloading, but a strong tide pushed her towards the reef's outer rocks. As Hunter put her about on another tack the wind suddenly switched direction and *Sirius* was swept stern first onto the rocks and wrecked.

On this extraordinary note, the regime of the first commandant of Norfolk Island, Philip Gidley King, came to an end. With some survivors from the *Sirius* he sailed for Port Jackson aboard the *Supply* on 24 March 1790. Accompanying him were his convict concubine and their two sons, Norfolk and Sydney.[8]

Mary Carroll's seven-year sentence was not due to finish until October 1793 – but King was back on Norfolk Island well before then!

From 21 December 1790 until 15 March 1791, King was in London where he was granted interviews with the Secretary of State, Lord Grenville, and the President of the Royal Society, Sir Joseph Banks. His frank discussions on the problems confronting New South Wales and Norfolk Island impressed them and contributed to his promotion to commander on 2 March 1791.

Despite his convict-born family, King married his cousin Anna Josepha Coombe on 11 March. They boarded the *Gorgon* together four days later to sail back to New South Wales.

In November 1791, after spending five weeks in Port Jackson, King left again for Norfolk Island with his wife. Also with them was a detachment of the New South Wales Corps, a formation specially raised to relieve the Royal Marines and to take over guard and garrison duties in the colony. It was commanded by Captain William Paterson, who had arrived at Port Jackson recently. King quickly resumed control of the island and by March 1793 he could report that a year's rations had been accumulated in the store. Extensive clearing had been under way that led to successful crops of wheat and maize (corn). He especially praised settlers who had stayed from the *Sirius* shipwreck, reporting they were good workers. As crime had decreased, it was a good period all round.

Life was changing on the island. Ships began to appear at more regular intervals with a variety of supplies and, of course, more convicts. Many of these were being transferred to the island as punishment for crimes they had committed on the mainland. The same ships also took away the freed convicts who did not wish to settle on the island, among them Mary Carroll. On 26 July 1794, she boarded the *Francis* for the journey to Port Jackson.

After returning to New South Wales, Mary faced the expiree's choice of trying to return to the life she had left behind in England or remaining in the colony. Free but without money, working a passage back to England was far from easy for a woman. A report by a Select Committee on Transportation published in the British Parliament described the dilemma women faced:

No difficulty appears to exist amongst the major part of the men who do not wish to remain in the colony, of finding means of return to this Country. All but the aged and infirm easily find employment on board the ships visiting New South Wales, and are allowed to work their passage home; but such facility is not afforded to the women: they have no possible method of leaving the Colony but by prostituting themselves on board the ships whose masters may chuse [*sic*] to receive them. They who are sent to New South Wales, that their former habits may be relinquished, cannot obtain a return to this Country, but by relapsing into that mode of life.[9]

Another alternative for Mary would have been to try and renew her relationship with John Nichols, but it is not known if she made an effort to do so. If she did, she may have discovered that John was already living with someone else, a convict hutkeeper, apparently a woman who was not chosen to be a wife.

Mary was probably fortunate that at this time the colony was being administered by the commander of the New South Wales Corps, Major Francis Grose, in his capacity of Lieutenant-Governor. Governor Arthur Phillip had returned to England earlier because of ill health. It was during Grose's tenure that private enterprise became established in the colony. Several officers of the New South Wales Corps were able to occupy influential positions. They and others were given grants of land. Under Grose's encouragement, the Hawkesbury area to the north and north-west of Sydney town began to be settled, and several former convicts took up land for cultivation.

Mary received a grant of land at Mulgrave Place near Richmond. This was some distance away from John's property at Prospect Hill. There was no established method of direct transportation connecting the two, although Grose had a good road made from Sydney to the banks of the Hawkesbury which went through Parramatta to Windsor, Richmond being a few more miles further on to the west.

Mary died on 3 April 1803, a year of serious drought throughout New South Wales. For some reason her burial was not registered until two months later on 8 June at St Philip's Church of England in Sydney. Her passing meant that John was legally free to marry again – if that happened to be his wish.

The colony's first chaplain, the Reverend Richard Johnson, travelled regularly to Parramatta where he held services in the open air and later, appropriately enough, in a carpenter's shop there. Johnson was joined in 1794 by the Reverend Samuel Marsden who became assistant-chaplain with his residence at Parramatta.

As a Church of England clergyman, Marsden adhered to a narrow interpretation of the scriptures and preached the 'suffering road' to salvation. Shortly after his arrival he became a magistrate and, following a line similar to his clerical teachings, he built a reputation for severity, earning the epithet the 'Flogging Parson'. As a landowner and farmer he was a success. Initially granted land in the Parramatta region, he later purchased more and by 1805 he had over 1,000 sheep on pasture. His skill in this regard established him as one of the founders of the Australian wool industry. Marsden had been two years in spiritual charge of Parramatta when, in 1796, two wooden huts were formed into a temporary church, and so St John's Church began its long, proud history.

At first when the church opened there were no pews, and in those days it was not feasible for the congregation to supply permanent chairs. The congregation had to bring their own rough and ready forms or seats of any kind. As time wore on, pews were furnished, and the townspeople assembled here together with the officers from the barracks when they were on duty. The soldiers and convicts were housed in the galleries and later, too, the children of the Protestant Orphan School. When The King's School was established, the boys trooped to the church every Sunday. At first the building was of brick, stuccoed. In time, two towers were added – when the church itself was removed and rebuilt of stone, these towers were left standing.

It was in St John's at Parramatta that John Nichols and Ann Pugh were joined in matrimony on 25 August 1803. The ceremony was performed by the Reverend Samuel Marsden.

John Nichols had prospered at Prospect Hill between 1791 and 1803, but the going had been far from easy. By the end of 1792 there were government farms at Sydney Cove, Parramatta and Toongabbie (an aboriginal word meaning 'meeting of the waters'), and the colony traded with England, Ireland, Calcutta and Batavia, as well as ports in China and the USA. The colonial population of New South Wales had increased to 3,108 and there were 1,115 on Norfolk Island.

Governor Phillip relinquished his command of the colony for reasons of ill-health and, on the evening of Monday, 10 December 1792, he boarded the *Atlantic* to return to England. He left behind a well-established colony that had overcome almost overwhelming odds to survive. 5,000 acres of land had been granted to 112 ex-convicts and fifty-five former Royal Marines, and 1,516 acres were under cultivation. As the population of the colony grew and land became a source of wealth the two original social classes of officers and prisoners were expanded to include free immigrants, the native-born who would eventually be called Currency lads and lasses, and expiree convicts, including John Nichols, who were frequently referred to as emancipists.

Major Francis Grose, commander of the New South Wales Corps, officially took control of the colony as Lieutenant-Governor on 31 December 1792.

Under Major Grose the influence of the military, the New South Wales Corps, was greatly enhanced. Civil courts became military courts. He increased the rations of the officers, introduced the granting of land to officers and permitted them to engage in speculative trading. This system was unique to New South Wales. It was of questionable legality. In other parts of the British Empire, civil and military officers were required to resign their commissions before being eligible for land grants.

Private internal trade had been established with markets at Sydney and Parramatta, but as there was a lack of currency most trading was done by bartering, especially among the poorer sections of the community. Coinage had not been included in the provisions of the first settlement on the assumption that a penal colony did not need supplies of minted money. The omission led to many problems, both monetary and social. Alongside bartering, the use of promissory notes became a standard method of exchange, a system that would last for several decades. It led to a trade monopoly run by the civil administrators and military officers. These people also became the principal traders in rum as a form of payment, and the practice spread throughout the colony.

Also under Grose, the New South Wales Corps determined to only carry out garrison duties, neglecting overseeing and policing. Officers devoted the remainder of the time to their private, more profitable, concerns. Constables and overseers had to be appointed from the better behaved convicts.

Settlers at Prospect Hill and around Parramatta complained repeatedly of being robbed by runaway convicts, but ironically in August 1793, John Nichols actually became the victim of runaway soldiers. The incident was recorded by David Collins:

Two soldiers were put into confinement on suspicion of being parties in a plan to seize one of the long-boats, were tried by a regimental court-martial on the first day of this month (August), and one was acquitted; but Roberts, a drummer, who was proved to have attempted to persuade another drummer to be of the party, was sentenced to receive three hundred lashes, and in the evening did receive two hundred and twenty-five of them. While smarting under the severity with which his punishment was inflicted, he gave up the names of six or eight of his brother soldiers as concerned with him, among whom were the two who had absented themselves the preceding evening. These people, the day following their desertion, were met in the path to Parramatta, and told an absurd story of their being sent to the Blue Mountains. They were next heard of at a settler's (John Nichols) at Prospect Hill, whose house they entered forcibly, and making him and a convict hutkeeper prisoners, passed the night there.[10]

Hutkeepers seem to have been those women who were not fortunate enough to be selected for wives 'which every officer, settler and solider is entitled to, and few are without.' Perhaps because John had been legally married in front of witnesses in the colony itself, as a respectable settler now he could only have a hutkeeper, not another wife, despite the fact he and Mary Carroll were separated and she was on Norfolk Island.

At another settler's they took sixteen pounds of flour, which they sent by his wife to a woman well known to one of them and had them baked into small loaves. They signified a determination not to be taken alive, and threatened to lie in wait for the game-killers, of whose ammunition they meant to make themselves masters. These declarations manifested the badness of their hearts, and the weakness of their cause; and the Lieutenant-Governor, on being made acquainted with them, sent out a small armed party to secure and bring them in, rightly judging that people who were so ready at expressing every where a resolution to part with their lives rather than be taken, would not give much trouble in securing them.

The parties who had been sent after the runaways, by dividing themselves fell in with them near Toongabbie on the 6th, and secured them without any opposition.

In 1794, Collins reported that, 'Prospect Hill proved to be most productive, some grounds there returned 30 bushels of wheat for one.'

John Nichols and his neighbours were determined to succeed but their difficulties were many. Not only did they have to contend with a completely different climate and possibly hostile natives, they also had to adjust to the completely unfamiliar flora and fauna. This was further complicated by their lack of experience in agriculture and farming.

Even the man who had been issued the first grant of land, James Ruse, who had been a convict on the *Scarborough* with John, ran into difficulties. The seasons were not as favourable to him as he deserved. In 1793, his crop having failed, Ruse sold his 'Experiment Farm' at Parramatta to Dr John Harris, whose properties would later form the adjacent suburb of Harris Park. In the following year Ruse took up farming on a thirty-acre land grant on the Hawkesbury River. After many years he sold this too, and he died in Campbelltown in 1837.

The two sow pigs that had been promised to John and the Prospect Hill settlers in 1791 were finally delivered and by 1795 were flourishing and reproducing. In 1996, John was one the suppliers of pork to Norfolk Island. Surviving records show that on 3 July he sold 506 lbs of pig flesh, and just over a month later, on 6 August, another 566 lbs. At sixpence a pound, John was owed £26 16s. How long this arrangement continued is not known.

Nevertheless, many settlers faced bankruptcy because of the exorbitant prices they were obliged to pay for their basic commodities and the low returns they received for their crops. By 1798 only six of the original thirteen Prospect Hill settlers remained. They were John Nichols, George Lisk, Thomas Martin, Samuel Griffiths, Joseph Morley and John Herbert.

In 1797 Governor Hunter, Phillip's successor, gave the settlers an opportunity to report on the effect the monopoly of trade and labour by the New South Wales Corps was having on them. The report was given to him the following year; in it was a petition from the Prospect and Toongabbie settlers, outlining their 'Grievances and Complaints'. The name 'John Nicholls' appeared along with five others on the petition. All of them were time-expired First Fleet convicts. The document was 'Signed in presence of Thos Arndell' on the '5th day of March 1798' and witnessed by the Reverend Samuel Marsden JP.

Despite such petitions, Hunter's efforts to do anything about the situation were ineffectual. The officers of the New South Wales Corps continued to amass a large percentage of the colony's wealth through their control of the rum trade and imports and their internal manipulation of favours.

One of those ambitious men who worked the system was John Macarthur. Born near Plymouth of Scottish parents, he joined the Royal Navy and received a commission as an ensign at fifteen. He later left the service for farming but rejoined the navy when he enlisted as a foundation lieutenant in the New South Wales Corps, which was being established in 1789. At the time, his aim was to gain promotion while in the colony to enhance his prospects in England. Arriving with the Second Fleet in 1790, he was posted to Rose Hill, later Parramatta, where he became Corps Paymaster in 1792, and Inspector of Public Works in 1793. That same year with a grant of 100 acres, he began his farming ventures. He named this property Elizabeth Farm after his wife. Within a few years he became the largest landholder in the Parramatta area and a foremost supplier of produce for the Government Store. He quickly established his reputation as a determined farmer and trader, which later included shipping interests. If necessary, he was ready to challenge authority in the pursuit of his goals.

By 1799, the officers of the NSW Corps owned an estimated 32 per cent of the colony's cattle, 40 per cent of the goats, 59 per cent of the horses and 77 per cent of the sheep. By 1800, Macarthur owned 1,610 acres.

Macarthur's temperament set in motion a chain of events that would eventually lead to him being declared 'The Father of the Australian Wool Industry'. In 1801, he fought a pistol duel with his commanding officer, Colonel William Paterson, who was wounded. Macarthur was sent to England to be court-martialled. He took with him samples of the wool he had produced at Elizabeth Farm, where since 1795 he had been breeding from some Spanish Merino sheep brought into the colony from the Cape of Good Hope.

English experts found Macarthur's wool to be 'equal to the best which comes from Spain'. At that time, the supply of wool from Spain was not reliable because of the Napoleonic Wars. Macarthur was therefore encouraged to continue with his experiments in producing wool in New South Wales. He resigned his commission in the New South Wales Corps and was free to return to the colony as an influential settler.

*

Ann Pugh had been placed on trial at the Herefordshire Summer Assizes on Tuesday, 16 July 1799, accused of stealing goods to the value of £2 12s 2d. Found guilty, she was sentenced to transportation to New South Wales for seven years.

Ann was taken on board the transport ship *Earl Cornwallis* commanded by Captain James Tennant, along with 193 male and ninety-four female convicts. The vessel left England on 18 November 1800. The journey took a tragic 206 days. By the time the vessel arrived in Sydney Cove on 12 June 1801, no fewer than twenty-seven male and eight female convicts had died along the way.

The arrival of female convicts was always eagerly anticipated because of the great imbalance between the sexes. There was a standard protocol in place.

A book called *A Brief Account of the Colony of Port Jackson* by an Ensign G. Bond was published in Southampton, England, in 1803. In it, the author described a typical selection procedure. First, on their arrival, the female convicts were 'well washed and furnished with a change of suitable apparel'. After that:

> The commissioned officers then come on board, and as they stand upon deck, select such females as are most agreeable in their person ... The non-commissioned officers then are permitted to select for themselves; the privates next; and lastly, those convicts, who, having been in the country a considerable time, and having realised some property, are enabled to procure the governor's permission to take to themselves a female convict. The remainder, who are not thus chosen, are brought on shore.[11]

They could then be sent to the 'Factory' at Parramatta prison. This prison for women convicts was actually a curious marriage bureau. It was half prison, half barracks, where the women were fed and clothed by the Government in return for their labour spinning and weaving wool into clothing and blankets. Well-behaved convicts in the colony were encouraged to choose a bride from the 'Factory'.

How and when John and Ann actually met remains uncertain but it is likely that it happened through one of these established processes, or she may have been simply assigned to him as a servant or hutkeeper under the system set up by Major Grose and continued by his successor Captain William Paterson. Ann was living with John before 1802 – it was sometime in the middle of that year that their first child, a boy, was born at Prospect. They named him John. In the muster of 1802, John Nichols was listed as a Prospect landholder supporting one woman and one child without assistance from the Government Store. For Ann, the arrangement had to have been an agreeable change compared with the life she left behind in England and what she had gone through. She had been so desperate that she used 'force and arms' to commit robbery; she had been arrested, placed on trial, imprisoned; and she had survived a lengthy journey by sea in which thirty-five of her fellow convicts had died.

By now, John was well respected and enjoying a measure of prosperity. The 1800 muster showed that he possessed forty acres sown with wheat; twelve acres planted with maize; 110 sheep, twenty-eight pigs and a horse. Musters were surveys of the people in the colony who were not government-employed or dependent on the Government Stores. Calls to attend the musters were placed up on public notice boards.

The years 1798 to 1799 were a period of severe drought in New South Wales in which wheat and maize crops failed, but this was followed in March 1799 by torrential rain. The Nepean–Hawkesbury area suffered dangerous flooding. Livestock and wheat stacks were swept away and one man was drowned. Many settlers spent a frightening night clinging to the roofs of their houses.

A survey in August 1799 showed that there were only ten horses and fifteen mares in the colony held by settlers. The price of a horse in 1796 was £90 ($180). How and when John Nichols obtained his horse is not known, however, it enabled him to lease his horse and cart out to other farmers for a fee.

John was also a constable. Constables were elected by the people of designated districts. Once elected they chose from among themselves a head constable for each district who had to report the number of inhabitants in his division, including births and deaths, to the Acting Magistrate each month. Other duties included suppressing gambling; enforcing respect for the Sabbath; and seeing that all persons in their district attended the general musters. They had the power to search houses for suspicious persons or concealed goods. For their service, constables and their families were placed on the 'Free Ration', received an issue of spirits, and occasionally clothing from the Government Stores when available. Constables continued in their elected role for twelve months and could be re-elected at the end of the term. John seems to have performed his duties to the satisfaction of his peers and the authorities because he held the position for at least nine years, probably from 1799, and at times was a head constable.

In 1800, Governor Hunter was replaced by the colony's third Governor, Philip Gidley King. During his second stint on Norfolk Island, King had been plagued by ill-health and he and his family left the island in September 1796 aboard the whaling ship *Britannia*. After convalescence, instead of returning again to his post as commandant of Norfolk Island, he was sent to replace Hunter as Governor of New South Wales.

Meanwhile, the eighteenth century closed with great unrest. Although halfway around the world from the 'Mother Country', events so far away overseas did have their impact on New South Wales. First, there was the bogey of French conquest under the leadership of Napoleon Bonaparte. Then rumours of a rebellion in Ireland in 1798 began to circulate throughout the colony. The Irish uprising was unsuccessful but many of its 'political malcontents' were exiled without trial to New South Wales.

If there was an uprising in the settlement, or an invasion in force by another power, or both, it was highly unlikely the New South Wales Corps would cope. Governor Hunter had believed extra precautions needed to be taken. He appealed to the 'patriotism' of the colonists, and the Loyal Sydney and Parramatta Associations were born in 1800 'to protect public and private property and to assist the military in the preservation of order.' There were fifty armed men in the Sydney association, all properly equipped and clothed in regimental dress, and the same number in Parramatta. The men in each association were chosen from free men of good character who possessed property.

King was authorised to take over the office of governor as soon as Hunter could arrange departure, but there were delays. He did not assume command until 28 September 1800. Before that, the Irish rebels were Hunter's problem.

He was wise to worry. A revolt was in the process of being planned on the Government Farm at Toongabbie. The plan involved taking Parramatta and dealing with the hated Anglican Minister and Magistrate Samuel Marsden, the 'Flogging Parson' who freely ordered punishment in the form of the cat 'o nine tails. After disposing of Marsden the rebels planned to kill the soldiers in their beds using self-made pikes, take their muskets and then march on Sydney. However, informants exposed the plan to Marsden, and when the rebel leaders learnt they had been betrayed they were quick to cancel the uprising.

Once aware of the planned uprising, fear of the Irish convicts spread like wildfire through the colony. Nor did failure dampen convict enthusiasm for rebellion. Another uprising was planned for September but again was revealed, this time to Captain John Macarthur of the New South Wales Corps. Macarthur advised the governor to wait for the convicts to rebel and deal with them in the open but that did not happen. The leading rebels realised their plan was discovered and cancelled it again. More floggings followed and those merely suspected of involvement with the rebels were made to watch.

Then, late in the year a dispatch arrived from Norfolk Island revealing that a conspiracy among the Irish exiles to seize control of the island had been suppressed. The ringleaders had been arrested and hanged as an example, and others allegedly involved in the plot were flogged. It was the beginning of the cruellest chapter in Norfolk Island's history.

In February 1801, four months after Governor King, assumed command, the transport ship *Anne I* (or *Luz St Anna*) arrived in Sydney with 178 convicts, sixty-nine of them former United Irishmen. King was uneasy, but the ship also brought more welcome news that Britain and Ireland had united in Union. It gave the Governor hope that the Irish exiles might feel greater empathy with the English in future and be more accepting of their situation in New South Wales.

Hope? Yes, but the situation had to be watched closely ... The New South Wales Corps was mainly concentrated in Sydney, with the other settlements only having small garrisons. Clearly, if there was trouble, the colonists in the Parramatta, Prospect and Toongabbie areas would be at most risk.

Governor King maintained the existence of the Loyal Sydney and Parramatta associations until August 1801 when he had them disbanded as fears of a rebellion seemed to decline. The following year, however, responding to reports of likely trouble, King authorised a search of dwellings and other buildings throughout the colony. All offensive weapons were confiscated although the settlers were allowed to retain one musket each. John Nichols at Prospect was listed as having two weapons in his possession, a gun (probably a musket) and a pistol.

Meanwhile, more ships arrived from Ireland. Each brought more exiles from the 1798 Irish Rebellion, and there were reports again of growing unrest. Then in 1803, when news reached Sydney of a renewed war between England and France, the Loyal Sydney and Parramatta Associations were re-established.

Volunteers in the associations were required to drill regularly and become proficient in the use of arms. The Parramatta volunteers had to attend each Wednesday and Saturday from 4.00 to 5.30 p.m. They were to conduct themselves with proper respect, keep their uniform and arms in perfect condition, and were to observe order and decorum whilst on duty. John Nichols was listed as being a member of the Parramatta Loyalist Association in 1810, the year in which the volunteer companies were again disbanded, but his name does not appear in its earliest years. When it was disbanded in 1810, the Parramatta Company consisted of thirty-seven men plus officers.

John and Ann's second child was a girl, born on 22 May 1803. They named her Ann. She was among the first to be baptised in St John's Church at Parramatta, the ceremony taking place on 26 June. Meanwhile, as Mary Carroll had died the previous April, John and Ann were free to marry, but there was some delay.

It could be that, although Mary Carroll died on 3 April, her burial might not have been properly registered. The Reverend Marsden, not a man to be trifled with, may have stipulated that he needed proper confirmation of her death before it would be appropriate for him to perform the marriage ceremony. This would account for the late registration of her burial at St Phillip's in Sydney on 8 June 1803.

John and Ann were married on 25 August, two months after baby Ann's baptism. The ceremony was witnessed by Timothy Hollister and Amelia Evans. Hollister had arrived in the colony aboard the *Albemarle*, one of the vessels of the Third Fleet. In 1802, he was a private in the Parramatta Loyalist Association and by 1804 he was leasing land in the Parramatta district.

John frequently purchased items from Rowland Hassall's store at Parramatta. Hassall was a former preacher with the London Missionary Society. Governor King made him the government storekeeper at Toongabbie and placed him in charge of the Parramatta Granary. By 1804, Hassall too was a member of the Parramatta Loyalist Association holding the rank of sergeant.

The year 1804 opened with the threat of another crisis looming in the colony, and Ann Nichols at Prospect Hill knowing that she was pregnant again.

The situation was at flashpoint. In Europe, the Treaty of Amiens in March 1802 had established an uneasy peace between England and France under Napoleon Bonaparte, but it had only lasted just over a year. There were fears of French naval domination of the Mediterranean and in the East Indies and West Indies. England imposed a naval blockade of the Continent. Napoleon began preparations for an invasion of England.

News of the renewed war reached New South Wales but Governor King was already preoccupied with simmering local concerns – rumours throughout the colony of another rebellion planned by the Irish convicts. Would the combined strength of the NSW Corps and King's re-established Sydney and Parramatta Loyalist Associations be enough to meet any emergency? On Sunday,

22 January 1804 the *Ferret*, a whaling ship, arrived in Sydney harbour. She was five months out of England and carried on board newspapers that were as recent as 22 August 1803 and these carried the first reports of a new uprising in Dublin.

Convict leaders at the Castle Hill Government Farm planned to rally the prisoners and march to Parramatta, enlisting other convict groups on the way. The leading groups from there would fan out in the area with the idea of converging on Parramatta and making it the spearhead of a huge revolt. After putting John Macarthur's Elizabeth Farm and Parramatta to the torch, they would then march to Windsor to join up with the rebels in the Hawkesbury area before marching on Sydney. Their plans were far-reaching and transmitted through secret messengers, but again authorities were alerted.

That night in Parramatta and Sydney, the military and militia were called to duty amid rallying drums and gun shots. At Parramatta, Samuel Marsden evacuated from the town by boat with his family and John Macarthur's family. John Macarthur was still in England. Marsden was an obvious target as his tyrannical penchant for flogging had earned the hatred of many convicts. The only thing settlers living near to Parramatta were able to do, if they were aware of what was happening, was prepare whatever defences they could, mount a guard and wait.

What precautions John Nichols took, if any, on the night of 4/5 March 1804 are not known. The boy John was nearly two years old by now, baby Ann just ten months, and his wife Ann about halfway into her third pregnancy. Being unable to read or write, neither John nor Ann could record anything down for posterity. In reality, all they could do was watch and wait like the others ...

The *Sydney Gazette* reported:

The alarm began at Castle Hill about 8 o'clock on Sunday night where there are upwards of 200 Irish Prisoners (sent here for Seditious Practices in Ireland), by setting a House on fire and ringing the Bell, when Cunningham appeared as the avowed leader, vociferating the cries of 'DEATH OR LIBERTY!'

Two hundred rebels overpowered the constables and broke into the Government Farm's buildings, taking firearms and ammunition, and any other weapons they could find. Two convicts dragged the Hills District flogger, Robert Duggan from under his bed and beat him unconscious. In two other separate incidents, the lives of constables were saved when muskets misfired. The rebels then went from farm to farm towards Parramatta gathering firearms and supplies, and drinking any liquor they discovered along the way.

At half past eleven o'clock on Sunday night, 4th of March, 1804, an express was received by HIS EXCELLENCY, from Captain ABBOT, Commanding Officer at Parramatta, with intelligence that the Prisoners at Public Labour at Castle Hill, and the Settlers' men, were in a state of Insurrection, and had already committed many daring Outrages.

Sydney was instantaneously alarmed, the Military and Inhabitants were under Arms; the Captain, Officers, Marines and Ships Company of His

Majesty's Ship CALCUTTA came on shore, in ten minutes after the alarm was given, and by the Governor's orders all Horses throughout the Town were held in requisition.

As information was received that the Insurgents were in several bodies, Major Johnston with Quarter-Master Laycock, & 25 Non-Commissioned Officers and Privates of the New South Wales Corps, accompanied by a Trooper and several of the Constables & Inhabitants, at half-past 6 proceeded by way of Toongabbee; Lieutenant Davis with an equal number of Soldiers proceeded along the Castle Hill Road, that place being appointed for the Rendezvous, in case nothing should occur to make those Officers alter the directions they were under.

Major George Johnston ordered his detachment to force-march to Parramatta. Meanwhile, Governor King immediately set off for Parramatta, where he arrived not long before Johnston and his men. One of King's first actions was to declare martial law. Towards daybreak, around 350 convicts armed with stolen rifles, crudely made arms and makeshift weapons were near Parramatta. At daybreak, rebel leaders were still waiting for a signal from the uprising in Parramatta, but it never came.

Rather than face the Parramatta garrison head on, the rebels decided to head north-west down the Hawkesbury Road to Windsor to meet up with rebels from the Hawkesbury, but daylight brought back a sobering reality. The thought of retaliation by the colonial authorities cooled the anger of many of those present. Some abandoned the enterprise, but a large contingent headed out to rally support from convicts at the Hawkesbury. They moved north-west and west and, importantly for John Nichols and his family and the other settlers in the area, away from Prospect Hill.

The *Sydney Gazette* again:

Major Johnston on arriving at Toongabbee, received information that a considerable Body were on their way to the Hawkesbury. Notwithstanding the fatigue of his small Detachment in marching up from Sydney, and the distance they had gone since, they immediately ran in good Order, with their followers, and after a pursuit of Seven Miles farther, Major Johnston and a Trooper, who had preceded the Detachment came up with the rear of the Insurgents at 11 o'clock, whose numbers have since been ascertained to be 233 men, armed with Muskets, Pistols, Swords, &c, and a number of followers which they had taken from the Settlers.

After calling to them repeatedly they halted, and formed on the rise of a Hill. The Major and Trooper advanced within pistol shot, and endeavoured to persuade them to submit to the Mercy that was offered them by the Proclamation, which they refused ...

Two requests to surrender were refused, including one from the convict priest, James Dixon, whom Governor King had sent along with the Corps. Major Johnston made the next move.

The Major required to see their Chiefs, who after some deliberation met them half way, between the Detachment and the Insurgents, when by great presence of mind and address the Major presented his Pistol at the head of the Principal leader (Philip Cunningham), and the Trooper following his motions, presented his Pistol also at the other leader's head, (Wm. Johnston) and drove them into the Detachment without the least opposition from the body of the Insurgents.

Major Johnston immediately ordered Quarter-Master Laycock to advance with the Detachment, &c, and cut the body to pieces, which immediately filed off and fled in all directions, pursued by the Detachement and followers; several shots were fired by the Insurgents without effect. As the pursuit was along the Road and on each side in the Woods, the number of dead are not yet ascertained; nine Bodies were found about the Road and several were known to be killed in the pursuit through the Woods. A number were overtaken and made Prisoners, among whom was the Leader (Philip Cunningham).

The uprising was over but the soldiers' blood was up. At one stage Major Johnston had to threaten his own men with a pistol to prevent more bloodshed. The pursuit went on all day up until 9 p.m., ranging as far north-west as Windsor. One rebel leader was hanged under martial law at Windsor's Commissariat Store, which he had bragged he would burn down.

The available men of the Parramatta Loyalist Association had taken on the role of the town's defenders. Rowland Hassall's name appears among those who were there, his store being at Parramatta. A few accompanied Major Johnston's detachment and parties of settlers to round up the rebels who were still at large. Over the next three days around 300 were eventually brought in.

During the remainder of the week, nine of the leaders were executed at Castle Hill, Parramatta and Sydney. The choice of these three locations was to press home to the inhabitants the judgment of colonial law. One leader executed at Castle Hill was then hung in chains, just outside Parramatta on the road to Prospect Hill. Another was executed at Parramatta and hung in chains there too.

Some of the convicts who had joined in the uprising were moved north to chain gangs at the new settlement of Coal Town on the Hunter River. The name Coal Town was changed soon afterwards to Newcastle.

*

William Cox had problems in his position as New South Wales Corps Paymaster. A deficiency of £7,900 had been found in his regimental accounts in 1803. He had been suspended from office. A sum of £2,000 was secured, and to pay the remainder his estate was assigned to trustees to sell for the benefit of his creditors including the army agents.

The debts touched many, including John Nichols. The trustees took John to court to recover £22 which he was obliged to pay within one month of

26 October 1805. By 1806, the creditors had been paid in full, but Cox was ordered to return to England under arrest 'to answer such charges as may be brought against him'.

An uneasy peace was eventually restored and life returned to normal, although on 7 May 1804 a number of communities including Parramatta, Prospect, and Hawkesbury were shaken by the shocks of a minor earthquake.

John and Ann Nichol's third child, a boy they named Charles, was born on 22 July. He was baptised at St John's Church, Parramatta, on 12 August.

During that year, the settlers of several districts, including Prospect Hill, were required to name three people from among themselves who held one hundred acres each or more by grant to be appointed as trustees of their respective commons. After being elected by their fellow settlers, the appointees would be recommended to the Governor by a Bench of Magistrates for final approval. The common land was to be used collectively to pasture the cattle and stock. Prospect Common covered most of what is now Blacktown. John Nichols was one of the three appointed trustees. Governor King gave his approval on 11 August 1804 and the trio received the grant on 21 December 1805.

Meanwhile, Governor King's efforts to break the rum trade were largely unsuccessful, although he challenged the monopoly by encouraging more competition. He established a government brewery to try to offer a substitute and encouraged the brewing of beer. He also continued the licensed houses started by the previous governor. Illicit stills were forbidden and if they were found incurred heavy punishment. Every farmer was required to lodge a return of the wheat he held so it could be compared with his sales and consumption to curb the use of wheat for distilling.

John Nichols' star was rising. He was prosperous and diversifying. In an account of beer brewed at Parramatta, he was shown to have brewed nineteen gallons during the period 10 December 1804 to 30 June 1805, possibly for personal consumption or sale, or perhaps both.

Governor King's relations with the New South Wales Corps were becoming increasingly strained, in a large part because of his efforts to curb the inflated prices charged by the monopolists. King imported produce for sale in the Government Stores and at the same time pegged the prices to put a stop to their excessive profits. He also strove to expand production in the colony by arranging settlement on larger holdings.

John took advantage of this to increase his own property. He acquired the lease on an allotment of land at Parramatta, which was registered in his name and witnessed by 'Philip Gidley King' on 1 January 1806.

John apparently decided then to let his original holding and advertised it in the *Sydney Gazette* of 13 April 1806:

> To be let and entered on immediately. A valuable farm at Prospect, containing 60 acres, all clear, with large commodious, and substantial dwelling, house newly built and shingled, fit for the immediate reception of a genteel family,

with good barn, stock yards, sheep shed, pig sties and all other necessary appurtenances, well supplied with water, and free from all danger of flood. Particulars to be had of John Nichols on the premises.

Rent on the property was ten shillings per annum. The muster of 1806 recorded that emancipist William Blower, who had arrived as a convict on the Albemarle in October 1791, was the person renting land from John at that time.

John and Ann's fourth child was another girl, Sophia, who was born on 10 March 1806. For some reason there was some delay in having her baptised. This did not take place until over two years later on 24 April 1808, again at St John's in Parramatta.

King also encouraged an increase in the number of independent traders which in turn contributed to reducing the number of colonists depending on government rations. The numbers dependent on government supplies dropped significantly, much to the approval of colonial authorities in England who were always keen to cut expenditure. However, his autocratic attitude often triggered an underlying hostility between him and the influential men of the New South Wales Corps. His attitude may have been aggravated by his declining health.

Philip Gidley King left office on 12 August 1806 and handed over to a newly arrived successor that had been recommended by Sir Joseph Banks in England. During his tenure as governor, King had worked consistently for the good of the colony and he left it a much better place than he found it. Three days later, when he boarded ship for the voyage home, King collapsed. He was not able to sail until 10 February 1807. Plagued by chronic ill-health, King died in England on 3 September 1808 and was buried in the churchyard of St Nicholas, Lower Tooting, London. His two sons by Ann Inett on Norfolk Island were both cared for and they rose to be lieutenants in the Royal Navy. By his wife he had one son and four daughters, one of whom died as a child.

King's successor was Captain William Bligh, late of HMS *Bounty*. Bligh took office as the fourth Governor of New South Wales on 13 August 1806. His reputation preceded him. He had been the captain of the *Bounty* when she sailed from England in the autumn of 1787 bound for Tahiti. Bligh was a difficult man who at times dispensed harsh punishments; from the very beginning, dissent was a feature of the voyage. After the lengthy stopover in Tahiti which lasted several months, Fletcher Christian, the master's mate, led a mutiny.

Bligh was held at sword point while he and eighteen others were transferred to an open longboat and set adrift. Remarkably, thanks to his strict rationing of the existing supplies and his skills as a navigator and sailor, he and the rest of his men survived the ordeal, except for one man who was killed by hostile natives on an island where they had landed for supplies. They drifted halfway across the Pacific Ocean and arrived in Timor in mid-June 1789.

Bligh returned to England from Batavia in the spring of 1790. At his subsequent court martial he was cleared of responsibility for the mutiny. He continued to serve in the navy and took part with distinction in some of Lord Horatio Nelson's campaigns, but among the men he was commonly called 'that *Bounty* bastard'. Then, in 1805, the authorities recommended him for the governorship of New South Wales to succeed King.

After taking office, Bligh became worried about the excesses he observed in the colony. At this stage, all in the colony, especially officials and military officers, were trafficking in spirits, particularly rum, for want of a proper currency. These were imported at a few shillings per gallon and bartered at 100 per cent to 200 per cent profit. Spirits were distributed according to the rank and influence of the individual, so the senior officials and those most favoured reaped greater profits. The New South Wales Corps became known as the 'Rum Corps'.

Besides prohibiting the barter of spirits, Bligh put an end to the many perks and privileges of the monopolists by refusing land grants and restricting the assignment of cheap convict labour. He became popular with the poorer settlers and small farmers, particularly those in the Hawkesbury area, by giving them access to cheap goods from the Government Store and endeavouring to keep the prices down, but this particularly antagonised the rich and influential.

He acted with the best of intentions and had some success in curbing the rum traffic. His reforms were urgently needed but he paid scant regard to the necessity of placating the colony's most powerful people. His inflexibility and wide-ranging regulation of colonial life, combined with his rash personal attitude, made him extremely unpopular with many of the most prominent and influential in the colony. They included wealthy landowner and businessman, John Macarthur, the 'Father of Australia's Wool Industry', and prominent representatives of the Crown including senior NSW Corps officers. They were defying government regulations by engaging in private trading ventures for profit. Bligh was determined to stop the practice.

John Macarthur was the most successful of the colony's businessmen, a person who was ruthless in the management of his affairs and, like Bligh, he was stubborn. That their clashes would deteriorate into an explosive situation was inevitable.

It erupted in December 1807 when Bligh summoned Macarthur to answer charges over a ship he part owned which had broken harbour regulations. Macarthur refused to answer the summons so Bligh issued a warrant for his arrest. A hearing was held on 25 January 1808 before Judge-Advocate Richard Atkins. Macarthur objected, alleging that Atkins bore hostility towards him, and the six officers appointed to assist the Judge-Advocate acquitted him. Because of their action, a furious Bligh moved to place them all on trial for sedition.

Acting quickly to counter this, Macarthur had Major George Johnston, the hero of the Castle Hill Revolt, demand that the governor resign. Bligh refused.

On 26 January, the twelfth anniversary of the First Landing, soldiers of the NSW Corps under the command of Major Johnston marched on Government House in Sydney and arrested Bligh. A petition written by Macarthur and addressed to George Johnston was written on the day of the arrest but most of the 151 signatures on the petition were gathered in the days after the overthrow. This bloodless *coup d'état* would become known as the Rum Rebellion – Bligh's term as governor of the colony was one of the shortest on record!

Bligh was held under arrest in Government House and there he remained until August. Major Johnston assumed the title of Lieutenant-Governor, his first official act. Further acts of rebellion followed rapidly. It seems that the object of the rebels was not simply to overthrow Bligh but to obtain complete control of all branches of government. Macarthur acted as Johnston's colonial secretary.

An Insurrectionary Committee was set up to examine the deposed governor's public and private papers in an effort to find incriminating evidence against him. There was none.

Despite the revolutionary events going on in Sydney, normal day-to-day life went on in the rest of the colony. John and Ann Nichol's fifth child, Mary, was born on 2 April 1808 but she died the following day. She was buried at St John's in Parramatta. The family's previous child, Sophia, who had been born two years earlier, was baptised three weeks after Mary's death, on 24 April. Again the ceremony was held at St John's.

George Johnston was superseded in his self-proclaimed office by the arrival of his senior officer, Lieutenant-Colonel Joseph Foveaux, on 28 July 1808. Foveaux decided to back the military junta that removed Bligh from office by continuing with the arrest and governing in his own name. He proved an able and efficient administrator, but he was more likely to follow his own inclinations rather than the letter of the law. His tenure continued until he was officially relieved by Lieutenant Governor William Paterson, who arrived from Port Dalrymple aboard HMS *Porpoise* on 1 January 1809.

Paterson assumed government of the colony on 9 January and held the position for the year, but he was in poor physical condition and regarded as ineffective. According to one account, Paterson in Sydney was:

> In a very bad state of health – almost a paralytic – from former intemperance; and now I am informed from good authority that he is drunk the greatest part of his time; so that, from imbecility when sober and stupidity when drunk he is a very convenient tool in the hands of McArthur, or of Foveaux and Abbott who see that his plans are executed while he keeps himself in the background to remove the offence which his actual interference would give many in the colony.

William Bligh was held prisoner until March 1809 when he was placed on HMS *Porpoise* to be returned to England. However, before he left Sydney, he received an Address of Loyalty from the Hawkesbury settlers which contained the names of nearly 900 colonists, including that of John Nichols. Bligh was thanked for his help and support.

Instead of sailing for England, Bligh took command of the *Porpoise* and sailed to Van Diemen's Land (modern Tasmania). There he tried to gain support from Lieutenant Governor David Collins for retaking control of New South Wales, but to Collins and the authorities in Hobart he was 'an embarrassment'. In effect, he remained imprisoned on the ship until January 1810.

Back in New South Wales, Paterson not only allowed the speculation of government property and the rum trade to continue, but he enormously increased the number of free grants of land at Foveaux's instigation to the point where the distribution of lands was made almost without constraint.

In a letter dated 13 October 1809 to Lord Castlereagh in London, Sir Henry Brown Hayes described the system of government prevailing under Paterson in New South Wales:

Forty thousand gallons of spirits ... were given away to the civil and military officers since Bligh had been deposed, and not anything to the peaceable, industrious individual. The officers and favourites have been finally enriched by this republican Government... Paterson gets drunk at Government House at Parramatta, and Foveaux is left at Sydney to do as he likes, and he gives pardons, grants, and leases to the whores and greatest thieves, 'till there is nothing left for any other Governor ... to give.

In the twelve months of his administration, Paterson issued 403 grants – more than King had made in almost six years!

One benefiting from Paterson's administration was John Nichols. John astutely gained approval for a license to sell spirits at Parramatta, and with word spreading that Paterson was granting land to almost anyone, he succeeded in obtaining a grant for another 100 acres at Prospect.

John was enjoying a period of prosperity. He was recorded as having forty six and a half acres under cultivation. This consisted of maize thirty acres; wheat six; barley four; oats half an acre; peas and beans; potatoes half an acre; pasture four and a half with an orchard and garden of half an acre. He also had fifty-three acres lying fallow. John held in hand ten bushels of wheat and eight bushels of maize.

His livestock consisted of two horses (one male, one female); one bull; three oxen; three rams; five ewes; one male goat, three female goats; and two hogs, one male and one female.

In his employ, he had two convicts and one free man who worked as a labourer.

Meanwhile, his and Ann's sixth child, Martha, was born sometime during the year, but there seems to be no existing record of her baptism.

*

The Rum Rebellion prompted His Majesty's ministers in London to devote at least a modicum of their attention to what was happening in New South Wales. The system by which naval governors had to depend for their authority on the goodwill of a military force, which distance made semi-autonomous in practice, was abandoned. William Paterson's tenure continued until the appointment of a new permanent governor from England – a Scotsman by the name of Lachlan Macquarie.

Macquarie was commander of the 73rd Highland Regiment, the unit assigned to replace the New South Wales Corps, which was under recall following its part in the Rum Rebellion. He and his wife, Elizabeth, reached New South Wales at the end of 1809 accompanied by two warships. His duties began on New Year's Day 1810.

Macquarie had instructions to revoke all of Johnston's and Foveaux's administrative actions, and he extended these to include those of Paterson. Their grants of land and pardons were regarded as not been awarded by the legal government and suspended. His proclamation for this was published in the *Sydney Gazette* of Sunday, 7 January 1810. It affected many people.

It meant that John lost possession of his 100 acres grant on Prospect Creek, but he did have the opportunity to reapply for it. A week after the proclamation in the *Sydney Gazette*, he lodged a memorial to the new governor to retain his property. All John could do after that was await the result. John's run of prosperity stalled. The new governor was starting afresh, even looking back to the years of King's tenure. He disposed of the grant of Prospect Common, which, it will be remembered, had been delivered into the care of John and others for the communal grazing of stock.

Macquarie also disbanded the Sydney and Parramatta Loyalist Associations that had been formed by Hunter and existed under King. John was a member of the Parramatta Loyalist Association. The volunteer groups had been active backing up the New South Wales Corps during the Castle Hill Revolt, and the commander of the 73rd Highland Regiment did not want, or need, semi-autonomous groups of armed militia in the colony.

John came under increasing stress financially as he waited for the result of his appeal to the governor concerning the property at Prospect Creek. Unable to meet various bills, he became involved in a number of court proceedings that obliged him to pay the damages and costs.

Much was happening within his family as well. Although John and Ann's sixth child, Martha, was born during 1809, there seems to be no extant record of her baptism during this difficult time of financial stress. Amelia, their seventh child, was born on 26 February 1811 and was baptised at St John's Church, Parramatta, the following 17 March.

At this time the family was living on the 100 acres at Prospect Creek which Paterson had granted in October 1809. They were living with the real possibility that they might be forced to leave. A decision still had to come from Macquarie. In addition, although the Hawkesbury River had flooded again in

1809, the drought conditions of 1809 to 1811 were said to be the worst since 1789. Crops were destroyed and a serious water shortage ensued.

Two days after John lodged his memorial to Governor Macquarie, William Bligh arrived back in Sydney. He had sailed from Hobart on 17 January. His intention was to collect evidence for the forthcoming court martial of Major George Johnston in England. He eventually departed for England on 12 May to attend the trial. Lachlan Macquarie was pleased to see him finally on his way. He reached England on 25 October 1810. The following year, Johnston was convicted of mutiny and sentenced to be cashiered, a form of disgraceful dismissal that entailed surrendering his commission in the Royal Marines without compensation.

Cleared in London of any responsibility for the Rum Rebellion, Bligh received a backdated promotion to rear admiral soon after Johnston's trial concluded. Bligh was court-martialled twice more during his career and acquitted both times. He went on to enjoy promotion to vice-admiral in 1814 and a more peaceful life in Kent before his death in 1817. Macarthur escaped prosecution and remained in England until the year Bligh died.

Lachlan Macquarie governed over New South Wales for eleven years (1810–21). His administration was paternal and stabilising but absolute, in the same way that some of his ancestors had ruled over their Scottish Highland clans. He encouraged merit wherever he found it.

Finally, after nineteen months of waiting, John's appeal to the governor was successful and on 18 October 1811, the 100 acre property at Prospect Creek was granted to him once again. The family's relief must have been palpable, but his financial problems were not over.

Another court case on 7 October 1812 resulted in him again having to pay damages and costs. The court's judgement may have been the cause of the Provost Marshal's advertisement in the *Sydney Gazette* on 12 December announcing the auction sale of pigs and wheat to be held on the premises of John Nichols at Prospect.

Worse was to come.

*

Governor Macquarie became renowned for ordering the erection of many fine buildings. Among those still standing are St James' Church in King Street, Sydney, the adjoining Hyde Park Convict Barracks and St Matthew's Church at Windsor.

Then there was Sydney's so-called 'Rum Hospital'. Its name was derived from the fact that at one stage Macquarie, in his efforts to stamp out the rum trade, sought to control it by granting to the contractors an official three-year monopoly for importing spirits. In return they built the Sydney Hospital. Only part of the elegant Georgian building still stands, serving as the Parliament House of New South Wales.

Even though wages for work on building the Sydney Hospital were paid in rum, Macquarie did succeed in breaking the power of the rum monopolists during his period of office. Nevertheless, bartering among the poorer sections of the community in conjunction with rum and promissory notes were still forms of widely used payment in the colony.

The variety of coins that were in circulation was as diverse as the ships calling in for trade. When Governor King had tried to value the assorted coins early in his governorship, Dutch guilders, Indian rupees and dollars were only some of those existing alongside Sterling.

In 1813, Macquarie tried to reduce the variety of coins in distribution by issuing two denominations: the Holey Dollar, valued at five shillings, and the Dump, valued at one shilling and three pence. These coins were made from a shipment of Spanish dollars valued at £10,000. Macquarie ordered the centre of the coin, the dump, removed. It led to a widespread saying that to be 'down in the dumps' meant that you were financially poor, but eventually it came to mean you were gloomy and melancholy.

There was plenty to be gloomy about at this time. A plague of caterpillars had destroyed crops of wheat, barley and vegetables in the Hawkesbury River area in 1810, and it happened again in 1812. The drought of 1809–11 was bad enough, but drought hit the colony again in 1812 and worsened over the next three years. Stock losses were extensive and the yield of wheat fell by two-thirds. Prices soared.

The years 1812 to 1815 turned into a period of almost continuous economic recession, not helped by the colony's overseas suppliers withdrawing credit because of a commercial crisis in Britain. As well as this, Britain, while still fighting Napoleon, was again at war with the United States after the three-pronged US invasion of Canada. During this, American traders imposed a trade embargo on New South Wales.

Susannah, John and Ann Nichols' eighth child, was born on 18 January 1814 at Prospect. She was baptised at St John's Parramatta on 20 February. In the 1814 muster, John was recorded as a landholder at Parramatta with his wife Ann and seven children: John, Ann, Charles, Sophia, Martha, Amelia and baby Susannah. As usual, the family was self-supporting, requiring no assistance from the Government Store, but times were becoming tougher, even desperate.

The drought was into its third year and there was little sign of relief. With the crossing of the Blue Mountains in 1813, new land became available for cattle and sheep but, although wealthy graziers looked forward to profit and the wool industry benefiting as a result, there seemed little prospect of improving fortunes among the smaller farmers whose crops were failing. Caterpillars appeared in plague proportion along the Nepean/Hawkesbury River. The Reverend Marsden's attempt to introduce honey bees brought from England into the colony was failing. Hungry wild dogs, dingoes, were reportedly causing widespread destruction amongst flocks of sheep in the Nepean River area and there were reports of arsenic baits being used to poison them.

Around this time, John Nichols made what must have been a difficult decision to move away from the Prospect/Parramatta district. In the *Sydney*

Gazette on 24 December 1814, and again on 7 January 1815, his original land grant was advertised for sale:

> To be sold by private contract 53 acre farm known by the name Nichols Farm, all cleared and contiguous to a large Common at Prospect Hill adjoining to Captain Bishop's and Mr. Broughton's. For particulars enquire of Mr. Howe, Sydney or John Nichols, Prospect.

It must have been a major upheaval for John was no longer a young man. He had been in the colony now for twenty-six years, the majority of them farming his own land. He was approaching the age of sixty and had a large family to support. John, the eldest of his seven surviving children, was in his thirteenth year and Susannah, the youngest, just one. His reasons for leaving probably arose from the harsh realities of trying to farm amid a seemingly unending drought, plus the financial trouble he was facing because of failing crops and falling land values.

John did have another property which he sold two months later. This was a sixty-acre farm at Prospect, land that Governor Arthur Phillip had originally granted to William Parish. John had probably acquired it before he was made a trustee of Prospect Common in 1804, a stipulation for appointment as a trustee being the ownership of 100 acres or more. If John had only possessed his original Prospect Hill grant at that time, he would not have been eligible for the position. The purchaser paid only £250 – a bargain. That the property was sold so cheaply suggests that John and his family were in urgent need of money.

Money worries continued to plague him. The following year, John was involved in a court case in which it was alleged he had not repaid a loan for goods as promised. There the matter rested for the next ten months until John lodged a plea on 12 February 1817 asking the court to rule that the action be discharged for want of prosecution. The case was dismissed.

At the same time, a summons concerning a similar action against him dated 1 July 1816 was continuing, and the only surviving evidence suggests that John lost the case.

John and Ann Nichols' ninth child, Thomas, seems to have been born after the family left the Prospect/Parramatta area. Most likely, if he had been born there he would probably have been baptised at St John's Church Parramatta, like his older brothers and sisters.

Their tenth offspring and last son, Joseph, was born sometime around 1816, but no baptismal records seem to have survived.

The eleventh baby, Eliza, was born on 8 June 1819 and was baptised at St Philip's in Sydney the following 14 September. John and the family seem to have fallen on difficult times since leaving Prospect and the 1819 muster of freemen in the Sydney district lists him as working as a 'labourer', although the following year he was described once more as a 'gardener'.

In another memorial to Governor Macquarie in 1820, John applied for a new grant of land. In it he indicated that the largeness of his family, whom he had always supported without help from the Government Store, had placed him in humble circumstances. Justice of the Peace William Cowper signed the document and added, 'I believe this Petitioner to be an industrious man.' It was noted that John was the holder of four acres of land in the district of Sydney; Governor Macquarie promised to grant him eighty acres.

Though Parramatta Road was the only land route from Sydney until the coming of the railway in 1855, in the early days people bound for Parramatta had the choice of coach or ferry. The ferry was more popular and enjoyable. The first travellers to Parramatta came via the river. The keel of a boat intended for a regular Parramatta service was laid late in 1788. Launched the following year, she was named the *Rose Hill Packet,* but was better known unofficially as *'the Lump'*. A regular service on the river seems to have been established in 1793. The fare was one shilling per passenger. Those who were sufficiently affluent could hire the boat for six shillings.

Meanwhile, a path or track to Rose Hill, later Parramatta, was formed shortly after the settlement was founded. In 1794 came the first attempt to make a proper road. This thoroughfare did not exactly follow the present line, but swept south of it from about Homebush to Granville. The next attempt at road building was in 1797 when a new line was formed, this time practically identical with the present road. The settlers were required to find the necessary labour. It was stated in 1805 that the road had become impassable and a public meeting was held to consider the question of repairing it. In 1806, a notice appeared in the *Sydney Gazette*:

> In consequence of the bad state of the roads leading from Sydney to Parramatta, and the danger of horses being lamed in the deep ruts near Sydney, it is hereby decided that all public and private carts and waggons passing that road (not otherwise loaded) do take a load of brickbats from the brickfields and drop them in the places appointed by the Overseer of Roads.

After Governor Macquarie arrived orders were given for the reconstruction of the road. Since that time the road has been remade repeatedly – the newspapers for over a century were loud in their complaints.

As early as 1803 efforts were made to establish a regular transportation system to Parramatta by means of a stage wagon. The attempt appears to have failed, and in 1805 one William Roberts made an attempt to run a stage wagon on the road. Fares for passengers were fixed at five shillings.

In his memorial to the governor, John gave his residence as the Five Mile Stone on the Parramatta Road. The *NSW Calendar and Directories* of 1832 gives an itinerary of roads and located the 'Cheshire Cheese' Public House on the right side, presumably the southern side, of Parramatta Road at the five-mile mark. McCaffery's *History of Illawarra* noted:

On board the First Fleet there were people of mixed trades, professions and callings. Just to mention four names, viz: John Moss, Edward Pugh, John Nicholls, and Rebecca Poulton. These people settled in time in Windsor, Parramatta, and at the *Cheshire Cheese Hotel*.

The muster of 1821 again showed John as a landholder and, in the same year, it was recorded that a grant of 100 acres was promised to him in the County of Cumberland, Parish of Saint George. The muster for the following year showed that he had eighty acres in the Sydney district at Petersham. Four acres had been cleared and another four acres were under cultivation as gardens and an orchard but he was not residing on the property. As well, he had livestock consisting of fourteen cows and a hog, and a convict assigned to work for him.

Sarah, John and Ann's twelfth child, was born around April 1822. Just eight months later, John passed away on Christmas Day. His burial service was performed at St Philip's Church in Sydney and he was buried at the Devonshire Street Cemetery, Surry Hills, a mile and a quarter from the centre of town.

Where this cemetery once stood, part of Sydney's huge Central Railway Station stands now. The locality was described in *An Illustrated Guide to Sydney 1882*:

> Redfern railway terminus fronts the corner of Devonshire and George Streets, the workshops and engine shed being placed near the eastern boundary of the ground. In Devonshire Street the second oldest general cemetery is situated, but it is now closed except to those who acquired a right to bury there before the Necropolis at Rookwood was established. The familiar names of many pioneer colonists are here recorded, forming a numerous contingent to that great army already passed into the Silent Land.

On John's headstone were the words, 'Sacred to the memory of John Nicholds who departed this life 24th December 1822 aged 67 years'. When Central Station became Sydney's railway terminus, the cemetery was moved to various other locations; Central Railway Station opened on the site on 4 August 1906.

Half of John Nichols' life had been spent in the colony. In those thirty-four years he had grasped with both hands the new start that transportation had forced on him in this unknown and foreign place so far away from London and the Old Bailey across the world. It had all started back there so many years ago. In those years, he had witnessed the beginning of the penal colony's transition into a living, breathing settlement that initiated its own growth and expanded at an accelerating rate. It was spreading to the north from the coal seams of Newcastle at the mouth of the Hunter River; it was sailing eastwards out through the Heads and across the globe, trading with the Old World, the Far East and the New; it was expanding westward beyond the old Blue Mountains barrier into the great plains around Bathurst and the Macquarie River; and it was pushing south along the coast into the Illawarra while at the same time Parramatta-born 'currency lad' Hamilton Hume and English settler William Hovell were setting out to explore the inland way south. In those years, John too had been transformed – from a convicted felon into an independent, respected pioneer farmer. He had prospered through his own hard work. He had experienced the growing pains of the colony with its revolts, and the harsh realities of its droughts and flooding rains. He had suffered the degradation of financial decline and moved beyond it towards recovery. And, along the way, he had earned the trust and respect of his peers.

The embryo of a new country was stirring. The work was just beginning, but John's contribution had been made and his days of toil were over.

Today, the lives of John Nichols and his family are regularly commemorated throughout Australia by generations of his descendents in the John Nichols Society.

*

It is tempting to speculate if Pat Hughes was aware of how close he was to his great-great-grandfather's original place of rest on the evening of 17 January 1936. Pat was at Sydney's Central Railway Station rushing to board the 8.20 p.m. train, The 'Limited', to travel to Melbourne, Victoria. Most unlikely. He was on his way to join the Royal Australian Air Force as a cadet at Point Cook, south-west of Melbourne on Port Phillip Bay.

His mind was likely on too many other things.

*

Pat Hughes was a direct descendant of Amelia Nichols, John and Ann Nichols' seventh child.

Amelia had been eleven when her father died at Sydney on Christmas Day 1822. She seems to have accompanied her sister Sophia and her husband, Alexander Philp, when they moved north to Newcastle in the middle of 1826. Alexander was a witness at her marriage to Charles Hughes on 23 July 1827 at Christ Church Newcastle. Alexander may have been the one who gave the necessary permission for Amelia to wed as she was still only sixteen.

Probably of Welsh origin and born about 1798, Charles Hughes had been charged with 'felonious assault on the King's highway' at the Old Bailey on 15 January 1817. In reality, he had picked somebody's pocket and stolen his watch and chain. For this he was sentenced to death, but this was commuted to transportation for life. Charles arrived in New South Wales on the *Larkins* on 22 November 1817. In early 1819, he was sent to Newcastle, the harsh penal settlement at the mouth of the Hunter River. There the convicts worked long hours mostly mining coal, felling timber and manufacturing lime from sea shells. On one occasion he received twenty-five lashes for gambling but his overall diligence and good behaviour in this difficult place attracted the approval of those in authority. Over time, he was appointed to the position of assistant pilot, the highly responsible job of guiding shipping through the treacherous, shifting sandbars of Newcastle harbour. As well, he was recommended for the salary of overseer.

Charles received his 'ticket-of-leave' on 31 May 1827. These were usually given to prisoners with life sentences after they had served eight years with one master, the approximate time Charles spent at Newcastle as Assistant Pilot. He could now acquire property and be self-employed – it was the first step towards independence for a reforming character.

Amelia and Charles married two months later. Neither could read or write their own their name. Although Charles later learned to form a crude signature, his near-illiteracy created huge difficulties in business. The couple's first child, a boy, was born on 20 May 1828 and, just over six years later on 10 July 1834, Charles received his conditional pardon. This removed his obligation to remain in the Newcastle area. Having no trade qualifications and little education, his opportunities were limited. Inn-keeping was an accepted way for ex-convicts to enter into the world of business. With a young, growing family to support, Charles paid £25 for a publican's licence for the Australian Inn on 30 June 1836. This was an established public house in Hunter Street, Newcastle, near the wharf. During his working life Charles became the licensee of several inns in Newcastle, Maitland and Black Creek (now Branxton) up to 1851 but his inability to read and write fluently placed him at the mercy of literate traders.

Charles and Amelia's eighth child was born at Black Creek on 12 September 1849 at a time the district began to suffer from the effects of a devastating drought. Their older children received schooling at Maitland, and in Black Creek the younger ones attended a small private school. Their sons began to work at an early age and Charles lived to see his four oldest children marry local settlers.

After suffering for six months from cancer of the stomach, Charles died at Branxton on 8 January 1869, aged seventy-one. Amelia lived on at Branxton for another fifteen years; she saw the marriages of her two younger children and the births of thirty-six of her fifty grandchildren. She died from acute kidney failure on 25 June 1884, aged seventy-three, and was buried with Charles in Branxton cemetery, an imposing stone marking their final resting place.

Jane Hughes, who was Charles and Amelia's third child and first daughter, coincidentally married John Hughes, who was no relation, in 1850. They had nine children.

*

Paterson (Percy) Hughes was born in 1894. He left home at the age of sixteen.

PAT HUGHES' RECORD OF SERVICE

With the kind permission of Pat Hughes' brother, the late Bill Hughes of Beacon Hill, Sydney, NSW, documentation of his service obtained from the Ministry of Defence and Public Record Office, London, is reproduced here.

RECORD OF SERVICE
OF
FLIGHT LIEUTENANT PATERSON CLARENCE HUGHES DFC (39461)

DATE OF BIRTH: 19 September 1917

PREVIOUS SERVICE:

Air Cadet, Royal Australian Air Force	20.1.36
Discharged	9.1.37

APPOINTMENTS AND PROMOTIONS:

Granted a Short Service Commission as Pilot Officer in the General Duties Branch of the Royal Air Force for 5 years   19.2.37
Flying Officer   19.11.38
Acting Flight Lieutenant   8.11.39
Flight Lieutenant   3.9.40
Killed (Flying Battle)   7.9.40

POSTINGS:

1 Flying Training School, Point Cook:	Flying training	31. 1. 36 to 8.12.36
R.A.F. Depot	Supernumerary	19.2.37

2 Flying Training	Flying training with Advanced Training Squadron	27.2.37
64 (Fighter) Squadron	Flying Duties	22.5.37
234 Squadron	Flying Duties	8.11.39
247 Squadron	Temporary Duties	1.8.40

HONOURS, AWARDS AND MEDALS:

Distinguished Flying Cross London Gazette 22.10.40
Awarded Flying Badge (Royal Australian Air Force) 8.12.36
1939/45 Star with Battle of Britain Clasp
Aircrew Europe Star
War Medal 1939/45

COMBAT CLAIMS

This list is compiled from direct reference to Combat Reports and the Operations Record Book of 234 Squadron RAF.

1940

8 July	1 Ju 88 Shared
27 July	1 Ju 88 (Unconfirmed) Shared
28 July	1 Ju 88 (Confirmed) Shared
15 August	1 Me 110
15 August	1 Me 110 Shared with P/O Doe
16 August	2 Me 109s
18 August	2 Me 109s
26 August	2 Me 109s
4 September	3 Me 110s
5 September	2 Me 109s
6 September	1 Me 109
	1 Me 109 (Probable)
7 September	1 Do 17 (Combat report of wingman)

TOTAL: 14 confirmed, 1 probable, 3 shared, 1 shared unconfirmed.

DISTINGUISHED FLYING CROSS

Acting Flight Lieutenant Paterson Clarence HUGHES 39461 (since killed).
    This officer has led his flight with skill and determination. He has displayed gallantry in his attacks on the enemy and has destroyed seven of their aircraft.
                                                  London Gazette, 22 October 1940

The citation for this award seems very Spartan in its formal brevity and underestimation. It should be realised, however, that in reality the citation is unfinished. The man preparing it, Squadron Leader Joseph 'Spike' O'Brien, was killed on the same day as Pat, and in the same battle. He had personally known Pat for only three short, hectic weeks. How much he was aware of Pat's earlier work is a subject for speculation.

    After three days of the heaviest fighting he had been so impressed with his flight commander's achievements (six, and very likely seven, victories) that he decided to put pen to paper – but he didn't finish. He didn't have time.

ABBREVIATIONS AND RANKS

AAF	Auxiliary Air Force (RAF)
AASF	Advanced Air Striking Force (RAF)
AFC	Air Force Cross, also Australian Flying Corps
AFLT	Acting Flight Lieutenant
AI	Aircraft Interception
AIF	Australian Imperial Force
ASF	Australian Striking Force (AIF)
AVM	Air Vice Marshal
AWM	Australian War Memorial
BBC	British Broadcasting Corporation
BEF	British Expeditionary Force
CFS	Central Flying School
CSIR	Commonwealth Scientific and Industrial Research
DFC	Distinguished Flying Cross
DP	Death Presumed
DSO	Distinguished Service Order
EFTS	Elementary Flying Training School
FIU	Fighter Interception Unit
F/Lt	Flight Lieutenant
F/O	Flying Officer
JG	*Jagdgeschwader* = fighter wing
KG	*Kampfgeschwader* = bomber wing
KIA	Killed in Action
LAC	Leading Aircraftman
MID	Mentioned in Dispatches
MU	Medically Unfit
NCO	Non Commissioned Officer
OKW	*Oberkommando der Wehrmacht* = Armed Force Supreme Command (German)
ORB	Operations Record Book
OUT	Operational Training Unit
PC	Permanent Commission

P/O	Pilot Officer
PDU	Photographic Development Unit
POW	Prisoner of War
PRO	Public Record Office (London), now National Archives
PRU	Photographic Reconnaissance Unit
RAAF	Royal Australian Air Force
RAF	Royal Air Force
RAFVR	Royal Air Force Volunteer Reserve
RAN	Royal Australian Navy
RCAF	Royal Canadian Air Force
RFC	Royal Flying Corps
RN	Royal Navy
RNAS	Royal Naval Air Service
RNZAF	Royal New Zealand Air Force
SSC	Short Service Commission
St	*Staffel* = Squadron
S/Ldr	Squadron Leader
ZG	*Zerstorergeschwader* = destroyer wing

The following list of Luftwaffe and RAF rank equivalents is necessarily approximate in certain cases: various German ranks existed which have no exact British parallel.

Flieger	Aircraftman (2)
Gefreiter	Aircraftman (1)
Obergefreiter	Leading Aircraftman
Hauptgefreiter	Corporal
Unteroffizier	Sergeant
Unterfeldwebel	
Feldwebel	Flight Sergeant
Oberfeldwebel	Warrant Officer
Stabsfeldwebel	
Leutnant	Pilot Officer
Oberleutnant	Flying Officer
Hauptmann	Flight Lieutenant
Major	Squadron Leader
Oberstleutnant	Wing Commander
Oberst	Group Captain
Generalmajor	Air Commodore
Generalleutnant	Air Vice Marshal
General	Air Marshal
Generaloberst	Air Chief Marshal
Generalfeldmarschall	
Reichsmarschall	Marshal of the Air Force

BIBLIOGRAPHY

Air Ministry, *The Battle of Britain — an air ministry account of the great days from August 8 to October 31, 1940* (Ministry of Information, London, 1941)

Baff, F/Lt K. C., *Maritime is Number Ten* (Baff, Netley, South Australia, 1983)

Barker, Ralph, *Aviator Extraordinary* (Chatto & Windus, London, 1969)

Bateson, Charles, *The Convict Ships 1787–1868* (A. H. & A. W. Reed, Sydney, 1974)

Bekker, Cajus, *The Luftwaffe war diaries* (Corgi, London, 1969)

Benjaminson, Eric, 'Undaunted by Odds', *Aeroplane* (July 2010, Vol. 38, No. 7)

Birch, Alan and David S. Macmillan, *The Sydney Scene 1788–1960*, (Hale & Iremonger, Sydney, 1962)

Bishop, Edward, *The Battle of Britain* (Transworld Publishers, London, 1961)

Bishop, Edward, *Their Finest Hour — the Story of the Battle of Britain 1940* (Macdonald, London, 1968)

Bowyer, Chaz, *Fighter Command 1936–68* (Sphere, London, 1981)

Bowyer, Chaz, *Bristol Blenheim* (Ian Allan, London, 1984)

Britts, M. G., *The Commandants – The Tyrants Who Ruled Norfolk Island*, (Herron Publications, West End, Queensland, 1980)

Burns, Michael, *Spitfire! Spitfire!* (Blandford Press, Poole, 1986)

Burt, Kendal and James Leasor, *The One That Got Away* (Granada, London, 1956)

Champ, Jack and Colin Burgess, *The Diggers of Colditz* (Allen & Unwin, Sydney, 1985)

Churchill, Winston, *The Second World War, Vols 1, 2, 3 & 4* (Cassell, London, 1964)

Claasen, Adam, *Dogfight – The Battle of Britain* (Anzac Battles Series, Exisle Publishing Ltd, Auckland, 2012)

Collier, Basil, *The Battle of Britain* (Fontana, London, 1969)

Collier, Richard, *Eagle Day* (Pan, London, 1968)

Collier, Richard, *1940 — The World in Flames* (Penguin, Harmondsworth, 1980)

Collins, David, *An Account of the English Colony in New South Wales*, (London, 1798)

Cooksley, Peter G., *1940 – The Story of No. 11 Group, Fighter Command* (Robert Hale, London, 1983)

Cumes, J. W. C., *Their Chastity was not too Rigid* (Longman, Melbourne, 1979)

Darmody, Tom, *Tales of the Monaro* (Tom Darmody, NSW, 1995)

Deighton, Len, *Fighter – The True Story of the Battle of Britain* (Triad/Panther, St Albans, 1979)

Deighton, Len, *Battle of Britain* (Coward, McCann & Geoghegan, London, 1980)

Dickson, Lovat, *Richard Hillary* (Macmillan, London, 1951)

Doe, Helen, *Fighter Pilot* (Amberley Publishing, Stroud, 2015)

Doe, Wing Commander Bob, *Bob Doe – Fighter Pilot, The Story of One of the Few* (Spellmount Ltd, Tonbridge Wells, Kent, 1991)

Fleming, Peter, *Operation Sea Lion* (Pan, London, 1975)

Foreman, John, *Fighter Command War Diaries – Volume 1: September 1939 to September 1940* (Air Research Publications, Walton-on-Thames, 1996)

Foreman, John, *Fighter Command War Diaries – Volume 2: September 1940 to December 1941* (Air Research Publications, Walton-on-Thames, 1998)

Foreman, John, *RAF Fighter Command Victory Claims – Part 1: 1939–1940* (Red Kite, Surrey, 2003)

Franks, Norman, *Wings of Freedom* (William Kimber & Co. Ltd, London, 1980)

Galland, Adolf, *The First and the Last* (Methuen, London, 1955)

Gelb, Norman, *Scramble – A Narrative History of the Battle of Britain* (Pan, London, 1986)

Gibson, Guy, *Enemy Coast Ahead* (Pan, London, 1955)

Halley, James J., *The Squadrons of the Royal Air Force* (Air-Britain, Tunbridge, 1980)

Herington, John, *Australia in the War of 1939–1945*, (Air) Vol. III, Air War Against Germany and Italy, 1939–1943 (Australian War Memorial, Canberra, 1962)

Hillary, Richard, *The Last Enemy* (Macmillan, London, 1942)

Hughes, Paterson Clarence, *Pat Hughes' 1936 Diary*, Australian War Memorial File: 419/049/038, 87/412, via Stephanie Bladen

Irving, David, *The Rise and Fall of the Luftwaffe* (Futura, London, 1976)

James, R. R., (ed.), *Winston S. Churchill, His Complete Speeches 1897–1963* Vol. II 1935–1942 (Chelsea House, New York, 1978)

John Nichols Family Society, *Without Rhyme or Reason – Poems By The Family Of John & Ann Nichols* née Pugh (Gosford, NSW, 2013)

John Nichols Family Society, *The Story of John Nichols First Fleeter and Five Generations of His Family* [by] K. Purnell, S. Tuck, S. Draper, B. Coleman, J. Marden (Sydney, NSW, 1988)

Johnson, Frank (ed.), *R.A.A.F. over Europe* (Eyre & Spottiswoode, London, 1946)

Jullian, Marcel, *The Battle of Britain* (Jonathan Cape, London, 1967)

Kreipe, Werner, 'The Battle of Britain' in Richardson, William & Freidin, Seymour (eds), *The Fatal Decisions* (Harborough, London, 1959)

London, Pete, *Flying in Cornwall* (Tor Mark, Redruth, Cornwall, 2011)

Long, Gavin, 'The AIF in the United Kingdom' in *Australia in The War of 1939–1945, (Army) Vol. I, To Benghazi* (Australian War Memorial, Canberra, 1961)

Macdonald, Emily, 'Kodak Moments Live On' in the *Townsville Bulletin*, 27 January 2012

McCarthy, John, *Australia and the Imperial Defence 1918–1939* (University of Queensland Press, St Lucia, 1976)

McClelland, James, *Where Australians Fought and Died* (McClelland, Silverdale, 1980)

McKee, Alexander, *Strike From the Sky* (New English Library, London, 1977)

Marks, Neil, *Australian People Australian Tales* (HarperCollins Publishers, Sydney, 1999)

Mason, Francis K., *Battle over Britain* (McWhirter, London, 1969)

Middleton, Drew, *The Sky Suspended* (Pan, London, 1963)

Morgan, E. B. and E. Shacklady, *Spitfire, the History* (Key, Stamford, 1987)

Mosley, Leonard, *Battle of Britain* (Pan, London, 1969)

Mosley, Leonard, *The Reich Marshal* (Pan, London, 1977)

Murray, Williamson, *Strategy for Defeat: the Luftwaffe 1933–1945* (Quintet, London, 1986)

Numeralla and District Community History Group, *'in those days...'* – *Numeralla-Countegany-Peak View and Surrounding Areas* (date unknown, via Stephanie Bladen)

Newton, Dennis, *A Few of 'The Few' – Australians and the Battle of Britain* (Australian War Memorial, Canberra, 1990)

Olive, Gordon DFC, (ed. Dennis Newton), *Spitfire Ace* (Amberley Publishing, Stroud, 2015)

Orange, Vincent, *Sir Keith Park* (Methuen, London, 1984)

Parker, Nigel, Luftwaffe *Crash Archive Vol. 1 – September 1939 to 14th August 1940* (Red Kite, Surrey, 2013)

Parker, Nigel, *Luftwaffe Crash Archive Vol. 2 – 15th August to 29th August 1940* (Red Kite, Surrey, 2013)

Parker, Nigel, *Luftwaffe Crash Archive Vol. 3 – 30th August to 9th September 1940* (Red Kite, Surrey, 2013)

Parnell, Neville and Boughton, Trevor, *Flypast – A Record of Aviation in Australia* (Civil Aviation Authority, Canberra, 1988)

Parry, Simon, 'The Reunion' in *Flypast* magazine (December, 1983)

Price, Alfred, *Battle of Britain: The Hardest Day* (Macdonald and Jane's, London, 1979)

Price, Alfred, *Luftwaffe* (Macdonald, London, 1973)

Price, Dr Alfred, *The Luftwaffe Data Book* (Greenhill Books, Russell Gardens, London, 1997)

Ramsey, Winston, G. (ed.), *The Battle Of Britain Then and Now* (After The Battle, London, 1980). Plus versions Mk II, Mk III & Mk IV

Ramsey, Winston G. (ed.), *The Blitz Then and Now*, Vol.1 (After the Battle, London, 1987)

Ramsey, Winston (ed.), *The Blitz Then and Now,* Vol. 2 (After The Battle, London, 1988)

Rawlings, John D. R., *Fighter Squadrons of the R.A.F. and their Aircraft* (Macdonald and Jane's, London, 1976)

Reeder, Joan, *Woman Magazine* (15 November 15 1980)

Ricketts, P/O V. A., *248 Squadron Line Book* (Unpublished, 1941, via John Hamilton)

Roberts, Tom, *Wingless – An Alphabetical List of Australian Airmen Detained in Wartime* (Thomas V. Roberts, Victoria, Australia, 2011)

Ross, David, *Richard Hillary* (Grub Street, London, 2000)

Saunders, Hilary St George, Richard Hillary and Cajus Bekker, *The Battle of Britain* (Tandem, London, 1969)

Semmler, Clement, (ed.), *The War Diaries of Kenneth Slessor* (University of Queensland Press, St Lucia, 1985)

Semmler, Clement, (ed.), *The War Despatches of Kenneth Slessor* (University of Queensland Press, St Lucia, 1987

Shirer, William L., *Berlin Diary 1934–1941* (Sphere, London, 1970)

Shores, Christopher and Clive Williams, *Aces High* (Grub Street, London, 1994)

Smith, Constance Babington, *Evidence in Camera* (Chatto & Windus, London, 1957)

Taylor, John W. R., Michael J. H. Taylor and David Mondey, *The Guinness Book of Air Facts and Feats* (Guinness, Enfield, 1977)

Tench, Watkin, *Sydney's First Four Years* being a combined reprint of *A Narrative of the Expedition to Botany Bay* and *A Complete Account of the Settlement at Port Jackson,* (Library of Australian History, Sydney, 1979)

Terraine, John, *The Right of The Line* (Hodder & Stoughton, London, 1985)

Thompson, Laurence, 1940: *Year of Legend, Year of History* (Collins, London, 1966)

Townsend, Peter, *Duel Of Eagles* (Corgi, London, 1970)

Trevor-Roper, H. R., (ed.), *Hitler's War Directives 1939–1945* (Pan, London, 1973)

Wallace, Graham, *R.A.F. Biggin Hill* (Four Square, London, 1958)

Willis, John, *Churchill's Few – the Battle of Britain Remembered* (Michael Joseph Ltd, London, 1985)

Wood, Derek, *Target England* (Jane's London, 1980)

Wood, Derek and Derek Dempster, *The Narrow Margin* (Hutchinson, London, 1961)

Wright, Robert, *Dowding and the Battle of Britain* (Corgi, London, 1970)

Wynn, Kenneth G., *A Clasp for 'The Few' – New Zealanders with the Battle of Britain Clasp* (Kenneth G. Wynn, Auckland, New Zealand, 1981)

Wynn, Kenneth G., *Men of the Battle of Britain Clasp* (Gloddon Books, Norwich, 1989)

Ziegler, Frank, *Under the White Rose* (609 Squadron) (Macdonald, London, 1971)

NOTES

1. PATERSON

1. London, Pete, *Flying in Cornwall* (Tor Mark, Redruth, Cornwall, 2011).

2. Phyl Campbell (Mrs), Cooma Monaro Historical Society, *Correspondence*, 23 April 1987, responding to an enquiry about Captain Lancaster and Mrs Miller by Mrs H. Bowditch of Normanhurst NSW (via David Hughes).

3. At the time of writing Chubbie Miller's flying helmet was in a picture frame mounted above the mantelpiece in David Hughes' study. David Hughes is Pat Hughes' nephew. Of it, David wrote on 2 May 2002, 'As they departed Cooma, the leather helmet belonging to Mrs Miller fell from the aircraft and was retrieved by Charles Hughes, my father. It has remained in our family since that day.'

4. Interview with W/O Jock Goodwin RAAF 421725, Canberra, 4 July 2011. In the Second World War, Jock served in 461 (Sunderland) Squadron, the Anzac Squadron.

5. Ashfield and Haberfield are inner western suburbs of Sydney.

6. Henry Lawson (1867–1922) was a famous Australian writer closely associated with the early days of the *Bulletin* weekly journal. Although he never produced a novel, his short stories, particularly those about bush life, are among the most noteworthy in Australian literature.

7. Adapted from the eulogy for Constance Olive Torbett, *née* Hughes (1915–2010) delivered by her daughter, Dimity, on behalf of herself and her sister, Sandra, on 30 July 2010.

8. John Nichols Family Society, *Without Rhyme or Reason – poems by the family of John & Ann Nichols née Pugh* (Gosford, NSW, 2013), p. 107–8

9. Laurence Lucas, *Correspondence*, 23 August 2013.

10. Amy Johnson achieved the first solo flight from England to Australia by a woman. She flew from Croydon to Darwin 5–14 May 1930 in a de Havilland DH60 Gipsy Moth (G-AAAH), which she named *Jason*.

11. William Morris Hughes was the eleventh Prime Minister of Australia, 27 October 1915 to 9 February 1923.

12. Janus, ancient Latin god honoured by the Romans. He has been depicted on coins as having two, and sometimes four, faces with the ability to look in as many directions.
13. Frankston is a suburb of Melbourne, Victoria.
14. Glenbrook is a village in the Lower Blue Mountains west of Sydney.
15. Hughes, Paterson, 'An Autumn Evening', *The Fortian* (June 1934), p. 39.
16. Pat Hughes' *1936 Diary*, Australian War Memorial File: 419/049/038, 87/412, via Stephanie Bladen.

2. POINT COOK
1. Olive, Gordon DFC (ed. Dennis Newton), *Spitfire Ace* (Amberley Publishing, Stroud, 2015) pp. 20–1.
2. The various de Havilland Moth aircraft were very similar to each other and were usually differentiated by the type of engine installed. The 'Cirrus Moth' had a Cirrus engine; the 'Gypsy Moth' had a Gypsy engine. The RAAF's 'A7' (First and Second) Series had both types in its inventory.
3. Pat's school mate, John 'Pete' Pettigrew.
4. Hauptmann Oswald Boelcke, credited with forty victories, was one of the most successful German aces of the early First World War and winner of the coveted *Pour le Merite*. He commanded *Jasta* 2 and among his prodigies was the fabled Red Baron, Manfred von Richthofen. He was actually killed as the result of a mid-air collision with another of his pilots on 28 October 1916.
6. Olive, Gordon DFC (ed. Dennis Newton), *op cit.*, pp. 25–6; in the Second World War, G/Capt John Raeburn 'Sammy' Balmer OBE DFC commanded 13 Squadron during 1940–41, 7 and 100 Squadrons in 1942 and 467 Squadron 1943–44, all RAAF units. He failed to return from a mission to bomb a military camp at Bourg-Leopold on the night of 11/12 May 1944.
7. Hughes, Pat, Correspondence to Constance Torbett late 1937, via Dimity Torbett.
8. F/O J. R. Paget was one of Pat's instructors at Point Cook. He had taken up a short service commission in the RAF in July 1931 and had recently returned to Australia.
9. Laurence Lucas, Correspondence with the author 23 August 2013.
10. Hughes, Pat, Correspondence to Constance Torbett, 10 January 1937, via Dimity Torbett.

3. ENGLAND
1. Olive, Gordon, *Unpublished Papers*.
2. *ibid*.
3. Olive, Gordon DFC (ed. Dennis Newton), *Spitfire Ace* (Amberley Publishing, Stroud, 2015), p. 33.

4. *ibid*, pp. 33–5.
5. Johnny Weissmuller, a US Olympic champion and star of the Hollywood *Tarzan* movies of the 1930 and 1940s.
6. Hughes, Pat, Correspondence to Constance Torbett, 28 March 1937, via Dimity Torbett.
7. The coronation of King George VI on 12 May 1937. The idea of a flight over London on coronation night by Pat and Gordon Olive apparently did not eventuate.
8. Hughes, Pat, Correspondence to Constance Torbett, 8 May 1937, via Dimity Torbett.
9. Olive, Gordon DFC (ed. Dennis Newton), *op cit.*, p. 36.

4. THE GATHERING STORM

1. Franks, Norman, *Wings of Freedom* (William Kimber & Co. Ltd, London, 1980), pp. 82–101.
2. Galland, Adolf, *The First and the Last* (Methuen & Co. Ltd, London, 1955), p. 19.
3. Hughes, Pat, Correspondence to Constance Torbett, November 1938, via Dimity Torbett.
4. Pat's twenty-first birthday was on 19 September 1938.
5. Pat's school mate, John 'Pete' Pettigrew had joined the RAAF in July 1937 and trained at Point Cook. He left Australia for an RAF a short service commission on 16 July 1938. His was the last group (of eight) to go under the system as the scheme was suspended because of the RAAF's own need to expand. However, RAF short service commissions did continued to be advertised in the Australian press but later volunteers were civilians without the benefit of Point Cook training.
6. Pat was promoted to flying officer on 19 November 1938.
7. John MacGuire was at Point Cook July 1933–June 1934. He left Australia to join the RAF on a Short Service Commission on 9 July 1934.

5. 234 SQUADRON

1. Hughes, Pat, Correspondence to William Hughes, 6 September 1939, via William Hughes, also known as 'Bill' and 'Will'.
2. Hughes, Pat, Correspondence to Constance Torbett, 6 September 1938, via Dimity Torbett.
3. Doe, Helen, *Fighter Pilot* (Amberley Publishing, Stroud, 2015), p. 51.
4. Doe, Bob, *Bob Doe – Fighter Pilot, The Story of One of the Few* (Spellmount Ltd, Tonbridge Wells, 1991), p. 11.
5. Wynn, Kenneth G., *Men of the Battle of Britain Clasp* (Gloddon Books, Norwich, 1989).
6. Wynn, Kenneth G., *A Clasp for 'The Few' – New Zealanders with the Battle of Britain Clasp* (Kenneth G Wynn, Auckland, 1981).

7. Doe, Helen, *op cit.*, pp. 48–9.

6. KATHLEEN
1. PRO, 234 Squadron RAF, Operations Record Book, AIR 27/1439.
2. PRO, 234 Squadron RAF, Operations Record Book, AIR 27/1439; PRO, 616 Squadron RAF, Operations Record Book, AIR 27/21.
3. Reeder, Joan, *Woman Magazine*, 15 November 1980, via Winston Ramsey.
4. Doe, Bob, *Bob Doe – Fighter Pilot, The Story of One of the Few* (Spellmount Ltd, Tonbridge Wells, 1991), p. 12.
5. Macdonald, Emily, 'Kodak Moments Live On', *Townsville Bulletin*, January 27 2012, p. 19.
6. Doe, Bob, *op cit.*, pp. 12–13.
7. Reeder, Joan, *op cit.*

7. ST EVAL, JULY 1940
1. A few Spitfires and pilots were actually sent to France but these were specially stripped and polished, unarmed machines used for high altitude photographic reconnaissance deep over enemy territory. Desmond Sheen was attached to the unit.
2. Roberts, Tom, *Wingless – An Alphabetical List of Australian Airmen Detained in Wartime* (Thomas V. Roberts, Victoria, Australia, 2011), p. 383; PRO, 151 Squadron RAF, Operations Record Book, AIR 27.
3. Long, Gavin, 'The AIF in the United Kingdom', *Australia in the War of 1939–1945 (Army) Vol. I, To Benghazi* (Australian War Memorial, Canberra, 1961).
4. PRO, 234 Squadron RAF, Operations Record Book, AIR 27/1439.
5. London, Pete, *Flying in Cornwall* (Tor Mark, Redruth, Cornwall, 2011).
6. Doe, Bob, *Bob Doe – Fighter Pilot, The Story of One of the Few* (Spellmount Ltd, Tonbridge Wells, 1991), p. 16; PRO, 234 Squadron RAF, Operations Record Book, AIR 27/1439.
7. PRO, Pat Hughes' Combat Report 8.8.40, AIR 50/89 4551.
8. This anecdote is the stuff of legends and may well be apocryphal as no final source has been traced.
9. Ramsey, Winston (ed.), *The Battle of Britain Then and Now* (After the Battle, London, 1980), pp. 746–7. In order to get married in 1940 Pat would have had to first give 'notice of marriage' at the local register office where couples had to prove there was no impediment to the marriage. Details were then 'displayed for a period of time' before the marriage could take place. (Letter to author from Cornwall Council, 2 April 2012.)

10. PRO, Pat Hughes' Combat Report 27.8.40, AIR 50/89 4551; Pat called himself 'Blue 1' in his combat report. For the narrative, 'Blue 1' has been substituted by the first person 'I'.

11. Matching combat claims with actual losses is always open to question. According to Francis Mason in *Battle Over Britain*, the Ju 88 was from I/KG51 and flown by Leutnant Ruckdeschel and crew. This is disputed in Winston Ramsey's *The Battle of Britain Then and Now*, which states that Leutnant Ruckdeschel was from 3/KG51 and that his plane ran out of fuel and force landed at Buckholt Farm, Bexhill, on 28 July 1940, i.e., the next day. *The Blitz Then and Now* by the same author/editors restates the later date and adds that a ball and socket MG15 gun mounting from the cockpit canopy of this aircraft, Ju 88A-1 9K+HL, is in Tangmere Aviation Museum.

12. PRO, Pat Hughes' Combat Report 28.8.40, AIR 50/89 4551.

13. Ramsey, Winston (ed.), *op cit.*, p. 550.

14. Bailey, G., Correspondence with the author, 5 January 1984.

8. THE IDES OF AUGUST

1. Doe, Bob, *Bob Doe – Fighter Pilot, The Story of One of the Few* (Spellmount Ltd, Tonbridge Wells, 1991), pp. 12–13.

2. See Appendix 2.

3. Mason, Francis K, *Battle Over Britain* (McWhirter Twins Ltd, London, 1969), pp. 570–1.

4. Baff, Flight Lieutenant K. C., *Maritime is Number Ten* (K. C. Baff, Netley, South Australia, 1983), pp. 41–79.

5. Newton, Dennis, *A Few of 'the Few': Australians and the Battle of Britain* (Australian War Memorial, Canberra, 1990), pp. 72–3.

6. PRO, John Curchin's Combat Report 8.8.40, AIR 50/171 65629.

7. Power, R., Correspondence with the author, 6 September 1983.

8. Willis, John quoting Alan Harker, *Churchill's Few – the Battle of Britain Remembered* (Michael Joseph Ltd, London, 1985), p. 128.

9. Doe, Helen quoting Keith Lawrence, *Fighter Pilot* (Amberley Publishing, Stroud, 2015), p. 62.

10. Willis, John quoting William Hornby, *Churchill's Few – the Battle of Britain Remembered* (Michael Joseph Ltd, London, 1985), p. 128.

11. Doe, Bob, *Bob Doe – Fighter Pilot, The Story of One of the Few* (Spellmount Ltd, Tonbridge Wells, 1991).

9. 15 AUGUST 1940

1. PRO, 234 Squadron RAF, Operations Record Book, AIR 27/1439.

2. Ziegler, Frank, *Under the White Rose* (609 Squadron) (Macdonald, London, 1971).

3. PRO, Bob Doe's Combat Report 15.8.40, AIR 50/89 4551.

4. *ibid.*
5. PRO, 234 Squadron RAF, Operations Record Book, AIR 27/1439.
6. Reeder, Joan, *Woman Magazine*, 15 November 1980, via Winston Ramsey.
7. *ibid.*
8. *ibid.*

10. 16 AUGUST 1940

1. Long, Gavin, 'The AIF in the United Kingdom', *Australia in the War of 1939–1945 (Army) Vol. I, To Benghazi* (Australian War Memorial, Canberra, 1961).
2. Champ, Jack and Colin Burgess, *The Diggers of Colditz* (Allen & Unwin, Sydney, 1985).
3. PRO, Pat Hughes' Combat Report 16.8.40, AIR 50/89 4551; PRO, 234 Squadron RAF, Operations Record Book, AIR 27/1439.
4. Reeder, Joan, *Woman Magazine*, 15 November 1980, via Winston Ramsey.
5. *ibid.*

11. 18 AUGUST 1940

1. Wynn, Kenneth G., *Men of the Battle of Britain Clasp* (Gloddon Books, Norwich, Norfolk, 1989).
2. PRO, Pat Hughes' Combat Report 18.8.40, AIR 50/89 4551.
3. PRO, 234 Squadron RAF, Operations Record Book, AIR 27/1439.

12. 26 AUGUST 1940

1. PRO, 234 Squadron RAF, Operations Record Book, AIR 27/1439.
2. Mason, Francis K., *Battle Over Britain* (McWhirter Twins Ltd, London, 1969), pp. 570–1.
3. PRO, John Curchin's Combat Report 25.8.40, AIR 50/171 65629.
4. PRO, Pat Hughes' Combat Report 26.8.40, AIR 50/89 4551.
5. PRO, 234 Squadron RAF, Operations Record Book, AIR 27/1439.

13. 4 SEPTEMBER 1940

1. Sheen, Desmond, Correspondence with the author, 25 October 1983.
2. Sheen, Desmond, Correspondence with the author, 25 July 1985.
3. Newton, Dennis, *A Few of 'the Few' – Australians and the Battle of Britain* (Australian War Memorial, Canberra, 1990), p. 136.
4. Jullian, Marcel, *The Battle of Britain* (Johnathan Cape, London, 1967); Sheen, Desmond, Correspondence with the author, 1 March 1984.

5. Newton, Dennis, *op cit.*, p.148.
6. PRO, 234 Squadron RAF, Operations Record Book, AIR 27/1439.
7. Hillary, Richard, *The Last Enemy* (Macmillan, London, 1942); Ross, David, *Richard Hillary* (Grub Street, London, 2000).
8. Fopp, D., Correspondence with the author, 6 November 1984.
9. PRO, 234 Squadron RAF, Operations Record Book, AIR 27/1439.

14. 5 SEPTEMBER 1940
1. Wallace, Graham, *R.A.F. Biggin Hill* (Four Square, London, 1958).
2. Jullian, Marcel, *The Battle of Britain* (Jonathan Cape, London, 1967).
3. PRO, Pat Hughes' Combat Report 5.9.40, AIR 50/89 4551.
4. PRO, 234 Squadron RAF, Operations Record Book, AIR 27/1439.
5. Mason, Francis K., *Battle Over Britain* (McWhirter Twins Ltd, London, 1969), p. 353.
6. PRO, John Webster's Combat Report 5.9.40, AIR 50/.
7. PRO, Pat Hughes' Combat Report 5.9.40, AIR 50/89 4551.
8. Munday, A. E., Correspondence with the author, 14 February 1983.
9. Stitt, John L., Correspondence with the author, 20 August 1990.
10. Ramsey, Winston (ed.) , *The Blitz – Then and Now Vol. 1* (After the Battle, London, London, 1987); Parker, Nigel, *Luftwaffe Crash Archive Vol. 3* (Red Kite, Surrey, 2013).
11. Ross, David, *Richard Hillary* (Grub Street, London, 2000), pp. 139–40.
12. Wynn, Kenneth G., *Men of the Battle of Britain Clasp* (Gloddon Books, Norwich, 1989).
13. Parker, Nigel, *op cit.*, pp. 330–42.
14. *ibid*, p. 337.
15. Price, Dr Alfred, *The Luftwaffe Data Book* (Greenhill Books, London, 1997).
16. Franks, Norman L. R., *Wings of Freedom* (William Kimber & Co. Ltd, London, 1980), pp. 82–101.

15. 6 SEPTEMBER 1940
1. PRO, Pat Hughes' Combat Report 6.9.40, AIR 50/89 4551.
2. Parker, Nigel, *Luftwaffe Crash Archive – A Documentary History of Every Enemy Aircraft Brought Down Over the United Kingdom*, Red Kite, Surrey, 2013), p. 345.
3. *ibid.*

4. *ibid*, p. 352; Ramsey, Winston (ed) , *The Blitz - Then and Now Vol. 1* (After the Battle, London, 1987), p. 627; PRO, Pat Hughes' Combat Report 6.9.40, AIR 50/89 4551.

5. Franks, Norman, *Wings of Freedom* (William Kimber & Co. Ltd, London, 1980), pp. 82–101.

6. PRO, 234 Squadron RAF, Operations Record Book, AIR 27/1439.

7. *ibid*.

8. *ibid*.

9. *ibid*.

10. Reeder, Joan, *Woman Magazine,* 15 November 1980, via Winston Ramsey.

11. Franks, Norman, *op cit*.

12. Willis, John, *Churchill's Few – the Battle of Britain Remembered* (Michael Joseph Ltd, London, 1985), p. 128.

16. 7 SEPTEMBER 1940

1. Reeder, Joan, *Woman Magazine*, 15 November 1980, via Winston Ramsey.

2. Willis, John, *Churchill's Few* (Michael Joseph, London, 1985), p. 135, Kay Hughes quoting comments from the *Hull Daily Mail*.

3. Semmler, Clement (ed.), *The War Diaries of Kenneth Slessor* (University of Queensland Press, St Lucia, 1985).

4. Willis, John, *op cit.*; Reeder, Joan, *Woman Magazine*, 15 November 1980, via Winston Ramsey.

17. WHAT REALLY HAPPENED?

1. PRO, 234 Squadron RAF, Operations Record Book, AIR 27/1439.

2. PRO, Keith Lawrence's Combat Report 6.9.40, AIR 50/89 4551.

3. Reeder Joan, *Woman Magazine,* 15 November 1980, via Winston Ramsey.

4. Ramsey, Winston (ed.), *The Blitz Then And Now – Volume 2 September 1940 – May 1941* (After The Battle, London, 1988), p. 52.

5. *ibid*, pp. 52–3.

6. Mason, Francis K, *Battle Over Britain* (McWhirter Twins Ltd, London, 1969); p. 366.

7. Reeder, Joan, *op cit*.

8. Bailey, G., Correspondence with the author, 5 January 1984; Newton, Dennis, *A Few of 'the Few' – Australians and the Battle of Britain* (Australian War Memorial, Canberra, 1990), pp. 166–7.

9. Parker, Nigel, *Luftwaffe Crash Archive Vol. 3–30th August to 9th September 1940*, Red Kite, Surrey, 2013), p. 360.

10. Ramsey, Winston (ed.), *op cit.*, p. 52.

11. Ramsey, Winston (ed.), *The Battle of Britain Then and Now* (After The Battle, London 1980), p. 428; Willis, John, *Churchill's Few* (Michael Joseph, London, 1985), p. 135.

12. One is reminded of the dramatic film sequence showing the torso of Dornier Do 17Z, F1+FH, of 1/KG76 as it spiralled down on Victoria Station minus its tail section and outer wings on 15 September 1940. See Parker, Nigel, *Luftwaffe Crash Archive Vol. 4 – 10th September 1940 to 27th September 1940* (Red Kite, Surrey, 2014), pp. 430–3.

13. John Foreman, *Fighter Command War Diaries – Volume 2: September 1940 to December 1941* (Air Research Publications, Walton-on-Thames, 1998), p. 16; John Foreman, *RAF Fighter Command Victory Claims – Part 1: 1939-1940* (Red Kite, Surrey, 2003), p. 199; Simon Parry, Correspondence with the author, 3 April 1987.

14. See Chapter 12, 26 August 1940.

15. See Chapter 14, 5 September 1940.

16. P/O Brian van Mentz, 222 Squadron, PRO, Combat report 7.9.40 AIR 50/85 114484; *Aeroplane* (July 2010, Vol. 38, No. 7), p. 23, 'Undaunted by Odds' by Eric Benjaminson.

18. AFTERWARDS

1. Shirer, William L., *Berlin Diary 1934–1941* (Sphere Books Limited, London, 1970), p. 392.

2. Laurence Lucas, Correspondence with the author, 23 August 2013.

3. Willis, John, *Churchill's Few – the Battle of Britain Remembered* (Michael Joseph Ltd, London, 1985), p. 137.

4. Reeder, Joan, *Woman Magazine*, 15 November 1980, via Winston Ramsey.

5. *ibid.*

6. Laurence Lucas, Correspondence with the author, 14 March 2012.

7. Geof Hartnell, Correspondence with Kay Hughes, 22 October 1980, via Winston Ramsey.

8. Geof Hartnell, Correspondence with Kay Hughes, 20 November 1980, via Winston Ramsey.

9. *ibid.*

10. Henry Hughes, Correspondence with Kay Hughes, 23 December 1980, via Winston Ramsey.

11. Jack Hughes, Correspondence with Kay Hughes, 30 March 1981, via Winston Ramsey.

12. Henry Hughes, Correspondence with Kay Hughes, 12 May 1982, via Winston Ramsey. AVM Henry Alfred (Bill) Hughes AO DFC passed away on 23 July 2005.

13. Adapted from a story by Dimity Torbett.

14. Reeder, Joan, *Woman Magazine*; 15 November 1980, via Winston Ramsey.

19. PAT HUGHES NIGHT

1. Doe, Bob, *Bob Doe – Fighter Pilot, The Story of One of the Few* (Spellmount Ltd, Tonbridge Wells, 1991); Doe, Helen, *Fighter Pilot* (Amberley Publishing, Stroud, 2015); Wynn, Kenneth G., *Men of the Battle of Britain Clasp* (Gloddon Books, Norwich, Norfolk, 1989).
2. Marks, Neil, *Australian People Australian Tales* (HarperCollins Publishers, Sydney, 1999), pp. 154–60.

APPENDIX 1: NEW SOUTH WALES: THE ANCESTRY OF PAT HUGHES

1. *The Proceedings of the Old Bailey*, Reference No.: t17840421-130.
2. Lord Sydney to the Lords Commissioners of the Treasury', Whitehall, 18th August, 1786, printed in the *Historical Records of New South Wales*, Vol. I, pt. 2, at pp.14–19.
3. Bateson, Charles, *The Convict Ships 1787–1868* (A. H. & A. W. Reed, Sydney, 1974), pp. 94–119.
4. *ibid.*
5. Collins, David, *An Account of the English Colony in New South Wales* (London, 1798), pp. 5–7.
6. Tench, Watkin, *Sydney's First Four Years* being a combined reprint of *A Narrative of the Expedition to Botany Bay* and *A Complete Account of the Settlement at Port Jackson* (Library of Australian History, Sydney, 1979).
7. *ibid.*
8. Britts, M. G., *The Commandants – The Tyrants Who Ruled Norfolk Island* (Herron Publications, West End, Queensland, 1980), pp. 9–25.
9. *House of Commons Papers for 1812*, Vol. ii, Paper No. 341.
10. Collins, David, *An Account of the English Colony in New South Wales* (London, 1798). David Collins was Governor Phillip's Secretary and Judge Advocate in New South Wales 1788–96 and a historian of the colony's early days. Later he became the founder and Lieutenant Governor of the penal settlement in Van Diemen's Land.
11. Bond, Ensign G., *A Brief Account of the Colony of Port Jackson* (Southampton, England, 1803); quoted in J. W. C. Cumes, *Their Chastity was not too Rigid* (Longman, Melbourne, 1979).
12. Cunningham, P., *Two Years in New South Wales* (London, 1827); quoted in Birch, Alan and Macmillan, David S., *The Sydney Scene 1788–1960* (Hale & Iremonger, Sydney, 1962).

ACKNOWLEDGEMENTS

I am pleased to acknowledge the help and cooperation of the many people and organisations who have given support and help while researching and writing this book.

First of all, my very special thanks go to Pat Hughes' nieces and nephews without whose marvellous support, association and ready access to their family memorabilia, the project could not have even been started: especially Dimity Torbett, who started me on the trail and pushed me (gently) along the way; Stephanie Bladen, who maintained the impetus and provided so much encouragement; David Hughes for his great hospitality and ready collaboration; Laurence Lucas for his perceptive judgement and astute observations; and Malcolm Booth for his guidance and direction.

Others who have helped along the journey include: Helen Doe; Keith Lawrence; Neil Marks; the family of Gordon Olive; Colin Burgess; Dick Power; Desmond Sheen; Simon Parry; Kenneth Wynn; Robert Glyde; Robert Burridge; John Hamilton; Chris Egan; Henry McDonough; John Wallen; Peter Thompson; David Innes; Winston Ramsey; Derek Wood; Stewart Wilson; E. A. Munday; Jock Goodwin; Bryan Philpott; Ron Lees; and my son, Scott Newton.

I am particularly grateful for the work of Jonathan Reeve and the team at Amberley Publishing, who have spent long hours editing and designing this book, and without whose skills it would have reached realisation.

Organisations that have assisted include: In Britain: Ministry of Defence, Public Record Office (National Archives), Commonwealth War Graves Commission, the Imperial War Museum, Battle of Britain Museum, Battle of Britain Fighter Association of Great Britain, The Caterpillar Club, The Goldfish Club; in Australia: the Australian War Memorial, Australian Archives, the National Library of Australia, the Department of Defence, the Battle of Britain Fighter Association – Australian Branch, Bull Creek Aviation museum WA, Aero Australia, Wings, NSW State Library, NSW Military

Historical Society, Aviation Historical Society of Australia , and especially the John Nichols Family Society.

No serious study of a pilot involved in the Battle of Britain could be made without particular reference to many outstanding books because of their originality, wealth of detail and accuracy. I owe a special debt to Derek Wood and Derek Dempster's *The Narrow Margin*; Francis Mason's *Battle over Britain*; Nigel Parker's *Luftwaffe Crash Archives*; Kenneth Wynn's *Men of the Battle of Britain Clasp*; and Winston Ramsey's *The Battle of Britain Then and Now* series, and *The Blitz Then and Now* series. I acknowledge in particular the help given to me by Winston Ramsey, the *After the Battle* editor, and his contributors.

To all of these people and organisations my sincere thanks. If anyone has been inadvertently omitted, I apologise for the mistake.

Finally, and by no means least, I give especially acknowledgement to my wife, Helen. Without her support and incredible patience, this work could not possibly have been finished.

LIST OF ILLUSTRATIONS

10. Richard Hardy's captured Spitfire. In the running fight on 15 August 1940, 234 Squadron's Red Section was overwhelmed by enemy fighters. Hardy's Spitfire was hit and he was wounded in the shoulder, probably by a cannon shell which hit struck the fuselage just behind the pilot's seat. Injured, short of fuel and far out to sea near the French coast, he headed for the nearest land where he managed to touch down safely on Cherbourg-East/Theville airfield, much to the astonishment of the Germans on the ground. (ww2images.com)

11. Pat Hughes' grave, carefully tended over the years by Mr Bert Knowes, Norman and Margery Shirtliff of Hull and also by Mrs Jean Holmes of Barton-on-Humber, apparently on behalf of the Spitfire Society. Both Margery and Jean corresponded for many years with Pat's closest sister, Constance Torbett, until her death at the age of ninety-five in 2010. Constance remained very grateful to them for their care and for the fresh flowers they laid there. (Dimity Torbett, Stephanie Bladen)

12. The memorial plaque on the wall of the house identifying where Pat Hughes fell into the backyard garden. The resident in 1940 was William Norman. (Malcolm Booth)

13. The telegram sent to the Lucas family informing them of Pat Hughes' death. (Laurence Lucas)

14. Pat Hughes' medals. Bill Hughes donated his brother's DFC and campaign medals to the Australian War Memorial for display. A photograph of them was placed on the dust jacket cover of *A Few of 'The Few' – Australians and the Battle of Britain*, the book published by the Australian War Memorial to mark the fiftieth Anniversary of the battle. (Author's collection)

15. Pat Hughes' nephew, David Hughes, in a similar pose to his Uncle Bill, displaying miniatures of Pat's medals. (Author's collection)

16. The cover of the Pat Hughes' Memorial Stone Service of 23 August 2008. Dedication of the Memorial Stone and the Memorial Stone Service were carried out by Shoreham Aircraft Museum in Sevenoaks on the initiative of the curator, renowned aviation artist Geoff Nutkins. (via Stephanie Bladen)

17. The Pat Hughes Memorial at Cooma NSW. This memorial was dedicated to him in Monahan Hayes Place in 2006. It is in the form of a glass topped font which contains the model of a Spitfire and a picture of Pat's last photograph. (via Stephanie Bladen, Laurence Lucas)

18. Pat Hughes' parents: Caroline Christina (*née* Vennel) and Paterson Clarence 'Percy' Hughes. (Dimity Torbett)

19. Family snap: Pat Hughes (right) with his brother William. William, of course, was usually called 'Bill' by his friends and relatives, but in his letters Pat addressed him as 'Will'. (Dimity Torbett)

20. Family snap: Pat Hughes with his sisters Marjorie (left) and Constance. (Dimity Torbett)

21. 'A' Course January 1936 entry at RAAF Point Cook. Left to right, back row: Cadets Paine, Rogers, Robertson, Dillon, Cooper, Jackson, Sladin, Fowler, Kinane, Good and Cameron. Centre row: Cadets Cosgrove, Yates, Hullock, Hughes, Armstrong, Wight, Grey-Smith, Gilbert, Power, Kelaher, Sheen and Brough. Front row: Cadets Johnson, Kaufman, McDonough, Boehm, Allsop, Hartnell, Olive, Marshall, Mace, Campbell and Eaton. Most subsequently had distinguished careers of in the RAAF and RAF. Of them, Pat Hughes,

39. Vincent 'Bush' Parker after his release from Colditz. After the war he stayed in the RAF but on 29 January 1946 he was killed in a tragic accident when the Hawker Tempest he was flying crashed into a hillside, cause unknown. He was deservedly Mentioned in Despatches the following 13 June. (Colin Burgess)

40. Ron Lees, the Australian CO of 72 Squadron. He remained in the RAF after the war and, on 3 February 1966, after thirty-five years of distinguished service, he retired as Air Marshal Sir Ronald Beresford Lees KCB, CBE, DFC & Bar. (RAAF Museum)

41. Desmond Sheen seated in the cockpit of his Spitfire. Out of the twenty-four RAAF cadets who chose to journey to England to join the RAF early in 1937, just three flew Spitfires during the Battle of Britain: Pat Hughes, Gordon Olive, and Desmond Sheen. This particular aircraft was Spitfire Mk. I, K9959/RN-J of 72 Squadron, Sheen's regular machine until he joined the Photographic Reconnaissance Unit (PDU) in April 1940. His personal emblem was a brown boomerang in a white circle. (Desmond Sheen)

42. Junkers Ju 88s. In 1940 the Ju 88 was the latest and fastest German bomber. Originally designed as a dive-bomber, it proved to be one of the most versatile types in the Luftwaffe arsenal and was always regarded by those Allied pilots who encountered it as a formidable opponent. (MAP)

43. Ju 88 under fire. (RAAF Museum)

44. Tally ho! At 6.15 p.m. on 8 July 1940, the three Spitfires of Blue Section, 234 Squadron, led by Pat Hughes intercepted a Junkers Ju 88 twenty-five miles south-east of Land's End. Pat's two wingmen were New Zealander, P/O Keith Lawrence as Blue 2, and Sgt George Bailey as Blue 3. (AWM)

45. Gladiator N5585 of 247 Squadron depicted with the 'Anzac Answer' emblem. The sketch is based on the diagrams in Francis Mason's book, *Battle Over Britain*. (Dennis Newton)

46. Pat Hughes and 234 Squadron at St Eval. The extra details on the photograph were added by Keith Lawrence who, with Pat, took part in 234 Squadron's first credited victory on 8 July 1940. He was also flying with Pat when the Australian was killed in action during the first huge daylight attack on London on 7 September 1940. Pat is seated on the left. (Keith Lawrence)

47. Pat Hughes at dispersal, as usual wearing his dark blue Royal Australian Air Force uniform. (Dimity Torbett)

48. Messerschmitt Me 109E. The Me 109 and Me 110 aircraft referred to by the Allies were actually the Bf 109 and Bf 110 respectively. (MAP)

49. A Messerschmitt Me 109E damaged to the extent that its port undercarriage has dropped down. Me 109s made up the majority of Pat Hughes' victories. (AWM)

50. Messerschmitt Me 110. Although fast and well armed with two 20 mm cannons and four 7.9 mm machine guns in the nose firing forward and one flexible 7.9 mm machine gun in the rear cockpit, it failed as an escort fighter when confronted by Fighter Command's fast and far more nimble Hurricanes and Spitfires. Later in the war the type was developed into a highly dangerous night fighter. Pat Hughes claimed three Me 110s in his most successful combat on 4 September 1940. (AWM)

51. Pat Hughes with a couple of pilots from 234 Squadron's 'B' Flight. (Stephanie Bladen)

52. Pat in happier times at picnic at St Eval in August 1940, before he found himself in the position of temporary commander of 234 Squadron. Pat led

INDEX

Yate, E. W., 35

Ziegler, Frank, 202, 269
Zurakowski, Janusz, 107, 141,
151, 152

PLACES

Abbeville, 83
Aberdeen, NSW, 123, 203, 204
Acklington, Northumberland, 67,
105, 131
Adelaide, South Australia, 9, 33,
60, 83, 135
Aden, 38, 39, 41, 146
Africa, 213, 214, 223
Albany, Western Australia, 188
Albury, NSW, 23, 35
Aldwych, London, 41
Amesbury Abbey, Wiltshire, 110,
160
Amiens, 83, 236
Andover, Hampshire,
48, 60, 86, 108, 110, 155, 160
Ardennes, France, 82, 83
Ashfield, Sydney, 13, 14, 16, 19,
264
Augsburg, Germany, 53
Australia House, London, 41
Australian Capital Territory
(ACT), 8, 36
Australian War Memorial,
Canberra, 200, 202, 203, 257,
265, 267, 268–270, 272, 275

Bad Godesberg,
Germany, 55
Balmain, Sydney, 18
Banff, Aberdeenshire,
Scotland, 153
Banks Farm, 146,
215, 241
Batavia, 229, 242
Bathurst, NSW, 251
Bayswater Road,
London, 41
Beachy Head, E Sussex 132, 136,
149, 151
Beacon Hill, Sydney, 203, 253
Bedfordshire, 51
Bega, NSW, 8
Belgium, 59, 78, 82, 83, 87, 98
Benenden, Kent, 153
Bentley Priory, 156, 157
Berchtesgaden, 55
Berlin, Germany, 55, 62, 72, 80,
125, 137, 148, 156, 195, 272
Berwick-upon-Tweed, 111

Bessels Green, 183,
184, 188
Beverley Arms, Beverley, 76
Biggin Hill, 107, 108, 113, 114,
116, 117, 125, 126, 130–134,
139, 141, 153, 159, 184, 187,
270
Birde Lane, London, 41
Birmingham, 153
Black Creek, NSW, 252
Blacktown, NSW, 240
Blue Mountains, NSW, 223, 230,
247, 251, 265
Bodmin, Cornwall, 92, 97, 108,
198, 223
Bolton, Lancashire, 69
Bombay, 38, 39
Boscombe Down, Wiltshire, 62,
69, 84, 86
Botany Bay, NSW, 207, 215, 217,
219, 220, 222, 273
Boulogne, France, 147, 199
Bournemouth, Bmouth, 107, 127
Branxton, NSW, 252
Bremen, Germany, 53
Bridge of Waithe, Orkney, 80
Brisbane, Queensland, 11, 26
Bristol Channel, 121
Bristol, 216
Broken Hill, NSW, 60, 157
Brooklands, Surrey, 69, 134, 137,
149, 152
Bude, Cornwall, 86
Burma, 200, 203, 206
Burnley, Lancashire, 73

Cairns, Queensland, 77
Calais, France, 88, 93, 133, 134,
156, 199
Calcutta, 229
California, USA, 10, 11
Cambridge, 65
Campbelltown, NSW, 231
Camperdown, Sydney, 17
Canada, 52, 110, 141, 247
Canberra, ACT, 8, 27, 200, 201,
264, 267, 268, 269, 270, 272
Cannock Chase, Staffordshire, 186
Cap Blanc Nez, 88
Cap Gris Nez, 122
Cape of Good Hope, 232
Carmarthen Hills, NSW, 222
Castle Hill, NSW, 237, 238, 239,
242, 245
Catfoss, Yorkshire, 47, 77
Catterick, Yorkshire, 67, 69
Central Railway Station, Sydney,
250, 251
Ceylon, 41

Champigneul, France, 80
Channel Islands, 87
Chatham, Kent, 113
Cherbourg, France, 84, 99, 100,
107, 111, 115, 124, 128, 148
Christ Church Newcastle, NSW,
251
Church Fenton, North Yorkshire,
56, 58, 63, 65, 67, 68, 81, 105
Cleave, Cornwall, 86
Colombo, 38
Concord, Sydney, 16, 18
Coogee, Sydney, 16, 17
Cooma, NSW, 8, 11, 12, 13, 14,
15, 16, 19, 44, 57, 205, 206,
208, 212, 251, 264
Cornwall, 9, 85, 86, 92, 98, 108,
127, 152, 155, 197, 223, 264,
267, 268
County Cork, 52
County Durham, 77
Coventry, 127
Cranwell, Lincolnshire, 42, 43, 52,
69, 71, 98
Croydon, 11, 67, 108, 116, 117,
130, 132, 133, 139, 160, 264

Darenth, River 185, 189
Danzig, Polish Corridor, 61
Darwin, Northern Territory, 10,
11, 33, 264
Deal, Kent, 93, 112
Debden, Essex, 126, 135
Denmark, 80, 98, 105
Detling, Kent, 99, 132, 134, 135,
145
Devonshire Street Cemetery,
Sydney, 250
Digby, Lincolnshire, 42, 43, 44, 45,
48, 67, 153
Doncaster, 68
Dover, Kent, 91, 93, 94, 104, 111,
116, 122, 125, 132, 133, 134,
136, 149, 150
Drem, Scotland, 68
Driffield, 105
Duddo, Northumberland, 111
Dunedin, New Zealand, 70, 113
Dungeness, Kent, 90, 134
Dunkirk, 83, 87, 91, 104, 110,
122, 142, 199, 223
Dunmanway, Ireland, 52
Duxford, Cambs, 123, 126

East End, London, 158, 181, 203
East Grinstead,
West Sussex, 145
East Malvern, Melbourne, 27, 32